SHAKESPEARE AT THE MOMENT

Shakespeare at the Moment

Playing the Comedies

Albert Bermel

HEINEMANN
Portsmouth, NH

Heinemann
A division of Reed Elsevier Inc.
361 Hanover Street
Portsmouth, NH 03801–3912
www.heinemanndrama.com

Offices and agents throughout the world

Library of Congress Cataloging-in-Publication Data
Bermel, Albert.
    Shakespeare at the moment : playing the comedies /
Albert Bermel.
        p.   cm.
    Includes index.
    ISBN 0-325-00206-1 (acid-free paper)—ISBN 0-325-00205-3 (pbk.:
acid-free paper)
    1. Shakespeare, William, 1564–1616—Comedies.   2. Shakespeare,
William, 1564–1616—Dramatic production.   3. Comedy.   4. Acting.
I. Title.
PR2981.B39   2000
822.3'3—dc21   99-44251
                                                                      CIP

Editor: Lisa Barnett
Production Coordinator: Elizabeth Valway
Production: Denise Botelho/Colophon
Cover design: Jenny Jensen Greenleaf
Manufacturing: Louise Richardson

Cover photo from *The Comedy of Errors*, Royal Shakespeare Company, 1983. From left to right: Richard O'Callaghan as Dromio of Syracuse, Paul Greenwood as Antipholus of Syracuse, and Paul Clayton as an officer.
Cover photo by Donald Cooper.

Printed in the United States of America on acid-free paper
04 03 02 01 00   DA   1 2 3 4 5

Contents

Works Frequently Cited
and Acknowledgments

In preparing a bookload of observations about stage interpretation of the comedies, I have eagerly consumed the scholarship of others, the nutriment of criticism. The quantity of Shakespeare commentary is staggering; so is its overall quality. One can luxuriate in some of the finest critical writing of the past four centuries.

Not everybody welcomes the opportunities to dip or immerse oneself in the currents and immensity of critical waters. A director friend, exasperated by the multiplying of appreciations and depreciations, said about fifteen years ago that the best thing that could happen to Shakespeare's plays would be for someone to bury them and let them lie undisturbed for several hundred years. Since then, the number of writings about the dramatist has frantically swollen. Anyone wishing to check out a selection of rubrics under which the writings can be sorted has only to look at the thirty-page, double-column bibliography in eight-point type entitled "Suggestions for Reading and Research" in a fairly recent sacroiliac-straining, brain-daunting anthology.[1] And the categories found there do not even include the all-encompassing "Miscellaneous." Nor does (or could) that bibliography list descriptive reviews of productions: these accounts, worldwide, often take issue with hardened literary and theatrical assumptions.

As is evident, I owe unrepayable debts to the notes, critical essays, and supplementary materials listed here, and feel especially grateful to

1. *The Complete Works of Shakespeare*, 4th ed., ed. David Bevington (1992), A-72–A-101. The categories include: Works of Reference; Life in Shakespeare's England; Shakespeare's Predecessors and Contemporaries; London Theaters and Dramatic Companies; Shakespeare's Life and Work; Shakespeare's Language: His Development as Poet and Dramatist; Textual Criticism and Bibliography; Shakespeare Criticism to the 1930s; Shakespeare Criticism from the 1940s to the 1970s; Shakespeare Criticism of the 1980s and 1990s, including New Historicism, Feminist Criticism, and Poststructuralism; Shakespeare in Performance; Dramaturgy; Comedies; Problem Plays; Histories; Tragedies; Romances; Poems; and the separate subheads for thirty-seven plays, four long poems, and the sonnets. The first two of the three historical groupings, especially "to the 1930s," understandably omit subcategories for the periods, and even the third one can mention only some "inclusions" of the more celebrated and rumbustious types. There are some eight publications that devote themselves to Shakespeare scholarship—which also appears in many general literary journals. Of the categories listed here, some contain fifty to eighty entries or more.

critics and editors with whom I have in places disagreed for providing grounds and opportunities.

Collected editions of the plays

The Complete Pelican Shakespeare. General editor: Alfred Harbage.

The Complete Works of Shakespeare. General editor: David Bevington.

The New Cambridge Shakespeare. General editor: Philip Brockbank.

The New Shakespeare. General editors: Sir Arthur Quiller-Couch and John Dover Wilson.

The Oxford Complete Shakespeare. General editors: Stanley Wells and Gary Taylor.

The Riverside Shakespeare. General editor: G. Blakemore Evans.

The Yale Shakespeare.

Single-play editions

The Arden Shakespeare. Current general editors: Richard Proudfoot and Ann Thompson.

The Oxford Shakespeare, reprinted in World's Classics series. General editor: Stanley Wells.

The Oxford School Shakespeare. Editor: Roma Gill.

The New Penguin Shakespeare. General editor: T. J. B. Spencer. Associate editor: Stanley Wells.

The Peter Alexander edition, as republished by the British Broadcasting Corporation, in association with Mayflower Books (New York), with new introductory material by John Wilders.

The Signet Classic Shakespeare. General editor: Sylvan Barnet. Most of these volumes appeared during the 1960s. In 1972 they were gathered into a collected edition, *The Complete Signet Classic Shakespeare*.

As of this writing a new complete series, *The Applause Shakespeare Library*, announced its first eight volumes for 1999. General editor: John Russell Brown. Additional editors include actors and directors, and scholars. Please refer to the Bibliography for other books and articles cited in text.

Such older editions as Kittredge's (1936) and Furness's New Variorum (1800s, various dates), and some "classical" editions of the seventeenth, eighteenth, and early nineteenth centuries, have been helpful for consultation. So have a number of anthologies of criticism devoted to single comedies, critical anthologies covering multiple comedies, the many critical works by single authors given over to comic aspects and themes, and essays in specialized publications. These are noted parenthetically in the text or end notes. Books that authoritatively display a modern (but not necessarily or wholly postmodern) critical spirit in their investigations of the comedies and other plays include John Russell Brown's *Free Shakespeare* (1974) and *Discovering Shakespeare* (1981), Gary Taylor's *Reinventing Shakespeare* (1989), and Maurice Charney's *All of Shakespeare* (1993).

I follow the usual method of referring to scenes and lines, but I prefer shortened titles of the plays and books to coldhearted initials. The line numbers cited correspond to those in Bevington's *Complete Works of Shakespeare*, fourth edition (1991). During the earlier period of research, writing, and revision it was the last-issued complete edition on the market. It has a few further advantages, particularly for college and high school students, such as illustrations of relatively recent stagings and films, adequate gutter margins (which some mass-market paperbacks and the New Cambridge Series lack), each speech in poetry set on the line below the name and each speech in prose beginning alongside the name, and spelled-out names for the speech headings. (I cannot understand why Arden and one or two other editions persist with curtailed names, when the First Folio and some Quarto editions have come back into facsimile printings for those purists who insist on the upper limits of historical authenticity.) I do not, however, subscribe to anything like all the editorial judgments in Bevington.

The Oxford series reprinted under the World's Classics rubric contains generous quantities of introductory and supporting material, including illustrations of productions and synoptic stage histories. In the New Cambridge series the editorial material is also of high grade, and Walter Hodges's line drawings, imagined reconstructions of Global proportions, have provocative value. It has become possible in recent years to reproduce halftones of performances well on reasonably good paper and the influx of photographic material is welcome in the newer editions.

The virtually boundless pastures of Shakespeare criticism only infrequently turn into genteel battlefields. Anyone who grazes in them sees how personal gripes and points of dispute seldom burst into anything but civil begging to differ, not like some of the open combat in Shakespeare's own era over the barbed Martin Marprelate missives and the War of the Theatres. Most of the exquisitely polite skirmishes make for compelling reading. In a public spirit Shakespeare scholars— not only the series editors—may selflessly lend their readings and conclusions to newcomers. In the 1994–95 World's Classics edition of *A Midsummer Night's Dream*, Peter Holland writes,

> My debt to the play's many editors, especially its most recent,
> Harold Brooks and Reg Foakes, is immeasurable; the acknowledging of this debt often seems a gesture of academic courtesy but here
> is genuine and heartfelt. (vi)

Professors Brooks and Foakes edited the directly competing editions published respectively by Arden (1979, revised 1983) and Cambridge (1984). Such reciprocity—in Holland's note of thanks—shows that the playwright, among his other triumphs, managed *à son insu* to create a community of learning of the kind his Henry of Navarre could only dream about.

To Shakespeare's drama I come as a playwright-critic, not an actor-critic, a director-critic, or a designer-critic, much less a scholar-critic. This statement is not a boast or even a claim, merely an admission of certain shortcomings, most of all a defensiveness about that author's likely dramaturgical motives. I do not put forward production concepts, only responses to the text and to productions of the (mostly) recent past that may prove helpful to somebody.

As a Briton by birth, I grew up on Shakespeare, imbibing the plays during classes devoted to printed versions of *Macbeth* and *Othello* in my very early teen years and, at about the same time, to jollied-up productions of *Twelfth Night* and *Dream* thought suitable for immature delight. Not much later, I began to trace some of the plays' soarings under the tutelage of an English teacher, Mr. Thorpe, and a French teacher, Dr. Stockwell (in those days teachers had no first names), at St. Olave's and St. Saviour's Grammar School on Tooley Street in Bermondsey-Southwark, a brisk walk from the site of the old and the reconstructed Globe Theatre. Dr. Stockwell put most of my friends and me into a school showing of *1 Henry IV*. From playing the king I learned I would never be an actor.

In these much later years students at Lehman College, the Graduate Center of CUNY, and the Yale School of Drama taught me much more about the comedies. So did six years of theatre reviewing for *The New Leader*, and I regret not having more time and room to expend on detailed looks back at productions worth reconsidering. Colleagues, sons, and friends deserve but probably will never come by some sort of recompense. So do Mildred Marmur, one of the great literary agents; Kurt Daw, who read the manuscript and offered valuable suggestions; and Lisa A. Barnett, who welcomed the manuscript at Heinemann and with whom I had merry e-mail exchanges. So too does Joyce, who has accompanied me to Shakespeares on stage for longer than I ought to mention in print.

Introduction:
Impulsive Behavior in the Comedies

. . . In the first scene [of The Tempest*]—a storm and its confusion on board the king's ship [bring] the highest and lowest characters together, and with what excellence! Much of the genius of Shakespeare is displayed in these happy combinations—the highest and the lowest, the gayest and the saddest; he is not droll in one scene and melancholy in another, but often both the one and the other in the same scene. . . . One admirable secret of his art is, that separate speeches frequently do not appear to have been occasioned by those which preceded, and which are consequent upon each other, not to have arisen out of the peculiar character of the speaker.*
(Coleridge, *Shakespearean Criticism*, ed. T. M. Raysor.)

Shakespearean Comedy or Shakespeare's Comedies?

Henri Bergson's classic essay (reprinted, together with "An Essay on Comedy" by George Meredith, in *Comedy*, edited by Wylie Sypher [1956]) purports to deal with "Laughter," its title, rather than with comedy, but it announces early on that he will study "the comic spirit," which he declines to define—wisely. But this most humanistically sensitive philosopher does separate out comedy of form (structure), of situation (together with comedy of form, this would cover most of what we think of as farce), of language, of gesture, and of character. He believes, as Meredith did before him, that comedies invoke intellectual detachment, while tragedies, by contrast, involve the emotions of the audience. Is this true? Even a truism? It sounds generally on target for tragic literature, including drama read as literature; but theatre experience often contradicts it, what with unpredictable conditions of performance and possibilities of manipulation by second and third parties, such as directors and actors (not to mention designers and dramaturgs) who come between the author and his public. One is bound to ask as an unfairly rhetorical question: Can a spectator, either an ice-hearted critic or a torch-carrier for Pure Entertainment, remain emotionally detached from the end of *The Shrew* or *Much Ado* or, come to that, any of Shakespeare's principal comedies or, come to *that*, Molière's, to which Bergson seems to have intended his essay to apply?

Each comedy by Shakespeare damages settled conventions, and in its own fashion, I prefer the plural form *comedies*. The word *comedies* says that, for me at least, no irrefragable pattern emerges from the assortment of plays taken to be comic. They don't all observe such ancient precepts as exposing errors or condemning vices and antisocial behavior among non-royals and lower-crusters.

In Romance languages the root word (*comédie, commedia, comedia*) means not only plays that are funny but also drama in general, just as the French *comédien* and *comédienne* mean actor. We can appreciate a comedy without laughing continuously or even laughing at all. Nor do people generally weep over a tragedy but more often over a comedy with an ending of reconciliation: forgiveness, gulping sounds, mutual apologies and self-recrimination, a wedding. Laughter, in short, can be linked to "the comic spirit," but so can spite or triumph or reconciliation—or tears. Thomas McFarland says that "laughter is merely a comic tool; it has no necessary relationship to the comic essence, which is the criticism of individuality by the standards of the group" (1972, 18). Well before McFarland Freud had gone much further than most recent writers on comic literature by asserting famously that laughter, anything but the token of benevolence associated with the grinning mouth of a mask, consists of "veiled aggression." And long before Freud, says M. C. Bradbrook, "Thomas Wilson, the author of the influential *Art of Rhetoric* (1553)—which Shakespeare himself was to read— saw all laughter as derisive" (1963, 38).

But if we restrict ourselves to the growth or structure of comedies—to the properties that inhere in their nature, as opposed to laughter, smiles, and other *consequences* of comedies, no overall definition I've met covers all or most of the cases that drift onto the screen of the mind. Bergson's famous and ingenious near-definitions refer us to human beings who behave like machines. But by the time Bergson published his essay in 1900, infant movies, especially by his countrymen the Lumière brothers and Méliès, had chanced to knock out some of the props from under it by displaying its obverse: machines and other theoretically inert matter, from ladders to hoses, that behave as mischievously as human beings. If *Le Rire*, although one of the most beautiful and rigorous writings on the arts, lacks free applicability, is a prisoner of its time like the bulk of theories, and is not, despite its title, a thesis on laughter, isn't there still room—still plenty of hope—for theories of comedy in the future? Yes. And the more of them that appear, the less hope there will be for a single dominant theory. So far, helpful statements have been broad and tentative, as definitions only partial. Some stretch out even more broadly, to embrace not only

Shakespeare's art but also that of his contemporaries: Matthew Arnold claimed that the Elizabethan age was "steeped in humor and fantasticality up to its very lips" and "can hardly bring itself to see an object quietly or to describe it temperately" (cited in Matthews, 1927, 211).

This book looks at (a) vexing, unsettled questions exhumed from past criticism of the comedies; (b) questions earlier criticism hasn't taken much notice of, if any; and (c) some productions that help clarify both sorts of questions. The book's gist is intended to be practical, rather than theoretical. But because so many superb theoreticians have taken part in the enrichment of Shakespeare studies, it borrows brazenly from theory.

Opinions

Luckily, Shakespeare's comedies, like other learning and pleasure, thrive on dissension. According to Susan Snyder, *Dream* and *The Merchant of Venice* demonstrate "that the old give way to the fertile, vigorous young." She adds, "Rites and plays alike are about life, not virtue" (1980, 24). Leo Salingar, however, says Shakespeare's comedies are not about life; they are "the unfaithful mirror" of life (1974). Marjorie Garber finds they offer an antidote to life when she points out the presence of death in every comedy by Shakespeare (1980, 121–26).

Even when buttressed by swarming footnotes per sentence, each critical theory rests on an unsteady foundation of personal preferences, not always revealed and not always known (or knowable) by the writer. Readers will similarly be swayed and repelled at least as much by their own prejudices as by the persuasiveness of others. Critical theory rears up on a groundsill of predisposition. Emerson remarks that, at a later stage than theory, "every reform was once a private opinion" (1940, i). When Bertrand Evans says that *Troilus and Cressida* has many dramaturgical flaws and Kenneth Muir rebuts Evans's contention and hotly defends the play, they both make persuasive advocates. The reader who agrees with one or the other will most likely do so on the strength of an attitude already taken toward the play or the roles. When Jan Kott proposes that the grotesque, horror-ridden world Shakespeare discerns from his time (and Seneca's) matches ours in horrors and grotesqueries, while McFarland disputes Kott's view of *Dream*, taking particular exception to the Kott-influenced interpretation by Peter Brook and the Royal Shakespeare Company—this play, says McFarland, spills over with happiness and takes place in a healing paradise—readers once again are likely to react because of opinions already calcified. Critical sparring, in which authors put forward opposed views fortified by solid evidence, appeals as blatantly to the sympathetic imagination and to memories of past productions as to the skeptical intellect, if those faculties are indeed separable.

In the disagreements that break out over every one of the comedies, and with especial tenseness in the cases of *The Shrew, The Merchant*, and *The Tempest*, we run into arguments over what the plays say and what they imply; over Shakespeare's deemed philosophical declarations, or the bearing of his total *oeuvre*; over what exactly happens in the action; over what inexactly happens offstage; over what the stage itself was, is, and might be; over what the characters are like and whether they are likable; over the caliber of the prose, blank, and rhymed verse; over its literal and figurative meanings; over its sources and the playwright's obligations to them; over the structural integrity in the sequence and emphases of the "beats," scenes, and acts; over how comic we judge certain encounters, speeches, and lines to be; over the mythological references and overtones, and other preoccupations. In current reviewing, critics weigh how bold or timid a staging is—and should be; they may gauge the results of cutting, transposing lines or scenes, adding production effects (what Hollywood calls "values"), accentuating words or whole lines. "Creative refashioning," lavishing effort on the fun quotient, and other doctorings go back to Betterton, Macklin, Cibber, and Garrick.

But change provokes resistance. Until recently critics and public alike had grown accustomed to a certain *mise en scène* for each comedy and tragedy, and believed it hallowed; they resented obtrusive novelties, such as slanting the roles or tinting them by inverting characterizations—Brook's treatment of Goneril and Regan (Irene Worth and Pauline Jameson) or on film, Polanski's of Ross (John Stride). Shakespeare moves about restlessly in our imagination. Today one seldom finds a Shakespeare comedy that directors have not to some degree modernized. They even jump today and the life soon to come, replanting *Macbeth* or *The Tempest* in soil of the far future a setting that never will be, but if played with conviction, such a show can entrance us— for at least the duration of the performance.

Some theatre people have tried to do away with the director, on the supposition that there was no such animal at the original Globe. Among other troupes, the Royal Shakespeare Company under John Barton experimented with undirected performing; the What You Will Company under the guidance of Patrick Tucker tried a similar modus operandi; and John Russell Brown advocated scrapping the director and turning the actors loose in *Free Shakespeare* (1974).

The treasury of critical approaches keeps opening up, thanks to scholars' calling on history (social, political, military, artistic), mythology, theology, sociology, political science (Marxism, feminism, power struggles), anthropology (especially the origins of comedy and tragedy), and—surely the most popular crutch of our times—psychology. Because roles are viewed as living personalities, Randy Rolf could write an article called "Hamlet, Prince of Co-Dependency" (*Changes*, March-April, 1982), and W. Thomas MacCary could look upon the pairs of young men in the comedies as unadmitted because unknowing lovers (1985). Investigations multiply well beyond the "pluralist criticism" envisaged a quarter of a century ago by S. E. Hyman in *Iago: Some Approaches to the Illusion of His Motivation* (1970). Hyman writes,

> On the theory of the symposium, that truth has a good chance to emerge out of the mutually corrective interplay of part-truth and error, one gets a richer sense of the critical problem—ultimately of the literary work—than any single critical vocabulary or method can give. (3–4)

This claim is unexceptionable. We might indeed hope to get continually closer to the truth, like asymptotes, except that as critical stances *and footwork* keep changing, the assorted theories may refuse to cohere.

A grand theory of Shakespearean art, or even of Shakespeare's comedies, much less an overarching theory of all comedy, stands little chance of solidifying—except under the ministrations of an astrophysicist or other mathematical wizard who draws up intricate patterns and paradigms, broadly applies them, and bullies followers into refraining from reinterpretations. Such a theory, or theorem, would doubtless have to be encapsulated in a mathematical formula, rather than in words. In what we take to be the far less complicated century of Aristotle, did he give up the task of compiling the treatise on comedy that would have partnered his synoptic work on tragic poetry? Or did it get lost? Or eaten, as in *The Name of the Rose?* About the best a critic can manage by way of theory these days is a partial definition, such as McFarland's, cited previously, proposing a critical function for "the comic essence." In this vein I offer a provisional separation of comedies from tragedies (both in the plural): comedies deal with fertility, tragedies with sterility. Those two words connected with the idea of generation—and genre—have implications I'll return to shortly. To stretch the contrast further, comedies resemble dreams of wish fulfillment, in which all finally comes right; they are a form of heaven while tragedies turn into nightmares or dreams of hell.

Freud and Stanislavsky

Sigmund Freud, born in 1856, about a month after Bernard Shaw, lived until 1939, twenty days beyond the outbreak of World War II. Constantin Stanislavsky, born Alexeyev in 1863, seven years after

Freud, died the year before Freud in 1938, a total of eight years un-
luckier. The overlap in these lives—of the doyen of modern psychology, who became the father of psychoanalysis, and the doyen of
modern directing, who gradually pieced together the acting "System"
originally meant for the Moscow Art Theatre—may explain in part the
psychological underpinning of the System and its stepchild,the Method, almost as many versions of which sprang up as there were heirs of
Stanislavsky, American and Russian. There is no need to posit a connection between the two masters or even to trace influences of Freud
upon Stanislavky: their ideas poured into the Psychological Century,
receiving exultant welcomes.

Among its other merits the System, like its derivatives, sought to
help actors unlock persisting motives, a through line in each role, as
well as a larger through line or "red line" or "spine" in the dramatic
sequence. Sometimes actors and directors, in their desires to rationalize acting, have gone so far as to construct life stories or even case histories for the roles, based on measly evidence from the action and on
intuition and guesswork. Whether because of imitation or common
notions adrift in the atmospheres of Vienna and Moscow, psychoanalysis similarly sought an understanding of a unified personality, the
shape of a life, in order to make sense of it and then encourage it to
adapt to its conditions. Failing that adjustment, a patient might try to
alter those conditions, if doing so seemed advantageous, and compel
them to adjust to the troubled personality—any actions redolent of
starting over: divorce, remarriage, a new job, going into teaching or
the theatre. And failing *those* adjustments, the patient who had not yet
committed suicide might go to drastic lengths to create a fresh set of
conditions, such as moving to another country or taking up the latest
cult or creating one.

If Freudian therapy incited patients to *live* to the best of their abilities, Stanislavsky's System and its derivatives incited students of acting and directing to *mimic life*—their own and that of others—to the
best of their abilities, and to put the imitations at the service of their
roles. In popularity Freud's theories and practices for a time out-
stripped the competition, principally that of Jung, erstwhile member
of Freud's inner circle; Stanislavsky's System for a time pulled well
ahead of alternative techniques created by, among others, Meyerhold,
who had once worked as an actor under Stanislavsky's direction.

The language used by the two teacher-leaders and their followers
and commentators has grown abused and muddied over the past century, especially the noun *identity*, which has become hard to avoid, despite its imprecision. But, imprecision is precisely what makes certain
words freely adaptable and popular (two current verbs: *resonate* and
focus). Freudians took identities to be in some ways intrinsic and so

fixed while in other ways moldable. Stanislavskyans scrutinized the identities of roles, which could be put on like costumes and worn for a run of performances.

Freud and Stanislavsky, subtle artists both, don't deserve blame for the pall of consistency draped over their conceptions by sincere admirers. Blame, rather, this century's determination to summarize and simplify during decades of jumbled information overload. What has developed? Assumptions that consistency is naturally superior to inconsistency—in temperaments, roles, manufactured products, scientific theories, theological tracts, and ripe fruit. And this despite the famous admonition from Emerson in his *Essays* that "a foolish consistency is the hobgoblin of little minds. . . . With consistency a great soul has simply nothing to do" (1940, ii). In introducing the Arden edition of *The Tempest*, Frank Kermode wrote: "Inconsistencies we should surely always expect. Shakespeare did not tidy his most careful plots . . ." (1963, xix). Sir Frank was thinking of accidents in writing and publication, and not what I mean when I refer to willful inconsistencies in the behavior of the roles.

But Freud and Stanislavsky alike took account of underlying and inconsistent motives in the formation of identity: Freud attributed them by and large to the treacheries of the unconscious, that shadowy hinterland of the mind; Stanislavsky, to the ironies in every play's subtext, the meanings between the lines, what the roles were "really" saying.

Among newer generations of actors, Stanislavsky has lately fallen into disfavor. The film and theatre writer and director David Mamet published a book of advice for raw actors; it deals with *Heresy and Common Sense for the Actor*, the subtitle, and with *True and False*, the title (1997). It's a dogmatic work, rather than heretical. Mamet ends his 127 pages by asking, "What is true, what is false, what is, finally, important? . . . It is not a sign of ignorance not to know the answers. But there is great merit in facing the questions." After the number of times he has urged actors, whom he treats as inexperienced dummies, to go headlong for the true and spurn the false, his conclusion strikes me as a cop-out. Still, I agree with many of Mamet's comments, especially with his disapproval of the Method. He doesn't want actors to concentrate in rehearsal on the play, but on the scene. I advocate concentrating more intensively yet on the moment. We're both thinking of not trying to summarize each of the roles all the way through the play, or to connect them with a spine or other link, but to think about how to deliver each of the lines, even or especially when these seem contradictory.

According to Mamet, there are no characters, no real people in the text, only words on pages. I concur. But Mamet goes indefensibly further; he says analysis of plays is a waste of time for actors, if not a downright misleading way of studying a part. He labels academics mere fakers—they know nothing about the stage or its potential. Yet he writes: "Any meaning past that supplied by the author will come from your *intention toward the person to whom [the lines written for you] are said*" (55, his italics). But how does an actor know the intention of the role or of individual lines without having analyzed a complex play by Shakespeare, Giraudoux, Sophocles, or Ghelderode and used the analysis (and some doubts) to seek guidance? What will an actor *intend* toward other actors on stage when she could use help in interpreting lines? Here Mamet in effect promulgates reverse snobbery: Don't pay attention to others; I'm the writer. I know, and you know, too, by instinct and by your innate skills, so there's no need to read or think about what academic and other charlatans have to say. But actors and many spectators know something else: that every Hamlet and every Medea is different from every other and for that reason many seek every production they can find of certain plays in a *search* for fresh interpretations. Playwrights who are honest with themselves soon become aware of how much they owe their collaborators. They may even see an actor reach personal discoveries that the playwrights had no idea were there, discoveries that may—a truly heretical find—*enlarge* the author's intentions.

Role, Character, Personality

Critical delvings for consistency in Shakespeare go back more than two and a half centuries before the birth of Freud. Leontes, Portia, Tamora, Bertram, Coriolanus, and at least a couple of dozen more roles—before we invoke the even more majestic names of Hamlet, Lear, and Othello—have been judged inconsistent and *therefore* less than likable and *therefore* challengeable as psychological entities. But what do we mean by a psychological entity in the theatre? Three words get bandied about with no distinctions generally drawn between them, and so I will invent some distinctions roughly based on usage.

Role: A part written by a playwright, consisting of dialogue to utter and stage directions for guidance in casting, costume, movement, behavior.

Character: The role after a particular actor wraps his or her body, heart, and intellect around it and after it has been colored by help and hindrance from interested or interfering souls, such as the director, designer(s), spouses, indispensable others, and the prompter—in other words, the actor's total showing in a performance. In previous writings about character and characters I treated them as mutable, not fixed, entities. Yet, I found that the word character, as it is generally spoken and written, implies insufficient plasticity, however carefully one qualifies it. Hence the distinction here between roles and characters.

Personality: The character onstage reminds a spectator of an actual person, dead or living, a celebrity, maybe, a relative, an acquaintance, a foe. Robert Brustein wrote a colorful column called "Character and Personality in Shakespeare," a review of two lectures given by Harold Bloom who, Brustein reported, "expresses the academic's age-old conviction that Shakespeare should be read aloud rather than performed." Brustein himself offered connotations of "character" and "personality" that correspond closely to current usage (The New Republic, 1.1, 1996, 27–29).

These three casual definitions encompass feelings and other marks of identification—dress, deportment, speech, physique, manners, mannerisms, and responses provoked by others. As understood here, a *personality*, created by life, differentiates a human being from a *role*, created on paper; both of these differ from a *character*, created on stage. An actor's contribution, the characterizing, may enliven and deepen a role. Or it may betray a role, because of inept casting or misguided interpretation. Roles, then, are appreciated by the reader; characters by the spectator. In the case of Bunraku or Punch and Judy or some other form of dehumanized acting (in body masks or with amplified speech), a puppeteer directs, as well as acts, but the puppet remains a character; its role exists only in a script.

Living personalities often behave unlike their recognized selves, in the short term as a result of exotic or perverse impulses, in the longer term because they have moved or acquired a new nationality or simply grown older. They change as they submit to the dictates of time. On a stage the roles may escape the confinement of a fourth wall, or all walls, but they cannot break out of the fourth dimension any more than personalities can. Consider the personality most commonly associated with the seventeenth century, Louis XIV, sometimes said to *represent* that century.

> The [youthful] King who climbed about the roofs of the Louvre at night to find an unbarred window in the quarters of the Maids-of-Honor was a very different man from the King [aged 46] who married Mme. de Maintenon; and for old courtiers it must have been difficult to realize that the new Louis was the same man who, when pinched *a tergo* by a pretty girl in full Court, sprang upwards with a shout of "Damn the bitch!" (W. H. Lewis, *The Splendid Century: Life in the France of Louis XIV*, New York: 1957, 40)

Similarly, in any play by Shakespeare—in anybody's play that doesn't traffic in cartoonlike figures—the roles change for successive generations as they become victims of time or victors of themselves over time.

The sum of each role amounts to its appearances and activities in a number of specified scenes, added to its absence (being purposely withheld) from other scenes, during which it may be talked about or deliberately not talked about, and may carry out some tasks offstage that affect the action onstage: Isabella and Mariana play the "bed trick" on Angelo; Fenton and Nan Page elope, to the consternation of her parents. But any *ambitious* role's presence in some scenes will prove inconsistent with that role's presence in others. I merely contend that such inconsistency need not cause alarm, complaint or, worse, smoothing-over. Percipient actors, whether trained in the pure or adulterated Method or some other source or practice, have always known that a role worth playing offers explosions of unexpected emotion. In act 1 of *The Winter's Tale* Leontes will grow incensed with jealousy—going beyond green to purple; in act 5 he will flicker among contrition, humility, gratitude, and devotion. How shall we find the concord of this discord? How do we reconcile Valentine's passion for Sylvia in act 2 of *Two Gentlemen* with his astounding gift of forgiveness to his faithless friend Proteus in act 5, "All that was mine in Sylvia I give thee," after Proteus has threatened to rape Sylvia? The answer in both cases is we don't, we needn't try, any more than we need try with, say, Ibsen's drama: Halvard Solness, the aging, domineering masher turns to Norwegian putty in the grasp of Hilda Wangel, who starts out as a cute kid in her sailor suit—or is it a mountaineering outfit?—and ends as the goddess Nemesis. In Ibsen's best-known turnaround, songbird Nora becomes her husband's stern judge before she slams the front door on him.

Striving to meet the demands of a hypothetical through line (by implication, straight and horizontal) or a "spine" (without curvature or slipped disks) may falsify a role by hemming it in. Shakespeare, the finest maker ever of multiple roles, apart from God, terrifies actors, who therefore love him. He surely could provide gradations between contrasting appearances of a role, but his sudden gusts, his flat contrarieties, seem intended to shake his audiences with surprises. If these self-conflicted *roles* are absorbed and transmitted by actors, without the flattening, surgery, or cleaning up that will make them supposedly more acceptable as they become *characters*, and if their acting lives up to the play's demands, they will bring to mind images of real people—*personalities*—precisely because of their inconsistency. I revert for an instant to Leontes. Arthur Sewell remarks that "Leontes is an acting part, rather than a character" (1951). Sewell says so disparagingly, but if by "character" he means approximately what certain directors and acting coaches and teachers mean when they use the word—a personality pudding with no lumps—he happens to be correct. Leontes the character takes on the role's insane and maddening instability—and possibilities—when the actor plays each moment of the character for what it calls forth in his preparation and temperament, letting it benefit from his own stock of impulsiveness.

We think of a role as a single human body, and in the case of Shakespearean theatre even the chorus (whether known as Chorus in *Henry V*, Gower in *Pericles*, Rumor in *2 Henry IV*, or Time in *The Winter's Tale*) consists of one narrator; but Shakespeare also gives us some collective roles, such as the crowd in *Julius Caesar* and *Coriolanus*. He goes out of his way to display the Roman mob's inconstancy, most tellingly during the speeches of Brutus, who with the aid of high rhetoric justifies the assassination of Caesar, and then Antony, who plays oratorical tricks to win the mob back to its worship of Caesar by exploiting its greed.

The inconsistency of roles in Shakespeare has further benefits: it denotes richer parts for actors to play and for spectators to savor. *Richer* may be too weak a word. Inconsistency shapes the roles, period. Proteus's cry, "O heaven, were man/But constant, he were perfect!" (*Two Gentlemen*, 5.4.110–11), wells up from the heart of male apology; but for "man" read "human being" and for "constant," not mere sexual reliability, anti-fickleness, but predictable speech, looks, and behavior—a constant attitude toward life—and the line swells into a yearning for a peace that passeth all understatement, and that, if it were miraculously granted, would destroy life's dramas as well as the theatre's. Roles are not finite, even in the crudest role-creating. Every sentence, word, inflection, gesture, face put upon them is a divide in a role, calling for choices.

We have all known all along that consistency is a misguiding light. But in criticism, as in directing—the most demonstrative form of criticism—we often go along with it, straightening and simplifying.

Performances of a Shakespeare comedy that yield to discrepancies and rough edges are condemned as romantic, "romanesque." And they often are. Such accusations may unnerve actors and directors, making them play down not only the comedy, but equally or more the primitive melodrama. They scorn the rewards of giving rein to excess.

Shakespeare Out of Time and Space

Shakespeare created his own Italy (or Italies), his own France and Spain and Illyria and Scotland; his own historical pinpointing in the Romes of Julius, Augustus, Coriolanus, and Titus Andronicus; the Englands of Lear and of a string of Plantagenet, Lancastrian, Yorkist, and Tudor rulers, as well as his contemporary England of the Ford and Page families. The cast of any one comedy also gives us a mix of nationals, the most varied sample being in *Dream*, laid in a very different

Athens from that of Timon. To ferret out consistency in the playing means seeking the unfindable. The company at the Globe went further than urging patrons to eke out their imagination: it teased their disbelief—and this in addition to having boys as women.

Most theatre troupes in the United States subscribe to nontraditional casting, although they do not always live by it as sedulously as they tout it. My own observations of audience indignation at unusual casting suggest that the *public* could benefit from rehearsals and coaching, understanding theatre as mimesis or impersonation, rather than as defective portraits of reality. Does it make any less sense for, say, a twentieth-century African American woman to play a twelfth-century Hamlet the Dane than it did for the Divine French Sarah in the nineteenth century or the original Englishman Burbage to do so? Is a white actor from London more "real" than a Hispanic American in the role of the Viennese Isabella of *Measure for Measure* or the Paduan Kate? Pretty well every assay at a Shakespeare role today invokes a flight through space and time, much as the role itself does between the start of act 1 and the cinching of act 5.

Some directors defend the mania for juggling with Shakespeare's times and spaces not to promote nontraditional casting, which has artistic advantages, but to make sitting through several hours more familiar, less of a strain. Other directors claim merely to have tired of the old ways of presenting the play. Perhaps so, but in theatre, as in politics and education, stale, discredited ideas still get trundled back into position, horse-drawn cannons renamed *challenges*, *agendas*, or *initiatives*. I see these as strivings for a consistency between the antique roles, the modern actors' persons, and the timelessness of sets and costumes—as a patronizing of patrons. Spectators who really crave the familiar comfort of a modern ambience stay home dozing in front of sitcoms.

The hoary story about prisoners who grew tired of reciting old jokes and started to call them out by numbers has some application to theatre, and especially to Shakespeare's, as it does to many other pursuits, and it has become a myth for our times. A new prisoner calls out four or five numbers but nobody laughs. The rookie prisoner is disappointed. From the next cell a veteran prisoner explains: "It wasn't the jokes; it was the way you told them." Theatre persons know the phenomenon. Comic material meant to be funny ("It broke us up in rehearsal") wins no reaction, not even a jeer. A scene not intended to be funny provokes raucous, embarrassing laughs. Theatre, even after previews and rewrites, rests on the vagaries of tone, timing, and response.

Here, before I embark on a description of the leading components in Shakespeare's comedies, is a note about the use of *plot* and *plotting* in this book. They are neither of them a synonym for *intrigue*. Conversational usage and professional criticism take the two words as rough synonyms for story or a skeletal version of the story. Previously I've drawn an analogy with a lighting plot in the playhouse, when the designer aims particular spotlights and floods onto the stage with colored filters. A closer analogy may be the parts written for orchestral instruments in combination, or singly, or, for the moment, not playing. So a playwright concocts a plot by means of presences and absences. The plotting of a given scene depends on which roles the playwright uses to create the scene and which roles are kept offstage. The main plot consists of the sequence of scenes in which the principal roles appear; the subplots pull together the secondary roles.

The Comedies' Characteristics

In Shakespeare comedies reveal roles as they contend with money, property, and other blessings and burdens; with friends, relatives, lovers, enemies (political and religious) in activities—eating, drinking, exertions of power and opposition to power; with distrust and superstitions, with oral stumbles, errors in identification, and mental blindness. The *dénouements* ought to be called *nouements* (by analogy with the coincidence between the meanings of *raveling* and *unraveling*), since dramatic traditions, in Shakespeare as elsewhere, insist on a final tying together, not untying, of the main plot and subplots to reinforce the echoes of, or comments on, similar happenings and images in the main and secondary plots. Spectators watch for this formal integrating signaled by the triumph of the decent (usually less vivid) roles over rascally ones, as well as over obstacles and setbacks. A wedding impends, a portal to fertility.

Beyond the overruling fertility motif in most of the fifteen plays to be discussed in the following chapters we find further characteristics:

1. At least one heroine, more spirited and trusting than her male counterpart, is buffeted by conventional opposition, but not to be turned away from her self-imposed mission. In some of the plays, the mission requires male guise for part of the action. But, says Kenneth Muir, "although disguise and mistaken identity are prominent features of Shakespearian comedy, they do not seem to be its essence" (1965, 3).

2. The female roles generally outsmart the males either in verbal conflict—Rosaline, Nerissa, Beatrice—or by capturing him—Helena, Julia, Rosalind. Portia outsmarts one and captures another. The patterns correspond closely to Hollywood's screwball comedies, or have been imitated by them, especially some of the finest written by Ben Hecht on his own or in collaboration with

Charles MacArthur, and by Preston Sturges, often directed by Sturges himself, Lubitsch, and Howard Hawks. (Subsequent film screenwriters and directors, men and women alike, from the 1950s to today, have almost surely taken their plot patterning not from Shakespeare but from screwball comedies and their direct predecessor, wisecracking Broadway and vaudeville of the 1920s.)

3. The marital wrap-up looks only questionably happy, resolved for the sake of children, that is, the future. We groan that if the hero was a person, rather than a role, he wouldn't deserve the heroine. In doing this we unconsciously project a "through line" to time to come; we assume that once a bum, always a bum: the fictitious figure cannot change. (And please see the "caution" that follows.) William Carroll remarks,

> . . . rarely if ever does Shakespeare show us a truly happy marriage in progress; we hear about them [it?], in the past or future, but even the few obvious exceptions cannot lay to rest the biographical ghosts lurking around this omission. (1985, 59)

4. There are at least two marriageable couples. One couple, not necessarily the secondary pair, is more broadly comic or even farcical than the other, as in *Much Ado About Nothing*. This device has survived in formulaic Broadway musicals to prove there is someone for everyone.

5. At least one role is taught a lesson (Malvolio, Shylock, Prospero's foes), but (a) the lesson may not be a positive, general one, a trowelful of wisdom to slap down in other circumstances and at other times; (b) the lessons are seldom cynical in tone or substance; (c) roles on the receiving end of a lesson, especially repentant evildoers, sometimes welcome the experience of being taught (Proteus), but an impenitent (Don John) may prove hostile or immune, not only because it entails punishment, isolation, or expulsion.

6. Adaptations abound: outright pilfering, marvels of reinvigoration from Greek and Latin writings, French, Spanish, abundantly Italian—commedia dell'arte and *commedie eruditi*, the latter including pastoral romances—Tudor and Medieval English, and from the playwright's predecessors and contemporaries. Almost every recent edition of the plays has documented these sources, some of them painstakingly dug up.

7. The action occupies two principal settings, sometimes contrasted, and a few subsidiary ones. Some paired settings are separated by geography, as in *The Winter's Tale* and *All's Well*. Others are close but distinct, such as the street and the abbey in *Comedy of Errors* or different parts of Windsor in *Merry Wives* or of Vienna in *Measure*

for Measure or of the royal park in *Love's Labor's Lost*. At least one environment promotes desirable results by being friendly to marriage and reconciliations, probably a "green world" (Frye 1965, 182), which appears in assorted shapes: a forest, a countryside, an island, a garden, a park, an "orchard," or simply as foreign terrain. The bucolic setting will very likely undergo (or expect) a seasonal celebration. In many recent productions, the action takes place in one abstract and modifiable set, which whatever the intent (simplifying, economizing, hewing to one theme throughout) often results in the imposition of a false consistency, which may be visual but may also fail to keep faith with textual inconsistencies.

8. A healing of social and personal wounds will follow from a night or nightmare, an endurance test or rite of passage, a social ritual or a mockery of one. Critics who apply ritualistic analysis to Shakespeare, such as Frye, C. L. Barber, and Edward Berry, distinguish between ritual (which amounts to a formalizing of everyday activities and may grow mechanical) and drama, which must *seem* improvised, unpredictable. Berry writes:

> The shipwrecks, banishments, and journeys that begin the plays may be compared with rites of separation, breaking apart lovers, families, and friends, and placing the protagonists in states of social and psychological alienation. The consistent use of symbolic geography in the plays—the movement of characters into the "holiday" or "green" worlds so important in the criticism of C. L. Barber and Northrop Frye—creates mysterious landscapes analogous to the sacred forests of initiation. In these enchanted places, Shakespeare's protagonists experience the dislocations and confusions of identity, the ordeals, and the education characteristic of the liminal phase [a transitional rite]. (1984, 5)

9. The playwright will manipulate different levels of awareness: Bertrand Evans calls them "discrepant awarenesses" of what is happening in the action between (a) some of the roles and others; (b) all the roles and the audience. The spectators are usually at least one up on the characters (1960). The practice calls on multilayered dramatic irony and often conspiracies, which are fertile only in generating plot variations.

10. Conflicts between generations are endemic in these comedies, no less than in other authors'. Young lovers defy and usually defeat paternalism in its varied guises; they also extract good terms—money and concessions. The comedies offer no outright sexual rivalry between fathers and sons (as in, say, *The Miser*), only a few conflicts between them, found in subplots: *Two Gentlemen; The Winter's Tale*; Lucentio and Vincentio at the end of *Shrew*; Bertram

and the stand-in for his father, the King of France. Most generation gaps hang between fathers and daughters, in the revered
Greek New Comedy tradition. Mothers are rare, although among
the pairs of heroines, some "mother" others (Rosalind and Celia).
In *Comedy of Errors*, the mother figure, who is also a mollifier, appears only in the last act but plays a critical role. The blameless,
accused mother of *Winter's Tale* disappears for most of two acts, her
place taken by a hardier mother figure (Paulina); while Mrs. Page
and Mrs. Ford in *Merry Wives* are themselves the heroines, although one has a marriageable daughter and the other a husband
more suspicious than a curmudgeonly father. The Countess in *All's
Well*, mother of the hero and guardian of the heroine, would love
to bring about the marriage between them that does eventually
take place. Beneficent super-mothers in the form of two goddesses
and Juno's messenger take part in a masque in *The Tempest*.

11. Further impediments to marriage are sure to crop up. In *Comedy of
Errors* these arise from the given circumstances: the unmarried
brother looks identical to the married one and the domestic servant looks identical to *his* brother, the servant from out of town,
to the bewilderment of the wife of one and the unpledged fiancée
of the other. In *Shrew* and *Much Ado* the principal female partner
becomes the obstacle; in *All's Well* and *Twelfth Night*, for different
reasons, the obstacle is the principal male partner; in *Measure* it's
an unexpected male suitor; in *Tempest* it's the father; in *Dream* it's
a hobgoblin.

12. Even though questions remain about the order in which
Shakespeare wrote his plays, one cannot help noticing in his
work, from *Comedy of Errors* on, a break with the comic form he
borrowed from Greek Middle Comedy as processed by Plautus and
Terence. A most startling subversion occurs in the last scene of
Love's Labor's Lost, but every play displays what must be regarded
as undercutting or overlaying of the comic form.

13. In every comedy—but not only in the comedies—we find the pres-
ence of at least one clown or fool, nearly always masculine: the
Dromios in *Comedy of Errors*; Dull, Costard, and Mote in *Love's
Labor's Lost*; Launce and Speed in *Two Gentlemen*; Sly and (in places)
Grumio in *Shrew*; Bottom and (to some extent) Puck in *Dream*;
Launcelot Gobbo in *The Merchant*; Dogberry in *Much Ado*; Jaques
and Touchstone in *As You Like It*; Feste in *Twelfth Night*; Lavatch in
All's Well; Pompey (and Lucio) in *Measure for Measure*; Autolycus
and the Old Shepherd's Son (explicitly called "Clown") in *Winter's
Tale*; Trinculo and, less definitely, Caliban in *The Tempest*. In *Twelfth
Night* Feste succeeds in proving Olivia a fool by logic (1.5.35–69),

but even as he does so, he proves she is not a fool-qua-clown by role, because he draws out of her not a glimmer of wit. Maria in *Twelfth Night*, Lucetta in Two Gentlemen, Margaret in *Much Ado*, and Mistress Quickly in *Merry Wives* take on roles that are not quite clown-fools, but similar in function as dispensers of humor (unmeant comedy) and wit. A clown and a fool are not conceptually the same—the clown, misusing language, misunderstands situations, while the fool is wise and at times witty, poetic, and cryptic—but in practice Shakespeare interchanges the titles fairly freely. Mostly the fool-clown is a servant, often with the privilege of speaking his mind without severe inhibition, though he can also take on the girth and knightly rank of Falstaff. But the clown-fool seems to stand for more than he embodies.[1] In a dictionary of symbols, under the heading of *Clown* we read the following:

> The clown is traditionally the figure of the assassinated king. He symbolizes the inversion of the royal proprieties in his accoutrements, his words, his attitudes. For majesty there is substituted drollery and irreverence; for sovereignty, the absence of all authority; for fear, laughter; for victory, defeat; for blows given, blows received; for the most sacred ceremonies, ridicule; for death, mockery. He is like the wrong side of a medal; the opposite of royalty: parody incarnate. (Chevalier and Gheerbrant 182–89, 263; my translation)

The ramifications of this symbolic "over-role" are momentous, especially for the staging of scenes in which one or more clown-fools appear—and even more especially when the plotting confronts them with a ruler who may stand for their conceptual past: Orsino for Feste; Duke Senior for Jaques and Touchstone.

14. Inconsistencies crop up when the principal roles alter under the impact of the plotting, to reveal new aspects of themselves. The alterations may look slight or drastic from scene to scene or line to line, and seldom accord with the dictates of nineteenth-century realism. Nevill Coghill writes, "He who holds too tenaciously in the study of Shakespeare to 'realism' and the Unities has left the punt and is clinging to the pole" (in Muir 1970, 198). Critics have pointed to not only the purloinings from Ovid's *Metamorphoses* but also the actual metamorphoses in the roles themselves between the early and later acts of each play, even between sequential scenes—or sequential lines. These metamorphoses do and should affect the acting, especially its sincerity. Shakespeare's zestful demonstrations of the plasticity of roles serve to witness the plasticity of the beating heart. William C. Carroll traces varieties of metamorphosis in Ovid and in Shakespeare's comedies, such as conver-

sions from human beings to beasts or monsters, male to female, the reverse, and lovers to haters. These changes may start out as literary conceits, but they require actors to play each moment wholly, without need to reveal residues of earlier states of being and without anticipating later ones. Playing the moment compares with living the moment, cherishing this performance because it will die and never come back to quite the same life. Janet Suzman, a consummate actor and teacher, writes:

> Acting is only alive when it is concentrated *in the moment* [her italics] . . . A face that is really concentrated is a beautiful thing to see. I think that is why athletes are so good to watch. And babies. They are in the moment. (1996, 34–35)

She further suggests: "The still and concentrated centre from which all art flows resides in a moment, the here and now" (152). But playing each moment doesn't mean continual overplaying; a performance needs varied emotional and vocal topography. Actors and directors trump their own hands when they flatten the acting to avoid exceeding a moment to come or try to conform with a moment earlier Roles don't lend themselves to a summing-up in one or two adjectives unless they speak only two or three lines and remain for one or two minutes on stage. It is possible to describe the Hostess who materializes at the beginning of the Induction to *Shrew* as "indignant" or "shocked" or "mercenary," because after exchanging a few lines with Christopher Sly, she disappears forever, that is, until this evening's performance. Because of changes, the evolution of a role, we best describe it when we say what place in the action we refer to.

15. In Shakespeare's theatre, as in other plays, structure, one of the trickiest words to pin down in theatre criticism, can mean the bones, the architecture, the sequence of acts and/or scenes, the order of the entrances and/or exits of the roles, a shift from instability of a dramatic situation to stability, and other formations that denote a comedy's framework. Some critics believe the overall movement of a play takes it from stability to instability and thence back to stability. I can think of only one Shakespeare comedy in which we witness an initial stability, and that very short-lasting: in *The Winter's Tale*. Initial stability as a rule *precedes* the action. As a Shakespeare comedy's action typically opens, a previously stable situation is already in flux and now a conflict (*Dream*) or tone of sadness (*Twelfth Night*, *The Merchant*) rules the scene. But what *determines* the structure? It has to do with attempts to manipulate the spectators' feelings. Structure depends on creating favorable expec-

tations: Kate will marry Petruchio against all odds; Rosaline will yield to Berowne; these expectations will be fulfilled or left unfulfilled. Irregularly resolved resolutions, common in Shakespeare's comedies, do not fully unify the play's strands; they may pull them together into a hasty clutch, but leave them unfused.

A reminder: not every comedy incorporates every one of the fifteen touchstones listed here. And a caution: it strikes me as dead-ended thinking to indulge in ethical criticism, approving or disapproving of the roles' stage behavior and speeches. They are what they are to make the comedy what it is. Such a statement sounds too elementary to bicker with, but surprising numbers of otherwise imaginative commentators frown on some of Shakespeare's most enthralling figures, like Tamora or Thersites or Timon, and even Falstaff. The reproaches slide from annoyance at what the roles *do* into moral judgments of what they *are*, as though to complain that they would be unwelcome at an office bash, in a family gathering, in church at Christmas, or on a witness stand. Pronouncing on the morality of roles that zealously carry out their tasks as miscreants, and occasionally suggesting how they might reform (the "if only he had realized" ploy), resemble the practice known in playmaking circles as script development or "workshopping," where dramatic art is blunted by reaching to realize "characters you feel for" and "situations everyone can believe in" and "writing about what you know"—by struggling to achieve blunt plausibility. Admiring one of the magnificently sketched villains in Shakespeare (or in Dostoevsky, Dickens, or Jonson) is not the same as praising criminality. Apropos of *2 Henry IV*, critic Allan G. Chester writes:

> We need not condemn Hal too severely [for brutally spurning Falstaff]. Good judgment would have taught Falstaff that the laws of England would *not* be at his commandment after the death of the old king, and delicacy would have forbidden him to intrude himself so abruptly into Hal's new situation. (Harbage 1969, 705)

Good judgment is about the last characteristic one would expect of any of Shakespeare's three Falstaffs, thank heaven.

As a possible result of well-meant character assassination on the part of critics, some directors now deconstruct comedies so as to lift the theatrical weight off role and character; to purge dogged realism and draw attention to the artificiality of plays; to relieve the audience of the strains of dubious characterization and narrative suspense by putting in their place an impersonal staging such as rituals, mystifying light and shadow, or patterned arrangements of the actors. The effects may prove pleasing, but relieving a comedy of colorful roles may equally relieve it of comic content. At the deconstructive end of today's theatre we find plays transformed into visual festivals featuring Craig-like sub-supermarionettes or, worse, statues. Gozzi liked to create statues in his Tales for the Theatre. In *The Green Bird,* Calmon, the King of the Statues, warns the hero, a brash philosopher, that if he keeps harping on the same few ideas he "will learn how like a statue a man can become" (1.10).

Unstable Labels

The original grouping of Shakespeare's comedies by Heminges and Condell, who, for all we know, were respecting the author's own classification, has undergone few refinements by scholars since the 1623 publication of the First Folio. *Comedy of Errors* and *Shrew* strike us today as being closer to farces than to comedies. It is hard to treat *1 Henry IV* as strictly a history play when its double main plot (Bolingbroke versus the Percy family and the King's displeasure with his heir, Prince Hal) almost drowns under the satiric (virtually Satanic) downpour of Falstaff. Can we still look on *The Merchant of Venice* as a comedy when neither its eponymous role nor its outstanding male role survives happily? I am certainly ready to scrap the term "problem play," apropos of *Measure for Measure, All's Well,* and *Troilus,* when every play by this author raises large questions of structure and genre. In the case of *Troilus,* sometimes referred to as a "problem comedy," the unhappy end of the action, with the blasting of the love of Troilus and the treacherous murder of his brother, works so strongly against the comic elements, such as the cynicism of Thersites and Pandarus, itself not altogether funny, that this extraordinary work deserves to be viewed as *sui generis,* an anti-Romance, if it has to be classified at all. My choice of comedies to discuss in this book almost lines up with the First Folio's, because I see no way of improving on it, except with the addition of *1 Henry IV,* which can still be a history, too.

In each subgrouping here the plays remain in something like the accepted chronological sequence. These groupings are not clearcut; every reader will realize that most of the comedies could live comfortably under the rubrics "Love, True and False" and "Woman vs. Man" and even, if less suitably, under "Justice." Nor do the plays, in my view, form a rising curve of accomplishment or a falling curve, whether one adverts to the quality of their prosody or complexity of the roles or rhyming slickness or integration of scenes or subtlety or profundity or any other declared standard I've seen. *The Tempest* is in my view *a* (not *the*) summit of its author's achievement and not his most serene work, despite its legacy to speechwriters who sweat their way through dictionaries of quotations.

The inconsistency of roles, which this book defends, is not a new idea. I keep running into one or another version of it adumbrated in the writings of others, and it appears to be implicit in most of my own earlier writings. It must have haunted me for years. Rather than offering us steady or settled portraits, the big and small roles display the equivalent of a series of pixillated takes, as in cinema when a number of frames are omitted and the actors' faces and bodies jerkily take on new expressions and postures. This technique does not correspond to the inevitability of gradualness created by superimposition, a stunt that a slick filmmaker like Victor Fleming relied on to turn Spencer Tracy from Dr. Jekyll into Mr. Hyde: a sneer added to the mouth, pouches under the upper lip, accentuated facial shading. The images I am thinking of are sudden, discrete, baffling, not motivated and morphed.

They come about from harsh clashes written into the roles and from milder repercussions of one role upon others; they also come from artistic and temperamental collisions between one actor and another in their scenes together, consequences of the mercurial nature of performers. Theatre boasts of being a matter of collaboration, and so it is: the more usual and jingoistic word is *teamwork*. But various forms of internal friction—*solowork?*—also supply contributions to enactment.

A Legal Gimmick?

Jekyll/Hyde, that two-headed Hydra, makes one think of the inclination among today's defense attorneys to plead "multiple-personality disorder"—a popular term that some specialists prefer to call dissociative disorder—in order to exculpate serial killers or lighten their sentences. The disorder's validity divides psychological practitioners, although it does find respected defenders, such as Daniel C. Dennett.

Some forty years before Robert Louis Stevenson's novel appeared, Poe's notorious stories had dealt with souls—like the narrator of "The Black Cat"—who feel helpless to prevent evil from straining out of them.

> Who has not, a hundred times, found himself committing a vile or a stupid action, for no other reason than because he knows he should *not*? Have we not a perpetual inclination, in the teeth of our best judgment, to violate that which is *Law*, merely because we understand it to be such? This spirit of perverseness, I say, came to my final overthrow. It was this unfathomable longing of the soul *to vex itself*—to offer violence to its own nature—to do wrong for the wrong's sake only—that urged me to continue and finally to consummate the injury I had inflicted upon the unoffending brute. One morning, in cold blood, I slipped a noose about its neck and hung it to the limb of a tree;—hung it with the tears streaming from my eyes, and with

the bitterest remorse at my heart;—hung it *because* I knew that it had loved me, and *because* I felt it had given me no reason of offense;—hung it *because* I knew that in so doing I was committing a sin—a deadly sin that would so jeopardize my immortal soul as to place it—if such a thing were possible—even beyond the reach of the infinite mercy of the Most Merciful and Most Terrible God. (1938, 225)

But did Stevenson know, when he concocted his *twinned* figure, of an actual case, something like what Yeats called an anti-self? He published *The Strange Case of Dr. Jekyll and Mr. Hyde* in 1886, five years before Wilde published *The Picture of Dorian Gray*, eleven years before Stoker published *Dracula*, but sixty-eight years *after* Mary Shelley published *Frankenstein, or the Modern Prometheus*, in which one might well see the monster as a "Hydden" version of Frankenstein who ultimately kills his creator, much as Hyde will displace Jekyll. I mention these books only: in many others there exist direct or implicit multiple personalities. Could Stevenson imagine the doubleness of Jekyll/Hyde distended by other novelists (and by screenwriters) into the wolf men and vampire men and spider women and evil, self-uglifying portraits? And into the three faces of Eve and later the umpteen faces of Sybil and then the further fragmentation of actual persons into distinct criminal personalities of both sexes (and maybe of intermediate or indeterminate sex), some of which "selves" could be called to testify against others?

Witnesses said that the person who robbed the Seattle-First National Bank branch in Vancouver, Wash., in July spoke with a deep, "male" voice so police were surprised to find Kristin Deane Pearsall, 29, inside a truck matching the one used for the robber's getaway. However, according to police, Pearsall admitted that the robbery was done by John, one of her five personalities. (Shepherd 1996)

The notion of multiple personae has come under widespread attack from psychologists, psychiatrists, and others. Thomas Szasz is quoted as having said that people display multiple personalities when they're unable to reveal their one personality. But the history of multiple personality disorder (M.P.D.) may have some more sinister undertones than Szasz implies. In a substantial magazine article tracing the popularity of the M.P.D. diagnosis and asserting that it almost always is applied to women, Joan Acocella protests that its supposed symptoms correspond to the commonest accusations men level at women and that it undermines the modern feminist movement (1998). Certainly by puffing up each mood or impulse of a person into a full "personality," M.P.D. theory exaggerates fragmentary mentality as it distorts each "fragment" into a mask, a persona.

The very suspicion that an element of deception, of deliberate performance, of mimesis, might account for the appearance in a court room of a man in woman's clothing and cosmetics to supply evidence against a different "self" of the opposite sex; for a woman grunting out answers in a temporary basso tremolo about how a mysterious "he" took over her faculties; for close relatives of such an afflicted (or sick or guileful) person growing so flummoxed they would tell reporters they did not know which personality to expect to meet next—this suspicion is worth a brief follow-up. Whether or not M.P.D. truly exists, even if a mental discontinuity is imagined to go no farther than a case of manic-depression, schizoid highs and lows, or even sustained rage or mere flashes of temper—loss of affective control—whatever makes a person temporarily unrecognizable and therefore estranged—the estrangement could serve as a potent tool for mimicry by actors.

Instead of striving to impose a through line on a complex role, an actor might consider subdividing it, scene by scene, or even beat by beat, into subroles that have their own names or descriptions, and then fully playing out every one as it occurs or recurs in the action, allowing personal traits—including movements, poses, gait, facial expressions, gestures, and voice to carry the only needed continuity, visible and audible, through the part. Or, as sometimes happens, a number of actors can share one role, playing it aspectivally at different moments in the action. Most of us already find it fascinating to observe a doubling up of roles among fewer actors in a cast, so long as each role receives its due. Many actors reinvent their roles for each scene without conscious thought that this is what they do when they play each scene differently and to its (and their) limits. The persistent popularity of *Kind Hearts and Coronets* is almost surely attributable to Alec Guinness's playing (and guying) of one female role and seven male roles in the D'Ascoyne clan.

The technique may go back several hundred years. Of the Globe troupe, Bernard Beckerman remarks:

> The company distributed roles not according to type, despite what T. W. Baldwin says, but according to their importance. The leading actors got the leading roles, and that was presumably because as leading actors they had unusual qualities of imagination, magnetism, and audacity to enable them to meet the extraordinary demands that the major Shakespearean roles make on actors. These roles ask actors to combine oddly contradictory traits in dynamic tension. To tease all these traits to life takes maturity and skill, and then to fuse these traits into a commanding performance requires no less than that special dimension we associate with stardom. (1986, 79)[2]

And the many comments of Bernard Shaw on his ideal actor include:

> My plays require a special technique of acting, and, in particular, great virtuosity in sudden transitions of mood that seem to the ordinary ac-

tor to be transitions from one "line" of character to another. But after all, this is only fully accomplished acting. (In Holroyd 1991, 357)

It seems hardly necessary to say that roles with "sudden transitions of mood" need not be sick—in disorder—out of psychological "order"; but it would take a firm hand to trace a line that analytically separates a living *personality* who is, to whatever extent, deranged, even criminally demented, from a cunningly conceived villain's role that evinces marked contradictions. Since at least Shakespeare's time, actors have known in their bones, or wherever arcane professional knowledge resides, that if they wish to plumb the drama for its greatest artistic rewards, they don't play the character, don't play the personality, don't play consistency. They play each moment—for all it is worth—when the action shunts it into place.

What Is the Moment?

Henri Dutilleux's composition, *Le Mystère de l'instant (The Mystery of a Moment)* reminds us—both the title and the multiple nature of the work itself—that we cannot draw satisfactory defining lines around a moment, any more than we can define its emotional requisites. It could consist of a speech, a beat, a fraction of a beat, two lines of dialogue, one line, a word; and its duration may be governed by a plausible reading—but plausible readings are likely to vary wildly in length, as in style, from director to director. Some extreme instances have to do with four heroine's roles. The long and final silences of Helena and Hermia, of Isabella, and of Hermione imply a range of acting and reacting choices, which partly govern the duration of some of the most critical moments in the plays.

Some Difficulties in Taking Stock of Shakespeare at the Moment

- **The internationality of the comedies.** Germany alone does more of his plays every year than Britain does.[3] Too many noteworthy productions take place to keep up with—and in a multitude of languages.
- **The historical order of composition.** With no fresh evidence to offer, I remain skeptical of dates and sequences, other than as a mind-sharpening pastime. A theory may not reckon with how artists create. After leaping years they can return to an old theme or story, an incident or a role.
- **Shakespeare's comedies on film.** I hoped to write a chapter on this, but a chapter wouldn't nearly suffice; I've settled for remarks

about film and television versions in the various chapters. Books and uncounted articles and dissertations have been devoted to the topic.[4]

- **The authentic treatment of a Shakespeare comedy.** Our research into Globe and Blackfriars productions is scanty, almost all of it open to question. Authenticity, if any, will end up, if anywhere, in the eye and mind of the beholder: do the acting, scenic effects, and other effects look right, feel right? But even when they do, the plays themselves warn us: appearances deceive.

Notes

1. See Gareth Lloyd Evans, "Shakespeare's Fools: The Shadow and the Substance of Drama," in *Shakespearian Comedy*, Stratford-upon-Avon Studies 14, ed. David Palmer and Malcolm Bradbury (1972, 142–159).

2. Beckerman's reference to Baldwin must allude to *The Organization and Personnel of the Shakespearean Company* (Princeton: 1954; 1961). A fold-out chart between pp. 228 and 229 of Baldwin shows the roles some twenty-nine actors may have played in Shakespeare's plays between 1588 and 1613.

3. According to an article in the *New York Times*, 30 December, 1995, by-line Stephen Kinzer, ll.

4. Among earlier books are Roger Manvell's classic, *Shakespeare and the Film* (1971) and *Shakespeare on Film* by Jack L. Jorgens (1977).

TWINNING

*T*he *Comedy of Errors* and *Twelfth Night, or What You Will* present the ancient muddles when look-alikes cross paths. Twinning opened Shakespeare's career, if *Errors* was truly his first comedy and first play. But even at that early stage of his playwriting he enriched the muddles by outdoing a plot derived from Plautus. To the twins who are masters he added twin servants; these not merely uphold a subplot but color the main plot too.

As his career went forward Shakespeare continued to exceed his sources. A number of times his plotting also drew on mistaken identity, usually in night scenes, and, as in *Much Ado*, at a distance, when Margaret is taken for Hero. But only once more did he resort to twinning. At his career's approximate halfway point, 1600, the year in which it is generally believed he completed *Hamlet*, he again enriched the look-alike, sound-alike theme by producing a twin made up of a boy and a girl. The groundlings in his theatre could swallow the who's-who more readily than we can, because boys played Viola-Cesario and Sebastian-Cesario.

Recent decades have seen attempts—some ingenious, some pathetic—to minimize the physical and vocal differences between the brothers Antipholus, the brothers Dromio, and the siblings Viola and Sebastian. Some of the most effective solutions have simply let the audience's incredulity dissolve under the spell of the actors' conviction.

The Comedy of Errors

In one of her many excellent essays Anne Barton writes, "At its ending *The Comedy of Errors* admits its own artificiality . . ." We might go further and say that the play *flaunts* its artificiality from its opening scene on, as Barton has already hinted when she says that Shakespeare

> pushes the story still further in the direction of that cloud-cuckooland of farce where, by special agreement between dramatist and audience, even the wildest and most coincidental plot structures become acceptable. (1974, 82)

Egeon, desperately talking to stave off a death sentence, says that when his twin "goodly sons" were born in Syracuse,

> That very hour, and in the self-same inn,
> A mean woman was deliverèd
> Of such a burden male, twins both alike (1,I. 54–56)

whom Egeon "bought, and brought up to attend [his] sons" (1,I. 68).

The artificiality of *Errors* resides in the traditional, Plautine elements of its coincidences, misunderstandings, and farce, not in the magic and physical transformations of fairy realms. R.A. Foakes possibly refers to the play's artificiality, temporal, geographical, and dramaturgical, when he calls it "the least romantic of Shakespeare's comedies" (1962, xvii). As further artificial "givens," or what Coleridge called "postulates," Egeon and one son, Antipholus of Syracuse, have landed in the same place, the port where the son's twin, Antipholus of Ephesus, and Egeon's wife, Emilia, live. The visitors arrive twenty-three years after a storm at sea and after the resident son and Emilia reached Ephesus. (Emilia herself adds a decade to the time lapse when she says near the end, "Thirty-three years have I but gone in travail Of

you, my sons"[5.1.401–02]. The rupture of the family has thus result-
ed in the split into mother and one son in Ephesus—although neither
knew the other had come ashore there—while father and remaining
son have sailed, separately, from their home in Syracuse and been parted for seven years. Not one of the four knows that any of the other
three are now there. To spice the complications, the two sons still have
their servants in attendance, the second identical pair, the Dromios,
neither of whom speaks of having any memory of a twin.

DROMIO OF EPHESUS . . . Will you walk in to see their gossiping?

DROMIO OF SYRACUSE Not I, sir, You are my elder.

DROMIO OF EPHESUS That's a question. How shall we try it?

DROMIO OF SYRACUSE We'll draw cuts for the senior. (5.1.419–22)

In the source play, Plautus's *Menaechmi*, which has one pair of twins
only, the sons, they began life with different names. When the father
thought one was drowned, he named the other after him, to keep the
memory green.

It also happens that Egeon has only a few hours to procure a sum of
money, while one son has just received that very sum in gold coin from
a merchant and given it to his servant to deposit at their inn. A law of
mutual hatred between the two ports in question has decreed that

> if any Syracusian born
> Come to the bay of Ephesus, he dies,
> His goods confiscate to the Duke's dispose,
> Unless a thousand marks be levièd
> To quit the penalty and to ransom him. (1.1.19–23)

Therefore, unless father and son meet before the literal deadline, and
unless the son, or some other great-hearted soul, pays the fine, Egeon
will hang for merely setting foot on Ephesian soil. Farce and melodrama, those blatantly artificial genres, here criss-cross, joining their
strength in places and, as always, thriving on flukes studiously arranged by the author.

Since either of the Antipholi and either of the Dromios will be
mistaken for his twin, further coincidences thicken the artificiality.
Because the four young men share two names, when the wrong one
of either pair is addressed by name, he will respond. And because each
young man looks *exactly* the same as his twin, we infer that he wears
exactly the same clothes, has exactly the same haircut, the same facial
hair (beard, mustache, sideburns, or the same absence of these), the
same voice and accent. At least two women intimate with the Ephesian pair accept the boys from Syracuse as substitutes. After Adriana,
the wife of Antipholus of Ephesus, has eaten lunch with her husband's

twin, she insists she lunched with her husband; so does her sister, who joined the meal. Dromio of Syracuse encounters a "mad mountain of flesh that claims marriage of me" (4.4.152), his twin's love match named Nell, who could tell him "what privy marks I had about me, as the mark of my shoulder, the mole in my neck, the great wart on my left arm" (3.2.150–52), so that the alikeness extends to warts, moles, and other "privy marks" that should assure identification. The Antipholi and their respective Dromios may not share the physical intimacy of sex partners, but they grew up together since birth; nonetheless, each repeatedly misidentifies his master or servant.

The play asks of the audience more willing suspension of disbelief: that Antipholus of Syracuse, who has spent years "to find a mother and a brother In quest of them, unhappy" (1.2.39–40), and his much more alert servant, who accompanies him, don't twig that they have come to the end of the search, even for a while after they see their brothers standing before them, and that the confusions arise from the presence in town of all four at the same time. In Plautus the recognition scene between the Menaechmi is even more strung out than in Shakespeare, but pays off richly in laughs.[1]

According to some critics, from Coleridge on, the extravagant artificiality declares the work a farce, rather than a comedy; it requires an interpretation broader than comic and with only limited characterizing of the roles. The belief has much to recommend it, although it may prove one-sided as an acting prescription, for the play does not lodge irremovably in farce, but rather veers in and out of it, so that one cannot confidently tell where the farcical borders begin and end. But then, *Errors* is atypical Shakespeare in most respects, not the least being a strained conformity with the hypothetical unities rivaling that of *The Cid*. It also does not partake of all the comic characteristics outlined in my introduction. In whatever directions the production is steered, the actors will need to keep adjusting their behavior and moods to match the demands of the roles.

But are the requirements as limited as is often suggested? Actors persuade their fellow actors, the audience, and the reviewers most effectively when they firmly establish their characters in a scene or subscene (a "beat") and adequately differentiate them from the other characters. Firmly establish, however, doesn't mean uniformly establish, any more than differentiation from the other characters means emotional separation from them. Even before the actors set foot, mind, and heart inside this play's roles, how do those roles alter in the course of this particular action? Not unpredictably at first. They respond to each situation as conventionally as most people might do. They do not baffle us—momentarily or forever—with the sort of surprise reactions we witness in, say, *Winter's Tale* or *Merchant of Venice*.

When Adriana, the wife of Antipholus of Ephesus, suspects her husband of infidelity, she rages. Her sibling, Luciana, faces women's matrimonial inferiority with such placid resignation that commentators frequently award her the sobriquet *raisonneuse*, and compare her lines with Kate's in the final scene of *Taming of the Shrew*. Like Kate, though, the sisters reverse themselves in the last act. Adriana, who accuses her spouse of madness, is tricked by his mother, Emilia, into admitting she might have nagged him crazy with her suspicions: "Thy jealous fits," says Emilia, "Hath scared thy husband from the use of wits" (5.1.85–6). At that point, Luciana defends her sister, turns against her brother-in-law, and chides Adriana: "Why bear you these rebukes, and answer not?" (5.1.89).

Characterizing these female roles consistently would demand that the two actors step out of character—for a few seconds, since they soon revert to their former "selves." But in both instances they have each had explicable motives. Adriana confesses she has played the shrew with her husband because she now sees that giving way to her jealousy will defeat its obscured purpose, to win him back. But she gets furious again—this time with a messenger (5.1.178–79)—who tells her that her husband is where he cannot be, doing what he is incapable of. In a similar fashion, Luciana defends *and* chastises her sister when she feels that Adriana came under unfair attack and may lose the chance to explain what happened.

Comments like the ones in the preceding paragraphs form much of the substance of discussions during rehearsals of a realistic play. But this is Shakespeare, his farce and comedy as well as melodramatic strokes; the artificiality inherent in the action stakes its claims, too. These women are not "straight men," not feeds. Their misapprehensions, rather than they themselves, amuse us. Luciana may strike some people as being sensible and compliant enough to warrant Shakespeare's using her as a spokeswoman, but she first justifies her brother-in-law's lechery, then gripes about his unreasonable doings, when, *in the action,* he has behaved neither lecherously nor unreasonably. All he did was lose his temper after he brought home a couple of business associates for lunch, only to have his wife appear to lock the front door against him, after which he went off to share a meal with a neighboring courtesan under the impression that Adriana was deceiving him. Luciana may, as a role, adopt a calm and rational manner, but since laughable mistaken identities figure in the action, Luciana mistakes the identities as often as other figures in the action do, and so becomes an early butt of those mistakes. The one role who makes no mistakes, Emilia, enters the action very late, as an abbess *ex machina*. A wise and mature lady, she knits (or knots) the last scene together when she proves to be the missing corner in the family quadrilateral;

she might also qualify for the spokesperson trophy, except that sprinkles of farce obviate the need for anybody to speak for this young author when he speaks so eloquently for himself.

Back to the play's artificial construct, the perfect look-alikes . . . How does a director cope with this fortuity? Refuse to do the play unless two pairs of identical twins or near-clones audition? They need only be similar in build and features and voice; the audience doesn't have to see birth marks—which, in any case, could be easily added. Or since the brothers alternate on stage, kept out of each other's way until the final, collective scene, one actor could play both Antipholi and one actor could play both Dromios, as in the BBC TV version of *Errors*—Michael Kitchen as both Antipholi and Roger Daltry, the rock singer, as the two Dromios. The director, James Cellan Jones, brought in two extras for the final scene to play the second brothers; they wore duplicate costumes and stood with their backs to the lens. The image worked satisfactorily for a film; there are several studio methods of presenting an actor on screen playing opposite himself and coping with the act 5 encounters between the Antipholi and the Dromios. But in a playhouse these and comparable devices amount to literal-minded simplifying. If the production is absorbing enough otherwise and if the other actors treat the Antipholi and Dromios as though they are physically indistinguishable, the audience will follow suit. The action needs to have, and to exhibit, an internal reality. A Dromio might, for example, peer into the face of the Antipholus who is *not* his master from a distance of three or four inches. Skeptical at first, he comes away convinced that the man behaving so erratically, so erroneously, so unlike his master, is his master. If he does it well, the audience accepts that the Dromio sincerely takes the stranger for his Antipholus; this is the only kind of believability the production calls for.

Or does it require even that? In the casting and staging a director may feel tempted to bring in at least one dramatic distinction between the brothers to help the audience sort them out. The Ephesian Dromio, for instance, might have machinegun speech, while the Syracusan Dromio stammers or drawls or has a different regional accent. But why should the audience be helped to sort them out? If at times it's as confused as the roles are, the production may benefit; the "discrepant awarenesses" discerned by Bertrand Evans—the perceptual advantage an audience has over the roles—will dissipate. Such a threat to the audience's safe distance from the play's events might fit in with the plans of a director who hopes to supplant the theatre's "real" reality with some virtual reality.

But do the two Antipholi inherently differ as roles? Some critics deduce so. Paul A. Jorgensen, who calls them "remarkably dissimilar for identical twins," elaborates:

> The Syracusian brother is melancholy, earnest, and almost tragically
> inclined. He speaks some of the most ardent poetry in the play and
> would probably, given the continued life, have developed into the copy
> of his father. The Ephesian Antipholus, on the contrary, is a prosper-
> ous, rather insensitive businessman, a respected citizen who expects
> his wife to behave with complete moral propriety while he himself
> tastes, in moderation, the pleasures of the town. He is also a realistic
> version of the husband with a nagging wife. (in Harbage 1969, 56)

But in Shakespeare's text the brothers' *situations* differ, and one can
easily misread into the roles characteristics that arise not for literary-
psychological reasons but from the force of circumstances. Even so,
the Antipholi are not all that dissimilar. They both feel out of place.
The Ephesian is a settled burgher, married and master of a household.
A goldsmith who does business with him, accounts this Antipholus

> of very reverend reputation . . .
> Of credit infinite, highly beloved,
> Second to none that lives here in the city.
> His word might bear my wealth at any time. (5.1.5–8)

This infinitely creditworthy gentleman keeps seven or possibly eight
maidservants, as well as Dromio and unspecified manservants. The
evidence for the bevy of servants is Dromio's call to anyone in the
house to open the door: "Maud, Bridget, Marian, Cicely, Gillian,
Ginn!" (3.1.31), plus Dromio's love, Nell (or Dowsabel), who does not
appear but is said to have a body as vast as the seven continents; she
may correspond to another maidservant called Luce, who does appear.
This Ephesian citizen has spats with his wife, but no spots on his reputation. He grows angry and vindictive when denied admission to his
home, and when the combined Dromios, to whom he and his brother
give contrary orders, cannot carry them out.

   But in the pure roles, neither brother has personal qualities that
mark him as distinctive. In tracing two differences between the Antipholi, Stanley Wells refers to the line spoken by Antipholus of Syracuse about his Dromio who lightens his "humor with . . . merry jests"
when he feels "dull with care and melancholy" (1.2.20–21). Wells remarks in his commentary:

> Antipholus of Syracuse is presented as more introspective and liable
> to melancholy than his brother. It is perhaps significant that this
> Antipholus soliloquizes whereas the other does not. (1980, 127)

Various other differences have been suggested, although some do not
lend themselves to stage realization. In the folio edition of the play,
1623, the Antipholi are referred to in the cast list by Latin tags as respectively *errotus* (wandering) and *serruptus* (seized or stolen).

We might sum up the Ephesian Antipholus by referring not to what he is but what he does: contend with constant frustration to find the familiarities of his daily existence turning unfamiliar. His brother, perplexed by this community, keeps running into locals who shower friendship and bounty upon him; they hail him affably and respectfully, know his name, invite him in for an affectionate midday meal. An unnamed First Merchant meets him soon after he arrives and hands him money from a transaction, then departs to do business elsewhere. Meanwhile, "his" Dromio, the only other person he knows in Ephesus and normally a "trusty villain," denies over and over having heard what his master asked him to do only minutes before. The sudden unreliability must be due to this other-worldly Ephesus, with its reputation as a haven for magicians, mountebanks, and witches of both sexes. But in spite of the spooky atmosphere of Ephesus, the brother from Syracuse has met and been entertained by two lovely sisters, one of whom entrances him. If only she would not inexplicably try to foist him off on her sister he'd feel more at ease when courting her. Still, thanks to his generally warm reception, he has a satisfied stomach and an eager libido—at first.

Then a courtesan, whose exterior looks winsome enough to house a devil, asks him for a chain he promised her. The goldsmith, Angelo, and another merchant want him to pay for the chain and even threaten to kill him. One of his erstwhile hostesses cries out for him to be spared because he is mad. Finally, being unable to get down to the harbor and sail away from this accursed port on the first available vessel, he and his Dromio must take refuge in the priory with the Abbess. She will shortly prove to be his mother, but for the moment, he reels from one mischance to the next. Even before his luck turned utterly sour, he yearned to escape.

> Here we wander in illusions.
> Some blessed power deliver us from hence! (4.3.43–44)

The Antipholi's father, the first member of the family we meet, did not enjoy even a temporarily friendly reception: he has come ashore on territory that bristles with hostility. The Duke thinks he is being merciful to Egeon when he grants him a reprieve until that evening:

> Try all the friends thou hast in Ephesus;
> Beg thou or borrow to make up the sum,
> And live . . . (1.1.153–55)

But we are not told of any friends Egeon has in this city. The Duke continues by saying, "If no, then thou art doomed to die," and orders the jailer to "take him to thy custody" (1.1.155–56). Egeon's hope for life appears to be nil. At last, after five hours of languishing in dread in his cell, or else wandering the streets in search of nonexistent friends, his Syracusan son recognizes him. That young man has committed the same crime and lived through the same peril as his father without being apprehended, thanks to his identical appearance to that hitherto-solid citizen, his brother. The brother, the Ephesian one, virtually a stranger to his father, thereupon offers the requisite sum to free Egeon. But the Duke abruptly reverses his stern death sentence and rejects the fine: "It shall not need. Thy father hath his life" (5.1.391).

This act, a single recognition scene with unexpected twists in motivation, seems to have served Shakespeare as a rough model for act 5 of *Measure for Measure.* In addition to the reverse turns in the last act, *Measure* resembles *Errors* in the approach of a wronged woman to the Duke and her cry for "Justice!" The Duke may swerve into his about-face because from the beginning he felt a sneaking sympathy for Egeon but had to conceal it behind a magisterial manner. In the colorful BBC TV production, Cyril Cusack as Egeon could hardly get out the woeful tale in act 1 of separation from his wife and a son, while spectators in the public square sniffled, and even the Duke (Charles Graves) wiped his eyes, so that when he nevertheless went on to impose the alternative, a fine or execution, a gasp went up from the listeners. The Duke may also feel awe for the abbess Emilia, who took command of the stage not long before and whose presence, as a Syracusan, offends the law as much as her husband's, although after the shipwreck Emilia came to Ephesus via Corinth and is probably thought of as a Corinthian; in any case, she has served in Ephesus for almost thirty-three years as the venerated abbess of the sacred temple of Artemis. And then, the Ephesian son tendering the money—now expressed in ducats, rather than marks—once, as he reminds the Duke, "bestrid thee in the wars and took Deep scars to save thy life" (5.1.192-93). The Duke may also feel relieved that everybody else feels relieved and he does not have to punish or reward any citizens, Ephesians or strangers, to conform with the brutal law. Or, more simply, as Harold Brooks says, he acts out of a spasm of mercy:

> More than justice is needed: without mercy, the godly prince is not himself. Now, inspired to what he had declared impossible, [he] freely remits the debt Egeon owes the law. (1961, 22)

Antipholus of Syracuse has the longest role in number of lines, but in performance the Dromios are likely to dominate the action. They align themselves with two commedia dell'arte traditions: they get drubbed for the smallest vexations they unintentionally visit on their masters, and they are brainier than those masters. But in several respects they break with commedia convention. Although smart, they are not cunning or at times malign like Arlecchino or Pulcinella; nor do they trump up the sort of schemes (to win money or a wife or a fight) that generally fall to pieces or yield unwanted results. They are loyal and long-suffering companions, never insolent, not even mildly disobedient. They therefore have all the more reason for resenting the ingratitude they both receive from their masters' sticks when they have each carried out the precise errands the masters demanded. In addition, they emit most of the play's wit and word play, rather than being responsible, as in commedia scenarios, for inordinate set-tos of bumping and bruising. They are, in a word, intellectuals—we might almost swear, scholars—who enjoy nothing more than concocting a jolly quibble or a phrase with three or more meanings and a literary allusion or two, a strong hint of bawdry, a Latin tag thrown in, whenever apt, and a preoccupation with punishment. An instance:

DROMIO OF EPHESUS Mistress, *respice finem*—"respect your end," or rather, to prophesy like the parrot, "beware the rope's end." (4.4.41–43)

And another:

ANTIPHOLUS OF SYRACUSE . . . If you will jest with me, know my aspect,
And fashion your demeanor to my looks,
Or I will beat this method in your sconce. (2.2.32–34)

DROMIO OF SYRACUSE "Sconce" call you it? So you would leave battering, I would rather have it a head. An you use these blows long I must get a sconce for my head, and ensconce it too, or else I shall seek my wit in my shoulders. But pray, sir, why am I beaten? (2.2.35–39)

The charm in this last quotation resides principally in the question delayed until the end of the speech. While his master hammers him around the stage, Dromio resists the pain and humiliation for long enough to throw off puns—concerning his head, where the pain and humiliation are being administered—before he would like to know why.

The Dromios are principal agents of farce in the action. If they suffer, we do not share the pain and humiliation. Farce has to stay remote from onstage happenings, nonenveloped, guilt-free. Playwrights have discovered manifold ways to accomplish such a distance for the spectator. And critics have mused busily over the entertainment quotient generated by twinning. Francis Fergusson writes,

> I do not know why two people who are identical are laughable, but they are, and if they are not only the same height and age and weight, but walk and sit in the same way at the same time, the comic effect is stronger. And if there are more than two, we are still more pleased with them. (1957, 146)

Further: a barber cutting hair is not necessarily amusing, but a view of a row of barbers performing the same motions in unison is worth a laugh. (Not so soldiers in ranks or dancers in coordination, because from them we *expect* matching movements, choreographed patterns.) Beyond a certain point, though, the multiplication of perfect doubles could become threatening, rather than funny. And if twins happen to be one female and one male, as in *Twelfth Night*, the effect may not be funny, either.

Fergusson does have a point, though, as numerous plays and movies about visually identical roles confirm (supremely, Chaplin's short *The Idle Rich* or Harpo and Groucho in the mirror scene of *Duck Soup*), even if the point grows sharpest in the final scene when the two Dromios stand together, as if for comparison. We seem to be close to Bergson's theory of automated human figures. As with miniaturization, enjoyment of small children or pets or other animals who behave like grown human beings and seem to satirize them, there is something quaint, not only amusing, about actual or appearing twins; they provoke laughter that has a flavoring of wonder in it. The relative proportions of those two ingredients, amusement and wonder, will vary with the scene. Harry Levin reminds us that "the actual predicament is that of two personalities forced into the same role, rather than that of one personality playing two roles, since the resident twin has the contracts and continuities, and the roving twin intercepts them, as it were" (1965, xxx). In the final moments, the four principal men meet, astounding one another and the onstage onlookers; the amusement factor overpowers the wonder, and the effects are stirred into a frenzy by the play's eagerness to wind itself tight into its apogee before undergoing an almost instant release.

The climax, as it arrives, has not passed through the transforming powers of a "green world"; nor does it reside in two principal settings, but in four, although these might be carelessly said to amount to a unity of place since all four belong in Ephesus. But we can hardly call the play literally atypical if, as I assume from available evidence, Shakespeare wrote it before the other comedies. *Errors'* (fake) unity might suggest that the action has clung to a unifying theme. Barbara Freedman, among others, talks about it as a dream. She points to Egeon as the dreamer because his two scenes of an execution-in-the-offing frame the action. Professor Freedman writes:

> That the action of cruel fate which separated Egeon from his wife was seconded by his own guilty wish for independence is further suggested by the fact that Egeon allows eighteen years to escape without searching for Emilia and is only motivated in his present journey to Ephesus by the loss of his Syracusan son. The crime of marital neglect, in the form of a failure to return home for a significant lapse of time, provides a genesis for the plot, explaining such problematic issues as Egeon's curiously passive acceptance of a decidedly obscure punishment, the

significance of the twins' prolonged punishment for neglected marital obligations at the hands of Adriana and Nell, and the means by which that punishment wins Egeon's redemption. (M. Charney 1980, 240–41)

She goes on to interpret the monetary debts in the play as "a disguised expression of the marital debt," while "the meaningful content of Egeon's debt is disclosed in the marital debts that his sons confront."

Egeon, an old man, finds himself in a foreign country. He has lost both sons; nobody knows him; he cannot evade the harsh sentence. He does not have enough time to seek help and borrow the fine. Even if he had more time, he might not know how best to employ it in these surroundings. He has not seen for five (or is it seven?) years the son he raised in Syracuse and has no idea that he is nearby.

That son, Antipholus of Syracuse, baffled at having landed in foreign, irritating circumstances, wonders if he is in hell—or in a nest of witchcraft and spells. Is he on enemy soil? (He will not learn until the end that the Duke's police or spies or military has caught up with his father but not, so far, with him.) Dromio keeps doing and saying things that confound him. The citizens here somehow know him, but he doesn't know them and is not sure how to respond to them. This woman claims him; that woman, whom he finds enticing, says he has to stay with the other one. He cannot obey either his early impulse or his subsequent yearning to get back onto a ship and escape and rebecome himself.

His brother, Antipholus of Ephesus, is on familiar ground, but for that very reason, all the more unstable. His wife locks him out; old acquaintances baffle him. Dromio follows instructions only intermittently. The wealthy citizen has lost his status as an respected Ephesian. His home has become a den of treachery.

In it, his wife, Adriana, fears she has lost her husband: that she looks too old, too homey and homely, especially when compared to the beautiful, carefree courtesan. Adriana would like, perhaps, to resemble what became known a few years ago in America as "the total woman," the voluptuous housewife; but everything she does to give vent to her feelings of loss and potential loss widens the rift between her and her husband. She, the one role who finds herself on the receiving end of a lesson, does not seem to resent its coming from her newly discovered mother-in-law. Adriana, also the one role who changes quite dramatically, from nagging her husband to thankfully accepting him, provides the play with its excuse for unloading an Ann Landers moral: Love thy hubby; in requital, he will love thee.

Adriana admits that she has sometimes failed to appreciate her husband's good features, but he has not lived a stainless life, either; and so she is not in the wrong for standing up for her rights. That it's the Abbess, like a shrink or a priest in the confessional, who chastises her doesn't negate those rights. Adriana does have a bolder, more admirable role than that of her conforming sister. Luciana suffers her own share of torment from the love pleas of her unmistakable brother-in-law, who attracts her but whom decency, training, and sisterly loyalty tell her she cannot have.

Nightmares settle foggily on the twin Dromios almost as densely as—but more persistently than—the one that surrounds Egeon. The servants can find no way of accomplishing their masters' orders without incurring beatings from the bouts of insanity that the Antipholi undergo. How does one cope with a boss who keeps rejecting what he just asked for and keeps saying he asked for something different?

Even one or two of the minor roles live out their own nightmares: an impatient merchant must catch the next boat out of Ephesus, as soon as he collects money owing from the goldsmith, money the latter cannot afford until he receives payment from Antipholus of Ephesus for a gold chain promised to both Adriana and the Courtesan . . .

Those fears of loss are precisely what support most drama. In tragedies and sometimes tragicomedies, they come to realization. In most comedies the losses are averted, as they are in most older farces like this one. We catch glimpses of them, before the resolution and the escape, and they bear heavily on the vicissitudes of the roles in Shakespeare's comedies no less than in the tragedies and histories. But the happy ending not only reintegrates the roles of Egeon and the members of his family, which arises reborn in the house called the Phoenix. At one time Egeon did steady business in Ephesus, where he is now treated as an enemy. But when Duke Solinus, after all his fuss, lets Egeon off without a penalty, it's as though the malevolent law has been repealed and a reconciliation, if not a trade pact and a peace agreement, struck between Ephesus and its fraternal twin city of Syracuse. The final celebration incorporates a general rejoicing in which we can imagine the entire populace of Ephesus taking part as though to make restitution to Egeon and his family for the nightmare through which they have voyaged.

Note

1. See scene 8 of Palmer Bovie's translation of *The Menaechmi* in *Classical Comedy: Greek and Roman* (Corrigan 1987, 331–40).

Twelfth Night, or What You Will

The title of an anonymous Italian comedy from the mid-sixteenth Century, *Gl'Inganni,* which became one of the likely sources of *Twelfth Night,* means *deceits* or *tricks* or *scams.* The Feast of Fools or holiday dedicated to misrule at that time of the year overturns authority in religious establishments and promotes a feeling of relief, an escape from the even colder discipline levied by the Church than that imposed on Olivia's residence by her steward, Malvolio.

For today's Christmas celebrants, "twelfth night," January 6, marks the burning or other disposal of greetings cards and fir trees. The date also ends musing and sermons about the birth of "the real king"—not at all the same figure as the one Orsino in the play calls the "one self king" (1.1.38), as he daydreams that Olivia will love nobody but him. He broods about becoming her master, although he may also think of becoming master of himself. The French call the play, and the night in question, *La Nuit des rois.* Some critics treat the self-king expression as part of a search by Viola and her twin, or by all the roles for a true identity, an innermost being, the Secret or Intrinsic Self in Others or in the Other or a Quintessential Identity—these capitals become infectious. Such an identity may not exist, but if it *were* found by the end of act 5, how might the audience learn of it?

Detecting an identity *for the play,* an integral theme that lends itself to "high concept," a summing up in a sentence, may increase one's respect for the playwright, as well as the critic, and make for some lively reading. John Hollander's essay *"Twelfth Night* and the Morality of Indulgence" takes the play to be a study of overstuffing, surfeiting of human appetites (desires included). It regards the opening scene and especially

Orsino's speeches as an announcement and résumé of the theme (Hollander, 1959). According to Hollander, the play is itself a nonliteral feast. Olivia and Orsino serve as its co-hosts. Olivia is enjoying a "feast of grief," while Orsino is overdosing on a mixture of lovesickness and melancholy, with a dash of self-pity. But how could this theme translate into theatre, since it isn't literal? The play is short of eating or drinking, which would be visible (and audible), if anywhere, only in 2.3 and perhaps 1.3, unless the director force-feeds these activities into other scenes.

For Nicholas Hytner, whose colorful production came to the Vivian Beaumont in New York in 1998, the theme appeared to be "water, water everywhere," according to a spectators' guide in the program and to four or five inches of blue water under boardwalks at the rear of the stage, a couple of pools downstage left and right, and a downpour of rain that drenched some of the dialogue. Since water shields us before birth and serves thereafter as our most common beverage, it has a starring role in everyone's life and gushes, both salt and fresh, through a number of Shakespeare's plays. But it no more distinguishes *Twelfth Night* than it does *Pericles*, say, or *The Tempest*.

The secondary title, the only one in Shakespeare, has come in for its own share of interpretation. The words are echoed in, or derived from, Olivia's command to Malvolio when Viola first appears as the proxy of Orsino: "If it be a suit from the Count, I am sick, or not at home: what you will to dismiss it" (1.5.105–06). The word *will* can mean wish for, feel like, intend. In 1600 it also connoted the penis. As a playful sobriquet for Shakespeare, it seems to have overtaken "the Bard."

The eighteen scenes in this shorter-than-average text for a comedy by Shakespeare—only *Errors, Dream* and *Two Gentlemen* are shorter—show us an Illyria that never was, even long before the Adriatic and Balkan regions were thrown and sewn together into a quilt called Yugoslavia—with a little Albania on the side. The cross-cutting that flicks between scenes, some of which might have alternated at the Globe between different levels, nowadays accommodates itself often to staircases and acting areas picked out by lighting or, as in Hytner's aquatic production, by gauze screens that descended from and returned to the flies. Illyria might well be a city, like Shakespeare's Ephesus or Vienna, or, come to that, an island like the one in *The Tempest*, since we hear of nobody's traveling to or from it by land. In "Come Hell or High Water: Shakespearean Romantic Comedy" David M. Bergeron twice calls Illyria "idyllic" (in Charney 1980, 113; 114). That spot, city, province may seem idyllic at the end for the two matched or mismatched pairs of lovers, but the other roles know it otherwise. This comedy's jests turn grave, its japes consequential, from Viola's disguise and banterings with Olivia to the Viola-Sir Andrew duel and the gulling and imprisonment of Malvolio.

The two principal settings, Orsino's palace and Olivia's mansion, with their ins and outs, may lie within walking distance of each other. The two scenes specified by Edward Capell's 1768 edition of the plays as taking place on the seacoast (1.2 and 2.1) also seem to belong in that city-port. Some recent editions prefer a vague location for 2.1, presumably to follow a hint in the play that Sebastian and Antonio did not just land but have been companions on shore for about three months. The HarperCollins volume (Bevington 1992, 337) situates the scene, "Somewhere in Illyria." I cannot help thinking of Orsino's ducal palace and Olivia's castle perched on the tops of steep, opposing hills, a run down and a stiff climb up the other side for Valentine, Viola, and Feste as they go between.

Some vividly three-dimensional sets for *Twelfth Night* revived the Constructivism of Exter, Popova, and their contemporaries in Russia after the revolution by inventively exploiting the stage's height, in addition to its width and depth. Other staging devices have also abstracted the look of Illyria: transverse belts that resemble moving sidewalks and allow actors to appear to walk or run without leaving the spot; turntables that bring on a succession of "pie slices" of setting; varieties of modified Baroque wings and backdrops, and modernized, pivoting *periactoi*, derived from Greek and Roman models. Using the latter, a 1948 London production had two squarish boxes on stage: they turned to reveal different faces and reminded reviewers of bathing machines, those one-person changing rooms that swimmers and dippers in the early years of being "beside the seaside" wheeled down to the ocean's edge to avoid exposing skin to prowling eyes. Eric Bentley called them "a couple of small collapsible, adaptable garden huts on separate revolving stages" (1953, 40). Jacques Copeau's *La Nuit des rois* in 1914 had the spare set, properties and simplified lighting associated with his artistry at the Vieux-Colombier.

> The upstage area represented a public room in Olivia's mansion, a rotunda with white walls, containing only essential furniture and two shrubs in green tubs. The rest of the action took place on the forestage, separated off by a pink curtain to indicate the palace of Orsino, and a yellow one for outdoor locales. (Rudlin 1986, 16)[1]

Certain director-designer teams have chosen a unified setting—in some ways representational, in others abstract—which fitted into restricted acting areas and saved money; although in larger spaces such a simplified design can arise from strictly artistic motives. As interpretations of the play multiply and alter—more accurately, darken—most directors still attempt to preserve a beautiful look for Illyria, if only to drape a beguiling, placid surface over troubling undercurrents.

In a comparison-review of two American productions, Michael Bertin describes the scenic design for the version directed by David Mamet at the Circle Repertory Company:

Fred Kolouch's deceptively simple setting was outlined by a high and decaying stone wall that broke off to blend with distant cliffs. The time seemed Mediterranean winter, and we were either in Olivia's garden or just beyond the garden gate. The gate itself was arched, fixing the scene with the prospect of a far and swelling sea. The green-blue sky and sea made the gray-brown rocks colder still. Though a potentially tragic land, however, the place held fast to hope and life, as did the lone and undulating rose vine that worked along the mountain path straining for the sun. The wall contained a mysterious empty statuary niche which was perhaps a muted echo of the unfulfilled life Viola—as "patience on a monument"—would miraculously evade. This was Illyria: antique yet modern in its ambiguity, beautiful yet potentially harsh, illusory yet real, informed by seriousness but happy in an unblinking way. (1981, 196–99)

One of the most elaborately geometrical, yet luxurious single-set Illyrias I have seen (only in a photograph), designed by Albert van Dalsum for a performance at the Stadsschouwburg in Amsterdam, consisted of an open-fronted gazebo perched on a low platform and pierced by Romanesque and other archways; it had Corinthian columns for support and arches retreating in a perspective *allée*, as one of the exits. A painting behind the platform depicted a figure on a white horse looking like an extract from a medieval tapestry, while snatches of background between several columns appeared to be a painted jungle in Douanier Rousseau manner, almost lapping up to and ready to surround the gazebo structure, like a threat. On the platform a throne intended for Orsino faced a tambour-shaped pouffe, presumably for Cesario to sit on, while another property behind it might be Olivia's seat. Dalsum's set, photographed by Teigen (1956, 136), like many another design sketch and photo that features slim, detached, or skeletal arches meant as disconnected entrances/exits, looks as if it could service more than one, if not all, of the Shakespeare comedies. Naturally, one can do no more than guess how Dalsum's three properties functioned during the show unless one does some serious Dutch record-dipping, but in the book illustration they suggest the triangle at the heart of the main plot.

That main plot of what one book by John Dover Wilson regarded as a sample of *Shakespeare's Happy Comedies* (1962) and what Leo Salingar describes as a "'comedy about comedy' and a kind of summing-up of [Shakespeare's] previous work" (1974, 173) might be simplified and diagrammed as three unrequited loves. Viola loves Orsino, Orsino loves Olivia, Olivia loves Cesario, an outward version of concealed Viola. Two of the loves never reach requital. The third, Viola's for Orsino, fructifies, as often in Shakespeare, in a final breakneck tidying-up—and peculiarly. The subplots will dramatize three more fruitless

loves: Antonio's for Sebastian, Aguecheek's and Malvolio's for Olivia—
if Malvolio really does love Olivia and not the possibility that she will
serve as a ladder to his lofty ambitions.

After the preliminary and sketchy part of the story, Viola has come
safely to shore after the ship she and her twin brother were on "did
split." Had the vessel sailed from Italy, which at that time governed Illyria? Viola cross-dresses in an outfit that matches her brother's and is
conveniently to hand. Assisted by the captain who helped her ashore,
she has herself presented "as an eunuch" to Duke Orsino. All of a sudden and between scenes (more scanty story), she becomes the number one adviser to Orsino, entrusted with his most sensitive and
cherished command, to purvey love messages to the unreceptive Olivia, thereby displacing Valentine, who was more aptly named for the
job but had no success with it. Viola, self-described as an intensified
portrait of the long-suffering good sport, does her best to transport
Orsino's sentiments intact, despite her own love for him. Or does she?
Viola's compliments can sound flattering beyond belief; but they can
play as cool or sarcastic, so that her manner belies her words. Ornstein
rightly stresses that Viola's visits to Olivia provide for a contest of sorts
(1986, 150). Olivia welcomes praise such as Viola's "Most radiant, exquisite, and unmatchable beauty" (1.5.166–70) and "Make me a willow cabin at your gate" and so forth (1.5.263–71); its effusive
ambivalence charms her, even though she has heard praise galore before and remained immune to it. Upon granting Cesario admission,
she swiftly ditches plans to extend her period of mourning for her
dead brother to seven years—a device surely dreamed up for fighting
off Orsino—and falls for Cesario in a Shakespearean trice. She may
never have heard that Cesario purports to be a eunuch—or, if she did,
she doesn't believe it. Viola, on the other side, apparently serves Orsino with fierce devotion and so enchants Olivia. Being unusually
sharp-witted, Viola does not fail to notice that Olivia says three times
in that one scene, "I cannot love him" (1.5. 252, 257, 275)—not she
doesn't, but she cannot. Viola may therefore go forward fervently with
the encomia, assured that Olivia will not reciprocate and that if she
can only bide her time, Orsino may yet be hers, Viola's. How could she
foresee that Olivia would be smitten by the vivid praises and by Viola's own unforced winsomeness? But she will: this lady in mourning
declares her love and, in Hytner's version, unable to resist Viola in
drag any longer, flings herself upon "Cesario" and brings her to the
ground while engaging her lips in lengthy suction. Nor can Viola guess
that she is readying the main plot to absorb the marriage of Olivia to
Sebastian and to achieve Orsino's acceptance of her, Viola, miraculously transformed into his "fancy's queen." Roger Warren and Stanley Wells believe that Orsino's early words about being helplessly in

love with Olivia ("My desires, like fell and cruel hounds, E'er since pursue me," [1.1.21–22]) reveal "a ferocity lurking beneath the artifice" that "prepares, incidentally, for Orsino's homicidal outburst when he thinks himself betrayed in the final scene" (1995, 28). Intellectually, the early words, spoken four acts previously, might serve as a preparation for one able to recall them during the turmoil of the final scene, but the memory of them is likely to be swamped by Orsino's vehement outburst, which usually seems called up from the lengthy frustration of being denied Olivia.

In a plotting nexus common to many Shakespeare plays—comedies and others—the Illyrian community accepts some roles and isolates or rejects others. The accepted, the new insiders, are Viola and Sebastian, who skim off the two most desirable partners in Illyria for wealth, power, and looks. Antonio remains an outsider, which he was previously in this duchy, as one of Orsino's enemies; Malvolio chooses outsider status for himself by promising in his exit line, "I'll be revenged on *the whole pack of you!*" (5.1.378, italics added). Aguecheek and Feste stay on the fringes, for differing reasons, not really in or clearly out.

Hardly any two people will agree on disentangling the knot of subplots. I put forward this breakdown with no feeling of finality.

Subplot #1, Malvolio's Fall

For a time Malvolio ("Ill-will") has the false letter that leads him to believe he will enjoy marriage to Olivia and promotion thereby above Toby to the rank of Count: precisely what he wants (what he will). He dreams of smashing through the class barrier, a seventeenth-century (and subsequent) equivalent of the class-glass ceiling, which was not impenetrable but seldom breached. Like Orsino, he hopes to become a self-king, attaining to both Olivia and his idealized self. He disapproves of house guests who do not behave like good children.

Maria paints him coldly enough to justify her intention, shared by Sir Toby, Fabian, and Feste, to humiliate him and have him dismissed by Olivia:

> The devil a puritan that he is, or anything constantly, but a time-pleaser; an affectioned ass, that cons state without book and utters it by great swaths; the best persuaded of himself, so crammed, as he thinks, with excellencies, that it is his grounds of faith that all that look on him love him; and on that vice in him will my revenge find notable cause to work. (2.3.146–52)

Shortly before this he threatens to tell on Maria if she gives Toby any more to drink (3.2.120–23); and sometime earlier, says Fabian, he "brought me out o' favor with my lady about a bearbaiting here"

(2.5.7–8). Like Toby, they have grudges. The humiliation succeeds. In the end Malvolio doesn't wait to be dismissed and estranged: he removes himself from the community. Incarcerated as a madman ("We'll have him in a dark room and bound," says Toby [3.4.137–38]), taunted by Feste, and laughed at by others in the household where he held sway, he goes off to an uncertain fate.

In *As You Like It* Rosalind remarks, "Love is merely a madness and, I tell you, deserves as well a dark house and a whip as madmen do" (3.3.390–91), implying that the dark house and whip belonged to the usual treatment of people judged mad. Explaining the letter and imprisonment, Fabian says,

> How with a sportful malice it was followed
> May rather pluck on laughter than revenge,
> If that the injuries be justly weighed
> That have on both sides passed. (5.1.365–68)

although it's unclear whether he means that the plot was a laughing matter for everyone who hears about it or that Malvolio ought to learn how to take a joke, such as being called insane and locked up in darkness.

The two lines that follow his exit leave Malvolio's future in abeyance:

OLIVIA He hath been most notoriously abused.

ORSINO Pursue him and entreat him to a peace. (5.1 379–80)

Whether the yellow stockings he dons in response to the fake letter are a sign of cowardice, which they were taken to be—and sometimes still are—or a token of narcissism, as Leslie Hotson claims (1954, 98)[2] they would certainly have looked outlandish and laughable for a steward at that time, much as they would for a butler or doorman today. Daniel Maclise's painting, once hung in the Tate Gallery, depicts a moment from 3.4, in a real-life outdoors, an ornamental garden. Malvolio kisses his hand to Olivia, who looks indifferent, rather than dumbfounded. Maria, behind her mistress, uses *her* hand to cover a smile, while a lapdog, seated nearby on its chair, appears to enjoy the steward's effusions. Maria, as the instigator of the trick message from Olivia, plays virtually the same game with Malvolio as is played in *Much Ado* on Benedick and Beatrice, but he discovers the message left in his path, instead of overhearing it, and her aim is to make him repellent, not to match him up matrimonially. She does it out of resentment of Malvolio, but it also diverts Toby and Andrew from their rowdy late-night antics. Or she may even do it out of *jealousy* of Malvolio if he is played as being more attractive than is customary and trying to rise above his station—and her. Or her motivation may be resentment of her mistress, a young woman with everything who seems to value nothing until the arrival of Cesario. Or maybe Maria plans to win Toby with her loyalty and ingenuity; he has openly dropped half-promises:

SIR TOBY I could marry this wench for this device.

SIR ANDREW So could I too.

SIR TOBY And ask no other dowry with her but such another jest . . . *Enter Maria.*

SIR TOBY . . . .Wilt thou set thy foot o' my neck? . . . Shall I play my freedom at tray-trip, and become thy bondslave? (2.5.178–81, 184, 186-87)

It's not surprising that Toby makes a fuss over Maria. She is one of that rare species, a female trickster, one step beyond the forest-smart pretender, Rosalind. Where the female trickster exists in Shakespeare, she generally retaliates for a trick played on her first (as with the merry wives, Ford and Page); or she might divert mischief from its target. Here she performs, like some of Molière's maids (Dorine, Nicole, Toinette), as a female equivalent of the commedia dell'arte zany. By the last act she has become Lady Belch. As for Sir Toby, he is to Olivia what a president's boozy brother is to a president or what the pointy-tongued mother of a speaker of the House is to the speaker. As a part-time embarrassment and a full-time parasite of the shameless Roman variety, Toby portrays a blustery talker, eater, drunk. The surname Belch earns a place in the action. Toby blames his burps not on drink, but on pickled herring. The first name Toby, short for Tobias, might have been connected with the Toby jug, once a common sight in any British pub and in many homes as a mantelpiece ornament and/or drinking vessel.[3] The role of Belch, once a favorite with British audiences for its Falstaffian appetites, today comes across frequently as a cadging blusterer and glutton, owing some features to the Spanish capitano or Roman parasite. After the first trick works on Malvolio, Toby manufactures the second, a swordfight between two unpracticed and inept duelers.

Subplot # 2, Sir Andrew's Wooing

Toby encourages the "foolish knight" (as Maria calls him, 1.3.15) to court Olivia. Later Andrew is persuaded to take Cesario for his rival in love and pays for his credulity: terrified by a duel with Cesario; wounded by Sebastian, the alternate fencer; blindsided; insulted; and nearly pauperized by his fat-living friend. "Aguecheek" seems to imply that he looks wasted and thin, a former plague case with a bad skin whose shape contrasts with Sir Toby's. But if an actor plays him in a routine manner, as too obviously an effeminate, a fop, a dotard, or an imbecile, he will find himself wooing not Olivia but cheap laughs. Max Wright, in Hytner's staging, could claim to be the perfect merry Andrew, with an equally admirable command of gracefulness and gaucherie.

Subplot # 3, Sebastian's Beaching

He has come ashore from the wreck, "bound to the Count Orsino's court" for some reason. His rescuer, Antonio, loves him feverishly, and urges him before they separate for an hour:

> Here's my purse . . . .
> Haply your eye shall light upon some toy
> You have desire to purchase. (3.3.38, 44–45)

During the crowded hour, Andrew takes Sebastian for Viola, and then Toby does likewise. In bewilderment, Sebastian invites them to draw and fight him. Later, Andrew moans, "He's broke my head across, and has given Sir Toby a bloody coxcomb too" (5.1.73–74), as though Sebastian had dropped a brick on his skull. The "broken heads" of the two knights might be a figurative description of their mental shortcomings. Olivia intervenes to save her beloved, as she thinks, from her uncle's ferocity. She yells at Toby, takes Sebastian into her mansion, hands him a pearl, and, while he waits, runs for a priest to marry them, giving the baffled young man no chance to break out of his compliant mood as he wonders at his new fortune and feels puzzled why Antonio, who could have advised him, failed to meet at the appointed place. Antonio has, of course, been arrested while defending Cesario. Olivia returns with the priest; Sebastian swallows his doubts; the marriage ceremony takes place offstage.

Subplot # 4, Antonio's Losses

Without his purse and friend, and as Orsino's enemy who may once have plundered Illyria, Antonio hopes to remain unnoticed there. Warren and Wells draw attention to the dispute in the lines over whether Antonio was a pirate (1995, 41). But seeing Toby and Andrew, who have engaged in the "brabble" with Viola, "the Count's youth," Antonio comes to Viola's help before the duel gets under way, taking her for Sebastian. According to 3.4, Antonio challenges the knights but doesn't get to fight them. His gallantry brings him into the open—and danger. Orsino's police recognize and catch him. In practice, this would mean skipping a contest between the two sword-flailers, Andrew and Viola, but no director would pass up an opportunity to win a batch of knockabout laughs. Antonio is finally pardoned by Orsino, only left forlorn. Intrusion after intrusion have cut off discussion of his fate—the arrival of Sebastian, the twins' recognition scene, the entrance of Malvolio. Olivia has captured Sebastian from him and the priest has attested to her ownership.

Subplot # 5, Unions and a Reunion

Sir Toby has wed Maria offstage, out of gratitude to her for having entrapped Malvolio with her masterly letter. The other pledges help to resolve the main plot. Sebastian abruptly consents to marry Olivia. In a later moment, Orsino pledges himself to Viola as soon as she can get back into her "maiden weeds." Then, as the ranking figure who asserts order, he gets to make the final speech. But the play's concluding words, a song, are entrusted to Feste.

Subplot # 6, Feste's Songs

These comment on the action, not only on life in the world outside the theatre. They will be discussed at more length.

The principal roles could be assigned to categories borrowed and enlarged by Shakespeare from Latin drama. Marvin T. Herrick lists the types of character in Terentian comedy as Young Man, Senex, Matron, Courtesan, Manservant, Parasite, Soldier, all of whom appear variously modified in Shakespeare's comedies, but not all in *Twelfth Night*. (1950). Or the roles may have descended from the ones Northrop Frye points back to in *Anatomy of Criticism*. These remain serviceable as components of *Twelfth Night*, and of other plays analyzed by Frye and subsequent critics. Frye writes,

> With regard to the characterization of comedy, the Tractatus lists three types of comic characters: the *alazons* or impostors, the *eirons* or self-deprecators, and the buffoons (*bomolochoi*). This list is closely related to a passage in the *Ethics* which contrasts the first two, and then goes on to contrast the buffoon with a character whom Aristotle calls *agroikos* or churlish, literally rustic. We may reasonably accept the churl as a fourth character type, and so we have two opposed pairs. The contest of *eiron* and *alazon* forms the basis of the comic action, and the buffoon and the churl polarize the comic mood. (1965, 172)

These types may also have galvanized twentieth-century playwrights into germinating new roles and ideas, as critical perceptions now and then do. But Frye breaks down the roles into creations with consistent behavior patterns, like the Roman ones—in other words, into psychological wholes. The roles in this play become as unstable as any in Shakespeare, elusive and fragmented. Trevor Nunn's movie of *Twelfth Night* (1996) fragments the action even more, much more, with cross-cutting between two scenes that doesn't help either one. Nunn sets the action in the late nineteenth century. At the beginning a luxury liner with Viola and Sebastian aboard crashes, requiring added dialogue and supplying strong visual implications of incestuous love between the twins. The acting, which with one exception is competent, explains the motives away and turns typological, as when Malvolio first appears inspecting the hands of the maids in Olivia's house and the last act turns into a hugfest as the roles crash into each other's arms. The exception is Ben Kingsley's Feste, an impenetrably wise figure whose poetic glances tell anything and everything. The period setting allows for one funny, added touch: Sebastian carries a Baedeker's guide to Illyria.

Rather than following Frye's tantalizing lead and distinguishing the roles by pure types or applied psychology, I prefer to sort them out by their functions in the plotting. Take Malvolio: here is a role, like Shylock's, that directors and actors in the past, especially in the recent past, have portrayed favorably or unfavorably, as the hero, as a villain, or as *the* villain. Leading actors from Bensley, Macklin, Irving, and Copeau to Olivier, Donald Sinden, John Woodvine, Alec McCowen, John Thaw, and Philip Bosco have tackled him and left their mark on criticism, preferring his indeterminacy to the larger role (by line count) but less controversial breadth of interpretation possible for Sir Toby.[4]

To those who regard the play as a festivity, Malvolio appears as a spoiler, maliciously putting an end to drinking, singing, and other pleasures in Olivia's household and alleging he does so for her sake. Yet while he plays her as the "heavy," he doesn't misrepresent what she wants. To others, he comes over as a pompous ass, a class snob, a buffoon, a morbid opportunist, a loyal lover, a desolate swain allowed a glimpse of hope . . . all the way to a victim crudely put upon or a willing prey of tragic impulses.

But Malvolio's *function*, whatever the sum of his psychological qualities in performance, compels him to become the sport of a conspiracy and to fight back, whether strongly or weakly. Precisely this function of *resisting being acted upon* gives a number of beholders a more arresting impression of his plight than of Viola's, and it makes Malvolio's subplot often outweigh the main plot's triangle. In the famous quotation from John Manningham's diary, used by many historians to establish the first date of *Twelfth Night*, the diarist identifies the play by Malvolio's mistreatment.[5] One can understand the desire of male actors for this part, just as it makes sense to choose Jaques in *As You Like It* and Parolles in *All's Well*—if one has the choice. The part has variety plus plasticity: it invites idiosyncrasies.

Viola declares herself a bider of time, not forcing anything to happen, only letting it happen ("To time I will commit," [1.2.60], and "O time, thou must untangle this, not I," [2.2.40]). But she is no patience on a monument like the sister she invents. She works hard for what she wants. If I had to find a maxim for her, it would be the First Witch's "I'll do, I'll do, and I'll do" (*Macbeth*, 1.3.10). As determined in her own fashion as Olivia to get what she wants, she doesn't perform as a shrinking Viola—and not only as Sebastian's birth twin but also Olivia's conceptual twin: their names would be anagrams of each other if Viola's had no second *i* missing.[6] Antonio (for the most part), Sir Andrew, and Sebastian, though, do serve as pawns, as captives of time and chance—or mischance. They differ from Olivia and Orsino, those two O's in authority who attempt to make things happen, wielding their power with motives that are here and there selfish or despotic or even (as they believe) selfless, disinterested. A third contingent consists of Sir Toby, Maria, and Fabian, the three who plot to bring Malvolio down. But Feste, Malvolio, and Viola: where do they belong in the Illyrian scheme of things? Feste keeps his distance from the others' company. Viola achieves her end without conspiring and with no authority. Malvolio turns into a displaced person.

Among all these functional types—procrastinators, authority figures, conspirators, a commentator, a feminist under male wraps, and a scapegoat—we cannot avoid perceiving gradations. Antonio exerts some dramatic pressure, but as a fugitive he cannot function positively. Feste joins in the conspiracy against Malvolio, but only for the Sir Topas episode and briefly in the final scene; through much of the play he remains outside the swirl of movement, trusting the whirligig of time to bring in his plural revenges. Granville Barker, in his preface to the play, remarks that "Fabian is added to take Feste's share of the rough practical joke and set him free for subtler wit" (1995, 177). Malvolio, who plots on his own behalf, believes he carries enough authority to join the authority group and enforce his orders, but in this belief, as in others, he misreads his place in Olivia's household. Sir Toby no less mistakenly sees himself as an authority figure, because of his knighthood; while Sir Andrew participates in the conspiracy, in his bashful fashion. He also drops quantities of money to win Olivia's favor, but, like Roderigo, gets "bobb'd" by his "Iago" into paying for unreturned affection.

The parents of the two pairs of lovers have died or go unmentioned: these youngsters, facing no family opposition, ought to enjoy more independence than their equivalents do in other comedies. Olivia has lost her brother, whom she may have worshiped as an older sibling to account for the solemnity of her mourning, if it's wholehearted. Viola believes her twin, the other remaining member of her family, is dead. The action opens up little of the twins' background. Their father died when they were thirteen, but he did mention the name of Orsino, who, Viola recalls, "was a bachelor then" (1.2.29). This last line could stoke speculation about why her father should mention that name and why she would recall it. Did the father (or Sebastian, who was heading for Orsino's court) hint at a future match between Orsino and Viola? Did Orsino seem old to be unmarried for a titled ruler? Is he what used to be called a *confirmed* bachelor, who woos Olivia in safety and as an excuse to soak in self-pity? Does he adore her because she stubbornly refuses him? And so on. And on.

Such speculation hangs on literal, rational motives for roles who do not behave according to reasonable lights. Some criticism has suggested that the four lovers are under twenty. I go along with the suggestion, choosing to ignore the contrary evidence about Orsino; and I would further suggest that Sir Toby, far from looking and behaving like the traditional stout old fogey, present us with a virile hedonist in his early thirties whose offstage marriage to Maria jibes with experiences in his past—and to come. To provide a welcome change a director might allot Malvolio's role to an actor in his twenties, not as young as the quartet but not too seasoned, either. If he had already won Olivia's regard and if he did become a count by marrying her, he would outrank Toby and become the equal of Orsino, who, for unplumbed reasons, is accounted a count in the dialogue and a duke in the stage directions.

Does the play really take place during Epiphany or does the season resemble an epiphanic outbreak in May or June, a love frenzy not unlike the spell of summer cast over *Midsummer Night's Dream* or *Miss Julie?* Before Olivia commits Malvolio in his yellow stockings and cross-garters to the "special care" of merciless Toby, she exclaims, "Why, this is very midsummer madness" (3.4.58). Viola, thrown ashore by the storm and restarting her life on foreign soil, elects to serve a man whose name she has heard and whom the Captain describes as "noble. . . in nature as in name" (1.2.25)—but what was noble about the name of Orsino, which suggests a bear of a man, a junior-sized bear, but lumbering and hairy, at a time when bear-baiting was a common pastime? (Olivia had banned it from being practiced by Fabian.) She dons her man's outfit, a duplicate of Sebastian's, not for its warmth as cloth but as armor, a coverall chastity belt of fabric. While she, apparently transsexualized, cozies up to Orsino, her twin brother basks (or grows itchy) for several months in the devotion of Antonio, his rescuer. Olivia's life is also starting over, and impulsively, as she plunges into a one-sided love. Orsino may well feel reborn if he believes his trusty Cesario can make (or has already made) more headway than Valentine did with the unflinching Olivia. For the occupants of Olivia's mansion it is time to rebel against Malvolio, while he, receiving the love letter, feels his hopes for a dizzying ascent supercharged.

One might also view these fresh starts as a sudden falling away of inhibitions, as though by contagion: "Even so quickly," Olivia asks herself right after Cesario's first visit, "may one catch the plague?" (1.5.290). Most of the roles are either mad for love or mad for revenge. Not clinically mad, if it still makes sense to talk about clinical madness, but theatrically mad. And since theatrical madness occurs in temporary bouts, the label "folly" fits it more properly, as many critics have decided in relating it back to *The Praise of Folly* by Erasmus. Feste, one exception to the folly, is of course the play's fool, the wisest person in sight and hearing. A second exception, Malvolio, suffers accusations from Feste, Maria, and Toby of being mad when he has followed, understandably, a line of hints that seems to prove his intuitions correct and his ambitions justified. Viola, who might be taken for sane, if not madly sensible, a young woman who copes about as deftly as one might expect of a castaway and whose name belongs to a flower and a mellow musical instrument,[7] keeps on her male attire even when it's her male attire that keeps her in trouble. (The Captain disappears with the clothes in which she comes ashore, and never reappears, let alone returns the garments. In those garments the rest of the roles never see her.) Her twin marries a woman he never set eyes on before. Olivia is said to have made up her mind to mourn for her brother for seven years. Is her grief noble, as Orsino thinks? Or fake? Or foolish, as Feste has already told her (1.5)? She backs away at top speed from her prospective seven years in black when she meets Cesario,[8] a switch as rapid as the King of Navarre's in *Love's Labor's Lost* when he and his gentlemen greet the Princess of France and her ladies after forswearing the company of women for three years.

Later Olivia accepts as her husband a man she doesn't know, *after* learning of her error. Feste addresses her as "madonna," which is good Illyrian and, like most of the names, not only Italian; but that first syllable jumps out at speakers of English because of the repetition in one line: "He is but mad yet, madonna; and the fool shall look to the madman" (1.5.134–35). As a model of inconsistency, Olivia plays a succession of different roles in the lengthy 1.5 scene, starting out when she humorlessly castigates Feste and argues with him over which of them is the greater fool, going on to her dissatisfaction with Malvolio's "self-love" and "distempered appetite," and thence to her and Cesario's counter ripostes, and, finally, to her vulnerable state as "he" departs, whereupon she can feel "this youth's perfections." In the exchanges with Olivia, here as elsewhere, Viola tries intently, but not bluntly, to establish her equality of rank, much as Julia does with Sylvia in *Two Gentlemen*.

Orsino at last takes for his "mistress, and his fancy's queen" a woman he's known only as a male youth (and a eunuch?); he announces his decision (rather than asking her) shortly after recovering from a murderous rage aimed at both her and Olivia. Antonio risks his life in a hostile environment for love of Sebastian. That young man, we know, looks astonishingly like his twin sister. The playwright may mean us to assume *not* necessarily that Antonio is gay but that for the first time a homosexual infatuation overpowers a heterosexual man because of a certain girlishness in Sebastian's mien and manner. Linda Bamber points out Sebastian's refusal to reciprocate: "In his very first scene Sebastian decisively turns away from Antonio, absolutely refusing his service. Sebastian's prose here [in 2.1] is almost too virile" (1982, 131). Bamber goes on to cite samples of Sebastian's almost-too-virile prose from 2.1. John Hollander, by contrast, considers Sebastian "characterized by an elegance hardly virile" (1959). In act 5 Sebastian does greet Antonio with affectionate warmth:

SEBASTIAN Antonio, O my dear Antonio!
How have the hours racked and tortured me
Since I have lost thee! (5.1.217–19)

However we translate Sebastian's lines into feelings, Antonio's passion for him grows so fierce and so affecting that it makes him an uncomfortable role to watch. The discomfort may explain why Shakespeare, unwilling to pursue it further during a complicated act-5 climax, supplies no resolution of Antonio's anguish in the maelstrom of parceling out other plot lines: he leaves the role *in vacuo,* even more neglected than the Antonio in *The Merchant.* I say "may explain" not to exonerate Shakespeare from a bit of untidiness, which seems to me negligible, but because critics sometimes reprehend him for omissions or errors that he didn't bother to rectify or that could have been caused for any of countless production or printing reasons. Richard Levin comes down hard on partisans who make excuses, some of which *are* lame, for Shakespeare's shortcomings. He complains of

> the disposition (or rather, lack of disposition) of Antonio at the conclusion of *Twelfth Night,* where he is left languishing in a legal limbo, [a defect that] is also representative of a large class of these loose ends, usually involving minor characters, that are found in the closing scenes of many of the plays. (in Charney 1988, 24)

The Antonio error might appear more grievous if we knew Shakespeare meant to compose a French, nineteenth-century well-made play. But directors do love to tidy up act 5. In Nunn's movie Orsino ends his enmity with Antonio by putting an arm around him as though to invite him to the double wedding.

But when did sanity, or even level-headedness, ever reign in drama that speeds up our blood? Madness in a role, that staple of stage motivation, doesn't mean the role behaves continuously like a lunatic, any more than many lunatics behave consistently like lunatics.

Madness comes over the role intermittently as spurts or waves. Viola's even emerges as delectable; not in the least does it obscure her cool charm and mettle. It is of the stage, but not stagy. She quietly supplants Orsino's personal emissary and other servants. Three days after becoming Cesario, she has raised herself to Orsino's confidant(e), without arousing evident dislike. She conveys (to us) her love for him most effectively when she takes momentary refuge in her true self as "all the daughters of my father's house" (2.4.120) and breaks with Orsino's crass claim that men suffer more in love than women do.

With the final act and its crammed recognition scene we run into the most severe complaint about the play: the improbability of identical male and female twins. Dr. Johnson (1765) thought the last act "well enough contrived to divert on the stage," but wanting in credibility. He also felt it does not "produce the proper instruction required in the drama," meaning it should exhibit a "just picture of life." The most obvious oversteppings of credibility are crowded events and an unlikelihood of an identical man and woman before today's sophisticated makeup. MacCary writes, apropos of his thesis of latent self-love in the comedies:

> To see the embrace of these actual twins on stage, one male and one female, should be a *coup de théâtre* unsurpassed in romantic comedy. Unfortunately, it seldom plays well, because the actor and actress do not look enough alike. The only scene which could surpass this in fulfilling the deepest narcissistic desires is if a mature lover could embrace his own younger, more beautiful self, since narcissism is essentially nostalgic. (1985, 190)

An endnote by MacCary cites as an example of such an embrace a late moment from Caryl Churchill's *Cloud Nine* (253).[9] But more than 80 years ago Granville Barker asked his readers to bear in mind that

> the most important aspect of the play must be viewed, to view it rightly, with Elizabethan eyes. Viola was played, and was meant to be played, by a boy. See what this involves. To that original audience the strain of make-believe in the matter ended just where for us it most begins, at Viola's entrance as a page. Shakespeare's audience saw Cesario without effort as Orsino sees him; more importantly they saw him as Olivia sees him; indeed it was over Olivia they had most to make believe. One feels at once how this affects the sympathy and balance of the love scenes of the play. One sees how dramatically right is the delicate still grace of the dialogue between Orsino and Cesario, and how possible it makes the more outspoken passion of the scenes with Olivia. (1995, 178)

In the modern playhouse, even with a woman playing Viola, who will in all likelihood be noticeably shorter than the Sebastian and have a higher voice and dissimilar features, implausibility as a rule melts away. Despite the rush of events toward closure in the single scene of act 5, *and* despite the identical outfits, *and* despite the accumulation of circumstantial evidence, Shakespeare puts off the embrace while she makes no incautious mistake in accepting this arrival as her brother and nobody else, that she is not the butt of another joke, like the challenge from Sir Andrew. If the director decides to stage an embrace, one of those familiar clasping matches in which the two roles seem to prop each other up, rather than to let the two young people stand paralyzed, marvel as they exchange stares, while we see their features—that embrace will break the tension; it will let the air out of the scene. When Antonio exclaims in wonder, "Sebastian are you?" (5.1.220), the audience will have already taken the phenomenon for granted. Besides, audiences delight in miracles as much as do devotees of recondite sects and have little difficulty in accepting the twins as theatrical doubles so long as the other roles appear to have done the same by attribution—as Barker says the Elizabethans did. An inspired demonstration of how an audience follows a director's adroit blocking occurred at the end of a 1994 performance mounted by the Rocky Mountain Shakespeare troupe in Alberta. As Orsino spoke of Viola's becoming "Orsino's mistress, and his fancy's queen," he laid an affectionate hand on Sebastian's shoulder to escort him offstage. Viola coughed a discreet "Ahem!" to make Orsino realize he'd almost taken the wrong twin.[10] *Pace,* MacCary, not the embrace but the error became the evening's *coup de théâtre* and made the audience aware of how similar Viola and Sebastian looked to the characters on stage.

Among the subplots of *Twelfth Night* I include the songs sung by Feste. It's worth recalling that Sir Toby also sings the odd line or fragment of either old or currently popular songs. And in the "madhouse" scene, between Malvolio's cries of "Fool!" Feste manages to sneak in a brief, unfinished verse about "Robin, jolly Robin," whose "unkind lady . . . loves another" (4.2.58–65). But I deal with the longer songs, and not so much as contributions to the action or the offstage story but as lessons the play attempts to teach, some more bluntly than others. The opening speech, incorporating the best-known sentiments from the play, drastically overmined for quotations and recited by Orsino ("If music be the food of love," etc), requires a musical accompaniment, as does his speech in scene 2.4 ("Give me some music. Now, good morrow, friends," etc), the twin themes of which are music and love. Neither of these *récits,* however, is a song. The first delivers a self-portrait of the lovesick young nobleman who can have everything but what he most wants, a familiar cause of grief for princes and other rulers, rather than a lyric about life's blessings, curses, samenesses, and surprises.

Like the sonnets and other poetry, these four songs—"O mistress mine" (2.3), "Come away, death" (2.4), "I am gone, sir" (4.2), and finally, "The wind and the rain," which substitutes for an epilogue—have undergone ample paraphrasing and analysis, line after line, sometimes word after word, by poetry critics. Here I will simply look at some of the songs' implications for the comedy and for the role of Feste.

Feste sings "O mistress mine" at the behest of Toby and Andrew, each of whom confers a testril, worth sixpence, on him for "a love song," rather than "a song of good life." The scene takes place in Olivia's home, but she, the employer, is not there. The lyric presents a swain whose beloved keeps evading him ("Where are you roaming? . . . Trip no further, pretty sweeting"), but the evasions are futile, for "journeys end in lovers' meeting." Meanwhile, she is not, in the familiar words, getting any younger. In the second stanza all six lines vary the warning of the final one: "Youth's a stuff will not endure," that is, *carpe diem*, make the most of the "now," translated crisply by the title of Saul Bellow's novel as *Seize the Day*, or, to put it in theatrical parlance, Play the Moment. Because of the pun on "mistress," he is also addressing Olivia, if *in absentia*, chiding her as he did in 1.5 for mourning her brother excessively so as to evade . . . what? Orsino? Love? The pleasures of youth?

"Come away, come away, death," another double stanza, aims itself squarely at Orsino, who has requested "the song we had last night . . . old and plain . . . . It is silly sooth, And dallies with the innocence of love, Like the old age" (2.4.42–48). The singer, "slain by a fair cruel maid," ends up pleading, "Lay me, O where Sad true lover never find my grave, To weep there!" Elizabeth Story Donno describes it as "clearly a folk song" and cites an authority on musical accompaniments to Shakespeare's songs. "Sung by women," adds Donno, "the words suggest patient devotion towards men who treat them badly" (1985, 83, n. 48).[11] If these assumptions are accurate, Shakespeare has slyly switched the sex of the singer; he mocks the overblown desolation in the lyric so as to make Orsino aware of the ridiculous figure he cuts. But Orsino has already said that when he heard it the night before, he thought the song "did relieve my passion much" (2.4.4). It seems to have worked as efficaciously this time as well, although not as Feste may have intended, for Orsino rewards him with money. We can assume, though, that if Orsino fails to see (and feel) Feste's point, Viola, Curio, and the other onstage listeners enjoy the dirge's sentiments and even more their master's boneheaded reaction to them.

On parting momentarily from Malvolio to bring him pen and ink, Feste sings "I am gone, sir, And anon, sir, I'll be with you again In a trice. Like to the old Vice," and ends on the words "Adieu, goodman devil!" (4.2.121–132), a slip of a song that has a theatricalist or self-referential coloring.[12] Does the song say or imply that Malvolio (or

Feste?) relates to the old Vice of medieval moralities or even the devil himself? Is it perhaps chanted to aggravate the imprisoned steward's fear, fury, bewilderment, sense of isolation, and helplessness? Can it be another late retort (like the whirligig of time's revenges) by Feste to the insults earlier tossed at him by Malvolio in front of Olivia: a "barren rascal" who was "put down the other day with an ordinary fool that has no more brain than a stone" (1.5.81–83)?

Feste's final song, consisting of five quatrains, has spawned a generous assortment of hypotheses from Hanmer in the eighteenth century, Halliwell-Phillips in the nineteenth, and in the twentieth, Hotson and countless others who have set about summarizing it, revising it, condemning it, picking through its meanings, checking out its mysterious linkage with *King Lear* through the Fool's single verse in the same meter in that tragedy, finding it exquisite, profound, cheerfully obscene, obtuse, and cosmogonal. But is it a confession about Feste's own life, as some critics—for instance, Ornstein—read it, or is it an impersonal Lesson About Life, a recapitulation of Jaques's Seven Ages of Man soliloquy? Quoting Touchstone, Jaques makes a parallel, equally downbeat remark in *As You Like It*: "And so from hour to hour we ripe and ripe, And then from hour to hour we rot and rot" (2.7.26–27).

It is all very well to ask actors to play the moment, but here and in music, how? Feste, the most elusive role in Shakespeare's comedies, gives away almost nothing about himself. When he speaks of begging or living by the church or wishing his sister had no name, we wonder what he is really saying. Even an ostensible private gripe disclosed at last, "the whirligig of time brings in his revenges," is couched impersonally. This walking enigma, unmarried, unattached, probably of an older generation, a wanderer between two households without finding—maybe without seeking—an identity, and remote from either house . . . . to what does he belong? To what principles does he subscribe? It is Feste who suddenly and open-heartedly, or ironically, commends Orsino for being inconsistent:

> Now the melancholy god protect thee, and the tailor make thy doublet of changeable taffeta, for thy mind is a very opal. I would have men of such constancy put to sea, that their business might be everything and their intent everywhere, for that's it that always makes a good voyage of nothing. Farewell. *Exit.* (2.4.73–78)

In this speech "such constancy" means "your inconstancy," an attribute that will show most dramatically at the end when Orsino snatches his long-lived affection from Olivia, as he thinks, and practically hurls it at Viola.

Feste's account of man's inexorable progress from a child's holiday realm of irresponsibility and joy into age, vice, disillusionment and

> death, draws upon an old, didactic tradition. Its basic pessimism is
> informed and sweetened, however, not only by the music to which
> it is set, but [also] by the tolerance and acceptance of Feste himself.
> (Barton 1974, 407)

So long as "vice" here is understood to include heavy drinking and
lechery, and so long as *thing, toy, bauble, man's estate, swaggering,* and
tosspots receive their due as licentious word-play, this seems to be a fair,
if scrubbed-clean, paraphrase.

But what does the song *do*? The departure of the two young couples and Fabian leaves Feste alone on stage with the audience. This
solitary farewell from the clown does not constitute a comedic novelty—at least, not for Shakespeare—for just as Oberon, the ranking figure in *Dream*, together with Titania and their trains, gives over the
stage to Puck, so Orsino, with his final speech, leads the rest of the
company offstage, surrendering the house to Feste, "of all Shakespeare's clowns the one most worthy of study perhaps." (Young 1948,
202; the quotation comes from Young's review of a 1941 staging by
Michael Chekhov and his Theatre Players). The innovation, rather, lies
in our doubts about the suitability of the two love pairings. In *All's Well*
and again in *Measure* doubts of this sort deepen as they, too, double-
cross the comic ending.

In his last quatrain the Fool moves away, disrespectfully, perhaps
even contemptuously, from the history of the world to the actuality of
theatre, the last dozen words introduced by "that's all one," a common
Elizabethan expression that Feste speaks more than once and hints at
an overriding unity in the work, if we can only retrospectively put it
together.

> A great while ago the world begun,
> With hey, ho, the wind and the rain,
> But that's all one, our play is done,
> And we'll strive to please you every day.

The clown, restored to his kingdom, again wears the crown.

Notes

1. Copeau designed his lighting in association with Louis Jouvet, who
also played Aguecheek. Duncan Grant designed the set. The company revived
the production in 1917–1918 during its residence at the Garrick Theatre in
New York and again in 1921, after the War, back at the Vieux-Colombier.

2. The narcissus is pale, like a diluted sister of a daffodil and thus in keeping with Hotson's idea and with the successive aspects of Malvolio's role as we
perceive their contributions to his anti-festive spirit. In clothing, a preference

for yellow is sometimes regarded by color analysts as a revelation of an untamed personality, but that interpretation relates to a deep or chrome yellow. Possibly Aldous Huxley had that notion of chrome yellow in mind when he titled his first novel *Crome Yellow* (1922), a pun on the name of the mansion in the story and possibly an allusion to its heroine.

MacCary, in his chapter on *Twelfth Night*, 177–91, proposes that most of the roles, but especially Olivia and Orsino, have narcissistic motives, and relates these to Freud's essay *On Narcissism*. Toward the end of his chapter, though, he remarks, "We all have narcissistic longings" [190], and he adds, "though few have twins."

3. The Oxford English Dictionary (O.E.D.) describes the toby jug as having "the form of a stout old man wearing a long and full-skirted coat and a three-cornered hat (18th c. costume)," the corners serving as lips for pouring beer. This second definition dates back to only 1840 in a citation from *Barnaby Rudge,* but it might go back farther orally than in print. The first definition is more promising: "The posterior, the buttocks: esp. in phrase *to tickle one's toby. slang,*" and this, traced back to a printed source in 1681, might have originated in Shakespeare's day or before.

4. For histories of actors' interpretations, and especially of Malvolio's departure late in 5.1, see Odell and other historians who are cited or alluded to in the Arden, New Penguin, New Cambridge, and World's Classics editions, and the treatment in Sylvan Barnet's "*Twelfth Night* on the Stage" (1986, 215–25).

5. See, for instance, the footnote in Herschel Baker's introduction to the Signet Classic edition, (1986, xxiv). Charles I also identified Malvolio as the protagonist.

6. Viola makes a play on Olivia's name during their first conversation: "I bring no overture of war, no taxation of homage. I hold the olive in my hand" (1.5.204–06).

7. The O.E.D.'s first citation of Viola meaning violet ("Swettest [sic] viola, that never shal fade") dates back to at least 1430. But when it means the "alto or tenor violin," its first recorded use, by Southey, was in 1797. Shakespeare may therefore have had the "shrinking" flower in mind.

8. In Lyly's *Gallathea* (1588?) two girls dressed as boys (originally played by boys) fall in love. Phyllida wishes Gallathea were a man; the wish is magically granted, like Pygmalion's wish that his Galatea statue might come to life. Olivia's love for Viola, although different from Phyllida's—she genuinely believes Cesario to be male—has been ascribed to Lyly's influence.

9. *Cloud Nine* has provoked much conjecture. My own discussion of it appears in *Comic Agony* (1993, 181–90).

10. Susanne Gillies Smith directed this Canadian production, Michael Kopsa played Orsino (and Aguecheek); Jillian Fargey, Viola; Allan Grant, Sebastian (and Valentine).

11. Donno's edition summarizes *Twelfth Night*'s resemblances to the other comedies (7–8). Ornstein also traces resemblances and contrasts in his chapter on the play (1986, 153–172).

12. Several of the play's celebrated remarks are also theatricalist: one is spoken by Fabian, "If this were played upon a stage now, I could condemn it as an improbable fiction" (3.4.129–30). Another follows Olivia's question, "Are you a comedian?" with Viola's reply, "I swear I am not that I play" (1.5.178 and 180). A third clinches the closing couplet of Feste's epilogue song.

WOMAN VS. MAN

Women come into conflict with men in nearly all the Shakespeare comedies, but four of them most strongly register contests between female and male. In the main plot of *Shrew,* the man wins the woman hands down, and she acquiesces—unless a company chooses to defy the lines of Kate's act 5 speech. *Love's Labor's Lost* looks as if it will turn into a fourfold marriage pledge between the Princess of France and the King of Navarre and between the three ladies in the Princess's retinue and the three lords in the King's prospective "little academe." The partnerships form as soon as the two quartets meet (2.1). In spite of some shilly-shallying by the women, no firm obstacles rear up until almost the end of the action with a startling announcement—the victory for neither sex amounts to a standoff. The main plot of *Much Ado* consists of an advance in the man/woman squabble, a truce artificially provoked and achieved with concessions from both sides and some men's repentance for the sake of a peaceful wedding ceremony. This looks like equality in love, more or less. *Love's Labor's Lost* and *Much Ado* dissent from the generalized interpretation of *Shrew*. But *All's Well* offers a more radical dissent, the triumph of a woman. Readers and spectators of both sexes who have feminist sympathies will continue to find this play's resolution as disturbing as that of *Shrew*. Helena conquers, but she has to stoop. No evidence will be put forward here that Shakespeare intended these plays to be taken as a group or a chronological cycle or to answer one another or to serve—any one of them or the collective—as his mouthpiece. Rather, the reverse.

The Taming of the Shrew

The main plot of *The Shrew* (pronounced *shro*) launches Petruchio's mercenary declaration to his friend Hortensio. He seeks

> One rich enough to be Petruchio's wife—
> As wealth is burden of my wooing dance—
> Be she as foul as was Florentius' love,
> As old as Sibyl, and as curst and shrewd
> As Socrates' Xanthippe, or a worse,
> She moves me not, or not removes at least
> Affection's edge in me, were she as rough
> As are the swelling Adriatic seas.
> I come to wive it wealthily in Padua;
> If wealthily, then happily in Padua. (1.2.66–75)

So long as the older, unmarried daughter of Baptista Minola, whom he soon hears about, comes in for a fat portion, she meets the rest of his lax requirements. Although early in the action he calls her, among other epithets, "an irksome brawling scold" (1.2.186), he promises to pounce on her eagerly. One of the suitors of her pretty, tractable sister cannot believe in this recklessness.

GREMIO . . . But will you woo this wildcat?

PETRUCHIO   Will I live? (1.2.195)

He has pledged to pull off the impossible. Some directors who mistrust the wit of audiences and insist on unclouded motives have allowed Petruchio a glimpse of Kate bullying Bianca and throwing a tantrum in the form of furniture before he spreads a marriage proposal before her father. But in the play, without having seen or heard her, he calls Katherina "fair and virtuous"—to her father's astonished face—and speaks of "her beauty and her wit, Her affability and bashful modesty, Her wondrous qualities and mild behavior" (2.1.48–50). Before long, his mercenary drive revs up as he asks Baptista Minola, "if I get your daughter's love, What dowry shall I have with her to wife?" (2.1.119–20). Her father has already proclaimed to Bianca's little swarm of adorers that he will not give them a decision until her older sibling is won; the suitors, led by Hortensio, have resolved to find Kate a husband. Hortensio comes up with this brash, impossible candidate. The action, meanwhile, teases the audience with that most gripping of prospects, irresistible force meets immovable object.

For Kate, we observe, is not merely a shrew, a man-hater, even a people-hater: she is also a torturer who wildly envies Bianca; she believes their father favors her sister and that for Bianca to gain a husband, he will sell her, Kate, to the first comer. She must resist. She is surely correct down to the last detail in her assumptions but that last detail is that she *can* resist a Petruchio. Past Petruchios often flourished and flicked whips, but no stage directions or dialogue in the play support such attempts to compel the comedy to "work." Directors who rely on physical abuse evidently believe that audiences will not accept Kate's conversion in act 5 by any persuasion other than might. They differ from Petruchio, who applies calmness, acts of unpredictability, and fulsome compliments besides mental punishment, frustration, hunger, and mockery but scorns physical abuse. He converts Kate into the feminine equivalent of being uxorious, for which no word seems to exist: a wife who dotes on her husband, perhaps, or a doormat—at any rate, far more accommodating to her new hubby than the play's other two new wives are to theirs.

A question insistently asked about this main plot is: Did Shakespeare choose some roles to vocalize his own opinions? If the answer is yes, then he pried Petruchio and Kate out of his sources and his imagination to serve him as spokespersons in a misogynistic play. If the answer is no, we can entertain a range of alternative meanings for the roles.

Petruchio takes Kate back to his scruffy mansion, where for a while he denies her food and sleep, the hat and gown she wants for her wedding, and his approbation every time she doesn't say and do exactly what he demands. If that mansion serves as the equivalent of the green realm in other Shakespeare comedies, an environment where roles are transformed, the green component here must come from mold and mildew. He does not beat her up; he does ill-treat her relentlessly. As has often been pointed out, in some of the play's sources the difficult or disobedient or "curst" woman undergoes much more brutal treatment from Petruchio's forebears than Shakespeare metes out to her, such as being flayed and then placed inside a horse's skin that has been liberally salted. Numerous works are cited as possible *Shrew* sources, most of which Shakespeare could hardly have read. H. J. Oliver writes:

> There were shrews galore in literature long before Shakespeare—tamed and untamed . . . in earlier English drama . . . and Old English verse and in Chaucer, in medieval tales, in Persian literature, in popular Italian stories, in Danish and other folklore; and probably there were shrews in many a stage farce. It is even possible to speculate whether there may not have been a stock costume to identify the character as soon as she appeared on the stage. (1994, 48–49)

One severe example of the humiliated shrew appears in the little French sottie called *Le Cuvier* (translated as *The Washtub* in *A Dozen French Farces,* 1997). A wife falls into a tub of scalding water and laundry; her henpecked husband refuses to save her until she swears to reform. Some adaptations of *The Shrew* in the seventeenth, eighteenth, and nineteenth centuries are also savage. They seem to imply that while Shakespeare was punishing a shrew, he missed the chance to carry out harm to her head and sensitive parts—to exploit the victim to her limits, or beyond. (The artistic and moral descendants of the adapters write our century's get-the-woman screenplays.)

Whatever one thinks about the Kate initially presented in the play, the Kate who electrifies act 5 with her 44-line monologue—that famous, final, servile-smelling speech—has proved an enigma. Is she her own woman? Drugged? Depleted? Is she, like Trilby or the Ann Todd character in *The Seventh Veil,* emotionally enslaved? Or is she like the reciter of *A Lover's Complaint,* the "fickle maid full pale," who tells her father

> That not a heart which in his level came
> Could scape the hail of his all-hurting aim,
> Showing fair nature is both kind and tame;
> And, veiled in them, did win whom he would maim. (309–12)

As an ancient (and I suppose anonymous) snatch of doggerel has it, "Shrewish wives Lead barren lives."

But before one can hope to clarify the ending, there is a prior puzzle to take account of: the Induction, a prologue that features Christopher Sly. A corresponding epilogue—there is none—would certainly affect the impact of Kate's speech, confirming, repudiating, or in some other way altering its meanings. Some directors have, like Jonathan Miller in his BBC TV version, omitted the Induction's two scenes, on the grounds that they peter out unresolved. Others have kept the Induction, but curtailed, to present it as a swift, almost independent curtain-raiser. Either way, directors feel embarrassed as a rule by the Induction's incomplete and separated characteristics; they wish to waste no time before getting down to business with the hearty conflict of the play that succeeds the playlet. But because of the Induction, bothersome issues abound when it comes to staging the full work. The inner play consists of five acts in Italy, while the Induction evidently has an English setting, the home of a lord without a name who decides to play a trick on the beggarly tinker Sly. But since neither the Induction as a whole nor the farcical romance between an inebriated Sly and the page who acts as his lady reaches consummation, logic suggests that either the ending of the Sly playlet has been lost or that no ending ever existed because Shakespeare realized (or was assured) that it enfeebled the robust climax of Kate's speech and its reception. Robert B. Heilman notes, after examining some explanations that have been offered for the disappearance of the Sly playlet, that

> there is no merit in the argument that the elimination of Sly prevented an anticlimax, for this begs the question whether a Sly epilogue would inevitably be anticlimactic. (1986, xxvii)

Heilman goes on to interpret the play as a farce throughout, because "it is the farcical view of life that makes possible the treatment of both Kate and Petruchio" (xxxvii). Others, including Oliver, believe the play is partly farce, partly realism, and that the two do not sit comfortably together in the same work. Oliver, who defends the play valiantly, takes farce to mean in this case "not slapstick, but a broader kind of comedy, not involving 'engagement' with the characters" (40). Later in the action, he proposes, we feel sympathetic toward Kate, and then the play has become "a young dramatist's attempt, not repeated, to mingle two genres that cannot be combined" (56). But two—or more—genres can be combined, and have been countless times, by almost every playwright of stature—and some without. Back to the first alternative: owing to time pressures before or during rehearsals, the playwright never wrote a Sly ending or, yet another alternative, could not come up with an ending that satisfied him.

The presence of Sly during the opening scene of the inner play as an onstage spectator, an occasional trespasser and commentator, seems to some directors to demand a corresponding phase-out of his prologue-subplot after act 5, some additions with discreet air-brushing that bring inner and outer plays into consonance. With this matching-up in mind, a few directors in the past have integrated the Sly play more tidily by having the role turn into Petruchio while the lord and his servants take on Baptista Minola and other roles from the inner play. Sly can wake up as himself after the extant act 5 to find that his treatment as a lord and his courtship and conquest of Kate were a dream of sexual power. After all, Sly doesn't speak after 1.1; he and the Page "sit and mark." Petruchio enters with Grumio at the start of

1.2. The dream interpretation was put forward by Sears Jayne (1966, 41–56). Thus the total work becomes a king-for-a-day dream. Such a recourse also takes care of the play's other big talking point or embarrassment: Kate's final speech, a demonstration of wifely obedience, not to say abject obeisance. Sly's vain dream, including the offensive speech, then need not be taken at face value.

Even if a performance keeps the Induction without grafting on a Sly tail, for some directors it has, in its vestigial form, the advantage of a theatricalist ploy—roles playing other roles. A theatrical interpretation resembles one arguing that Shakespeare derived the roles-playing-roles notion, as well as the Bianca subplot, "from George Gascoigne's play *Supposes* (1566), a prose version of Ariosto's *I Suppositi* (1509)."[1] Theatricalizing puts esthetic weight on the disguising of five roles of the inner comedy. Lucentio plays Bianca's philosophy tutor Cambio; the valet Tranio takes over the role of his master, Lucentio; the pageboy Biondello takes over the role of Tranio; Hortensio, the friend of Petruchio, disguises himself as the music and math teacher, Litio; and a straying Pedant assumes the role of Lucentio's father, Vincentio. The theatricalizing also offers a hint to anyone willing to pick it up that all the roles are playing other roles, that Petruchio and Katherina[2] take refuge behind personality pretenses throughout the action, that inner and outer plays elucidate each other while seeming more elusive than ever. The temptation for the cast to seize upon so appealing a hint strikes me as folly, as theatrical suicide—a field day for "indicating," winks, not-so-secret language, and cute, look-at-me-I'm-only-kidding mannerisms.

If the staging of *The Shrew* raises healthy questions for any theatrical imagination, another reason may be the tissue of doubts over the reliability of the text.[3] Although I'd like to ease past them, it seems unavoidable to allude to the three main areas of contention. First, disputes arise over Shakespeare's sources—his contemporaries and predecessors, British, French, and Italian. Second, was Shakespeare the sole author? Current scholarship concedes that contributions (or interference) may have sullied the most dependable text, the First Folio, but that Shakespeare made the substantive final revisions, even if he had to do so hastily and even if minor alterations or corrections by others took place in the seven years between his death and the publication of the Folio. Third, and linked to the first two groups of questions, how does *The Shrew* relate to a very similar work, *The Taming of a Shrew*, known for short as *A Shrew?*[4] The latter may have preceded *The Shrew* or have been drawn from a source common to both plays, an ur-*Shrew*. More likely, says much recent publication, *A Shrew* is a bad quarto version of *The Shrew*. Into this chapter *A Shrew* obtrudes

briefly not so much because of the variants in text or spelling or imagery but because it does what *The Shrew* boldly declines to do: it
wraps up the outer play. ("The Sly scenes in *A Shrew*" form Appendix
II to the Arden edition of *The Shrew,* [1981, 303–305], and also Appendix A to the Oxford edition, [1994, 233–35].) In a swift final scene, Sly
(spelled *Slie*) is dumped outside the inn by two bouncers "where they
found him"; he awakens, hung over, and is disabused about his dream
by the inn's Tapster, who offers to escort him home to his wife. She
will curse him, but Slie, after this "best dream That ever I had in my
life," will tame her, using the Petruchio dream method.

To insist on the probability of comedy here, as opposed to the possibilities of farce, would make Sly's intellectual ability and literacy level, from what we see of them, no match for the sophistication of his
dream. One corps of critical opinion believes that *A Shrew* was also
written by Shakespeare for performance by another company, Pem-
broke's Men, and that *The Shrew* therefore precedes it in performance,
if not in composition. In the New Cambridge edition Ann Thompson
agrees, after looking at available evidence:

> it seems wisest to assume that it was Shakespeare who was respon-
> sible for the complex structure and interweaving of materials that we
> find in both *Shrew* plays." (1984, 9)

But whether Shakespeare reckoned with the disparity between Sly's
mind in his waking moments and that of his dream-self, and whatever the provenance of *A Shrew*, if it really is in part a later reconstruc-
tion from memory or a "reported text" or some other corrupt form of
The Shrew, the mystery remains: *The Shrew* lacks an epilogue.

With the Induction overridden for the time being, we can switch
back to the inner play and fairly easily disentangle the main plot from
the three principal subplots. The title tells us what the main plot consists of. Bianca, her suitors, and other secondary roles then comprise
the subplots, which depend at first on the Petruchio-Kate tussle, later
separated from it like distributory waters at a delta, when the latter
pair departs for his home (3.2), the grungy green world at the center
of the action. Main plot and subplots reunite into a single stream after
the return to Padua (5.1).

Of the three subplots, which involve secondary roles, two are
straightforward: the family conflicts among Baptista, Kate, and Bianca; and the friendship between Hortensio and Petruchio, which leads
the former to arouse the latter's sudden passion for Kate's dowry.

The third and most complex subplot, the courting among rivals of
Bianca, begins in the opening scene. Lucentio has just arrived in "fair
Padua, nursery of arts," to improve himself with "that part of philoso-
phy . . . that treats of happiness By virtue specially to be achieved"

(1.1.18–20). Then he sees Bianca, her father, sister, and Bianca's pair of suitors. The philosophy of virtue goes out the window, instantly replaced by the mechanics of wooing.

> Tranio, I burn, I pine, I perish, Tranio,
> If I achieve not this young modest girl . . . (1.1.156–57)

The prescription for instant love—here, as in *Romeo and Juliet*, and in *Two Gentlemen*: one look and you're hooked—requires that in short order Lucentio joins Gremio and Hortensio, already suitors, but in the guise of a tutor of philosophy. He also instructs Tranio to court Bianca formally under his own name, Lucentio, so that he has two chances, not one, out of four. Tranio thereby acquires a large role in the play, second to Petruchio's in number of lines and longer than Kate's. Tranio does not, however, become the operative servant figure, the playwright within the play or principal instigator, as found in many other comedies; despite the size of his part in words, he remains a subsidiary figure. As if to tame him, as well as the heroine, the author never puts Kate and Tranio or Tranio and Bianca together in a scene by themselves. Hortensio similarly adopts a new guise. While Lucentio poses as Bianca's philosophy teacher, Hortensio plays her teacher of music.

In this same wooing-of-Bianca subplot, Lucentio's father, Vincentio, walks all the way from Pisa to Padua to check up on how diligently his son is pursuing his studies and, if the young man deserves it, to reward him with a sum of one hundred pounds, a generous parental blessing in the late sixteenth century. He is first affronted by being called a maiden and later affronted by being treated as an impostor: the Pedant from Mantua, passing through the city, has agreed to stand in for Vincentio and so displace him, an enraging circumstance for the old man after so tiring a walk. Tranio tells the Pedant, "'Tis death for anyone in Mantua To come to Padua" (4.2.82–83), because of a quarrel between the respective dukes, a comparable situation to the trade enmity between Syracuse and Ephesus in *Errors* that nearly costs Egeon his life—only, in this case, the quarrel is a fiction and part of a plan to lend authenticity to Tranio's abortive plan to substitute for his master.

Shakespeare may make the head of many a spectator spin with the names Lucentio, Vincentio, and Hortensio. Did he willfully mock Italian vowel endings, multiple syllables, and rhymes? They certainly contribute to the farcical effects in the text but they also work to the benefit of the plotting as he cleverly uses the role of Vincentio to reintroduce the Lucentio and Hortensio subplots to the main plot at a point when they had drifted apart. Petruchio, on the road back to Padua, addresses the old man as "gentle mistress," and then Kate, at her husband's urging, submits to wifely discipline and gushes, "Young budding virgin, fair, and fresh, and sweet" (4.5.27 and 36). In the next scene

(5.1), old Vincentio has recovered from this "merriment," only to face accusations in Padua of being a madman—neither the father of his son, Lucentio, nor the master of his servants, Tranio and Biondello. As the prelude to this additional humiliation, his visit to Padua serves to bring his traveling companions for the last leg of the journey, the two principals and Hortensio, back to the city for the banquet that celebrates three weddings. To round out this subplot, two of Bianca's suitors, who helped finance Petruchio's wooing of Kate in order to speed up the availability of Bianca, both lose her. Old Gremio gives up; Hortensio pulls out of the competition when his chances look hopeless, and somewhere between acts 4 and 5, he weds a widow. That marriage comes as an unexpected announcement by Hortensio in the disputed final couplet of act 4: "Have to my widow! And if she be froward Then hast thou taught Hortensio [to be?] untoward" (4.5.77–78).

The larger general statements deducible from the main plot and subplots boil down to three. First, marriage is obedience. It appears as a master-servant connection, not a partnership. Petruchio rudely bullies Grumio and his other servants in acts 1 and 4 as if in training for threatening, haranguing, and countermanding his wife in acts 3, 4, and 5, at times with exquisite politeness. Second, marriage will not happen unless money changes hands. The dialogue harps on dowries, the relative wealth of Bianca's suitors and Petruchio as he crudely trades offers with Baptista Minola. Money also winds its way through the segments of the action not having to do with marriage. Vincentio, "a merchant of incomparable wealth" (4.2.100), brings his son a cash present. The Pedant has "bills for money by exchange From Florence" (4.2.90–91). Third, getting what one wants, marriage included, requires not only money but also duplicity, especially deliberate lying and posing. Apart from the outright impersonations (and not counting the ones in the Induction), Kate and Petruchio are taken by some spectators and critics to be faking, putting on false faces—she not to be obliged to accept her father's choice of a husband, he to look fearsome and invincible. All this role-playing leads many literary critics to write that the play is "about" loss or change of identity. The widespread and growing conspiracy to reduce drama to sociological platitude almost surely arises from the misapprehension that roles, unlike personalities, must stay consistent.

The most blatant inconsistency, the one everybody cannot help noticing, shows up in the role of Kate.[5] At the end, the performer may wink at the camera (Mary Pickford) or rush off into an impenetrable crowd (Elizabeth Taylor) leaving Petruchio baffled for once; but at the beginning, if she softens the role, if she doesn't play the termagant, the play has no force: her misanthropy forms the mainspring of the early scenes and the yardstick by which the later ones are experienced and gauged. The early Kate could fit into a scenario by Molière. Like Harpagon, Arnolphe, Alceste, or Henriette, she is a superlative—in the old British expression, "out on her own." She ties Bianca's hands and strikes her, in some productions drags her by the hair, screams, hurls sizable props around—and these tactics seem like defensible additions to the text—then rails at her father.

> I must dance barefoot on [Bianca's] wedding-day,
> And for your love to her lead apes in hell.
> Talk not to me, I will go sit and weep,
> Till I can find occasion of revenge. (2.1.33–36)

The image of leading apes in hell, *of being compelled to do so*, is operatic, like one of the extravagances uttered by the Elektra of Hofmannsthal. Kate gives the impression, not so much of being unfortunately rejected (or repelled) by men as deciding she will give them no grounds for liking her. She may envy her good-girl sister for being daddy's pet, but she also feels superior to Bianca in not knuckling under to her father who, to her, personifies male authority. (No mother is mentioned.)

Petruchio puts her through the affective mill. As well as subjecting her to hunger, humiliation in front of her family and his servants, and other hardships, he keeps her psychically off-balance by talking and acting arbitrarily, at times crazily, so tyrannizing the servants and two merchants in his mansion that she cannot bear to witness what appears to be his unjust seizures. He resorts to something analogous to homeopathic medicine or holding up a mirror in order to cure her. How, then, can she genuinely love him at the end?

By the last quarter of the nineteenth century, before even the Suffragette movement, let alone modern women's lib, many people, Bernard Shaw among them, objected vociferously to the second scene of act 5, much as George Eliot objected to the last scene of *Two Gentlemen*. Why does Kate make that speech? Has she fallen in love with Petruchio, or is it an act? Jérome Savary's 1994 production (*La Mégère apprivoisée*, literally "The Shrew Tamed") at the Palais de Chaillot in Paris, proclaimed in its program notes that "it's not Petruchio who checkmates the shrew but she who overcomes him," to imply that she controls the "game" throughout.

Or might she obey him out of fear? In 1975 in London Charles Marowitz directed a cut version called simply *The Shrew*, in which Kate, played with superb conviction by Thelma Holt with eyes gelatinous and voice a barking monotone, recited the speech as though a victim of the Soviet purge trials of the 1930s uttering self-condemnations. If Kate does love Petruchio, it has been proposed, she may have had her first sex with him, the sort of initiation certain slimy therapists have been known to advise; on the strength of this hypothesis, in act 5 she is living in the afterglow. But Petruchio says he railed at her all night, gave her no sleep—here Marowitz's hollow-cheeked, brainwashed purge victim makes some comparable dramatic sense. And since one of the sources of the play may be Petrarch, it is easy to link the names Petrarch and Petruchio with one of today's favored-target words *patriarchy*. Some historians have said that in the late sixteenth century it was widely believed that women should subordinate themselves to their husbands for the sake of domestic tranquillity; such a sentiment does find an illustration near the front of a 1635 printed version of *A* (not *The*) *Shrew*, and reproduced in *The Riverside Shakespeare* (109). If the belief was indeed current some forty years earlier, we are forced to wonder why so many wives proved refractory and so many men felt it necessary to write poems, stories, and plays about the need to hurt them. I am disinclined, in any case, to believe in broad historical assumptions. Anne Barton comes closer to dramatic truth when she points out that Kate's reproachful words ("Fie, fie! unknit that threatening, unkind brow, And dart not scornful glances from those eyes To wound thy lord, thy king, thy governor" [5.2.140–42]) mean she is doing the same to Bianca in act 5 as she did in act 2, namely, teasing. Northrop Frye agrees: Kate is teasing again, only now in a socially acceptable fashion.

As another explanation of that final speech we might go back to the second of the play's broad statements, that marriage means money changing hands. If Petruchio has told Kate in the story, offstage, that he is going to bet a nice sum on her, she may share in the proceeds by winning the wager: he collects two hundred crowns from Lucentio and Hortensio (5.2.71–76). In this fashion we can continue to rationalize the ending or try to turn it upside down by planting motives in Kate's nonexistent (and therefore nonresistant) mind. The speech still does seem willed, and shocking, when it is actually conforming, all too willingly, with a comic reconciliation, like Anne's surrender to Richard III's wooing. Very likely the speech means no more than it says, that this inconsistent role permits her to announce that henceforward, doing her best to be loving and lovable, she commends her example to other wives.

Some critics pounce on Bianca, saying that Kate shames her—shows her up for a hypocrite. It is true that this heroine with a pale name (mentioned in some word-play—5.2.190) is bland and innocent at first, the object of a sibling rage and four men's attentions, three of them serious; and that she is sharp-witted enough at parsing musical love messages from Lucentio; and that late in the play she comes out with a couple of mildly bawdy remarks (5.2.40–41 and 46–47). When her new mate Lucentio "bids" her come back into the dining room, she declines, whereas Kate, when "commanded," not only comes instantly but goes back out again and hales in the other two wives by main force. Kate's affection for Petruchio looks more genuine than Bianca's for Lucentio, but it seems pointless to accuse Bianca of being "loathsome" and an icy-hearted spouse-snatcher (Leggatt 1974, 48–62). She is a role, not an immoral person susceptible to our chastisement, although she may well serve as an anti-model for the virtuous and as a model for the vicious, who surely don't seek models. Roles, like people, can clash with their earlier selves. Besides, the comic ending is more satisfying, even for those who do not use the Bible as a handbook of etiquette, when the good-girl daughter looks not so good and the prodigal daughter carries the day. As for the Widow, suddenly found married to Hortensio, he evidently rounded her up in a hurry since, as a sympathetic role, he deserved a wife. Some wife, any wife. Like Célimène, who is a widow at twenty, this role can also be allotted to a young actress. In Jonathan Miller's television film the Widow looked like Hortensio's mother, as though he had sought the first woman who crossed his path and was another soldier of marital fortune. The Widow is also needed to make up a trio of wives. Kate's fidelity—or spirited submissiveness—becomes more telling when contrasted with two fractious wives than with one.

Petruchio's role, like Kate's, invites bravura acting, nothing like the wooden, fake-heroic posturing practiced by Howard Keel in the film of *Kiss Me Kate* (1953, directed by George Sidney), or the braying of Richard Burton in the Zeffirelli movie of *Shrew* (1967), in which the character starts out drunk and becomes progressively less sober. Petruchio, no lush, is a fanatic, almost a monomaniac, who has independent wealth but as much determination to marry money as the scion of a banking corporation; who leaps at the task of taming the apparently untamable; who will succeed, to his joy, in turning his convert into a converter. Despite the occasional glimpse of a figure acting with controlled consciousness and candor behind the near-hysterical facade, as when he announces his intention in a soliloquy to put pretty constructions on Kate's faults (2.1.168–80), or in another soliloquy defends "a way to kill a wife with kindness" (4.1.176–99), or tells Hortensio in an aside to pay the belittled tailor (4.3.160), he does refer to his "rule" and his "reign" and gloats over his victories. An actor should have no qualms about painting Petruchio cruel. A number of critics insist on striking a positive or negative attitude toward him, almost as many as do with Kate. W. Thomas MacCary descries Petruchio as a narcissist who "emasculates" Kate—spectacular surgery even in quotation marks. He has, says MacCary, no young male "other," like the ones other young males in Shakespeare can count on to confirm their masculinity. But he does: his friend Hortensio. And unlike Lucentio, MacCary points out, Petruchio lacks a living father, a "protective older man." As he does. He thereby differs in another respect from the heroes of other Shakespeare comedies. For MacCary the conclusion is "inescapable" that there is misogyny in the play, as there is. But he does not distinguish between the role's attitudes and guesses at the author's (1985, 121–28). On the other side of the approval-disapproval barrier, J. Dennis Huston holds Petruchio up as a fairy-tale knight who frees the heroine from the monster of the sociopathic manner in which she is trapped when he teaches her how to play with the world (1981, 58–93). Teaching and play are taken up by Leggatt, although he goes beyond them and beyond the obvious meaning of "taming" into a program of training.

> Katherina is trained quite literally, as one would train a hawk. (In contrast, Bianca is described in the following scene as a "proud disdainful haggard" [4.2.39] who will not be tamed.) . . . The taming of Katherina is not just a lesson but a game—a test of skill and a source of pleasure. The roughness is, at bottom, part of the fun: such is the peculiar psychology of sport that one is willing to endure aching muscles and risk the occasional broken limb for the sake of the challenge and the pleasure it provides. And the sports most often recalled throughout the play are blood sports, hunting and hawking—thus invoking in the audience the state of mind in which cruelty and violence are acceptable, even exciting, because their scope is limited by tacit agreement and they are made the occasion for a display of skill. . . . The appeal to our sense of sport also has important implications for the development of Katherina herself: we watch her progress, not just as a wife, but a player in Petruchio's game. (Leggatt 1974, 56; 59)

But does Kate ask Petruchio to train her and to do so "quite literally?" Does she express a wish to undergo grueling preparations for becoming a black-belt wife? Leggatt's view is compatible with Germaine Greer's.

> He tames her as he might a hawk or a high-mettled horse, and she rewards him with strong sexual love and fierce loyalty. Lucentio finds himself saddled with a cold, disloyal woman who has no objection to humiliating him in public. The submission of a woman like Kate is genuine and exciting because she has something to lay down, her virgin pride and individuality: Bianca is the soul of duplicity, married without earnestness or good will. Kate's speech at the close of the play is the greatest defense of Christian monogamy ever written. (1971, 206)

As psychological and, even more, psychoanalytic interpretations creep into dramatic criticism and comment, roles undergo treatment as case histories, and despite the high order of discernment in the writings just cited, they are likely to lead us out of the action into the much murkier background of the unstaged story, not so much between the lines as behind the scenes. We could imagine that after the marriage, in that untenanted world that succeeds act 5, the initial shocks of love, and the profit from the wager, Petruchio will still have to contend with a shrew, partially reformed perhaps, while Kate will find herself confronted with a far harsher paternalistic figure than her father. But come to that, while we are imagining, we can imagine whatever we please about the subsequent marriage, even that the training subsequently wore off or that Petruchio decided to shorten the "jess" worn by his "hawk." But in cold fact, when the play ends, the roles have died.

Still, is Kate the only "shrew" in the action who has submitted to a "taming"? What about Petruchio himself? Does Kate mean to fool him with her speech of capitulation? Or does she mean every word? Either way, she has apparently pushed him out of his initial sarcasm into what looks like genuine affection, not to say love.

Perhaps because of the performers I have seen, I always visualized a substantial gap between the ages of the two principals. I'd cast Petruchio as a philanderer verging on middle age, despite his magnificent energy quotient—very likely fortyish, an experienced man about Northern Italy who has conceivably even tried out his taming more than once on less promising material. (His buddy, Hortensio, would then probably be of the same age.) Kate, on the other side, probably ought not to be more than twenty-five, old enough to give her father pangs that he'll never marry her off, but youthful by just about every other standard. H. J. Oliver writes:

> Shakespeare may well have thought of [Kate] as about sixteen. She is older than Bianca—but then on the evidence of other Shakespeare comedies Bianca would be thought marriageable at fourteen—and Kate's tantrums as well as Petruchio's treatment of them may seem rather more credible if she, too, in her own way is a spoiled child. (1994, 53)

Kate's insolent manner in the early scenes, however, denotes either confidence that comes of more practice than a teenager could lay claim to or recklessness because she believes she may be too old for marriage. Besides, a strong-mouthed woman is more intimidating to men than a shrill girl. Not one of these ages receives backing in the text, but they do have a small bonus to offer, a reason why two of the principal roles who become husbands enter Padua with contrasting ambitions: young Lucentio to "institute A course of learning and ingenious studies" (1.1.8–9); seasoned (or leathery) Petruchio to make money.

Petruchio carries the longest role (in number of lines) and the most strenuous. The continuous bravura required of the actor may account for the relief afforded him, before his entrance for the marriage ceremony, by giving the pageboy Biondello responsibility for the gorgeously colored description of the groom's pending arrival (3.2.43–62 and 64–70). A visual and physical enactment of this account could scarcely measure up to the author's verbal pyrotechnics here. Petruchio starts out under high pressure. He looks like a hot-tempered loony when he walks into Padua and the action, wringing Grumio's ears when the poor fellow doesn't respond to his master's feeble word play on *knock*. Why does he keep so dimwitted a servant? The answer: he doesn't. Grumio shows himself to be intelligent—indeed cunning—and capable of carrying out far trickier orders. As a swaggerer, Petruchio invites the audience to capture his quirkiness in a first impression, even though role-drawing in Shakespeare, however rich, always plays second fiddle to the requirements of the action. One role he resembles, the Miles Gloriosus or Capitano from Italian popular comedy, will prove a false analogy; so will our expectation of him as another fixed part, the innamorato who relies on his servant's wit to get him the girl. With Petruchio's first appearance, we see a misleading man.

As the profusion and confusion of the names ending in *io* suggest, most of the other roles spring more directly from Italian popular traditions, and so does one of the *ia* roles, Bianca's. Lucentio, the would-be philosopher (whose name alludes to light), does personify an innamorato who, like his descendant Count Almaviva, feels unequal to carrying off his heart's desire without instruction and help. Since he comes from Pisa he leans on his servant. But he finds he has a talent for communicating secretly with Bianca when in disguise, and he doesn't need the clever servant after all. In the guise of Cambio ("change") he lets fall no eccentricities. A very young man, he retains his philosophy studies fresh in his mind and regurgitates his lessons for Bianca's sake. He couches his sweet somethings in Latin, which she has to "translate" in both senses of the word. Thanks to his father, he has means; he can play host for the critical scene in the pleasant house he has rented. Hortensio, his rival and the other innamorato, makes a limited impact unless an actor with some striking personal crotchets secures the part.

Two of the servants have remote connections with commedia zanies, most of whom were rogues or fools or rogues who were foolish and therefore inept, although they vary wildly, depending not only on the tasks levied on them but also to some extent on the cities they come from—Naples bred the most outrageous rascals. As zanies at one remove, Grumio and Tranio are pretty innocuous; still, the former takes on some of Petruchio's cruelly courteous manner when he tortures the famished Kate (4.3) by offering foods he doesn't intend to give her. He also boils with resentment at his master—"Fie, fie on all tired jades, on all mad masters, and all foul ways! Was ever man so beaten? Was ever man so rayed? Was ever man so weary?" (4.1.1–3)—but never to the heat of rebellion. His opposite number, Tranio, despite quick reactions and the heft of the role, pretty much vanishes: as the play's invisible figure, he serves the plotting but displays no foibles that make him stand out as himself or as his master when standing in for Lucentio. He doesn't instigate conspiracies like a true zany; he carries out orders. And since his false courtship of Bianca runs parallel with Lucentio's, he seems unnecessary. But his role-playing as Lucentio is thankless compared with Lucentio's as Cambio: the servant is stuck conducting negotiations with the maiden's parent while the master gets to woo the maiden. Despite the apparent lack of color in Tranio's overall role, he remains onstage for so long and contributes so much bulk—flavorless fiber—to the dialogue that while a scrupulous Tranio goes unappreciated by the audience, a weak Tranio undercuts the production.

Of the four other commedia-derived parts, two of the older men present Pantalones and two *dottori*. Gremio and Baptista Minola resemble merchants now in retirement. Gremio plays Pantalone as an aged and hopeless suitor who offers himself as a partner for a child-woman, and gets laughs from being decrepit and incapable. Baptista plays a Pantalone whose female offspring must make profitable matches to alleviate or (with luck) avert the expense of dowries. In some commedia scenarios and related plays, these two Pantalones live in one body. Baptista's functions include a readiness to lose self-possession, an open mouth, and gasps at Petruchio's flamboyant claims and the remaking of Kate. Vincentio and the Pedant bear faint resemblances to the other two, partly owing to their age and, in the case of Vincentio, his wealth. The title *Pedant* alerts us to this role's function as being closer to that of the *dottore* who, in spite of this one's coming from Mantua, is a product of either the University of Padua or the University of Bologna, source of some of the more virtuoso Latin-spillers. The dispute between him and Vincentio (5.1.16 ff.) sounds like a scholarly debate—nothing to do with scholarship, mostly with name-calling.

Kate in her early scenes seems less of a commedia persona than a descendant of the shrewish wife of medieval playlets: for a conspicuous instance, Noah's wife in the Chester cycle, although there are abundant examples of the type, some of them doubtless written by browbeaten husbands.

The question remains unresolved: Is this an anti-woman or anti-wife play? At the end Petruchio gets what he wants in (and out of) Kate. His tyrannical vision of a marriage partner

> I will be master of what is mine own.
> She is my goods, my chattels; she is my house,
> My household stuff, my field, my barn,
> My horse, my ox, my ass, my anything (3.2.229–32)

even allowing for rhetoric, doesn't jibe with Kate's vision of a wife's role:

> Thy husband is thy lord, thy life, thy keeper,
> Thy head, thy sovereign; one that cares for thee,
> And for thy maintenance commits his body
> To painful labor both by sea and land. . . .
> Such duty as the subject owes the prince
> Even such a woman oweth to her husband. (5.2.150–52 and 159–60)

And when Hortensio wonders "what it [Kate's obedience] bodes" he draws from Petruchio the reply

> Marry, peace it bodes, and love, and quiet life.
> An awful rule, and right supremacy,
> And to be short, what not that's sweet and happy (5.2.112–14)

leading us, if not Hortensio, to wonder further *whose* peace and quiet life and sweet and happy "what not" Petruchio has in mind since he is also talking about the same person's awesome "rule and right supremacy."

Kate may not envisage anything like as slavish a relationship as he does, but she certainly speaks of the desirability of wives' becoming subordinated to husbands; and in making the speech, she illustrates the kind of self-abasement she evidently means:

> Place your hands below your husband's foot,
> In token of which duty, if he please,
> My hand is ready; may it do him ease (5.2.181–83)

the kind that bears no resemblance to the modern ideal (seldom realized) of sharing. She sounds as if she's proclaiming unselfish love from wives to satisfy a general male wish for order in society, in other words, for all persons to know their place. If Shakespeare meant her plea to the other two wives to be taken ironically we'd see or sense more irony in the content or undertones.[6] He can be not only the most subtle of playwrights; he can also be the most dramatically direct. Unless alterations or cuts (by omission or deliberately) were made, we must assume the play means what it forcefully says, not what it might or ought to mean.[7] Her speech is a willful shock blow delivered by the dramatist. There's no defending or excusing the sentiments so openly expressed with an apology that the author was a man of his time and his time was more brutal to women—and more openly—than ours is; the extent of wife-beating and related abuses in our era is only just beginning to enter the common consciousness, as are handicaps and frustrations in many women's lives that in some measure have always accounted for shrewish behavior. Nowadays we politely speak of "taming" not a human being but an animal. A literal shrew, however, is a species of animal. Some years ago a play called *The Shrike*, which won a Pulitzer prize, had commercial runs in several theatre capitals. It featured a female role who was much more of a "castrator" than Kate is at first. By coincidence, shrikes kill and feed on shrews, among other prey.

The reaction to *Shrew* by audiences appears to be that Kate has turned from an antisocial being into a social being, from an outcast to one who longs to belong. She now accedes to her lot, even if only for the time being, while Petruchio registers his own warm satisfaction with her oratory. In Miller's BBC TV production, John Cleese as Petruchio (inspired casting) closes his eyes in relief as she arrives at the final lines, as though unsure up to the last second whether she would dry up, skip lines, or commit a blooper—whether she'd pass the test. Petruchio has played, or been, the misogynist or worse, so long as doing so gets him what he wants. Soon after his first entrance, Grumio says, in front of his master,

> Why, give him gold enough and marry him to a puppet or an aglet-baby or an old trot with ne'er a tooth in her head, though she have as many diseases as two-and-fifty horses. Why, nothing comes amiss, so money comes withal (1.2.77-81)

and Petruchio does not contradict him. Conclusion: any rich woman would have done for Petruchio. But in Hollywood parlance, after the pair of headstrong souls have met cute and had time to undergo their joint ordeal, he falls for her, at least in part because of her exceptional compliance.

No honest critic can gloss over act 5's about-face. But not only Kate's. The four principal lovers have reversed themselves, have become their opposites. Petruchio was a spiteful master earlier. Kate was a shrew. Bianca was an innocent. Lucentio was a devout student of philosophy whose "great desire" was to "see fair Padua, nursery of arts" (1.1.1–2). And act 1 will always be what it is: it can never be undermined by act 5. Shakespeare's drama, I have already said (or should have said by now), frequently refers back to Ovid's *Metamorphoses*. The four role metamorphoses need no further explaining; they are stage magic. Yes, Petruchio starts out as a woman-abuser, even if he doesn't actually hit Kate. And yes, she starts out as a shrew. And no, Shakespeare doesn't by implication advocate an extension of the Petruchio treatment to all women; he doesn't even recommend it for a Kate. He doesn't say that somebody who is not the early Petruchio could succeed with Kate or with any other woman—Bianca, say, or

the Widow. His play doesn't amount to a recipe and home demonstration for taming or training or otherwise coping with an uppity woman. Or with a misogynistic man. He explores what might take place
when two imaginary bodies collide. The comic instability, the pliability, the opportunities keep revising the roles. These refashionings bring
us close to the male dream of molding a woman to one's fancy or requirements. (The opposite, a woman's dream of molding a man to
one's fancy or requirements, is seldom articulated openly, though a
show-stopping number in *Guys and Dolls* comes close: "Marry the man
today And change his ways tomorrow.") Leggatt and Greer may think
Petruchio trains Katharina like a hawk, as if for blood sports—and
hunting imagery does recur in the dialogue—but he is not that dense.
While working on her, he trains her into wifely acquiescence; and as
he does so they enter the worlds of Agnès and Arnolphe in *The School
for Wives*, Eliza and Higgins in *Pygmalion*, the Richard Gere and Julia
Roberts roles in *Pretty Woman*.

Petruchio engineers a fantasy, and the two other new husbands
instantly envy him. The morphing device is not a literary conceit but a
structural principle in Shakespeare. It governs Adriana in *Errors*, the
King and his three lords in *Love's Labor's Lost*, Proteus in *Two Gentlemen*,
and it determines what happens to Falstaff and Ford in *The Merry Wives*.

The Shrew has galloped through this century like a frolic: in the
1927 modern-dress production at the Garrick in New York; cavorted by
the Lunts in 1935 in another Broadway house; at Stratford, Connecticut, in the 1950s with Katharine Hepburn and Alfred Drake; when
staged by William Ball and the American Conservatory Theatre in the
1960s as a brawl choreographed in an arena that looked like a boxing
ring; in several films; and on the threshold of the 1990s, Tracey Ullman
versus Morgan Freeman in Central Park's Delacorte Theatre, which itself played America's West of the 1880s. *The Shrew* speaks (or whispers)
to an innate combativeness in both sexes and, at the same time, to a
hope for reconciliation. If we pine for a balance of power between the
sexes in a Shakespeare comedy we must look for it in a subsequent
play, *Much Ado*, and if we insist that a woman triumph over a man we
must turn to an even later comedy, *All's Well*. The variety of relatedness
to these two comedies is discussed in the following chapters. Whether
the author meant them to appear related—to be staged and seen as a
triptych—is anyone's guess, but two of them do represent retorts of a
sort to *The Shrew*. Which does not spare us male bullying.

> The subjection of women to men, though patently unfair and unjus-
> tifiable [writes Ann Thompson in the introduction to the New Cam-
> bridge edition, 41], is still virtually universal. It is the world which
> offends us, not Shakespeare.

Notes

1. See, for example, Ann Thompson's introduction to the New Cambridge edition of the play (1984, 10). See also *Shakespeare's World of Images* by Donald Stauffer (1949), 43–46), C.S. Seronsy's "'Supposes' as the Unifying Theme in *The Taming of the Shrew*," *Shakespeare Quarterly* No. 14 (1963, 15–30), and Richard Hosley's "The Formal Influence of Plautus and Terence" in *Elizabethan Theatre*, eds. John Russell Brown and Bernard Harris (1966, 131–45).

2. Different editions of the play spell *Katherina* with an *e* as the middle vowel (e.g., Arden, Folger, Pelican, Riverside) or with an *a* (e.g., Oxford, HarperCollins). The Signet Classic refers to her throughout as Kate.

3. In this chapter I have not alluded to the play's variety of writing styles. For a compact and penetrating discussion of the prose, blank and rhymed verse, as well as other matters relating to the dramatic language, see Oliver (1994, 56–64).

4. The literature on these three topics is so vast and varied that I refer readers to essays by two of the most prominent recent scholars and their bibliographies. Richard Hosley's "Sources and Analogues of *The Taming of the Shrew*" in *The Huntington Library Quarterly*, XXVII, 1963–64, reprinted in Heilman's Signet Classic edition, concludes with a summary of the most likely sources; so does Hosley's introduction to the play in *The Complete Pelican Shakespeare*, (80–83). The introduction by Brian Morris to the Arden edition of *The Shrew* (1981, 12–88), questions at least one of these sources.

5. See Thompson for a rundown of *The Shrew*'s textual inconsistencies, omissions, and ragged ends (1984, 161–62).

6. Coppélia Kahn makes a powerful case in favor of an ironic reading: that Shakespeare is pointing out that a married woman is "a subhuman being who exists solely for the purposes of her husband" (1981, 104–18). The quotation comes from p. 112. Ann Thompson weighs the pros and cons of Kahn's thesis in the introduction to the New Cambridge edition (38–41).

7. Brian Morris says that the three compositors identified by Charlton Hinman as typesetters for the First Folio ("the only text which has authority") worked together, "in this instance, to produce a reasonably clean text with no more than the average scatter of misprints" (1981, reprinted 1993, 1).

Love's Labor's Lost

Hunting he loved, but love he laughed to scorn
—Venus and Adonis

A critic's determination of the order in which the plays were written or produced usually relies not only on what looks like the hardest evidence available but also on the thesis being established about some aspect of Shakespeare's work as a whole. Thus, C. L. Barber in *Shakespeare's Festive Comedy* eloquently defends *Love's Labor's Lost* as Shakespeare's third comedy, not his second, because Barber takes it to be the playwright's first connection of dramatic form to social customs like holidays, as Barber himself has done. (1963, 11; 13; 87–118). Maybe, maybe not. I see no reason not to date it from the late 1580s as a production for a boys' company, revised with some slipshod editing and/or copying in the later 1590s for the King's Men.

Like *Errors*, it forms a structural and verbal oddity among the comedies. It features not the two or occasionally three or, in one case, four love pairings of other comedies, but five, though admittedly two couples are principals and two subsidiaries from the main plot, while the fifth pair belongs to a subplot. It flaunts seven odd secondary roles, more than are usual in Shakespeare; *Two Gentlemen*, for example, has only two, the servants, Launce and Speed. Yet most of the action moves at a ceremonial pace, luxuriating in the contemplative and self-indulgent tone of the speeches: the author refrains from febrile stage activity of the kinds we associate with the comic conventions he adopted and refurbished. Nor does it occur in anything like the threatening circumstances found in the later comedies. The *préciosité* of much of its language looks suspiciously like either an inheritance from Lyly, an imitation of Lyly, a tribute to Lyly, a parody of Lyly, or, as a poetic, sixteenth-century equivalent of graffiti, painting the Lyly; although according to Richard David in the Arden edition of the play (1968, xxxi), the language in *Love's Labor's Lost* is closer to that of Sidney's *Arcadia* than to Lyly's. Its wordplay, occasionally nearly as deplorable as that in the previous sentence, can flower into imagery as glorious as that of any of Shakespeare's later lyricism, and as reckless as almost any in twentieth-century literature. Frequent wordplay becomes the very objective of encounters and even entire scenes. Apart from metrical games, such as the frequency of sonnet forms within speeches, the play toys with matching sequences. Berowne, taking off from the King's mention of "vain delight," goes on in the opening scene to hurl a mind-numbing succession of *light* at the audience:

> Why, all delights are vain, but that most vain
> Which, with pain purchased, doth inherit pain:
> As, painfully to pore upon a book
> To seek the light of truth, while truth the while
> Doth falsely blind the eyesight of his look.
> Light seeking light doth light of light beguile;
> So, ere you find where light in darkness lies,
> Your light grows dark by losing of your eyes.
> Study me how to please the eye indeed
> By fixing it upon a fairer eye. (1.1.72-81)

Here *light*, as adjective or noun, takes on a spray of meanings, from *light in weight* to *lighthearted, slight, bawdy, light-colored, illumination*, and sometimes two of these in one. A passage that matches these lines consists not of a single speech but some bantering between Katharine and Rosaline at the other end of the play in the lengthy final scene (5.2.15 ff). Juggling not only words, Shakespeare broaches so many dramatic possibilities, several of which he would later capitalize on, that the play quivers with experiment, throwing off delectable novelties, which have energized stage presentations in the past quarter century.

The conflict is not the usual dramatic kind, the clash of roles with opposed motives, but a verbal war between four male nobles of Navarre and four ladies of France—skirmishes conducted in varied poetic meters, rhetoric, and vernacular excesses. The language strains to overflow denotative necessities and the disciplines imposed on them: the meter, the rhyme, the arcadian formalities of the setting, and the proprieties observed by the nine court habitués in the main plot.

That the main plot has nine roles—not three threes but four twos and an odd man out, Boyet, the chaperon for the four ladies—creates a healthy asymmetry. The laconic stage directions call for three (or are there two?) additional lords to escort the ladies into scenes 2.1 and 4.1—but not for their entrance in 5.2—and for one of them who goes unnamed to speak three words, twice, in the second act. Probably those slight roles were expunged during revisions—but not thoroughly—or, as Hibbard theorizes, Shakespeare may have "come to see that he could make better use of the two actors playing these supernumerary parts by giving them new roles," that is, those of Holofernes and Nathaniel, and so allowed himself to "carry much further that exploration and exploitation of linguistic fads and eccentricities which he had begun through his creation of Armado" (1994, 32).

Productions today generally omit the Princess's lords and assign the six words to the ladies and/or Boyet. The sometimes verbose movements of the main plot comprise a quadrille with the four pairs of not quite, not yet, not exactly lovers executing four dance figures as the last four acts of the play: roughly equivalent to the stanzas of a song. The final lines of act 5 point up this equivalence for they consist of four verses that include some of the poet's most memorable tropes—a song, rather than what we find in most of his other comedies: the prelude to a mating ritual and an entreaty for applause. The "dances" in the different acts resemble measures that take two steps forward and three steps back. The men, the King of Navarre and three lords, make some headway, then are coyly rebuffed by the women, the Princess of France and three ladies.

Apart from the interventions of Boyet, the diplomat of the Princess, who calls him, "our best-moving fair solicitor" (2.1.29), and whose presence works as an irritant on the men, and most evidently on the most forthright of them, Berowne (who speaks sarcastically of "honeytongued Boyet"[5.2.335]), the four promising courtly love matches display an unorthodox balance. No rivalries, much less jealousies, upset the pattern. Each lord grows instantly infatuated with the lady of his choice, like Romeo spotting Juliet at the Capulets' ball. Not one of the men is taken by the other three women, and the women have decided early on they feel attracted to the very men who want them. The early lineup remains unaltered: the pair of royals, the King and the Princess; the most talkative, if not long-winded and snippy, Berowne and Rosaline; Longaville with Maria; Dumaine with Katharine. The only ruffling of the placid arrangement will occur when the men put on disguises as Muscovites to entertain the women more boldly than they would do in their own clothes and accents, whereupon the women swap masks, to fool the foolers, and all eight young people find themselves dancing and chatting with the choices of others: that is, cross-addressing. The women trick the men because, according to the Princess:

> The effect of my intent is to cross theirs.
> They do it but in mockery merriment,
> And mock for mock is only my intent . . .
> There's no such sport as sport by sport o'erthrown,
> To make theirs ours and ours none but our own.
> (5.2.138–40, 153–54)

Such elements of conflict as we can pry out of this main plot are fivefold and mild. First, the male quartet renounces for three years all interests in life but scholarship in order to promote an academy of self-denying seekers of truth. They have in effect sworn to forswear the world (women), the flesh (women), and the devil (women), but when the female quartet comes on the scene the men abandon the sweeping ambition almost as soon as they have adopted it. Second, Berowne breaks with his three companions for a time when he protests that giving up the company of women and other pleasures is impractical, undesirable, and unnecessary, most of all because refusing to mingle with women means the men will forfeit a large packet of their education. However, he yields, for the sake of peace or unanimity, and takes the oath in favor of cold, hard learning or, as he later puts it, "to fast, to study, and to see no woman" (4.3.287). Third, the women, when approached, tease the men and outwit them, in part to teach them not to be spiteful with their wisecracks and in part to take revenge on the King who, to uphold his oath, has left them to camp out on the grounds of his park, rather than receive a full welcome in his palace. But they reject the men's vows unemphatically enough in act 5 to give the impression of a tame mating game that could in years to come work out satisfactorily for all. The fourth muted conflict consists of the Princess's business for coming to Navarre: to ask the King, on behalf of her father, for the return to France of the province of Aquitaine and repayment of a sizable cash loan. Still, the dispute, moderately heated at first, is forgotten until near the end of the last act, and then dropped when the Princess thanks the King for her "great suit so easily obtained" (5.2.735)—offstage, it must be. Fifth, the Princess learns suddenly in act 5 of the death of her father. The news wrenches the play into a dark mood: she and her ladies now feel uncomfortable even talking about matrimonial prospects. As the men pledge their love anew, the women ask for time out; they wish to postpone their decisions for a year. The men concede: instead of the three years of hard mental labor they had sentenced themselves to, they will now get off with one year and a day of socially responsible witticisms. Love's labors in truth are not altogether lost but placed on parole. Berowne has to endure this penalty from Rosaline:

> You shall this twelvemonth term from day to day
> Visit the speechless sick, and still converse
> With groaning wretches; and your task shall be
> With all the fierce endeavor of your wit
> To enforce the painèd impotent to smile. (5.840–44)

In all five soft-centered conflicts a jagged edge rises into view from time to time, but there are no big issues at stake to jar the etiquette for long. After a stunned initial reaction to his social work task, "to move

wild laughter in the throat of death? It cannot be; it is impossible,"
Berowne accepts it with good grace: "I'll jest a twelvemonth in an hos-
pital" (5.2.845–46, 861). These eight roles, who comprise the main
plot, do galvanize the dialogue, however, and so compensate for the
tempered drama in the scenes. Verbally speaking, all the punsters in
(or, in Boyet's case, beyond) the quadrille are bright, fast-stepping
hoofers on the alert for racy openings. Among them Berowne stands
out because he has easily the most lines, 591 out of a total of 2667,
says a useful table in *The Complete Pelican Shakespeare* (Harbage 1969,
31), as well as eighteen captivating monologues. For this purpose I
define a monologue as a speech in prose or verse that consists of at
least eight lines. Some of the monologues run much longer. The other
roles, including the King (eight monologues), the Princess (also eight
monologues), and Berowne's opposite number, Rosaline, are only
lightly differentiated and will depend for distinctive impact on the director and performers, unless these choose to make them not particularly distinguishable and so underline the play's diagrammatic
qualities and, as a result, its occasional cartoonishness.

Into the secondary slots or plots Shakespeare places the more eccentric and sharply defined roles, who stand further down the social
scale and look less conscious of their dignity and place as they live
their own lives, rather than existences decreed by their rank and by
that opportunistic deity, Chance. They add up to a sprinkling of rural
life, nothing like a cross-section: only one woman and no wives, merry or otherwise, as in Shakespeare's Windsor. For the purposes of the
action the kingdom of Navarre is both royal estate and tiny community—possibly a village—populated by several cousins of commedia
clowns, from the almost-literate peasant zanies Costard and Constable
Anthony Dull, who may both have additional roots in French and
British folk plays, to two middle-class pedants, the sum of the local
intelligentsia. (Richard David has summarized the debts to the commedia masks—Arden edition [1951, xxxi–xxxii].) The curate
Nathaniel dogs and worships Holofernes. That schoolteacher parades
his learning, pickled in his own brand of Latin, with crude possessiveness. He will not concede all local grandiloquence to the grandee, Don
Armado, who crossed Navarre's Spanish border and stayed, apparently because of Jaquenetta. She, the girlfriend and sleeping partner of
Costard, derives not from the commedia but from French farce, the
sottie. Rarely onstage, she is more an object (of Armado's and Costard's
affection) than a subject in her own right; but like several of Shakespeare's other minor lasses, she can make an entertaining presence of
her role with the aid of dumb show. Finally, there is Armado's page,
Moth, a teenaged wise guy and unmagical tryout for Puck and Ariel,
another opportunity for a perky boy actor of the late sixteenth and

early seventeenth centuries, and said by some critics to refer oblique-
ly to the writer Thomas Nashe, Shakespeare's younger contemporary.[1]

Five of these worthies (omitting Dull and Jaquenetta) form a little performance group that will present the traditional Pageant of the
Nine Worthies, exemplary figures from history, for the gratification of
the King, his guests, and followers, nine unworthies. At first the King,
still smarting from the ladies' sarcastic reception of his lords and himself in the guise of Muscovites, resists the Nine Worthies as an entertainment: "They will shame us," he says. "Let them not approach"
(5.2.509). But he is overruled by Berowne and the Princess who, like
hounds on the hunt, scent more victims for their "sport." When the
performance does begin and suffers ruthless interruptions and ridicule
from the ladies and especially the lords and Boyet, we see these men
at their worst. Here we have one of those scenes in which Shakespeare, supposedly as enigmatic as he is noncommittal, and sometimes
looked on as a monarchist and traditionalist, reveals a gentle contempt
for aristocracy, as indeed he does throughout the play. In calling the
performers within the performance the Nine Worthies, a historical
name, he implies that the group has set out to satirize the nine figures
in the main plot: the four couples and Boyet. Instead, the "worthies"
unintentionally bring out the pettiness of the interruptions by the
lords, ladies, and royals.

Love's Labor's Lost has other unusual characteristics:

- The division into acts, which dates back to the Folio edition of
1623, if not earlier, is uncommonly uneven, cramming a heavy
dose of material into act 4 and even more, much more, into act 5.
Act 1 consists of 484 lines; act 2, 258; act 3, 203; act 4, 673; act 5,
1,070. (These figures also derive from *The Complete Pelican Shakespeare* [Harbage 1969, 31.]) Since the last two acts are twice as long
as the first three, the intermission is often taken after act 4.

- The text falls into many declamatory speeches, some of them love
poetry of the pre-Metaphysical era. These speeches often contain
entire sonnets, some in dialogue form, so that more than one
speaker cooperates in fulfilling the sonnets' patterns. Some
speeches are long enough to contain more than one sonnet or one
plus a succession of rhymed couplets. The proportion of rhymed
lines amounts to more than 43 percent, a total exceeded only by
that of *A Midsummer Night's Dream* (45.5 percent)—but then,
Dream is a play openly about spells and enchantment, for which
rhyme is an advantageous instrument. (The next play down the
rhyming list, *Pericles*, has a much smaller percentage of rhymed
lines, just over 22 percent.). Frye went so far as to say that for
Shakespeare in general, "the subject matter of poetry is not life, or

nature, or reality, or revelation, or anything else that the philosopher builds on, but poetry itself, a verbal universe" (1965, 173).
The sentiment flatters Shelley's unacknowledged legislators and
would more likely be true, if it were true at all, of *Love's Labor's
Lost* than of almost any other play. If poetry, and especially rhyme
worlds away from being doggerel, becomes so prominent, almost
dominant, in this play, does it demand overdone elocution, rather
than the conversational manner many recent directors of Shakespeare have striven for? I would say it does, not only for the sake
of audibility but also because much of it also calls for good-natured caricature—of surviving types rather than only of the playwright's contemporaries.

The likely targets, if any, of the innocuous-appearing phrase
"school of night" and sundry other references may make for tantalizing historical speculation, but even when beautifully enunciated these references will carry little association for most spectators. Should they be retained? How to effect the most telling surgery on this play for performances remains open to guesswork and
taste. In 1951 Richard David tackled the question, apropos of an
Old Vic production at the New Theatre (174–85), and offered
some alternatives that still sound feasible, but for an American
audience half a century later substantially new considerations
come into play.

This remains a difficult play to get across. The BBC TV production directed by Elijah Moshinsky, very likely the most widely circulated version, sets the entire action indoors, even the scenes in
the tent into which the women have been shunted. Moshinsky
contrived other flaccid novelties by casting and dressing some of
the actors strangely: a well-spoken Moth (John Kane), but aged
about forty; a Holofernes garbed and enunciating like a judge; a
colorless Jaquenetta; two singers for Winter and Spring whose lyr-
ics were unintelligible. As an exception to the general drabness,
Mike Gwilym played a spirited Berowne. He also demonstrated
that the actors need unusually fluent articulation, for the meter
varies more than in the other comedies. Rapid changes take place
in, for example, 2.1. Nimble-tongued actors will have to switch
out of the iambic pentameter, which has evolved into an orderly
progression, and into some quick exchanges.

BEROWNE Now fair befall your mask!

ROSALINE Fair fall the face it covers!

BEROWNE And send you many lovers!

ROSALINE Amen, so you be none. (vv. 123-26, *Iambic trimeter*)

And shortly, after a return to the governing meter, into:

ROSALINE Alack, let it blood.

BEROWNE Would that do it good?

ROSALINE My physic says, "ay."

BEROWNE Will you prick't with your eye? (vv. 186–89, *Anapestic dimeter.*)

More variations and irregularities follow until Boyet moves into a rollicking meter, which takes the act almost to its end:

Why, all his behaviors did make their retire
To the court of his eye, peeping thorough desire . . . etc.
(vv. 234–35, *Anapestic tetrameter*).

Other rare meters include trochaic tetrameters (4.3.100–119) and a British alexandrine, or iambic septameter, in an improvisational, mildly dirty tongue-twister spoken by Holofernes (4.2.57–62) about a pricket in a thicket.

- All the scenes unroll in the same general setting, although not the same specific spots. Renaissance critics would probably accept the royal park as a unity of place. But the French ladies have their private colloquies; so do the lords of Navarre, and so also do Navarre's other citizens. Whether the scenery suggests the open air (with regal tents, maybe), interiors (such as anachronistic glassed-in buildings), or abstractions, some visual links between the successive locales will assist in unifying the action and delivering constant reminders that the little country of Navarre, neither French nor Spanish, a separation between Gascony, Castile, and Aragon, has an isolated, insulated situation. According to McFarland and Giamatti, the word *park* has semantic connections with *paradise*, which does imply nature tamed. Navarre is an island of peace, says Huston, in a troubled world. The entry of the Princess with her entourage brings closer the past and present troubles of that world: the King's father gave the Princess's father a loan to wage war on an unspecified enemy, and the loan may or may not have been wholly or partially repaid. Aquitaine, controlled by Navarre, lay directly to its north, was a much more extensive land, and would have amounted to a valuable prize for strategic and other reasons. But that intrusion of the world beyond with its property disputes may fade and diminish as the action continues to dwell in its idyllic surroundings—until the shattering entrance of Marcade:

MARCADE I am sorry, madam, for the news I bring
Is heavy in my tongue. The King your father—

PRINCESS Dead, for my life!

MARCADE Even so. My tale is told. (5.2.715–17)

Here a perfect pun, "Dead, for my life!"—a double meaning, not a mere word-association—combines with her anticipation of the bad news and unlike its imperfect predecessors turns the mood sober, even grave. Death has crossed the border and laid open Navarre's paradise-like remoteness.

As one of the peculiarities of this pastoral landscape, it does not accommodate conventional pastoral business and roles. In place of a shepherd-shepherdess wooing, what goes on between Jaquenetta and Costard, with contributions from Don Armado, seems like a prelude for Audrey, Touchstone, and William in *As You Like It*. In place of placid livestock grazing the hills we find wild animals like deer being hunted. The fourth act opens with the French party peering outward and up.

PRINCESS Was that the King that spurred his horse so hard

    Against the steep uprising of the hill?

BOYET I know not, but I think it was not he.

PRINCESS Whoe'er 'a was, 'a showed a mounting mind . . . .

Does this exchange exist for the sake of the Princess's pun? Why does the author have Boyet almost deny that she saw the King unkindly spurring his horse uphill? What is a bookish monarch doing on a hunt, anyway? A bit later in the scene the Princess voices her unease with slaying. As a royal personage, she is expected to handle a bow expertly and win admiration for doing so, while she confesses that, not for food or even the satisfactions of pursuit and murder but "for praise alone" she "now will seek to spill The poor deer's blood that my heart means no ill" (4.1.34–35). The scene does not stop at decrying the cruelty of hunting from the Princess's point of view but, in an insulting, if not acidic, exchange between Rosaline and Boyet goes on to elaborate upon a comparison between hunting an animal and hunting down a sex partner, and a likeness between a murderer and the invisible performer in every Shakespeare comedy: Cupid.

It may have been the hunting scene that prompted Pater to say of the play, "It is as if Shakespeare had intended to bind together, by some inventive conceit, the devices of an ancient tapestry, and give voices to its figures" (1885; reprinted in Signet Classic edition, 156). Medieval and later tapestries sometimes portrayed successive moments in a chase after a real or mythical animal, such as the famous wounding and death of a unicorn preserved at the Cloisters in upper Manhattan. In two of the productions I have seen—John Barton's in 1978 for the Royal Shakespeare Company and Michael Langham's in the early 1990s at the Theatre for a New Audience—the directors deployed the actors to take advantage of the width of the stage and, in that respect, too, to resemble a tapestry set in motion, as well as implying the vast extent of the park. The pastoral redolence of *Love's Labor's Lost* and the analogy between what the play almost calls seeking a deer and seeking a dear do not result in any slaughter, though possibly in a wounding of lords and ladies. But then the play proclaims no finality. It defers consequences.

To revert to the theme of this book: the principal male roles, palely defined as they are, do change under the impress of the women and one another, almost to their opposites and then almost back again to the originals. The first changes arise in the course of one of the playwright's most ingenious and challenging scenes (4.3), a multiple eavesdropping, during which each of three members of the quartet in turn, believing himself alone, reads aloud the missive in verse he has penned to his beloved—love's labor's spelled out—and goes on to have grave doubts as to its efficacy and his own mental health.

Berowne precedes them onstage. He gave a powerful hint of his change of heart in the previous act when he exclaimed in a soliloquy, "And I, forsooth, in love! I that have been love's whip"(3.1.172); he announced with helpless fury, after ranting about his lack of self-control, the "plague" being spread by Cupid,[2] and Rosaline's paltry but irresistible attractions. He will now, he says, behave like your regular, heartsick swain and (in a line of splendid monosyllables), "love, write, sigh, pray, sue, groan" (3.1.172 and 202). We have by then heard his sonnet, which fell into the wrong hands and voice, recited—void of feeling or with the wrong kind of feeling, and therefore parodied—by the parson Nathaniel, whom Berowne scornfully calls a "hedgepriest." Berowne, a lord of mockery, enters the scene dropping word associations like a highschool junior building a vocabulary:

> The King, he is hunting the deer; I am coursing myself. They have pitched a toil; I am toiling in a pitch—pitch that defiles. Defile! a foul word (4.3.1–3)

and so on. He exults over the sonnet he sent Rosaline by way of Costard the clown—"The clown bore it, the fool sent it, and the lady hath it—sweet clown, sweeter fool, sweetest lady!" (vv. 14–16)—when the King appears with his poem addressed to the Princess. Berowne darts into hiding (up a tree, behind a bush, in the shadow of a statue) while the King recites *his* rhapsodic sonnet of fourteen lines plus one heroic couplet all dedicated to his love. Scarcely has he finished than Longaville appears, sonnet in moist hand. Hastily, "the King steps aside," into some niche or nook not occupied by Berowne, who continues to have the superior vantage point for viewing and also for listening as he overhears the King's and Longaville's words considerately spoken aloud. The game of hide-and-speak grows more complicated with the arrival of Dumaine and his twenty rhyming lines and some chiding of him by Longaville. But the scene has not reached its climax. After the King reveals himself, mocks Longaville and Dumaine, and warns them about Berowne's sarcasm if he finds them out, Berowne advances, proclaiming, "Now step I forth to whip hypocrisy" (147) and tongue-lashes the three "men of inconstancy" (176), until his own script comes to light and proves him the most hypocritical of all. Each of the four feels relief at not being the only victim of love.

Their poems serve as witnesses to the agonies, not the ecstasies, of love. The four sassy youngsters of act 1, forebears of Evelyn Waugh's titled idlers of the 1920s, versify in act 4 about their bewilderment and mundane inadequacy in praising the ladies' divine gifts, especially their ineffable eyes, which mirror vast ranges of emotion and are convenient for rhyming. Berowne's sonnet (4.2.104–17), crudely paraphrased, says, "You're magnificently worth studying. I could learn so much from loving you, you heavenly creature." This is a fairly positive statement to the effect that loving is a better labor in the service of learning than pure learning is. The King's sixteen lines (4.3.23–38), more plaintive in tone, say in effect, "You look gorgeous, with your shining eyes, which defy comparison with the greatest sights in nature, while, look at my eyes, all tearful, because there's no way to do justice to your qualities." Longaville, less cheerless, declares (4.3.56–69), "You're celestial, a sun, while I'm earthbound. I'm not breaking my oath to give up women when I love you, because you happen to be a goddess." Dumaine grumbles (4.3.97–116), "I'm forbidden to pluck this rose. How unnatural for a redblooded young fellow like me, when the king of the gods himself couldn't have resisted you."

The trio of three young lords picked out and selected by the King for their accomplishments and charm to join a court that "shall be a little academe" (1.1.12) at which "the mind shall banquet, though the body pine" (25) have turned into stammering, inept apprentices at love, more like the quarries than the hunters after fame they started out to be. A number of critics have questioned the lords' sincerity, and they do seem to have stumbled into the extremes of pastoral and chivalric self-decrial—to have fallen, as the old lyric and even older cliché have it, in love with love.

The Princess and her ladies do not appreciably change until the news of the King's death; then they subside. Afterward, they veer away from the sarcasm and bantering they have accustomed us to—and grow demanding. The men shall serve a penance. Rosaline in particular abruptly sprouts a conscience, spares a care for the welfare of the "speechless sick" and other "groaning wretches," although in decreeing that Berowne shall serve them, she does not volunteer her own supervision, assistance, or even attendance.

In contrast to the perfumed sentiments and the volleys of wit (intended funniness) that rattle out of the mouths of the titled youths and the recipients of their adoration, the scenes between the other roles depend for the most part on humor (*un*intended funniness). The author doesn't exactly pillory the roles in the subplots more than he does the roles in the main plot, but other things like responses being equal, humor will as a rule be zestfully comic, liable to raise a laugh, whereas wit will as a rule raise a knowing smile or a tolerant moan. Holofernes and Don Adriano de Armado look upon themselves as wordsmiths, and they are at least as word-proud, or word-conscious, as the aristocrats when they attempt to out-play and out-display each other's flowery lines. Their toying with language differs, one's from the other's. Hibbard (1994) argues in his introduction to the World Classics edition, first, that these two serve to make fun of the lords of Navarre's pretentious talk; second, that they both have accompanying audiences, Armado being

> furnished with a sharply critical one in Moth; Holofernes with an effusively adulatory one in Sir Nathaniel . . . the Spaniard's great stand-by is the periphrasis; whereas the pedant relies mainly on the synonym. (32)

As a further distinction, Holofernes treats Nathaniel and, indeed, the whole world as pupils, thereby asserting his superiority; but Armado, conscious of being a foreigner, uses the prolixity to try to overcome his feelings of the outsider's inferiority—at home with the tongue yet able to ply it exotically. We laugh openly at the effusions of them both, such as the Don's love letter to Jaquenetta, intercepted by accident and read aloud by Boyet, so that its exaggerated, backward logic, rhetorical figures, and catechistic form are soaked in Boyet's sarcastic manner.

> "He came, saw, and overcame." Who came? The King? Why did he come? To see. Why did he see? To overcome. To whom came he? To the beggar. . . Shall I command thy love? I may. Shall I enforce thy love? I could. Shall I entreat thy love? I will. What shalt thou exchange for rags? Robes. For tittles? Titles. For thyself? Me. (4.1.70–74; 80–83)

Nathaniel's sycophancy will similarly impose itself on Berowne's synthetic sentiments when the former reads the latter's letter. Holofernes, blessed with a dictionary compiler's love of language and cursed with a pedant's craving to explain while listening greedily to his own utterances, judges himself witty and is taken to be so by his disciple:

> The deer was, as you know, *sanguis*, in blood, ripe as the pomewater, who now hangeth like a jewel in the ear of *caelo*, the sky, the welkin,

the heaven, and anon falleth like a crab on the face of *terra*, the soil, the land, the earth. (4.2.3–7)

He congratulates himself for being so clever.

> . . . This is a gift that I have, simple, simple—a foolish, extravagant spirit, full of forms, figures, shapes, objects, ideas, apprehensions, motions, revolutions. These are begot in the ventricle of memory, nourished in the womb of *pia mater*, and delivered upon the mellowing of occasion. But the gift is good in those in whom it is acute, and I am thankful for it. (4.2.65–71)

But to us he radiates humor, not wit; he labors to sound impressive, not comic, while we laugh precisely at his straining for impressiveness.

Nathaniel, who fancies himself a qualified votary of Holofernes, reacts to the latter's scholarly sallies and dead-weight modesty with the obsequiousness of a teacher's pet.

> Sir, I praise the Lord for you, and so may my parishioners, for their sons are well tutored by you, and their daughters profit very greatly under you. You are a good member of the commonwealth. (4.2.72–75)

What makes him and his rural co-savant humorous is that they commit their double entendres such as "their daughters . . . under you" by accident, not willfully, as the nobles do. Another reason for not laughing freely at the nobles' sexy wordplay—what editors like to call "bawdy quibbles"—is that these are either corny, after nearly four centuries of repetition and variation, or elusive, thanks to the death and rebirths of euphemistic slang.

Among the "low-comedy" types, Costard, Dull, and Jaquenetta, most of the humor issues from misused, misspelled, and mispronounced words and phrases. The playwright makes fun of the trio's semiliteracy but in a good-natured fashion. The two men enter the action as early as the opening scene, while Jaquenetta, the prime topic of their appearance, remains offstage in the story and scenery. Armado, lodging a complaint with the King, sends it by way of Constable Dull. It arrives just when the King and his lords have been talking about the "sport" they hope to extract from the rivalry between Armado and "the swain Costard" and shortly after they have been talking over the royal order to abstain from sex. The King reads Armado's appeal, another instance in this play of making the roles play roles, become actors and enacters of the messages of others. Armado wishes to instruct his majesty that he observed Costard, "contrary to thy established proclaimed edict and continent canon," in the company of "a child of our grandmother Eve, a female," namely Jaquenetta. He presents this intelligence in grotesquely overblown cadences, concluding, "Thine, in all compliments of devoted and heartburning heat of duty, Don Adriano de Armado," which Berowne finds to be "not so well as I looked for, but the best that ever I heard" (1.1.257–58, 268–70, and 271–73).

The King thereupon sentences Costard to fast for a week "with bran and water" (Costard would "rather pray a month with mutton and porridge") and appoints Don Armado his "keeper." In the final scene, during the Pageant of the Worthies, Costard (playing Pompey) tells Armado (playing Hector) that Jaquenetta "is gone! She is two months on her way . . . the child brags in her belly already. 'Tis yours" (5.2.669–670 and 673–74). A duel would follow between the two men if it were not for two drawbacks: first, Costard challenges Armado to fight in his shirt, but Armado answers, when pressed, that "the naked truth of it is, I have no shirt"; and, second, Marcade interrupts with his news about the King's demise. Later, Armado will "have vowed to Jaquenetta to hold the plow for her sweet love three year," in other words, to become a farmer, a literal husbandman, on her behalf while he refrains from making love to her, or—in yet other words—to let himself (without realizing it) be cuckolded by Costard for that period, after he has (without realizing it) become the father of Costard's bastard.

By this time several transpositions have taken place in the secondary roles. They have played some of the nine parts of the Worthies and become comic stand-ins for those figures but the lords and ladies have allowed them to utter hardly a line without literal, bloody-minded heckling.

COSTARD "I Pompey am—"

BEROWNE You lie; you are not he.(5.2.543)

And in addition, bickering and intervening:

ARMADO

  "The armipotent Mars, of lances the almighty,
  Gave Hector a gift—"

DUMAINE A gilt nutmeg.

BEROWNE A lemon.

LONGAVILLE Stuck with cloves.

DUMAINE No, cloven. (5.2.641–46)

Armado has to plead with the highborn young men to refrain, intoxicated as they are with their discovery of free association: "Sweet chucks, beat not the bones of the buried" (5.2.659–60). Holofernes has already protested a succession of jibes: "This is not generous, not gentle, not humble" (5.2.626). The secondary roles, playing heroic figures, which they have cut down to puppet size by their deficient playing, are made to look even more foolish by the humiliations heaped upon their tribute to the King and the Princess. A similar but even more

pointed fifth-act scene will display the callow behavior of the youths
Demetrius and Lysander toward the "mechanicals" in the performance
of "Pyramus and Thisbe." Here, however, we see the harmless braggarts Holofernes and Armado taken down a few pegs, turned into new
roles, but the effect is unexpectedly sad, in keeping with the turn of
the main plot toward its end as the lords and ladies feel humbled by
death's intrusion into the kingdom. Moth, that bumptious little bump-
kin, referred to by Armado as a "most acute juvenal" (3.1.65), lauded
by Costard ("An I had but one penny in the world, thou shouldst have
it to buy gingerbread," 5.1.68–69), and a reminder of the nobles with
his smartass talk, has vanished from the action: he came briefly onstage as Hercules the baby who strangled a serpent in his cradle, said
not one word, and was washed away as an inapt presence by the
play's last sorrowful exchanges of dialogue.

Over the length of the action the only secondary role—indeed, the
only role who noticeably improves his standing—turns out to be Costard.
He has won the hardly-seen Jaquenetta, who, since Jaquenetta seems a
comely lass, will be cast by directors from among busty auditioners, and
will probably remain in sight for longer spells in production than she
does in the text. Costard has ensured that he will not have to pay for her
upkeep or her (his) child's. He comes triumphantly out of any crossfire
of quips he engages in. He has the play's nearest approach to a show-
stopping sequence (3.1), when Armado hands him a tip of three farthings
(three-quarters of a penny) for delivering a note to Jaquenetta and calls
it a *remuneration*, after which Berowne allots him a tip of one shilling
(twelve pennies, sixteen times as much) for delivering a note to Rosaline
and calls it a *guerdon*. After he has exulted at how much more profitable
a guerdon is than a remuneration, Costard takes each letter to the wrong
party. All in all, he seems to be the secondary plot's answer to Berowne
in the main plot—not as expansive a role and not at all comparable to the
effusive lover's, but more rewarding as comedy. Berowne must squeeze
whatever joy he can from the suppression of his love for twelve months
(he will write about it incessantly), from the prospect of cheering up
some blighted lives, and from his sportsmanlike admission of defeat to his
colleagues: "Speak for yourselves. My wit is at an end" (5.2.431).

And then—the closing song, epilogue or envoi. Armado introduces a

> dialogue that the two learned men [Holofernes and Nathaniel] have
> compiled in praise of the owl and the cuckoo . . . This side [of the
> stage] is Hiems, Winter, this Ver, the Spring; the one maintained by
> the owl, th'other by the cuckoo. (5.2.875–76 and 881–82)

Armado's language, now stripped to the bone, depicts him as a foreigner or a man influenced by Costard when he substitutes *compiled* for *composed*. But *maintained* is one of Shakespeare's miraculously suited finds.

Each season has two stanzas of the "dialogue" to sing, followed by paradoxical refrains. First, the frisky spring, Ver. The singer, a woman no doubt, pays tribute to nature and humanity preparing, dressing up, for the year. But the refrain sounds a different note:

> The cuckoo then on every tree
> Mocks married men, for thus sings he: Cuckoo!
> Cuckoo, cuckoo! O word of fear,
> Unpleasing to a married ear. (5.2.897–901)

"Mocks married men." Not married women. So far as I can discover, there is no word in our language for a female cuckold. Do women in life play around so much more than men, as the drama seems to imply and life to deny? The cuckoo's reminder of cuckoldry can mar the spring, the time of burgeoning and hope. Implicit here we notice not just a threat, but a promise, aimed at the four marriageable young men and at Armado, who will be his cuckolder's keeper for a year and may have him under the same roof. The lords and their king will certainly not take note of the promise of cuckoldry as they pine for their partners-to-be, twelve months distant. They, the ones subjected to a lesson, may not have absorbed it.

And then the winter, Hiems. He sings of freezing cold, "when blood is nipped, and ways be foul." But the refrain takes the opposed tack to the ominous refrain of spring:

> Then nightly sings the staring owl:
> Tu-whit, to-whoo! A merry note,
> While greasy Joan doth keel the pot.

The "staring owl" lets out sounds that are "merry," an adjective that would never occur to anyone who has listened to an owl's lugubrious plaints. But one could force "Tu-whit, to-whoo" to signify "thou wit, thou who?" or "thou wit, thou what?" as a comment on the linguistic striving of the condescending upper-class men and women. (Virginia Woolf, of another mind, declared that "theirs is the word-coining genius, as if thought plunged into a sea of words and came up dripping.") Peasant Joan meanwhile stirs and skims the hot repast cooking in the pot. But greasy? If the refrain in both cases contradicts the verses, that one word puts some dubious coloring on the otherwise happy picture. The final statement, usually given to Armado, sustains yet another ambiguous ending by countering Apollo with Mercury: "The words of Mercury are harsh after the songs of Apollo. You that way; we this way." Does he mean that the spectators ("you") go out by one exit, the actors by another? Or that Winter and Spring (a different "you") leave by a different door from the rest of the cast?[3] Or that the audience lives in a state of prose ("Mercury") while the theatre aspires to a condition of poetry or music ("Apollo")? Questions remain hanging in the air, an answer to the play's declamatory opening lines:

> Let fame, that all hunt after in their lives,
> Live registered upon our brazen tombs . . . .

But this closing song sums up the mixed tone of the play, its comedy constantly undercut by serious notes and its serious business undercut by comic touches. It tells of experiences of growing up. The men try to brush aside pains and responsibility and then, at last, realize that the events of the action have changed them, and not only because of the death that crowds in from the great outside onto their tiny, nature-cosseted realm.

Notes

1. Disputes have arisen over the name Moth, pronounced "Mote" at the time and spelled Mote in some writings. The arguments are summed up by Hibbard, who prefers Moth (Appendix D in World Classics edition [245–46]). Hibbard, who rejects the allusion to Nashe, also adopts several alternative spellings of role names: Biron, Longueville, Marcadé. But for the Princess's speech heading after she learns of her father's death he uses QUEEN, a title she has no right to before a formal coronation.

2. Compare this line with Olivia's self-directed question after her first encounter with Cesario-Viola: "Even so quickly may one catch the plague?" (*Twelfth Night*, 1.5.285).

3. A number of editors put the words, "You that way; we this way" into square brackets to support their belief that this final instruction was a stage direction erroneously absorbed into the spoken text by a compositor.

Much Ado About Nothing

There are at least two peculiarities about this play. Shakespeare hints at them but, at the same time, partially suppresses them. One coastal, the other political—or imperial—they meet in the setting.

Messina lies at the northeastern tip of Sicily as the island's nearest city of any consequence to the southern tip of Calabria, at the toe of the Italian boot. Along the coastal fringes of the Straits of Messina were the infamous rock Scylla on the Italian side and the whirlpool Charybdis on the Sicilian side, which gave their names to two of the predacious monsters in *The Odyssey*. In at least one production of the past (1858, by Charles Kean) Messina was represented in the opening scene as a port and harbor (Arden 1981, 39, and footnote). In that first scene a messenger says that Don Pedro, who is visiting Messina, "is very near by this [time]. He was not three leagues off when I left him" (3–4). In order to be just under "three leagues off," Don Pedro would have to be aboard a vessel in the perilous Straits of Messina or beyond the Straits, on the Italian mainland, the Calabrian peninsula—or else approaching Messina and the coast from the opposite direction, from the hinterland of Sicily. The last possibility seems likely. We hear separate mentions by Beatrice (1.1.39) and the Messenger (v. 44) of "these wars," without any identification of the two sides or where they fought. We may be confronting another instance of either Shakespeare's deliberate reticence or his geography of the imagination. We know that the Pedro team suffered no losses of "gentlemen," thanks in part to the bravery of two of them, Claudio and Benedick: more details are not easy to deduce.

The imperial issue complicates the plotting. Over Messina's nearly four thousand years of history, various European and North African powers, Christian and Muslim, contended for control of the strategically placed settlement, later the city; they wrought destruction and heavy death tolls, set it afire many times, ravaged and plundered it. If the Don Pedro of Aragon in this play corresponds to Pedro the Third of Aragon who captured the city for a time, then the play's events take place, at least in theory, during the thirteenth century, perhaps not long after the uprising in 1282 in Palermo known as the Sicilian Vespers against the forces of Charles I of Anjou. In the play Don Pedro has defeated his bastard brother, John, not the historical Charles, in battle. John, the fifth member of Pedro's party, is now outwardly "reconciled to the Prince" (1.1.149), although we do not learn what happened to John's forces; two of his followers, Borachio and Conrade, seem to have met up with him in Messina, where they are residents, not soldiers. But on Pedro's side Claudio and Benedick, noblemen and evidently mercenaries, have fought on his behalf and become his close companions, together with the songster Balthasar. The first two are Italians, not Spaniards: Count Claudio from Florence; Signor Benedick—unlike Petruchio, who came to wive it wealthily in Padua—*from* Padua. Like another Shakespearean predecessor, Berowne, Benedick at first safeguards his standing as a bachelor. When he does get around to contemplating a wife, he remarks, "Rich she shall be, that's certain" (2.3.29), as her first qualification—but we do not find out if Beatrice will bring a plump inheritance or dowry into marriage.[1]

In Messina, Leonato carries the title of Governor, while his niece and daughter are addressed as My Lady, but without any specifying of their rank. We also hear of a duke, presumably the overall ruler of the island, to whom the Watch, that primitive police force, is responsible (3.4.19), but who does not show up in the action.

When Claudio, the youthful, romance-saturated battler (with the temerity, diffidence, and other defects those qualities imply) meets Hero, Leonato, and Beatrice, he utters not one word until all those present but Benedick and him have left the scene; then he bursts out, "Benedick, didst thou note the daughter of Signor Leonato?" He must instantly dwell on the beauties and virtues of "such a jewel" (1.1.150–51; 174), despite Benedick's acidic replies. Without a breath of doubt or hesitation, Claudio has come, seen, been overcome, and caught the scent of a nice dowry.

Don Pedro, though, knows Leonato and his family and appears to be on affable terms with them, whether because Leonato is a "dear friend" (1.1.142) or an Aragon appointee or because the two men have compatible temperaments (so far). But when Leonato leads a welcoming party to meet the quartet of warriors, Pedro's greeting to Leonato has a curiously awkward tone: "Good Signor Leonato, are you come to meet your trouble? The fashion of the world is to avoid cost, and you encounter it" (1.1.91–93). We can assume that, "Are you come?" means something like, "Why did you step forward so eagerly?" since he, Pedro, is the one who has just come; and why would he refer to himself as "your trouble," unless he was a superior officer on a tour of inspection or some other act of official spying, or a commander seeking to billet himself and his officers, compulsorily, for a free vacation after some hard scrapping—a member of a governing nation, who must be accommodated *and well,* whatever the "cost'? Leonato responds with admirable smoothness—compliments beyond the fringes of civility: "Never came trouble to my house in the likeness of your Grace, for trouble being gone, comfort should remain; but when you depart from me, sorrow abides, and happiness takes his leave" (94–97). Don Pedro, to sustain his faint sarcasm, cannot refrain from adding, "You embrace your charge too willingly." A charge— meaning a duty? After this conversation, we learn from Pedro, who intends "to stay here at the least a month," that Leonato "heartily prays some occasion may detain us longer" (1.1.143–45). The formality of the welcome and Pedro's words, delivered *de haut en bas,* set up a slightly charged atmosphere that productions seldom observe.

Kenneth Branagh's movie version went the other way. Admirably cut and shaped for the most part, it oversold the warmth and excitement of the arrival of Pedro and his party, with frenzied editing of running figures, yelling men, screaming women, low-angled shots of galloping horses kicking up dust, and naked actors of both sexes flinging their bodies into communal bathtubs, some in crosscut slow motion and performed to the noise of galvanic music. But as a prelude to this roisterous welcome, Emma Thompson as Beatrice recited the lyric of "Sigh No More" in a slightly hissing voice. This song Balthasar sings in 2.3—shortly before Benedick is gulled—about "the fraud of men" who "were deceivers ever."

Claudio can hardly withhold a gush of tributes to the most winsome girl he ever set eyes on. Well, not exactly. He did catch a glimpse of Hero before he went off to battle but hardly took note of her then. At that time was she still an adolescent? How long did the battle last? Beatrice and Benedick give the youngster no opportunity to speak as they slip easily into the first of their verbal skirmishes, as though nobody else was listening: the first skirmishes in the action, that is, not in the background story. The two B's make it obvious that they have crossed tongues and stings before.[2] We further suspect from some of Beatrice's lines that precede this bitter little contest, and others' lines that contribute to it, that she was at some time in the past let down by him and now employs ferocious self-protection to keep him at wit's distance. Her most explicit reference to one or more previous entanglements with him comes when he walks out uttering the nasty remark— one of several that he and she make in connection with eating and enduring the other's presence—"O God, sir, here's a dish I love not." Don Pedro then tells her she has lost Benedick's heart. She replies, "Indeed, my lord, he lent it me a while, and I gave him use for it, a double heart for his single one. Marry, once before he won it of me with false dice. Therefore your grace may well say I have lost it" (2.1.261–68). The phrase, "a double heart for his single one" sounds a swift regret, which covers layers of pain. To her Benedick appears a known quantity ("I know you of old," she mutters [1.1.139–40]), even though, as we see repeatedly, there is hardly any such creature as a known quantity in Shakespeare worth paying any mind to. But she remains wary of him, decisively puncturing such boasts of his as, "It is certain that I am loved of all ladies, only you excepted."

With adequate (or superior) actors in the contending roles, audiences as a rule dote on this play as the one that fires off salvoes of the author's most glittering sallies, exceeding the winnowed best of Congreve, other Restoration masters, Sheridan, and Wilde. But critics now and then come down hard on *Much Ado*, mostly for what they perceive as structural deficiencies and inconsistencies or—their bogy when it comes to playwriting—implausibility. Let me quote from two of the finer critics in English of the past hundred years, Bernard Shaw, writing in 1898, and Francis Fergusson, writing in mid-century. Shaw purports to find the work not implausible or rife with discontinuities but obscene.

> The main pretension in Much Ado is that Benedick and Beatrice are exquisitely witty and amusing persons. They are, of course, nothing of the sort. Benedick's pleasantries might pass at a singsong in a public-house parlor . . . . From his first joke, "Were you in doubt, sir, that you asked her?" to his last, "There is no staff more reverend than one tipped with horn," he is not a wit but a blackguard. He is not Shakespeare's only failure in that genre. It took the Bard a long time to grow out of the provincial conceit that made him so fond of exhibiting his accomplishments as a master of gallant badinage. . . .
>
> Precisely the same thing, in the tenderer degree of her sex, is true of Beatrice. In her character of professed wit she has only one subject and that is the subject which a really witty woman never jests about, because it is too serious a matter to a woman to be made light of without indelicacy. Beatrice jests about it for the sake of the indelicacy. There is only one thing worse than the Elizabethan "merry gentleman," and that is the Elizabethan "merry lady."
>
> Why is it then that we still want to see Benedick and Beatrice, and that our most eminent actors and actresses still want to play them? (1899, 422–24)

Shaw answers the last question by saying that, although a paraphrase of the ideas in the lines would show them up as coarse and self-evident, they are saved, even sanctified, by the music that inheres in Shakespeare's dialogue. His point is, I believe, a little misplaced. Shakespeare's manipulation of language—whipping it around, undercutting and refashioning meanings—doesn't need the blessing of being musical; it may not resemble a ringing of celestial chimes; it displays word-verve, tricks, and surprises, and these are more than enough for listeners who savor semantic ingenuity and not only sonorous sentences.

Shaw's emphasis on Shakespeare's music may have made for a more salutary approach to the plays in the 1890s—a reminder that plays are art, not documentation—but in the hands and mouths of English teachers since, worrying the musical-poetic implications of words has often led to neglect of the *dramatic* sequences in the scenes in question. Microanalysis of this sort can drive students crazy, or to sleep. Benedick's "first joke" about doubts as to Hero's legitimacy not only functions as a kidding retort to Leonato's previous comment about his wife, Hero's mother, but it is also uttered in the presence of John the bastard, who could hardly help showing discomfort or outright embarrassment. Still, I think a different misgiving about Benedick and Beatrice lurks in Shaw's unease with the play—other than what he sees as open vulgarity and banality—and that is a temptation it offers its leading couple to declaim in a self-congratulatory manner, which can become unendurable. In the same review, Shaw accuses the Beatrice, Julia Neilson, of rattling off her lines unfeelingly and archly. Ellen Terry, Shaw's favorite actress (and correspondent) and reputedly far and away the finest English Beatrice of her generation, also disliked "arch" acting. She looked back with a critical eye over her varied performances in this role and decided, "But at least I did not make the mistake of being arch and skittish." (1932, 97).[3] Anybody who has seen the play a few times must have witnessed a similar calamity, poseurs who deliver Lady Top and Lord Fop with suffocating superfetation, possibly taking too much to heart Leonato's remark in the first scene about "the merry war" between the two B's.

As for Shaw's other remonstrance, that Beatrice flaunts sexual remarks that "a really witty woman never jests about," it seems obvious that Beatrice, like some other heroines (not only Shakespeare's), does her best occasionally to outdo men in masculine choices of conversation. If Shaw is alluding to Beatrice's coldness, her hostility in the early scenes, where she is not as spiteful as Kate is but openly contentious, that very hostility draws Benedick to her. Each looks on the other as a subject for one or another sort of conquest. In their mutuality, they each regard themselves as a knife and the opposite number as a whetstone, although their names (Beatrice: blesser; Benedick: blessed) suggest more felicitous images. In Branagh's film, Beatrice and Benedick both wear red hair, Emma Thompson's verging on auburn. The his-and-hers heads may portend a match of hot tempers. Or was this a fashion touch, an updating effect that hints at the popularity of hennaed hair in Europe these days? I wouldn't want to ascribe the co-coloring to a fluke of studio hairdressing.

Fergusson draws attention, as earlier writers had done, to the abundant confusions that arise from disguised identities and motives. Margaret fails to clear the name of her mistress, Hero. Don Pedro inexplicably proposes marriage to Beatrice ("Will you have me, lady?"[2.1.310]), after Antonio has reported to his brother that "the Prince discovered to Claudio that he loved [Hero]" (1.2.10). Beatrice should affirm that Hero could not have made love to Borachio. Such patterns of misdirection can be ascribed to structural defects. After suggesting that "high school productions are likely to be terribly embarrassing," as though *Much Ado* were a novelty in that respect, and "I do not even like to think of the play's pathetic vulnerability on Times Square," Fergusson concludes:

> The play demands much from its performers, almost as much as Chekhov does. It demands a great deal from its audience: a leisurely and contemplative detachment which seems too costly in our hustled age. Perhaps Shakespeare should be blamed for all this: if *Much Ado* does not easily convince us on the contemporary stage, perhaps we should conclude, as Eliot once concluded of *Hamlet*, that it is an artistic failure. But on that principle we should have to rule out a great deal of Shakespeare. It was his habit, not only in *Hamlet* and *Much Ado*, but in many other plays, to indicate, rather than explicitly to present, his central theme and to leave it to his performers and his audience to find it behind the varied episodes, characters, and modes of language which are literally presented. Everything which Shakespeare meant by *The Comedy of Errors* is immediately perceptible; the comic vision in *Much Ado* will only appear, like the faces which Dante saw in the milky substance of the moon, slowly, and as we learn to trust the fact that it is really there. (1957, 144–57)

If Shaw comes at the play armed with a reviewer's wealth of experience—not that all experience enlightens a reviewer—Fergusson makes assumptions from reading it "in the security of one's own room, indulging in daydreams of an ideal performance," conditions in which, he says, "it is possible to forget the practical and critical problems which surround the question of the play's viability in our time." My own difficulty in accepting the "viability" *of the problems themselves* is that they do not, in performance, obtrude, possibly hardly exist. The word *problem* has become an easy refuge for literal-minded doubting (on the critics' part) over the absolute credibility of every aspect of the play considered not as invention, as art, as artifice, but as life, when we should rather seek for its *inner* credibility: not a play's truth to the ordinary happenings in life but its truth to its extraordinary self. In practice, we go back to the same Shakespeare plays again and again in the happy expectation that a new company will shed new light on shady places—but also on places we considered well illuminated. I will return to some of the doubts later in this chapter.

If we could isolate and unify our questions about the play's "serious" burdens and their success, for a time, in overpowering the comedy, we might well end up asking ourselves, as with *Two Gentlemen,* who is the villain? We would surely come close to those post–World War II plays and films that traded unblushingly on communal guilt: We are all responsible for war, prejudice, social catastrophes . . . We are all murderers . . . One day a gatekeeper like St. Peter or an apparition like Priestley's Inspector will pronounce our doom. The distinction between well-meant performance tracts and Shakespeare is that he doesn't posit lessons for audiences but restricts the instruction to the roles in the play—and keeps it comic.

Don John, the originator of the intrigue, who meant to embarrass Claudio and Don Pedro by shaming Hero, trusts Borachio to carry it out. Borachio relies on Margaret's cooperation. John and Borachio will be detected, thanks to the bumbling vigilance of Dogberry's subordinates. Margaret, a flirt (with Balthasar in 2.1; with Hero and then Beatrice in 3.4; with Benedick in 5.2), receives no chastening and remains strangely quiet when, as Fergusson and others complain, she might have come clean about her part in the intrigue. The complaint seems justified, even if her confession might have ruined the end of the play. J. Dennis Huston raises "the question of Margaret's apparent inconsistency of character" (1981, 125). In Branagh's film version, Margaret looks astonished on hearing Claudio's attack on Hero and then so embarrassed that she runs away, horrified by what her escapade with Borachio has led to, but afraid to confess. But a play does not amount to a real-life trial, even in a foreshortened version. The consequences remain unaffected by our knowing if Margaret was "innocent," as Borachio pleads, or somehow culpable. The playwright keeps whisking the action away from John and his followers. Subsequently, it will turn sharply toward cruelty when Don Pedro and Claudio make one of the gravest mistakes committed by Shakespearean roles: they believe the evidence of their eyes and ears.

As a result, Claudio not merely abuses Hero but delays and hoards his condemnations and spits them out at the most painful moment for her, at their wedding ceremony; he contrives at a performance that will excruciate her—has announced his readiness to do so *beforehand* if he witnesses any proof. He calls her "this rotten orange" (4.1.31). Don Pedro, who backs him up, alludes to her as "a common stale" (v. 64). Leonato then wishes somebody would stab him. Further, he wishes his daughter dead, on the strength of someone else's accusation. He speaks of "her foul-tainted flesh" (v. 143) and "her foulness" (v. 153), a harking-back to his tasteless remark in the first scene about her mother. Antonio, his brother and Hero's uncle, similarly accepts the charge against her, although he later challenges Claudio to a duel, as the two oldsters decline into a pair of laughable semblances of Pantalone. Hero's plight has on occasion been compared with that of Juliet, perhaps because the Claudio-Hero love match proves to be just shy of tragic, comic only in its final moments. Juliet, however, is cursed by both her parents and abandoned by the Nurse, who urges that after Romeo's banishment the girl would do better to switch her affection to Paris. Juliet has no allies other than timid Friar Laurence; but Hero has support from Beatrice, Benedick, Ursula, and—too long delayed—from her father and uncle. Beatrice, choked up by rage and grief, demands vengeance—"Kill Claudio,"—even if Benedick, whom she now confesses she loves, gets outdueled. He in turn, choked up by love and bewilderment, volunteers to fight his best friend and comrade in battle. The guilty, the gullible, and the furiously defensive all behave "out of character"—and from the audience's indignant vantage point, with superb dramatic sense. The jury almost bleeds for the defendant. Among the principals, the least blemished heroine to emerge is Hero. Who, then, is taught a lesson?

Everyone else. If the Hero of act 5 has learned anything (from the four men who lose trust in her), she displays no new understanding but goes on to submit to Claudio meekly for the second time. As corresponding gestures by Claudio himself, he twice swallows Don John's lies, believing on the first occasion that Pedro is wooing Hero for himself, and on the second occasion that Hero had an affair with a servant—and worse, that she will throw herself at any man. Bertrand Evans differs from some earlier writers, observing that Shakespeare evidently "intended to drop the Claudio-Don Pedro conflict and to make the slander of Hero his principal matter" in the Hero-Claudio plot. Evans writes of "the very excessiveness of his initial emphasis on the alacrity of persons to perpetrate practices [deceptions] and to be deceived by others' practices" (1960, 72).

How can a play with so many claimants to selfish and obstinate roles be such a golden entertainment? The deceivers, the deceived, and the incompetents like Dogberry, Verges, and the Messina Watch (immigrants to Messina from English village life) all ask to be played with charm and conviction, particularly the two roles spectators most like to dislike, Don John, the plot founder, and Claudio, his target. These roles may let slip a spasm or two of rage and nastiness, but the audience needs to watch them effectually persuade the other roles before it, in turn, is persuaded. In the BBC TV production of *Much Ado*, Don John comes across as a refined older man, not a figure visibly seething with resentment over his bastardy. When he speaks of "Leonato's Hero, your Hero, every man's Hero" (3.2.100–01), Claudio hurls wine in his face. John blinks, then goes on so earnestly with his charges that we are not sure he is lying. I would argue in favor of a calm and polished John despite Beatrice's severe "How tartly that gentleman looks! I never can see him but I am heartburned an hour after," and Hero's milder "He is of a very melancholy disposition" (2.1.3–5). John may seem retiring, to put the kindest face on his taciturn moments ("I am not of many words" [1.1.151]), but when he is up to some of his beloved mischief, he can be—and is—a winning speaker. His revenge on Pedro for the defeat in battle takes on a peculiar, nonfratricidal twist: he will jealously punish not the brother but the brother's favorite.

If the Claudio-Hero courtship brushes up against treachery and melodrama, the parallel love affair, between Beatrice and Benedick, remains stubbornly comic up to the quick exchange:

BENEDICK Come, bid me do anything for thee.

BEATRICE Kill Claudio.

BENEDICK Ha! Not for the wide world!

BEATRICE You kill me to deny it. (4.1.287–90)

At which point the lower jaws of everyone, on stage and off, drop, not from horror, but astonishment: "Kill Claudio" is one of the playwright's most resounding commands. It compares in shock value with, say, Iago's "But let her live" (3.3.490) when Othello has not yet even contemplated killing Desdemona, let alone spoken of it. Spectators at times are too embarrassed to take in the two words. Have the "bears," as Claudio calls them (3.2.72), driven themselves back to act 1, scene 1? No, the dogged love affair will return to its accustomed comic tracks.

What do those tracks consist of? Many people who write about *Much Ado* see it as a series of rounds in the Sex War or, for younger generations, the Gender War, but in either case a bartering of offensive remarks that may not be sincerely intended. Ornstein and other writers assume that the play has a genial opening. To them it's clear that Beatrice loves Benedick, although, as stated previously, she says she has had at least one bad experience (2.1.265–68) with this proclaimed bachelor-till-death, this "professed tyrant to the [other] sex" (1.1.162). Huston feels Beatrice and Benedick "hide their love for one another behind their merry war of insults" (124). David L. Stevenson alludes to their "self-conscious role-playing" (1964, xxix). Must the standoff between the two lead to a foregone reconcilement? If so, it presupposes saying one thing and playing another, coyness, the "arch" acting abhorred by Shaw and Terry, which implies, "I have a secret and you spectators out there can guess what."

Playing the moment means disposing of leaden pointers. Like Kate in the opening scene of *Shrew*, Beatrice has plenty of bite. If the actor hints that she'll accept Benedick, even love him, and if he reciprocates, much ado will go for nothing in their encounters and most of all in how these two hard-shelled specimens listen to what they overhear in the eavesdropping scenes. Beatrice says she knows Benedick of old but the first two and a half acts suggest that they suspect they do not know each other. How could they when they break up into a succession of Beatrices and Benedicks who misread one another time after time? Beatrice may have become wary and therefore peremptory toward men because of unknown happenings in the past, and she will shed some prickles, but not all, and certainly not all at once. By comparison, the untamed Kate is far fiercer, letting her barbs fly in all directions. Kate, as actors say, "opens at twelve o'clock" and should not at any point be romanticized. Gradually and following the play's title, she yields to the taming pressures until, at the act 5 feast, her graciousness amazes onlookers. Everybody who has been out in the world has worked in at least one office that housed at least one male or female misanthrope, with at least one or two of the antisocial traits of the early Kate. Beatrice is, from the start, more literate, more self-possessed, encased. Her vehement defense of Hero is, in its own way, as impassioned and startling as Kate's final speech, but not for the same reason: she wakens (or reawakens) to Benedick's love—but then, right after the glow from that feeling, comes the accusation from the men defaming the cousin she believes incorruptible.

By extension, a dual portrait of Beatrice and Benedick standing together against the rest of the world through most of acts 4 and 5 may make for a noble impression, but it is less dramatic than the play. The temporary collapse of the marriage between Claudio and Hero does not strengthen the union between Beatrice and Benedick; it endangers it. Indecision sometimes serves a play more faithfully and artistically than decisiveness does. Therefore, when Benedick goes to challenge Claudio and to affront him and Don Pedro (5.1), he falters, and the actor does well to recall his instant response to "Kill Claudio": "Not for the wide world." If he shows himself invulnerable to his friends' nasty joshing or bloated with righteous indignation (because of the humiliation visited upon Hero) and with bravery (because he has undertaken a mission on behalf of his beloved), he looks ridiculous.

At a number of points in the play Benedick is already ridiculed, mostly by Beatrice's retorts. But in 5.1 the actor has to be wary of letting his characterization slip into Don Armado's or Petruchio's, a variation of the braggart Capitano, which Benedick is not. At those moments of ridicule Shakespeare has given him the chance to remain silent and therefore dignified for fairly long periods under the rain of

Pedro's and Claudio's taunts. We ought to perceive the division of his loyalty between the urging of Beatrice and his feelings for these comrades, with whom he has risked his life. Such a division might well undercut his resolution. Besides, despite *Much Ado*'s reputation as an oral battle between a woman and a man, it includes scenes in which Beatrice or Benedick exercises wit at the expense of others or of the conventional wisdom. These comic portions do not consist only of their duets and are not all good-natured. Her strong resentment—jealousy even?—of his male comrades comes to light in the first act: "Who is his companion now? He hath every month a new sworn brother" (1.1.67–68) and "Is there no young squarer now that will make a voyage with him to the devil?" (76–78).

The two courtships run parallel and intertwine. The third, unresolved affair, the subplot involving Margaret and Borachio, alters them both in differing degrees. But do we need to follow most commentators and pick Claudio-Hero as the main plot over Beatrice-Benedick?

> *Much Ado About Nothing* is a fascinating play, and finally satisfying if we allow our attention to shift from the romantic protagonists, Hero and Claudio, in the main plot to the narcissistic subordinates, Beatrice and Benedick. (MacCary 150)

One can hardly imagine actors who would audition with a preference for the roles of Hero and Claudio over those of the "narcissists," Beatrice and Benedick. It is even more difficult to conceive of a director who would decide to do the play on the strength of having found a wonderful Claudio or Hero or both. Beatrice and Benedick carry the play, especially to its frolicking conclusion, while Hero and Claudio accidentally provide obstacles to that conclusion and at last reinforce it. The two affairs stand against each other for the sake of comparison and contrast—that is, for our delectation. In the Hero-Claudio plotline Friar Francis supervenes with his scheme for Hero's spurious death and rebirth as her "cousin." Yet the Hero-Claudio affair bears heavily upon the Beatrice-Benedick affair, as a good subplot should do on a main plot, and most notably when it pits Benedick against his fellow-officer, even if he never gets around to trying to kill him, as Beatrice orders. We see no correlative opposite, though. Hero and Claudio play emphatic parts *as individuals* in the eavesdropping scenes in the orchard when they fool the two B's, but for these purposes they belong to the main plot; their subplot, that on-and-off-and-on marriage, remains shelved for the moment.

Striking differences also emerge *between* the affairs. Claudio *noticed* Hero but "with a soldier's eye" (286) before he went to the war. Now, on his return, he cannot help *seeing* how fair she is.[4] In 1.1, when he gawps at her in the action, neither of them says a word. Later, after being struck momentarily dumb, he will observe, "Silence is the perfectest herald of joy" (2.1.292). He thinks she is great-looking and remains unwon by her wit or goodness or other nonphysical traits, although he does check swiftly into her financial prospects before he tells Don Pedro that he is smitten. He doesn't seem to be asking about future relationships with a brother-in-law.

CLAUDIO

> Hath Leonato any son, my lord?

DON PEDRO

> No child but Hero; she's his only heir.
> Dost thou affect her, Claudio? (1.1.282–84)

Hero in turn accepts him unquestioningly once her father approves of the match. As a comrade and protégé of Don Pedro, Claudio is an imperial superior. After her reincarnation she obediently accepts him again.[5] But she does feel heavy-hearted before the wedding, as though she foresees a bad end to the day (3.4.23–24). Her insistence on wearing a particular rabato, or stiff collar-ruff, for the ceremony hints at yet another wrong choice. Or else she may wish to go into this marriage angrily, punishing her neck and refusing to celebrate her future. She finds Margaret's inane putdowns (uttered in the spirit of competitive wit) exasperating. Zitner regards Margaret as an intelligent young woman trying to rise above her class. This characteristic does peer out at a number of points in the play. Possibly she hopes to elevate her standing through an affiliation, not necessarily marriage, with Borachio, who comes on strongly as a courtier at times; he in turn hopes to rise by backing Don John.

The Beatrice-Benedick match illustrates a Fabian inevitability of gradualness; but the inevitability becomes apparent only when one looks back from the end of act 5, not from the start of act 1. Almost as soon as the action gets under way, they squabble like fowl until Benedick gives up, out of exhaustion of his imaginative faculties or his stock of spite: "But keep your way, i' God's name; I have done" (1.1.136–38). He yields similarly in an exchange with Margaret ("I give thee the bucklers" [5.2.16–17]), who evidently likes to joust with anybody who will take her on, as she endeavors to flatten all comers. It takes time for Beatrice to override her mistrust of this "Signor Mountanto," as she calls Benedick in her first reference to him. The male chauvinist pig needs taking down a grunt or two, and she exults at every chance she gets to depress his morale. Benedick, on the other side of the spiky equation, seems bewildered (like Berowne) as this silken tigress resists his sexual vibrations. By the start of 3.2 the action has jogged each of them into awareness, not of the other's good looks, virtues, or talents but of imaginary pangs of nonrequital. Yet these orchard eavesdroppers hear themselves accounted heartless, and they give way, then and not before, to a humane—even a compassionate—reaction.

Now, it happens in the two eavesdropping scenes that the Claudio (in 2.3) and the Hero (in 3.10) prove to be the liveliest Claudio and Hero we meet. They play new conspiratorial roles—a worthy backup love team when we add them together. Claudio, for instance, can invent an image of an overwrought Beatrice that will shame the listening Benedick:

> Then down upon her knees she falls, weeps, sobs, beats her heart, tears her hair, prays, curses: "O sweet Benedick! God give me patience!" (2.3.150–52)

And Hero, after being coached by Don Pedro, can speak of "little Cupid's crafty arrow . . . . That only wounds by hearsay" (3.1.22–23). In those scenes, Benedick and then Beatrice lose their self-possession, suffer a change of heart, and go giddy. "Man," Benedick remarks, "is a giddy thing" 5.4.106), but so is one woman: and not just giddy but also dizzy. Their heads, and very likely bodies, go into a spin. In Branagh's movie Benedick whirled, danced, splashed ecstatically in a fountain, while Beatrice, superimposed, rocked wildly back and forth on a child's swing. Benedick does, after all, explicitly ask himself after he hears that Beatrice loves him, "But doth not the appetite alter?" And then submits that "a man loves the meat in his youth that he cannot endure in his age" (2.3.234–36).

We are looking at two different kinds of love in this quartet. About Hero's one can, like her, say little, no more than that Benedick "is the only man of Italy, Always excepted my dear Claudio" (3.1.92–93), a remark preceded by the even more dutiful reference to "my new-trothèd lord" (38). She has several memorable tics in the play, especially when she speaks with disdain about her clever disdainful cousin, who finds any excuse for discommending a commendable man (3.1.59–70). Again, her silent response to Claudio just before she swoons causes women and men alike in the audience to seethe at Claudio's and Pedro's and Leonato's stupid credulousness. And yet again, when she fulfills Friar Francis's deception by seeming to rise from the dead. In many of her other moments she portrays a trained pet more than a person in love. As a role she radiates none of the dazed or jealous character of a lover. What does Claudio see in her looks? Enough to excite him into a desire to possess her, and more than enough to launch a typical match today in Hollywood, say, whose star faces and bodies keep switching keepers for a year or two. At such blunt points the characterization depends almost entirely on Hero's actor's initiative. Claudio conforms pretty well with Theodor

Reik's "ego-ideal." Criticism derived from psychoanalysis has its limitations. But Reik, like many of the original Freud circle, is a poet, not
a dogmatist or jargon-splurger. In his justly celebrated book, love is a
"substitute for . . . the struggle toward self-fulfillment, for the vain
urge to reach one's ego-ideal." Thus, "love is really a second best" and
we exchange "the ego-ideal for an external object, for a person in
whom are joined all the qualities we once desired" for ourselves; it is
"a form of projection." Moreover, "we admire in this manner someone
whom we either wish to be like *or to own*" (my italics, not Reik's). The
reverse of this admiration for the love-object," Reik adds, "is [not hate
but] envy" (1974, 40; 41; 45; 46). I am quoting here from the first essay, "A Psychologist Looks at Love.") On the distinction between a
psychoanalytic poet and scholar, Reik himself writes of "poets, who
always push forward in advance of psychological research" (52). Reik
finds an element of dissatisfaction with oneself, even self-hatred, in
love based on the ego-ideal.[6]

As against this selfish and strictly erotic kind of love, Benedick displays what Rollo May calls "giving ourselves to our beloved" yet "pre-
serving what center of autonomy we have." It involves a virtual
"reunion with the other half of oneself." May also dissents from some
of the joyless conclusions reached by Freud and certain of his followers: "When I fall in love I feel *more* valuable, and I treat myself with
more care" (1974, 83; 113). More than a quarter of a century ago May
wrote: "We have emasculated sex." How-to books on sex and love
"deal with the topic like a combination of learning to play tennis and
buying life insurance." Such literature "sidesteps Eros" (65). Beatrice
subscribes similarly to Benedick's upbeat type of love, if in a slightly
more complicated fashion: she not only gives but also demands, although the demands are not exerted purely on her own behalf. Thus,
even after the B's continue to spar during the final moments of the
play, Benedick once again backs off, after he kisses her to stop her
mouth, saying to Don Pedro, "Dost thou think I care for a satire or an
epigram? No. If a man will be beaten with brains, 'a shall wear nothing handsome about him" (5.4.100–03). The line is susceptible to varied readings, but I take it to imply, among other things, that for a man
to strive to win the last word in an argument with a brainy woman is
senseless when the very striving will draw ridicule down on him. Besides, Benedick seems to realize that the mixture of the two of them
strengthens both, that benedictine and brandy together deliver more
of a kick than does syrupy benedictine on its own.

The third plotline has two sides to it: Don John with his sharp-witted
aides and on the other side the blunt-witted Messina constabulary loyal to Dogberry and his doddering "compartner," Verges. The astounding

contrivance that Conrade and Borachio discuss the latter's duplicity in front of the men of the Watch and then surrender to them is dramatic irony at its most insolent. It further inserts a little farce-cum-melodrama into a comedy that has been taking a gloomy turn, bringing it to a finely rounded comic end. In Dogberry's lines it also beguiles the language into a fetching new English that is at the far end of the scale from the tempered ripostes swapped by Beatrice and Benedick.

The action introduces Don John, Conrade, and Borachio early, mostly I would say to sound a threatening note.

DON JOHN . . . Though I cannot be said to be a flattering honest man, it must not be denied but I am a plain-dealing villain. . . .

And then, when Borachio reports that he can supply "intelligence of an intended marriage," John promptly asks, "Will it serve for any model to build mischief on?" (1.3.28–30 and 41–44). John is sometimes dropped into the same role-basket as Iago, and said to be possessed of motiveless malignancy. But besides his determination to foil and, if he can, injure Claudio, and through Claudio, deal a blow to his half-sibling and former enemy on the battlefield, John belongs in the ranks of practical (and impractical) jokers. Like them, he lacks a sense of humor. In Branagh's film version, John may have another, clearly detectable motive. Passing Hero at one point, he stops, hesitates, seizes her hand, and kisses it. The gesture implies that he is in love with her and regards Claudio as a more successful rival in the affections of Hero and also of his half-brother.

Dogberry's guardians of the peace, who will undo John, appear later than the Don John trio, and in only four scenes (3.3, 3.5, 4.2, and 5.1), some of which they share with Conrade and Borachio. Borachio changes drastically from moment to moment. After mentioning the impending marriage to John he comes up with the greedier notion of earning himself a reward from John of a thousand ducats by using Margaret to play Hero, knowingly or not. In this same scene, 2.2, John confirms his hatred of Claudio: "I am sick in displeasure to him, and whatsoever comes athwart his affection ranges evenly with mine" (5–7). Just before Borachio brags aloud, into the outstretched ears of the Watch, about his performance with Margaret (3.3.130–37), he turns social commentator as he embarks on a colorful condemnation of "the deformed thief"—fashion. Later, this scamp and Conrade protest before the Sexton that they are "gentlemen," by contrast with the humble Watchmen who captured them. He reforms himself yet again as he sincerely tells Claudio and Don Pedro about his deception and the "false accusation" of Hero because he believes he caused her death (5.1). He also exculpates Margaret, who "always hath been just and virtuous In anything that I do know by her" (297–98). Thus he runs a gamut from conspirator to loving penitent.

Several of the other characters undergo transformations under the influence of the play's nearest environment to a "green world," namely the garden or park or orchard. On this miniature landscape, often scenically translated into an arcade paced by the successive conspirators, parallel to a grove demarcated by statues and overarched with vines, where the eavesdropping subject of each conspiracy crouches in hiding or scampers back and forth in order to hear better under the delusion of not being detectable, first Benedick, then Beatrice will undergo a spiritual conversion from cynical *railleur* to unconditional and, now and again, ecstatic lover. The second eavesdropping episode, following hard upon the first and having the same dramatic progression does not resemble it in language, but rather complements it as a theatrical poem. But this is also the spot from which two more eavesdroppers will watch and listen to lovemaking between Borachio and Margaret from a distance that lends opacity to sound and sight. As a result, Don Pedro and Claudio will turn into icy delators.

The other roles of consequence, Leonato and Antonio, those amiable senior cits, change into misogynists and enemies of youth out of—what? Grief? Hardly. Self-pity, more likely, with a tinge of conscience at having been ready to believe the worst of Hero. But in the insults they offer the Prince and the Count—"Boys, apes, braggarts, Jacks, milksops!" (5.1.91)—could they not also be indulging in an outbreak of pique at their imperial masters, mere juveniles? Not that Leonato sticks to his guns. In the final scene when the Friar insists that he always felt Hero was innocent, her father, the lickspittle, replies: "So are the Prince and Claudio, who accused her Upon the error that you heard debated . . ." His argument: one must excuse the Prince and Claudio, for if they could be wrong, why, so could any man, myself included. In delivering the challenge to Don Pedro and Claudio, the aging brothers yell and foam at the mouth. If they felt less ashamed of their earlier, taken-in selves when addressing imperial masters, they would in all likelihood tremble, quaver, and forget about so sedulously upholding family honor.

Beatrice will not prove nearly as forgiving. Earlier, in venting her desire to be a man who could avenge Hero, she reviles princes and counts, possibly out of a resentment of nobility (which includes Benedick, whom she's addressing), but also as an anti-imperialist outcry. I surmise, with not a shred of proof, that the desire to take account of the imperial strain in the text led John Barton to set his 1976 Royal Shakespeare Company version of *Much Ado* in India during the "Raj." Like all Shakespeare's other plays, *Much Ado* has been helped by numerous directors and designers into assorted periods and places, after they asked themselves, "What's Messina to my public or my public to Messina?" But colonial India strikes me as an appropriate locale for a British troupe and its audience.

The one role that hardly changes, Dogberry, gives us a serene assassin of words who behaves with the utmost courtesy, even toward his prisoners. Unlike the Falstaff of *2 Henry IV*, he is not witty in himself, deliberately funny at the expense of others, but the reverse: unconsciously humorous and prone to turn gags back against himself. But he resembles Falstaff in being "the cause that wit is in other men," when, for example, he turns the Prince by mimesis that has nothing to do with envy into a clown:

DON PEDRO Officers, what offense have these men done?

DOGBERRY Marry, sir, they have committed false report; moreover, they have spoken untruths; secondarily, they are slanders; sixth and lastly, they have belied a lady; thirdly, they have verified unjust things; and to conclude, they are lying knaves.

DON PEDRO First, I ask thee what they have done; thirdly, I ask thee what's their offense; sixth and lastly, why they are committed; and to conclude, what you lay to their charge. (5.1.209–19)

When we hear or read this and other speeches by Dogberry as he recites the same old warped assonances, the same old mistaken opposites, the same old fractured sentences and misplaced words and transpositions, these four-hundred-year-old expressions are still liable to shake us to our stomachs with laughter. But at Branagh's worst casting gaffe in his film, Michael Keaton's Dogberry, we do not laugh; it is hard even to force a smile out of habit. Keaton, generally an actor with gumption, looked out of touch with the words he spoke and the awkward blows he inflicted on Verges.

Dogberry and his little troupe have an additional function, which is structural. They interrupt the flow of the action by getting in the way of the regular cross-cutting. The Watch apprehends Conrade and Borachio during 3.3. Two scenes later, when Leonato is in a rush, late for the wedding, the effusions of Dogberry which would, in the fullness of time, work their circuitous way around to telling him about the conspiracy against Hero, are not given the chance to be heard: Leonato, in a more figurative sense than he could imagine, has to leave to give his daughter away. And in 5.1, when he is eager to get on with the restoration of Hero to Claudio, there stands Dogberry, impossible to dismiss. Give him a purse of gold and an impatient shove and try to escape in the opposite direction: he will still delay you with an array of extravagant, misspoken compliments.

Much Ado, as is almost invariably pointed out in printed comments, has no cross-dressed heroines, no miracles or supernatural superventions (the editor of the Signet Classic edition calls it Shakespeare's most realistic comedy, xxii), and thus it remains uncharacteristic. And so do all the others. But it leaves a few perplexities dangling, and it may be worth looking at two of them, which have to do respectively with Don Pedro and with Margaret. For sundry critics, Huston among them, the Don Pedro perplexity invites a double question. They wonder why he volunteers to propose to Hero on behalf of his young Florentine adjutant (and why Claudio consents); they wonder further at the significance of the unfinished (that is, interrupted) scene between Don Pedro and Beatrice. In both cases, though, the question of rank obtrudes; Pedro is a prince and Sicily has not one lady who, by class, could suitably match him. Could he simply be getting into practice—rehearsing—in order to plight his troth later to some princess or other? At one moment he asks Beatrice a direct question.

BEATRICE . . . I may sit in a corner and cry, "Heigh-ho for a husband!"

DON PEDRO Lady Beatrice, I will get you one.

BEATRICE I would rather have one of your father's getting. Hath Your Grace ne'er a brother like you? Your father got excellent husbands, if a maid could come by them.

DON PEDRO Will you have me, lady? (2.1.304–11)

Here Beatrice flirts suggestively, even naughtily, as she chooses to hear his, "I will get you one" as "I'll beget a son for you to marry," and speculates about whether "a maid could come by [the brothers]."

She might also be taking a dig at Don John when she affects to admire Pedro's father's progeny in the plural. Pedro may be replying in kind, although it is hard to conceive of how an actor would read that last line of his comically, unless he lightly hit the word "have" so that it meant "accept me in bed." Or he might "interpret" the reading so that the line sounded strictly like a compliment, rather than a request, and meant, "If I, a Prince, ask for your hand, wouldn't any man of lower rank jump at the opportunity?" But I would argue for bantering dialogue again. Pedro engages a woman of exceptional vivacity in bright conversation and enjoys responding to her coquettishness—will even propose ambiguously to see how she takes his question; and he will go thus far for the sake of his other protégé, Benedick. He likes wooing nubile women.

But depending on exactly how the sequence of the masked ball is staged, her uncle appears and brings the conversation to an abrupt end: "Niece, will you look to those things I told you of?" Did Leonato catch any of their words? Is he willfully separating the two? Does he consider Beatrice unsuitable for the Prince? Or, most likely, is he getting her out of the room so that he and the Prince can talk confidentially about her for a while and enhance the possibility of a royal marriage?

DON PEDRO By my troth, a pleasant-spirited lady.

LEONATO There's little of the melancholy element in her, my lord. She is never sad but when she sleeps, and not ever sad then; for I have heard my daughter say she hath often dreamt of unhappiness and waked herself with laughing.

DON PEDRO She cannot endure to hear tell of a husband.

LEONATO O, by no means. She mocks all her wooers out of suit.

DON PEDRO She were an excellent wife for Benedick.

LEONATO O Lord, my lord, if they were but a week married they would talk themselves mad. (2.1.326–37)

At which point Don Pedro, the tentative matchmaker, having sounded out both Beatrice and her uncle, switches his attention to Claudio and, with no further ado, douses any royal marriage when he broaches his scheme to perform "one of Hercules' labors, which is to bring Signor Benedick and the Lady Beatrice into a mountain of affection th' one with th' other" (347–50). Couldn't he have been exploring around the edges of that labor before launching himself right into it?

Then we have the Margaret enigma, a worm that has wriggled persistently in the minds of writers, from Lewis Carroll to A. R. Humphries. (Carroll's troubled letter to Ellen Terry is reprinted in the Signet Classic Shakespeare edition, 138-39. See also Humphries, [1981, 65–67].) Here there does seem to be a dramatic lacuna: during the accusations in church, Shakespeare doesn't give Hero and Beatrice a chance to refute Claudio's and Pedro's "evidence"; but more seriously, at no point, then or later, does Margaret speak up. Perhaps the playwright felt that he was going to sink into unnecessary complications if he embarked on a cross-examination of this secondary role. He merely allots Leonato a line and a half to close 5.1 ("We'll talk with Margaret, How her acquaintance grew with this lewd fellow" [325–26]). He brings her on almost immediately in 5.2—as pert a tease as ever (with Benedick), who does not show herself regretful, if she really has been "talked with" in the interim offstage, and not in the least fearful if she knows that the "talking with" is still to come. The enigma remains, but the dramatist's judgment is unexceptionable: audiences clearly do not require illumination from Margaret as much as critics do; she is thought of after the performance, if at all, as having been no more than a minor plot element.

By the end, whether or not there is any author's point to make about imperialism, the conquerors' employees have doubly intermarried with the conquered. As the play pauses to take stock of its disguises, masks, duplicity, and misunderstandings, Don Pedro, who intervened on behalf of both young ladies, may look emotionally stranded, odd man out. Benedick, whom he (perhaps sarcastically) calls "the married man," cannot resist incorporating a last, lightly off-colored line in the sympathetic wish that offended Shaw: "Prince, thou art sad. Get thee a wife, get thee a wife. There is no staff more reverend than one tipped with horn" (5.4.120–22). In a note to these lines Zitner remarks,

> The seriousness of Don Pedro recalls the isolation of Antonio at the end of *The Merchant of Venice* [and of the other Antonio at the end of *Twelfth Night*]. Benedick's advice is bitter-sweet: there is honour in marriage although the staff of rule (here male domination) may also be a symbol of betrayal, i.e. tipped with horn rather than gold. (1993, 201n)

But here we run into one of those uncertainties that allow a director tests as well as opportunities. Has Benedick observed sadness in Don Pedro's mien or face? Does he describe *what he sees*? Or is he getting his own back after Don Pedro's and Claudio's earlier teasing in the same scene?

DON PEDRO

> Good morrow, Benedick. Why, what's the matter
> That you have such a February face,
> So full of frost, of storm and cloudiness?

CLAUDIO

> I think he thinks upon the savage bull.
> Tush, fear not, man, we'll tip thy horns with gold . . .

DON PEDRO How dost thou, "Benedick the married man?" (5.4.39–43 and 97–98)

Does the Prince indeed feel "isolated? " Or happy because of the occasion? He initiated both courtships and went to some trouble to push them toward consummation. As the play's most assertive matchmaker he may feel some relief as he yields instinctively to the dancing and cheerfulness, thereby helping to promote the comic happy end. And while we are on the subject of uncertainty-and-opportunity, does Beatrice, who used to mock her wooers out of suit, now laugh or frown or snarl? There is no time to tell. A messenger brings news of the capture of Don John. Benedick will devise "brave punishments for him," and sweeps her into a celebratory dance.

This remarkable close may also find spectators asking themselves and one another who exactly did what to whom in this second entry in Shakespeare's sex war. The main plot, as I see it, an equality in love, forms a complementary reply to *The Shrew*. (And the second, more radical reply will consist of *All's Well That Ends Well*—the triumph of a woman in that play's disconcerting comic resolution.) Although none of the roles has been tamed, the eavesdropping scenes shamed the two B's into matrimony. Shaming has replaced taming. The Prince and Claudio were shamed into mourning privately (in the absence of Leonato's family) at the presumed tomb of Hero (5.3). Claudio, with an offensive vow, has extended his penance by consenting to wed whomever Leonato decreed: "I'll hold my mind, were she an Ethiope" (5.4.37). Borachio spontaneously shamed himself into a regretful confession (5.1.225–37). The duel between Benedick and Claudio, in which audiences expected the latter to be tamed, never took place. In the penultimate moments, while Beatrice and Benedick resume their tongue-crossing in public, rather than admit that they are in love, Hero and Claudio again shame them by producing papers on which the B's have inscribed their affection for each other.

Because of outstanding Beatrices and Benedicks of the past, and sometimes not in the same production, critics have often been provoked into declaring one or the other role the center of the play. (Benedick has more lines than Beatrice—as do Leonato and Don Pedro—but does not have as many as Berowne or Petruchio do in their slightly longer plays.) The striking differences of opinion over this centrality suggest that those two roles sustain an equality and an interdependence—an example of sheer interplaying—unmatched elsewhere in the comedies.

Notes

1. F. H. Mares briefly addresses the matter of Beatrice's dowry (1988, 31).

2. Apropos of the two B's, the Quarto version of the text, which was considerably relied on for three subsequent Folio editions, had "many characters in *Much Ado* (Beatrice, Benedick, Borachio, Balthasar, Boy, Brother [Antonio], Bastard) whose names begin with 'B,'" writes Sheldon P. Zitner (1993, 80). The compositor's shortage of capital B's among his fonts has given editors many chances to speculate about speeches emerging from 'B' roles.

3. A synopsis of Terry's succession of Beatrices during her stage life and of other performances, together with sources, is given by Zitner (58–70), who mentions among other topics an adaptation that may not have been atypical in the seventeenth and eighteenth centuries: "Charles Johnson's *Love in a Forest* (1723) [which] was a mélange of *As You Like It* with insertions from *A Midsummer Night's Dream, Love's Labour's Lost, Twelfth Night,* and some forty lines from *Much Ado* of Benedick's witty resistance to love from the end of 1.1" (60).

4. In this chapter I neglect the word-play between the *Nothing* of the title and the assonance in Elizabethan pronunciation of *noting* (i.e., *noticing*), which

has been amply discussed in the criticism and is connected with the perennial Shakespearean theme of misapprehension through trusting one's eyes and ears. The verb *note* in its active form first appears in 1.1, courtesy of Claudio:

> CLAUDIO Benedick, didst thou note the daughter of Signor Leonato?
>
> BENEDICK I noted her not, but I looked on her.

More word-play between *note(s), noting,* and *nothing* occurs in 2.3.51–56.

5. Hero seems to be another motherless daughter. As has frequently been mentioned, in quarto and folio editions of the play, Leonato's spouse, Innogen, is listed but does not appear in the action.

6. René Girard in *A Theatre of Envy: William Shakespeare* ingeniously unravels the concept of "mimetic envy" as the sequence of feelings in Claudio's role, having to do with Claudio's self-contempt and a pattern of mimetic behavior between him and Don Pedro. But Girard, to make his concept work, interpolates events that do not occur between scenes in the action—that is—he creates a story not in the play—in order to construct a psychological whole for the roles, another case of helping the author along with a plausible through line.

All's Well That Ends Well

A century ago the tag "problem plays" settled like a curse on *All's Well, Measure for Measure,* and *Troilus and Cressida.* The words came from F. S. Boas in his lectures and book, *Shakespere and His Predecessors* (New York: 1896 and 1908).[1] They seemed to signify irremediable flaws; but in recent years the curse has more or less lifted as directors and critics came to look on these plays (and *Cymbeline*) as boundary-stretching experiments by the author. Some scholars still had reservations, though. G.K. Hunter, in editing *All's Well,* found its "rhetoric . . . contorted and gnarled by the pressure of thought in a way which is totally unlyrical" (1962, xxi). I disagree that the language is not lyrical, totally or partially; in places, to split a hair or two, it retains some lyricism even where hard to penetrate. But is it a comedy? It certainly ends as one. In the first two-thirds the action clings to the comic genre mostly by means of the sayings and doings of the military dandy Parolles and the clown Lavatch, but it finally throws off a flurry of hasty moral readjustments that are amenable to a happy ending. En route to that ending it invokes more melodrama, more forgiveness, more manipulation by the heroine, and heavier reliance on fate, luck, chance, serendipity, or synchronicity (that is, cagey plotting) than Shakespeare cared or dared to exploit in his earlier comedies.

Recent attempts at dating, which have to take account of contradictory facts, conclude that a preliminary form of the play was written in the late 1590s—say, not long after *The Merchant*—and revised possibly as late as 1603 or 1604. Hordes of spectators and critics have looked on Helena as a nitwit, wasting her young life on securing a husband glaringly unworthy of her. Still, even allowing for the relative sparsity of stage activities for its length,[2] *All's Well* spins a drama of a woman's love more impassioned, more unremittingly pursued, more self-denying and at the same time more self-affirming than any other by Shakespeare, including the tragedies and the delayed consummation of *As You Like It*. It constitutes a credulity-straining follow-up to the male domination of *The Shrew* and the equalizing of sexual power in *Much Ado:* heroine succeeds against odds in act-5 capture of reluctant (and surly) quarry. If Helena had lived to 1928 or later, her theme song could have been "I Must Have That Man."[3]

The action in the main plot has a twofold purpose. Helena submits to an irrevocable task: she must succeed in adjusting to Bertram's social level—abasing herself not precluded—to win his love and to win him away from his own badness, thereby redeeming them both. As a subsidiary purpose of this mission, she will resuscitate her father's reputation as a physician-cum-wizard and demonstrate that, though dead, he lives again, his medical magic revived through her.

She has to compete with Parolles for influence over Bertram: the contest between them opens in the first scene with their ambiguous and unsettled argument over virginity. In the course of the action Helena's fortune mounts, most markedly after she cures the French King's fistula by administering the pre-antibiotic resources handed on by her father or possibly by arousing his desire for her. Several critics have raised questions about a sexual encounter between Helena and the ailing king. In the BBC TV version there were unmissable signs of foreplay between Donald Sinden's King and the deliberately dowdy Helena of Angela Down. That fortune of hers, though, does suffer setbacks, while the fortune of Parolles stays on an even keel before skidding into a severe decline. Not that Helena defeats him; he defeats himself with slanderous lies and the assistance of a group of French soldiers. In the play's final scene, Helena and Parolles will become partners in bringing about the rehabilitation of Bertram—not a very explicit one—when Parolles, now a remnant of his old self, gives evidence against his former friend and superior officer.

The triangle of these two men and a woman structurally resembles that in *Othello*, written at about the same time as the postulated revision of *All's Well*. Hunter (1962, xxv) argues for "a tentative dating" of 1603 to 1604, as mentioned previously, a loose date that corresponds to a generally accepted dating for *Othello*. Some critics have interpreted *Othello* as a Christian document, with Desdemona as a Christlike exemplar and Iago, on "the dark side" of Othello, as the Tempter. Hunter does not draw the parallel between the *Othello* trio and the *All's Well* trio, but he does say that "Parolles and Helena are arranged on either side of Bertram, placed rather like the Good and Evil Angels in a Morality" (xxxiii). In her undoubted goodness and trusting love, Desdemona does bear resemblances to Helena, despite her wealthier upbringing, greater passivity, and more limited intelligence—emphasized when she pleads for Michael Cassio's restoration without noticing (or caring enough) how her pleas inflame Othello.

Three of the four secondary but consequential roles, those of the Countess, Lafew, and the King, all situated in the upper strata of French society, contribute to this main plot, but the connections between them and the three principals do not reach significantly into any subplots. As the fourth of these well-defined secondary roles, Lavatch does engage his employer the Countess in four scenes (1.3, 2.2, 3.2, and 4.5), and he does converse at times with Helena and Parolles, but like other clowns in Shakespeare, most markedly Feste, he strikes one as being self-involved, often removed from the action proper, although now and then he spoofs others, caricaturing what they are or stand for. Lavatch (sometimes spelled Lavache, à la française) is an unusual figure for a Shakespearean clown. Some women critics take him to be misogynistic, and he does appear so in his conversations with the Countess. He served under her husband, just dead, and she kept the clown in her service, a sentimental retaining of a retainer.

The brothers Dumain, referred to as First Lord and Second Lord, similarly step outside the action for some scenes, in which they comment on the other roles and the politics of France and Florence. They ease back into the action when they let us know that they have hardly more liking for Bertram than they do for Parolles (4.3.1–35), particularly because Bertram "hath perverted a young gentlewoman here in Florence, of a most chaste renown" (13–14). The First Lord also collaborates with the "five or six other soldiers" in the first of the play's two subplots, the ambush of Parolles: the two brothers then help to discredit him in the eyes of Bertram.

In the other subplot, Diana, her widowed mother, and two other Florentine women join forces with Helena to work the venerable bed trick, which depends on the curious assumption that, in bed and with the candles out, all women are more or less the same. Sir Arthur Quiller-Couch colorfully calls the bed trick, as it has become generally known, "the substitute bed-fellow" (1929, 1955). "Q" disliked this "rather nasty play" (xxxi), with its "hopeless skrimble-skramble" (xxiv)—"one of Shakespeare's worst" and a travesty "upon a fine prose-story" (xxxv).

As a contrast to most of the comedies, which inhabit two general locations, one preliminary, one principal—a spot to settle into—*All's Well* skips at times back and forth across France from Bertram's newly inherited castle in the province of Rossillion[4] in the south, not far from the Spanish border, to the court in Paris in the north, and later across other borders of city-states on the way to Florence, with one return stop at Marseille. It upholds suspense by scenic alternations or cross-cutting. No other comedy shifts its grounds, geographical and ethical, quite so restlessly, not even the one it most nearly resembles in structure, *Two Gentlemen*. Eight scenes take place in Rossillion; five in Paris (all early in the action), nine in Florentine locales; and one in Marseille. For the final two scenes, the action returns to Rossillion, where it opened.

Dissatisfied reviewers and spectators have framed the play's leading question roughly as follows: If persevering girl homes in on sullen boy until she gets him, has she won anything worth having? Behind the question lurks the conviction that he doesn't deserve her. From the mass of instructive commentary a different leading question arises: How does Helena operate—by sheer willpower, by divine ordinance, or by a mix of flukes and guesses? Anyone determined enough to pursue one or another of these possibilities as doggedly, say, as Helena pursues Bertram, might decide that the author was serious, was fooling, was indifferent to the action's principal engine. Did it amount to individual resolve, or God's will, or the Devil's, or some quite different source of belief and behavior, such as a premature and rudimentary form of naturalism, that late nineteenth-century belief in environmental determinism? Two critics of distinction from relatively early in this century, Sir Edward Chambers and Hazelton Spencer, collide head-on. Chambers asserts "the simple truth that the play is drenched in irony" (1925, 202), while Spencer says fifteen years later, "Certainly there is no trace of irony or skepticism in Shakespeare's handling of this very romantic plot" (1940, 293). Robert Ornstein brought the two essays together, reprinting Spencer right after Chambers, in *Discussions of Shakespeare's Problem Comedies* (1961).

Two later high-caliber critics, G. Wilson Knight and Russell Fraser, like others, come to opposed conclusions, either of which could have rich implications for the play's staging. Knight chooses lines from the text implying that Helena is a chosen vessel for God's message of love, goodwill, and trust, in addition to other lines that seem less corroborative but susceptible to an interpretation that supports the thesis (1958, 131–57). Fraser, though, picks lines not only from this play but also from all over the canon to explain that Shakespeare says a body (in this case, Helena's) rules its wearer's conduct (New Cambridge Shakespeare edition [1985, 1989] see especially "The Play," [8–28]). I find myself swayed by both Knight's and Fraser's arguments, without accepting either author's identification of an Ultimate Motive, because Shakespeare supports them both, as well as others, in various places— out of various mouths or out of the same mouth at various points in the action. Fraser, adducing lines from many plays to the effect that Shakespeare believed in the futility of human *and* divine will, makes a richly textured case. He draws attention to "recurrences in language and the juxtaposing of complementary scenes," so that roles that are unlike use identical words in successive scenes.

But other lines from the same roles or from other roles offer themselves as refutation. Isolated lines, or even lines in a generously reproduced context, will not tell what a play *is*, owing to the selectivity of the process. What keeps Shakespeare alive? Surely, the multiple deductions possible, the battles of ideas, the wealth of implications. Still, I feel indebted to both these theses: Knight's because it presupposes a driven young woman, when, for example, she says she will empty France of herself so that Bertram can return to his country without feeling inhibited by her or indebted to her. Yet, I sympathize with Fraser's thesis because he allows for "equivocal" roles—good and bad Helenas populating the stage, to mingle companionably with bad and good Parolleses and Bertrams. In Knight's book, Helena qualifies as a saint, an earthbound angel. But a source quoted by Fraser, Mrs. Charlotte Lennox in 1753, calls the role "cruel, artful, and insolent" (14).

The remaining roles display less pliability, although we can count on future directors and actors to come up with readings that apparently go against the grain. The Countess, Lafew, the King, Lavatch, and the Dumain brothers, all substantial parts, carry weight in the action by their effects on the central trio, rather than as studies in themselves. Anne Barton points out that the Countess, Lafew, Parolles, and Lavatch (I would add the King) "have one thing in common: they operate in their different ways, throughout the comedy, to raise Helena in our estimation and to degrade Bertram" (Evans 1974, 500). In their sympathy for Helena, Lafew and the Countess behave unlike conventional members of the nobility, as does the King, although he appears less sure of himself toward the end of the play. In affirming his ranking role in act 5 he predates the role of a later French king, Louis XIV, whom Molière casts as a Louis ex machina in *L'Impromptu de Versailles* and *Tartuffe*.

Susan Snyder confirms Barton's belief that the author went out of his way to paint Bertram's flaws fully and honestly (1994, 44-48). Among other critics, Snyder more or less accepts Bertram as a transferred portrait of the beloved, evasive object of some of the sonnets. Impassioned Helena can be read as a substitute, a persona and voice of the Shakespeare who is the unavailing "I" of those sonnets, languishing for not the Dark Lady but the fair young man, Bertram seen as another variation on the naive fighting-machine, spiritual brother to Fortinbras and the Claudio of *Much Ado*.

The attention given to folktales and fairy tales by W. W. Lawrence (1931) introduced what for the time was a set of new considerations in adjudging *All's Well*. Barton reminds us about a feature of many myths and fairy stories: that they arose from a popular belief about virginity. It not merely required keeping oneself physically and spiritually intact but also, and more dramatically, it could confer on its practitioner magical properties, courtesy of Artemis/Diana. In the opening scene Parolles and Helena banter about this topic. He urges her not to remain a virgin; she, in response, keeps him at bay by asking him how it's possible to keep men at bay. We understand that she is saving herself for Bertram but also hinting that she would like to know how to make her virginity serve her purpose, show her a way into his affections: whether, say, she ought to spend it in a good cause (winning him) or remain chaste (honoring herself). Barton jogs us into understanding further that Helena could not have successfully applied her father's miraculous cure to the King's ailment if she had not been a virgin. In the BBC TV version, while Parolles insolently asks, "Are you meditating on virginity?" Helena sits picking out a melody on a harpsichord, also known at that time as the virginals.

In her mission, is Helena alone?

> Boccaccio's heroine [Giletta in the ninth story of the third day of the *Decameron*, whose story resembles Helena's] is not, like Helena, a loner by nature as well as circumstance. From the beginning Shakespeare makes Helena a solitary figure, one who grew up alone on the periphery of a great household in which she had no assured place or station. Accustomed to this aloneness, she does not reach out to anyone except when an alliance with the King or with Diana and her mother will further her goal of obtaining Bertram. (Ornstein 1986, 180)

Given the backing of the Countess (against her own son), the King, and Lafew, if the young woman does look like a loner, she has chosen to be or cannot help being so. She may have lost her natural father, but she has a substitute father in the King, a substitute mother in the Countess, a substitute uncle in Lafew, and substitute lovers, if she would sanction them, in the young lords she teases among the royal retinue before she declares Bertram her choice (2.3). For a time she resists accepting the Countess as her mother and she resists implying that Bertram is her brother, but later she yields: she says to Lavatch, "My mother greets me kindly. Is she well?" (2.4.1). And in the final scene, the trial by pregnancy, when she notices the Countess among the courtiers, she cries, "O my dear Mother, do I see you living?" (5.3.320), a line in which she could be expressing relief that she has lived to have the joy of seeing the Countess again or relief that the Countess has not died. Only with the substitute sibling does she undergo strain in what communications specialists today call "interpersonal relations." Though she vehemently denies to the Countess that Bertram is in any sense her close blood relation, he behaves almost exactly like a jealous brother, strikingly in his first farewell to her, which is an order, void of affection—"Be comfortable to my mother, your mistress, and make much of her" (1.1.77–78)—and in his scornful shortness toward her in subsequent scenes. When she picks him for her future partner, he does not respond to her but addresses his protests to the King, as though refusing to acknowledge her presence in the throne room. He fastens onto a class distinction to justify his distaste, but the snubbing for that reason also marks his refusal to admit her to his family. He plays the far opposite of a man who pledges to help his sister find a husband. When he finally submits to her paternity suit (addressing the King again, not Helena), he does so guardedly, suspiciously, in a couplet often cited to vilify this play's verse.

> *If* she, my liege, can *make* me know this *clearly*,
> I'll love her dearly, ever, ever dearly. (5.3.316–17, my italics)

This, his final statement in the action, may repeat "ever" and "dearly" in the second line, but the three words I have italicized in the preceding line seem, in their triple caution, to point forward to the King's

> All is well ended, if this suit be won,
> That you express content. (Epilogue, 2–3)

The monarch, now an actor, is shilling for applause, as every epilogue reciter does, but might "this suit" also allude to Bertram's unloverly, unbrotherly, taciturn persona and caviling commitment and Helena's almost as "iffy" response, her last words to him?

> If it appear not plain and prove untrue,
> Deadly divorce step between me and you! (318–19)

To corral him Helena humbles herself more than her boosters approve of (vide Professor Snyder). Some performances may suggest that, with the benefit of a pink follow spot or some other unmistakable sign, she appears triumphant at the end of her brief appearance in 5.3 and her eleven and a half lines therein, but the text doesn't confirm that with the aid of gloating, self-congratulation, or compliments, as we would expect at the rounding-off of a comedy. Rather, we notice her sense of relief (not unlike Petruchio's in *that* act 5)—the task is over, thanks to the curtain—and the relief of the others, some of it due to her not being, as the rumor had it, dead. She is reborn, a little spuriously, as the destined (or unavoidable) mate for Bertram and as the undoubted mother of his child and possibly subsequent children. Unlike her namesake in *Midsummer Night's Dream*, she got him without the aid of puckishness or dependence on drugs. She may appear as humble as before, not without some suppressed pride at having been the play's internal playwright and director, and also a rehearsal mistress for Diana, coaching her as sedulously as any modern defense counsel does a defendant. She has taught Bertram a lesson, in the manner of comedy, but what he learned from it remains open to question. Susan Snyder wants attention paid to "what ought to stand out at the end—Bertram's recognition of his sin and repentance for it" (42), but however abjectly the actor hangs his head the audience will surely feel that he is yielding to the recognition that he's boxed in by a woman for whom he has no love, rather than genuinely regretful. Anne Barton remarks that Helena, on the other side of the marriage equation, is "prized by her elders" as a "living example of the attitudes of the past." Those upper-crust elders do indeed behave democratically. They take her for what she makes of herself, a virtuous young woman who knows her place but never grows discourageable; they do not confine her to the class she has emerged from, as a country physician's girl.

Even so, her very modesty tells of a wattage of masochism that glows at certain moments only. There may be mild masochism in anyone who goes along so conformably with the rules of society as these apply to rank. The action does not really dramatize fears of loss, as say *The Winter's Tale* dramatizes those of Leontes (or, at the start, of Hermione and young Mamillius). Rather, it hints at fears of gain that have built up in Helena since childhood, a misgiving that she may not match up to her belief that she ought to succeed if she tries hard enough. She gives private voice to the belief early on, and it has a distinctly masochistic ring.

> Th' ambition in my love thus plagues itself;
> The hind that would be mated by the lion
> Must die for love. (1.1.92–94)

And again in the same scene:

> Impossible be strange attempts to those
> That weigh their pains in sense and do suppose
> What hath been cannot be. (224–26)

Helena does not weigh *her* pains in sense. Cost what they will, she must endure; and she feels reassured that she will not be the first woman to have socially declassified herself. In this connection, her name has a comic ring. In the Folio she is called Hellen, except once. At various places in the text, the King, the Countess, Parolles, and Lavatch speak of or to her as Helen. Lavatch conjures up Helen of Sparta (and Troy) in his song.

> "Was this fair face the cause," quoth she,
> "Why the Grecians sackèd Troy?
> Fond done, done fond,
> Was this King Priam's joy?" (1.3.70–73)

Clifford Leech observes that this "Helen" does go to Paris ("The Theme of Ambition in *All's Well that Ends Well*," in Ornstein, *Discussions*, 56-63). It looks, however, as if Shakespeare *contrasts* her with the mythical Helen, who had every man running after her; this one elects to run after one man who doesn't want her.

We revert to the old questions, and one or two new ones. Does the audience feel let down? Feel satisfaction in seeing Bertram defeated? *Is* he defeated? Is the end anticlimactic? Bathetic? Did Helena waste her heroic efforts on a titled ne'er-do-well? Would we prefer to see Helena disdain the corny bed-trick, get over her infatuation, grow up, or even be in a position to spurn him? Anne Barton, looking beyond the action and into the never-to-be-unlocked story that follows it, as act 5 tempts us all to do, speaks (with reverberations back to the other Helen) of a "pyrrhic victory."

As Maurice Charney maintains in introducing his collection of criticism about "bad" Shakespeare, there is no need, no reason, to defend every one of Shakespeare's badnesses. Bardolators (Shaw's coinage) find it almost as easy to justify each badness as to condemn it. What puzzles me is *what makes* Shakespeare so easy to defend. Conclusion: when turned over and around like a flawed stone, even an excessive badness has a way of putting on a good facet. Critics who tackle this play especially are liable to feel at times, many times, that the author plays willful, posthumous games with those who poke at his mysteries. Some of them find the mysteries too gritty or refuse to look on them as mysteries, and depart in dudgeon. Others discern meanings less in general, resounding statements than in the sheer clash of roles. Does anybody still heed T. S. Eliot as a critic of Shakespeare? It may also be that Shakespeare just does know better than his unfavorable critics, that he tried some neat endings and didn't like them or tired of the trim wrap-up—as Molière later made fun of conventional openings and closings—found them less provocative, less artful than what he finally gives us.

But then that other type of critic, the director, cannot afford to call a scene or a moment a "problem" or "problematic." "Problematic" and "problematical" have become unlovely, pretentious stand-ins for the semantically abysmal "problem."[5] If directors think a difficult scene or line excisable, they cut it. If they think it excusable—it slows the pace of a performance but says something or some things worth saying—they do their best to justify it. In the last scene, Helena seizes Bertram, let us say, and plants a kiss so deep that it takes his breath away. After the news of her pregnancy, he cannot stop himself staring at the protrusion of his child to be. The Countess and the King take Bertram by either arm and lead him into the arms of Helena. Or—an old Hollywood trick—Helena smiles, goes on to laugh at first lightly, then uncontrollably, affecting Bertram . . . With friendly regrets offered those who wish to rework act 5, I feel we must view it as another risky realignment of the comic ending. Chambers exaggerates when he writes that "the issue of the thing is not Helena's triumph but Helena's degradation." He exaggerates less when he calls this

> a comedy from which all laughter has evaporated, save the grim
> laughter which follows the dubious sallies of Monsieur Lavatch and
> the contemptuous laughter which presides over the plucking bare of
> the ineffable Parolles. (39 and 38)

And Leech remarks that "there is a good deal of acid in the play's
thought" (61). Yes. Much acid and a scarcity of carefree laughter.
Leech's statement comes in his detection of what he calls "an aesthet-
ic problem"—

> of the dramatist's failure in imagination. A traditional story and real-
> istic characterisation can be fused, as in *Lear*. So, too, we feel no un-
> ease when a Christian colouring is present along with a sharply criti-
> cal view of the world, as I think in *Macbeth*. But here there is no fu-
> sion. (61–2)

Once again a critic sets up a hypothetical, retrospective standard—the
difficulty of combining realistic roles with a critical view of the
world—and then accuses the artist of having lacked the imagination to
conform with it. I believe the play goes along with enough tokens of
what we regard as a comedy to qualify for the genre. If we dub it a
romance, rather than a comedy, it lacks the pastoral elements associated with romances. But Paris, Rossillion, and Florence fail to meet the
requirements of a "green world." They seem like traps for Bertram,
two of them likely to crush any of his individuality the author may
have intended but concealed in him, and the third liable to corrupt
him because it's a foreign country where "those girls of Italy" (2.1.19),
as the King warns, stand or sit or lie, poised to pounce and, in all probability, pass on a disease.

Richard P. Wheeler, among others, calls *All's Well* a comedy of forgiveness, forgiveness of Bertram by Helena, the King, and the Countess, and also by Lafew of Parolles (Bevington 1992, 362–65). Edward
Dowden looks upon the action as a process of healing. Joseph
Westlund, in a psychological interpretation, says the play is about rep-
aration (984, 121–146).[6] The action does confirm these namings and
emphases. The first scene opens with mourning for Bertram's father
and the grief of Helena and the Countess at the son's departure. When
the Countess goes into her advice and instructions, even though she
is nothing like Polonius as a parent, we understand why Bertram is
anxious to escape from home to Paris (just as we understand the flight
of Laertes to the same permissive city), eager to use Paris as a launching pad for the glorious wars in Italy on the side of either Siena or Florence, it doesn't matter; anything for a decent battle. Bernard Shaw
takes the role of the Countess as a character, perhaps based on one
he'd seen by, say Ellen Terry, when he writes:

The most charming of all Shakespear's old women, indeed the most charming of all his women, young or old, is the Countess of Rousillon. . . . It has a certain individuality among them which suggests a portrait. Mr [Frank] Harris will have it that all Shakespear's nice old women are drawn from his beloved mother; but I see no evidence whatever that Shakespear's mother was a particularly nice woman or that he was particularly fond of her." (Preface to *The Dark Lady of the Sonnets*, Vol. 4, "definitive edition")[7]

The last scene closes with Bertram's having been constrained to buckle down with a suitable mate he doesn't love but is too available. He has, however, won pardons and hopes on the part of the three senior citizens and the heroine who will assist him in upholding his father's and family's reputation. Shakespeare keeps Bertram harsh, not to say repellent, but he possibly does so in line with the traditional versions, especially the biblical one, of the tale of the prodigal son.

Whether as critics or members of the reading and theatrical public, we have every right to judge a play's roles, even harshly. Yet disliking a work, as so many critics in the first few decades of this century did, because one dislikes one of the roles whom the action doesn't punish but only puts through a trial, may mean missing one purpose of the author: pointing out that people in real life behave this way. Bertrams retain their unwilling hold on Helenas by spurning them. Many are worse; they ill-treat them with fists, threats, and weighty objects. And with actual weapons. In much the same way, Kates do surrender to Petruchios, no matter how furiously we chide them for doing so. Othellos believe Iagos, although we who watch know we would be much too wise to let ourselves in for the same painful results. Lears bad-mouth Cordelias, who remain loyal to their senile or spiteful fathers. If we have normal, hard-working consciences, we would like nothing better than the chance to barge into the action like a Buster Keaton to rescue these voluntary victims. If we could, we'd go so far as to legislate on their behalf. But however pressing our urge to save them, the roles assist us in recognizing that figures who spite themselves continue to exist and suffer exploitation and disappointment.

Most of the inconsistencies in most of the roles in *All's Well* do not strike us as being arbitrary or sudden. The action accounts for them, especially the relationships. Bertram comes across in print as being almost too skewed for his act-5 self to defy convincingly the self we met in act 1. But the author has provided a stepping stone, for those who feel they need it, his excitement at being alone with Diana, whom he calls "a titled goddess, And worth it, with addition!" (4.2.2–3), before he pleads with her, "Stand no more off, But give thyself unto my sick desires, Who then recovers" (34–36). Thus speaks the "sick" suitor, newly promoted to General of the Horse in the Florentine cavalry, who, learning of his elevation, swore devotion to "Great Mars" and called himself a "hater of love" (3.3.1–11). When he says in the last scene that this same Diana is "a fond and desperate creature Whom sometime I have laughed with" 5.3.178–79) and "a common gamester to the camp" (189), do those epithets mean he was insincere when he hoped to bed her? Very likely, but if he appears so to the audience in the scene in question, it will falter: he will establish no real distinction between his hopeless surrender to Helena and "sick desires" for Diana. In critically reconstructing the role, one can try to make a consistent whole out of his "sick" and other desires, but an actor who knows his business will want to take greedy advantage of the role's unmediated extremities.

The part of Lafew, Bertram's escort to Paris and the King's trusted counselor, has more latitude than some critics and directors allow when they pin him down as a benign, sage Pantalone who dodders and is losing his hearing. Beginning as a stern guide, he melts into Helena's most effusive male admirer, the most open censurer of Parolles, and later a model of tolerance toward that wayward, fallen blusterer. Lafew's remarks in praise of old times and generations gone lend themselves to exhibition by folk who snatch them off the lips of the role and stuff them into the mouth of Shakespeare, whom they then accuse of being conservative, of disapproving of youth's energies and excesses, of deploring lapses in recent fashion or taste, even of "lookism," when Lafew calls Helena "pretty lady."

The Countess of Rossillion, although referred to as "Old Lady" in the stage directions introducing scenes 4.5 and 5.3, cannot be aged or cranky enough to serve as decrepit spokesperson for a reactionary Shakespeare. A typesetter may have confused her speech heading with that of Diana's mother, who is sometimes called Old Widow and is probably also in her thirties or early forties. Women of that age might have appeared old as real people when the play was written, but the stage directions could also serve as acting instructions to the boys who originally undertook the roles. Lately widowed, the Countess seems reluctant to part with her teenaged son, the new Count, whether because she loses him to the Court right after losing her husband or because she doesn't trust him to live independently or submit without question or hesitation to the wishes of the King, his new guardian. She asks Lafew to advise the "unseasoned courtier" (1.1.71).

Her adoption not long before of Helena, on the death of *her* father, her affection for this "daughter-in-law," after Helena's confession of her love for Bertram, without so much as a mention of differential rank (1.3), mark her as unorthodox for an aristocrat. When she hears Helen read the letter, the "dreadful sentence," written by Bertram in an attempt to dismiss his wife forever, she disowns him: "I do wash his name out of my blood, And thou art all my child" (3.2.67–68). But she cannot resist asking after his whereabouts, even though Helena "deserves a lord That twenty such rude boys might tend upon" (80–81). When Helena quits France so that Bertram may return and not feel out of place in his native land, the Countess's "heart is heavy," because she wants Bertram back but not at the price of losing Helena. She cannot tell "which of them both Is dearest to me" (3.4.38–39). All in all, the Countess does not change markedly. Most of the action unloads more grief on her than on either Helena or Bertram, largely because she is a witness, a comforter for Helena when she can be, but not an operative figure. In the end she might shed her gloom, or a fraction of it, for the sake of her two united children, but how confident she feels about their prospects only each actor who portrays her can say.

Nor does the King of France change much over the course of the action. Kings in general have mercurial temperaments, as does this one. They issue commands; they expect instant compliance; they rant if they do not get it. Zitner writes about this King's feeling that he knows his place and believes that he fits it better than anybody else. Such an attitude, a by-product of supreme power in a state, can lead to abuse of authority. This King is on the side of the angel, Helena, whom he must have for his son-by-proxy. His most visible transformation is from enervated sickness to his ecstatic basking in the miraculous recovery. And being obeyed to the letter.

Lavatch, whose role the author has sprinkled through the action into six scenes, plays in a more sour temper than Shakespeare's other clowns, most of whom, nonetheless, have their crotchety moments. People writing about the play pick up the two adjectives from the Countess's early reproach: "Wilt thou ever be a foulmouthed and calumnious knave" (l.3.56–57), as though he were an unusually beastly joker; but he puns on copulation and cuckoldry with Shakespearean vivacity and without exceptional vulgarity (for the author's time or ours). He belongs with Feste and Touchstone, not with Bottom, Costard, and Dogberry, those Spooner ancestors, in that he displays the verbal assurance of an educated person who has fallen on hard times. His first substantial speech, which provokes the Countess's criticism, tells her that he wants to marry his Isbel so that he can attract friends who will enjoy her and take over some of his marital obligations: "He that ears my land spares my team and gives me leave to in the crop. If I be his cuckold, he's my drudge" (1.3.44–46). The Countess is understandably shaken by a man who professes to welcome the state of cuckoldry, rather than cower at the prospect of it. He goes on to insult women, and before a woman—only one of them in ten is "good"— and to deplore that he, a man, "should be at woman's command" (1.3.91). He will pick up this line of polite insolence later. Scene 2.2

serves him as a pretext for exclaiming "O, Lord, sir!" as an answer that "will fit any question" asked at Court, articulated with variety so as to let the actor show off, and even make a brief bravura turn out of an encounter that hardly affects the plot line. He arrives in Paris (2.4), brings Helena a letter from the Countess, and banters with her and Parolles, relying on the kind of word quibbles that clowns never resist. When he returns to Rossillion, bearing from Bertram the letter that tells his mother, "I have wedded her, not bedded her, and sworn to make the 'not' eternal" (3.2.21–22), Lavatch has grown disillusioned with Isbel after experiencing the Court at first hand: "Our old lings and our Isbels a' the country are nothing like your old ling and your Isbels a' th' court" (3.2.10–12). In glossing "old lings" as salt cod, Fraser says, "The Clown's joke remains obscure, but it appears to suggest that his own appetites have become more mercenary since he was at court" (93). Whether it was the openness of the sexual activity there or its opulence, he has lost his own zest for sex. Clowns must match wits with other roles in as many talk contests as can be accommodated without unduly interrupting the flow of the play. In a fairly extended exchange (4.5.) Lavatch remarks cryptically to Lafew that he serves the Black Prince (Edward, father of Richard II) or the prince of darkness (the devil)—or does he mean the prince of the world, who keeps a court and might be either another sobriquet for the devil or the reigning King of France? Lafew, not wishing to plumb further into the clown's verbal murk, dismisses him hastily. But he has given him a purse and admits to the Countess, who has been a bystander, "I like him well" (4.5.68). In a final appearance, Lavatch meets with Parolles, now "muddied in Fortune's mood" and smelling "somewhat strong of her strong displeasure" (5.2.4–6). He introduces him to Lafew, for whom Parolles intends a pleading letter, and walks out of the play with a humane farewell: "I do pity his distress . . . and leave him to your lordship" (5.2.25–26), ending the jagged line of his inconsistent climb from cynicism to compassion.

Parolles himself was, and remains, the role male actors vie for, although I can envisage its yielding rewards in laughter and other accomplishments for a contralto. It calls for precisely the quality Bertram lacks: charm. Helena grants him that in the first scene. His "fixed evils sit so fit in him That they take place when virtue's steely bones Looks bleak i' th' cold wind" (1.1.104–06). That Shakespeare intended Parolles as the male lead seems confirmed by his participation in a colloquy at the start that has nothing to do with exposition but bites into a dominant theme. During more than the play's first half he holds over Bertram a spell not unlike in some respects the one wielded by Tartuffe over Orgon and his mother—although clearly much less villainous, with no plain, overriding motive. But the start of the action denotes a new phase for Parolles: we too can find him charming, even after we see him roundly put down by Lafew, but as of the time the action gets under way, the figures matched with him, playing against him scene by scene, begin to see through the charm. In the end, Lafew's and Lavatch's pity for him seems apt: out of the several motives we have glimpsed in Parolles as a live personality, the most prominent one was his desire to create and leave favorable impressions. The mask of Mars he wears keeps slipping to reveal the face of complaisance, eager for respectful salutation—one might say, eager to be loved or, failing that, to please. In the few productions I have seen, Parolles, like him or not, steals much of the play. His is a success role: he does make a favorable impression as a harmless crook, even a lovable rogue, not a fearsome warrior. He has something like the impact, though not the persona, of Autolycus. But he exerts the charm on the audience: with the other roles in the play, as with many critics, he doesn't get by, let alone succeed.

Comparisons of Parolles with other outgrowths of the *miles gloriosus* of Plautus and the commedia dell'arte's Capitano, from Armado to Pistol to Corneille's Matamore, are inevitable. He may not exactly suffer from such comparisons, but he doesn't benefit from them, and least of all from any of the Falstaffs, the braggart-poltroons most expansively conceived. And sometimes embodied. Here is one role whose views it is almost unthinkable for even the most didactic critic to mistake for Shakespeare's own, for Parolles's function (not his manner), resembles that of Lucio in *Measure* in being a false narrator. The scene in which he is publicly shamed as a coward incorporates some of his finest lines, in which he unloads some poisonous hatred and jealousy, ending with the memorable soliloquy that returns him to himself, the survivor:

> Yet am I thankful. If my heart were great,
> 'Twould burst at this. Captain I'll be no more
> But I will eat and drink, and sleep as soft
> As captain shall. Simply the thing I am
> Shall make me live. (4.4.332–36)

Is Parolles an impotent? The remark by Lafew suggesting, "Thou wert best set thy lower part where thy nose stands" (2.3.250–51) might hint at that. He mocks, not women exactly but rather, sexual activity. He could also be played as having a gay attachment to Bertram; some critics think that by advising Diana to get her money from Bertram beforehand, he tries to frighten her off. He could be fearful of losing Bertram. His flashy garb with scarves decorating his sleeves and his occasionally fancy language ("capriccio, kicky wicky") could be taken as the playwright's mockery of the French. He is, after all, the

only Frenchman addressed as Monsieur, and may be good in the Jacobean era for jingoistic-xenophobic laughs. He faces his cowardice
and hypocrisy so candidly (to himself in a soliloquy, 4.1.26–31, 34-43)
that the First Lord thinks, marveling, "Is it possible he should know
what he is, and be that he is?" (4.1.44–45). Like Malvolio he undergoes a severe humiliation; unlike Malvolio, he's anything but defiant:
"Simply the thing I am Shall make me live." He will strive to become
a professional fool by cringing; swallow his pride; come to terms with
his lower social status.

The last of Parolles is his part in the trial of Bertram. When the latter hears that his former companion will testify, he bursts out:

> What of him?
> He's quoted for a most perfidious slave,
> With all the spots o' the world taxed and debauched,
> Whose nature sickens but to speak a truth.
> Am I or that or this for what he'll utter
> That will speak anything? (5.3.205–10)

But in this scene it is Bertram who proves the liar. Parolles acquits
himself less shabbily on the witness stand than his garb would suggest.
He asserts that his "master hath been an honorable gentleman. Tricks
he hath had in him, which gentlemen have" (5.3.40–42). He goes on
to admit that he himself "did go between" Bertram and Diana and that
Bertram "loved her, for indeed he was mad for her, and talked of Satan and of Limbo and of Furies." He concludes, "I will not speak what
I know" (259–67). He has swung from ostentation to discretion—or
secretiveness.

To the last remark of Parolles during the trial the King retorts,
"Thou hast spoken all already" (268), that is, You've given us as much
as we're likely to get from you. Attention then turns back to Diana. If,
as the King remarks, Parolles is "too fine" in giving his evidence, Diana appears even more evasive, contradicting herself. Why has she
accused Bertram?

> Because he's guilty, and he is not guilty.
> He knows I am no maid, and he'll swear to't;
> I'll swear I am a maid, and he knows not.
> Great King, I am no strumpet by my life;
> I am either maid or else this old man's wife. (5.3.290–94)

The exasperated King cries out, "She does abuse our ears. To prison
with her!" The audience may well feel sympathetic to him. Diana does
indeed spin out the scene. Harold S. Wilson explains why:

> The whole thing has been obviously contrived; but we have been al-
> lowed to see enough of the contrivance, in Helena's earlier prediction:

> . . . You, Diana,
> Under my poor instruction yet must suffer
> Something in my behalf;

> and in our knowledge that Diana's petition really comes from Helena, to realize that Diana is acting on Helena's behalf. This is all the warrant we need for her conduct, and we can see its effect upon Bertram. But that Helena herself should bring this pressure to bear upon Bertram would be out of the question. Diana is a perfect substitute. (Wilson in Ornstein 1961, 53–54)

The explanation seems indisputable, if incomplete. Diana's drawing out of the last scene corresponds to the lengthy act-5 remarks by Touchstone about the seventh cause or Duke Vincentio's act-5 game-playing with his subjects. These serve the purposes of supporting realistic motives while heightening suspense: rather as the Duke obviously—to the audience—lures Lucio further into a trap and swells Isabella's gratitude to him as her savior.

Much as Touchstone gives Rosalind time to transform herself and makes his listeners impatient for her return, so Diana's testimony works on Bertram while it delays the confrontation between him and Helena. If Diana seems to pre-empt a larger role at the end than she is entitled to, that is because she prepares for Helena's last entrance *and* represents a figuration of Helena, as the name Diana and the opening scene's virginity theme, that goddess's province, tell us. Wilson catches this correspondence when he says Diana "is acting on Helena's behalf." If the play were a movie we might imagine her in any of her earlier scenes detaching herself corporeally from Helena, with that technique that goes back at least as far as the first Topper movie, but without turning transparent (like a spirit abandoning a corpse), because Diana must also exist as a role in her own right. Although Helena may never become an Everywoman, in places she does appear exalted, a character (given by the actress) who is not a folktale memory, as some critics would partially have her, but rather one who creates her own myth as she continues to exist, a conjuror, medical or tactical when she needs to be, her own matchmaker against all odds, who can create and disperse images of herself.

Partly because of Helena's resolve, partly because of her flexible tactics, *All's Well* may appear to suffer from a broken back. Snyder, in considering what might be its "right generic context" notes that some critics find "a disjunction between the miracle tale of the play's first part and the intrigue comedy of the second" (41, 40). It may be worth recalling that Euripides was and still is accused of such a dissociation of the two halves and the switch in direction of some of his plays. Between the play's realistic elements and its invocations of magic one can envision an earthbound Helena half-enviously watching a Helena who departs from her becoming a gentler version of that frantic pharmacist, the Medea of Euripides, as she flies away in triumph and in the chariot, not of the sun god but of the moon goddess.

Note

1. The tag, picked up by many scholars, is varied slightly in the title of what is otherwise a useful collection edited by Robert Ornstein, *Discussions of Shakespeare's Problem Comedies* (1961), which includes an essay by Boas on *Troilus and Cressida*.

2. *All's Well* is about 90 lines longer than *Measure for Measure* and about 95 lines longer than *Love's Labor's Lost*. But *The Winter's Tale*, which I treat as a comedy, though most editors place it, like *The Tempest*, under "romances," runs about 185 lines longer than *All's Well*.

3. One of the few protagonists in literature whose tenacity compares with Helena's is Florentino Ariza's in Gabriel García Márquez's *Love in the Time of Cholera*. Ariza waits more than fifty years for the opportunity to marry his beloved.

4. Most editions follow the English spelling, as here, from the 1623 Folio; others choose the French Roussillon. For one reason or another, various editors and critics prefer a single *s* or *l* or *i* and retain or reject the *u* from French.

5. Some writers even use *problematic* as a noun. Senator Arlen Specter of Pennsylvania once coined a neologism that is barely pronounceable, *problemsome*. The obverses of problem and problematic are brilliance and brilliant, accolades awarded when writers haven't quite decided what they are praising.

6. Abridged reprint in Signet Classic edition, ed. Barnet (1988, 189–201).

7. As an alternative interpretation of the opening scene and especially of Bertram's motives, Sheldon P. Zitner writes, "*All's Well* opens with a social thunderclap which has been muffled by the passage of social history. . . . The Countess is losing her son, not because in the ordinary course of the life of a peer he must go off to the kind of civil finishing school constituted by court attendance, but because his father has died. What adds to her grief at the loss of her husband is that the Countess is being treated as a non-mother, for purposes of law an un-person, and her son—foolish as she knows him to be— made a kind of artificial orphan . . . Bertram, too, in going mourns again his father's death because of its effect on his future: if only the old man had lived until Bertram was twenty-one! (Like Helena he overlays mourning with a more selfish reflexive grief.)" (Twayne's New Critical Introductions to Shakespeare: *All's Well That Ends Well* [1989, 45–46]). Despite Zitner's fondness for "problematic," his treatment of the play is helpful throughout.

JUSTICE

L ike the Woman vs. Man theme, justice (the ethical triumph of right over wrong) belongs to the very structure of comedy. Here I apply the word to deal with that favorite genre, the melodramatic trial, a genre prostituted in the performing media of this century by the courtroom setting and a tedious retailing and repetition of a few lines of evidence. ("So you did see the accused entering that house after midnight, as you and other witnesses have stated and restated?") The big scene in *The Merchant of Venice* does take place in a courtroom, the hero—almost unthinkable for the time—a woman as a prosecuting attorney and one who switches sides. *Measure for Measure*'s trial takes place out of doors, near the gates of Vienna, and is surely one of the strangest legal proceedings recorded in fact or fiction, when one "inside playwright" takes over as prosecuting and defending attorney, witness, judge, and, for a few minutes, defendant. *All's Well* too has some claim to consideration as a play about justice and, to prove it, concludes with a trial scene that, as in *Measure*, doles out twists and surprises.

The Merchant of Venice

The Merchant of Venice appears to have used up its main plot by the end of act 4. In this comedy, written in the mid-1590s, as was *Dream*, the final act dangles on a thin thread of suspense. Shylock's departure softens the action's dramatic pressure by wiping out the central conflict and thus the main plot. Some critics regard Bassanio's wooing of Portia and her wealth as the main plot; they would then take the rounding-out of the game with the rings in act 5 as the main plot's final convulsions. I read the Shylock-Antonio enmity, consummated in the trial sequence, as far weightier dramatically than the Bassanio-Portia romance, whose outcome is foretold in act 1 by Nerissa's and Portia's show of delight in Bassanio as a suitor (1.2.110–119).

As act 4 draws to a close the firestorm of the trial has burned itself out, leaving three subplots warm and waiting to be extinguished: the mischievous game by Portia and Nerissa with the rings, the fate of Antonio's argosies, and the union of Jessica and Lorenzo. The revenge drama, meanwhile, lingers in the minds of spectators and readers; it has easily overpowered the ups and downs of wooing. But the final wooing is what earns the play its place among the comedies.

As act 5 closes, memory rekindles the questions about the other acts, questions long asked. Is it necessary to force Shylock to renounce Judaism and turn Christian? Why make him so unbendingly cruel in trying to enforce the bond when, if he is a devout Jew, the tenets of Judaism forbid killing, maiming, or other willful injuring? (After the assassination of Yitzhak Rabin in Israel in November 1995, right-wing, purportedly religious groups in Israel sympathetic to the murder and the murderer claimed biblical and other justifications, which less rabid Hebrew scholars immediately refuted.) Did Shakespeare truckle to the bigotry of his audiences based on legend and outright lying? Few of

them could have seen, let alone known, a Jew since an unconverted
Jew could not *officially* reside in England from the end of the thirteenth century until halfway through the seventeenth; they would
have possibly encountered only *marranos*, who, like the Iberian *conver-
sos*, practiced Protestantism outwardly, Judaism in secret. The word
marrano, used by Inquisition zealots, means "swine." Did Shakespeare
then actively indulge Britons' passive distrust of strangers and outsiders for the sake of laughs, horror, applause? Was he biased against
Jews? (The term anti-Semitism did not, of course, exist in the 1590s.)
If Shakespeare lived up to how we would like to imagine him to have
been, an altruistic, broad-minded artist, even an equal-opportunity
creator of roles, why did he not adapt the material from his sources so
that the moneylender was, like the later Harpagon, no longer a Jew?[1]
Plays and tales had long circulated about rascally moneylenders who
practiced Christianity or some other faith or no faith (e.g., Munday's
Zelauto, 1580); and the murderous bond existed in other literatures
that date back to before the Christian era and are unconnected with
Judaism or any other religious affiliation. Whatever the author intended *The Merchant* to be, why should anyone outrage some segments
of the populace by performing it in these post-Holocaust years? Come
to that, why bend to its popularity and perform it even in a politically
correct version, with a gang of sinister Christians on one side and on
the other a sanitized Shylock who sports a white carnation in his but-
tonhole alongside a neat triangle of breast-pocket handkerchief, a
mensch who enunciates like a nobleman and has been embodied in
such a guise by, among others, Henry Irving, George Arliss, Laurence
Olivier, and Sydney Walker? May not any showing whatsoever—one
argument runs—incite Jew-haters and Jew-baiters and ignite other
muck-stirrers? Dan Isaac writes of a production that

> fully resolved the problem of the anti-Semitism implicit in
> Shakespeare's text. It was, I believe, the summer of 1966 at the
> Stockbridge Playhouse in the Berkshires, in a production directed by
> George Tabori—quite probably influenced by Peter Brook's *Marat/
> Sade*—that placed the entire action inside a German concentration
> camp, where *Merchant* was being performed by the Jewish inmates as
> entertainment for the SS officers. Viveca Lindfors portrayed a woman
> so empty and drained that she could bring no emotional affect to her
> performance of Portia, but only walk through the role as though she
> were the ghost of herself. Alvin Epstein performed Shylock wearing
> the stock trappings of the medieval stage Jew as demonic clown, a
> costume that included red wig and yellow nose. But when this Shy-
> lock is discovered to have a *real* knife in the courtroom scene—only
> *imagined* props were used by the imprisoned performers—the Nazi
> guards who nervously patrol the aisles of the theatre, rush the stage,

wrestle Shylock to the ground, and stab him to death with his own knife. Quickly, the potato-sack curtain is pulled across the stage. No fifth act of moonlight and music. No curtain call. The audience of summer vacationers in the Berkshires were left stunned and confused. And when they finally realized that the 'play' was over, they stumbled and groped their way out of the theatre. (1992, 352)

The stage history of this play and the parallel critical history consist of many similar tiltings and rapes of the text to explain, regret, or rectify its social and artistic defects and missed opportunities.

A person who ponders those questions about Shakespeare's and Shylock's motives will quite likely resent some lines spun off Shylock's tongue, most notably "How like a fawning publican he looks! I hate him for he is a Christian. . . . If I can catch him once upon the hip, I will feed fat the ancient grudge I bear him" (1.3.38–39, 43–44), and his words to his daughter, "I'll go in hate to feed upon The prodigal Christian" (2.5.15–16), and the self-excusing monologue that begins "Hath not a Jew eyes?" and ends with "I will better the instruction," at the heart of the play (3.1.50–69). These sentiments scorch his listeners' ears and have become more memorable, more characteristic of *The Merchant of Venice* than are any other speeches, even Portia's "quality of mercy" plea. To someone who looks askance on the play, the lines in the "Hath not a Jew eyes" speech seek to justify Shylock's hardly sane passion for revenge, to reek of a contemporary lawyer's reminder to a jury that his murderous client suffered a dreadful upbringing. The lines provide a rationale—but no justification. It's all very well for a Jew to protest the bigotry in society and deem it imitable, but society should not forget that this role is still a pound-of-flesh bargainer and, to any reader or spectator who harbors anti-Semitic feelings, a residual or potential Christ-killer. Among the countries of Western Europe, Britain has long had a comparatively large ration of anti-Semites; perhaps for this reason British directors and actors, not necessarily Jewish ones, like to use the play to flay the surreptitious and the open prejudice.

Members of the public who for personal or (if there is such a thing) impersonal causes dislike the play tend *not* to feel mollified when they see a staging with its emotions tempered and its impact softened by political and psychological "balancing," much less a version that heroifies Shylock. Such repairs and renovations strike them as attempts to defend an indefensible work and let Shakespeare off the hook. The opinions on both sides have grown so firmly irreducible at times that any production promoting strong convictions one way or the other will not escape censure.

If a role professes sentiments that a critic dislikes, while another role—or the same role—professes sentiments the critic approves of, for

that critic every argument in a play gets accounted a rift in the playwright's soul, or worse, hypocrisy, instead of its being a dramatic conflict for the stage. And if Shakespeare believed that one cannot escape
one's birth rank, why did he buy the title of gentleman for his retirement? If he frowned on bastards and other lower-class or classless
people, how did his daughter Susanna, who got herself born only six
months after his wedding, manage to remain a member of his family?
How did he contrive to create such plebeians as Bottom, Launce, the
twin Dromios, and Dogberry, who shine positively in the plays they
inhabit? If a speech in *Coriolanus* or *Julius Caesar* harps on the filth or
fickleness of the mob, the sentiments reflect the feelings of the role,
not necessarily the playwright's. In his famous, widely reprinted essay,
"Shylock," written in 1911, E. E. Stoll makes the unprovable assertion
that "Shakespeare, by temperament, was not a satirist," as if an artist
need be a satirist to detach his views from those of his creations.

In contrast to the indignant Stoll, MacCary warmly endorses
"Shakespeare's manipulation of plot and character," but Stoll would
surely not dissent from the first sentence of this citation from MacCary:

> Central to any interpretation of the play is "the Jewish question."
> Many critics have too readily accepted the historical solution to
> this,—that Elizabethans had a genuine prejudice against Jews and
> persecuted them without compunction. . . . I do not favor this kind
> of historical reading of a literary text: it tells us only how it was writ-
> ten, not how it must be read. I think in this particular case we must
> follow the lead of Jan Kott and read the horrors of our own times
> back into Shakespeare, appreciating all the while that these horrors
> are somehow predicted in Shakespeare's text. An issue in the play is
> certainly the use of the scapegoat, and one of the finest examples of
> Shakespeare's manipulation of plot and character is the exchange of
> places between Antonio and Shylock. It is historically the Jews' role
> to be whipped, excluded, and sacrificed, but Shakespeare—playing
> with the historical Jewishness of Jesus—makes Antonio, a rich,
> gentle Christian, assume that role. It is Jews who are traditionally
> circumcised, but Shakespeare threatens the Christian's flesh. It is
> Jews who were early forced into commerce because they could not
> own land, and their commercial practices gave rise to their general
> characterization as parsimonious and greedy, but Shakespeare shows
> us Christians finally learning to "fast bind, fast find." (1985, 160–61)

In saying that "Elizabethans had a genuine prejudice against Jews and
persecuted them without compunction," MacCary must be alluding to
Dr. Rodrigo Lopez, a professed Christian from a Sephardic family, who
had served as a physician to the Earl of Leicester and whose name has
survived in critical literature largely because of *The Merchant*. Lopez
was accused of poisoning Elizabeth I, and publicly hung, drawn, and

quartered in 1594, probably not long before *The Merchant* was written and produced. Apropos of his remark that "Shakespeare goes on to threaten the Christian's flesh," MacCary proceeds to quote Leslie Fiedler to the effect that "in Elizabethan minds circumcision was confused with both castration and cannibalism" (165). He also quotes from *The Genealogy of Morals*, II, 5, in which Nietzsche states that in Roman law "the creditor could inflict every kind of indignity and torture upon the body of the debtor; for example, cut from it as much as seemed commensurate with the size of the debt" (248). MacCary describes Shylock's seeking a pound of flesh as an attempted "castration of the heart" (1985, 167). Well, we could not return to an Elizabethan audience and conditions, even if we knew for sure what they were:[2] it is difficult enough to cope with the range of spectators' idealistic or ugly preconceptions that theater faces in our own days.

Before commenting on these critical reservations, I'd like to trace certain features in the dramatic structure and then the sequence of motives—especially Shylock's, but not only his. At the beginning, if we put aside figures like the Duke of Venice, the court officials in act 4, and some servants and bystanders without lines, the action selects three groupings of roles. The first consists of the Christians of Venice: Antonio, Salerio, Solanio, Bassanio, Gratiano, and Lorenzo.[3] We meet Antonio, the eponymous merchant, in his house (1.1), and the others as his visitors or in the Venetian outdoors. We have no notion of whether any of them other than Antonio have homes or businesses, and if not, what they do. It's a fair assumption that they belong to the idle rich or the idle middle. The only one with a title is Bassanio, a lord with debts, a member of the noble poor. Antonio, his kinsman, close friend, patron, and (a disputed assumption) lover, is a commoner, but his standing as a trader on the Rialto entitles him to the salutation *Signor*. These friends alert themselves to the tradings in Venice, that liveliest of ports in Renaissance Europe, with its labyrinthine form intercut by the canals and its labyrinthine commercial spirit. They patrol the business district, exchanging market gossip, if not information, so that they never fail to come up with a ready answer to Shylock's question (1.3.35–36), and later Solanio's (3.1.1): "What news on the Rialto?" Today they might, like the people constantly quoted on the business pages of our newspapers, associate with investment watchers and call themselves *analysts*. Antonio forms the nucleus of the group. The others respect him enough to sponge on him, but, with the exception of Bassanio, they do nothing on his behalf when his wealth appears suddenly to have disintegrated.

    Shylock, the adolescent Jessica, and the clown Launcelot Gobbo make up the second grouping and occupy Shylock's house, which may lie in a restricted area of Venice, a ghetto, although the play doesn't say so. Whatever its location, Shylock is house-proud; he *wishes* for segregation of sorts, an insulation from outside noises like the squealing of the fife during carnival and masques. He belongs to the synagogue congregation, and the play contains one hint only, apart from his suffocating ethnic pride, as to whether he or other Venetian Jews keep a kosher home. The text is not explicit on this point. The hint occurs when he declines to dine with Bassanio and Antonio (1.3.30–35). He says he objects to the *smell* of pork, suggesting that Christian food might be cooked in pork fat. He behaves at least as inconsistently as other roles in Shakespeare do, and remains atypical as a Jew, individualized.

Belmont houses the third grouping; here Portia, Nerissa, sundry servants—including Balthasar and Stephano—and the gold, silver, and lead caskets reside. Bassanio's rivals for the hand of Portia stop by in act 2 (Morocco) and act 3 (Arragon). Its name taken from one of Shakespeare's sources, it may be an island reachable only by boat or uncommonly strong swimmers: "I saw Bassanio under sail," says Salerio, after the indigent lord departs to try his luck with the caskets (2.8.1). Belmont's name, however, implies an idyllic setting in the alpine foothills, north of Padua, where Doctor Bellario dwells—the lawyer, Portia's mentor, cousin, and benefactor. Portia and Nerissa must cover the twenty miles from Belmont to Padua in one day by coach (3.4.82–84). Accessible by traveling against the current of an imagined, wide, swift-flowing tributary of the Po, Belmont has some of the countrified characteristics of a green world, but it is not as blessed and does not promote transformations, except of Bassanio, who becomes suddenly intelligent and sensitive when confronting the caskets.

By the last act a certain amount of shifting and shuffling between the groups has taken place. Gobbo has gone over to Bassanio, who has gone over to Portia, together with Gratiano. The latter, being a parasite, may secure quarters in the Belmont mansion to share with Nerissa, if Portia still requires the services of a female companion after marriage, as she probably will do for dressing. Jessica and Lorenzo are also domiciled in the mansion for the time being, while waiting for Shylock to die so that they can take over his "sober house" and other property in Venice. Antonio will shortly recover his wealth. Although twice welcomed by Portia's mouth he will probably not be asked to stay on as a perpetual guest, a prospect that would, in any case, pain him. By the time the action ends, act 5 has subsumed three marital pairings and several partings; it has also shifted the tone of the action from the initial fretfulness of Antonio (1.1) and Portia (1.2) to a less than blissful shift of the Belmont population into the mansion to take part in "inter'gatories" and explanations. In production we generally see Antonio standing on his own, once again sad, either abandoned when the others go inside or separated by his own choice. Jessica, who has said not long before, "I am never merry when I hear sweet music" (5.1.69), looks in the dumps as she probably wonders, like Portia, whether she has tied herself to a mercenary playboy. But dumps and doubts mean less than the three pairings as conventional signs of fertility, as well as the legal and financial salvaging of Antonio, and confirmation of Shylock's defeat. These fix the play in the comic column.

Nevertheless, this comedy has terminal melancholy. It results in part from Lorenzo's dreamy, philosophical, and astronomical mood. He tries in vain to get Jessica to share it as he compares the two of them with great lovers of the past. In part it comes from Jessica's determined undercutting of him, claiming he's already unfaithful as, "like a little shrow," she continues to "slander her love," as he puts it. Critics who find the tenseness between Jessica and Lorenzo fond teasing or banter choose to read against the grain of the lines. Further sadness flows out of Antonio; he can see that Bassanio's capture of Portia means he must give up his beloved, his "heart," even though he has retained the pound of flesh surrounding the other, anatomical heart. After he has sworn, "I dare be bound again, My soul upon the forfeit, that your lord Will nevermore break faith advisedly" (5.1.252–53), Portia hands him the ring, saying, "Then you shall be his surety. Give him this, And bid him keep it better than the other" (254–55).

As soon as Antonio has taken that oath to remove himself as Portia's rival, she produces an envelope by way of reward. It contains the good news about his argosies, although she informs him, "You shall not know by what strange accident I chancèd on this letter" (278–79). Her words could be construed as Shakespeare's attempt at a less strenuous wrap-up of the comedy—but they proceed from one of the two principal roles and must be given their due weight. They amount to a concessive compensation for his acceptance of the loss of Bassanio on the part of the man Portia has called "the bosom lover of my lord" (3.4.17), whatever that meant in Elizabethan English. Even if Antonio trips offstage exuberantly, against his wont, and Jessica decides on reflection that Lorenzo and she have a fated union, and Portia reassures herself because Bassanio is at least good-looking, and Bassanio feels virtuous at having offered Portia's money to redeem Antonio from debt and death, we still have a jocular but slightly nasty last line from Gratiano. In act 1 he had proclaimed, in challenging Antonio's sadness,

> Let me play the fool.
> With mirth and laughter let old wrinkles come,
> And let my liver rather heat with wine
> Than my heart cool with mortifying groans. (1.1.79–82)

In his and the play's last couplet, the replacement for an epilogue, he remarks, "Well, while I live I'll fear no other thing So sore as keeping safe Nerissa's ring," a resolution in which *fear, sore, safe,* and *ring* have to protect his marriage while they equally protect his wife from his cuckoldry. (And "sore" hints at a vulgarity.) Does he stay on stage and in thought after the others have gone in? Is he, even figuratively, biting his nails?

But the mood of mist that invades act 5's celebration arises overwhelmingly from the absence of the most vivid role in the play. With Shylock gone, the temperature of the action has slid dramatically down the scale, despite the mouth-delighting, ear-relishing word-music written for this rounding-off of the subplots. An air of unease, the need for resolution, hangs over the Belmont exterior. At times during this final act it sharpens into rage and spite, especially before the clinching of the "rings" episode. Portia devised the deception to test Bassanio; he failed the test by giving the ring to the "young and learnèd doctor" called Balthasar, a name she borrowed from a servant. When he shows her his ring-bereft finger, she exclaims, "Even so void is your false heart of truth." Kenneth Myrick reads this brutal line as a joking remark, as part of "the women's harmless teasing of the men" (1965, xxxviii). And no doubt an actor could exert every milligram of her charm in delivering the line so that she appeared to be more entertained than chagrined by the feelings that prompted it. But she would be faking, theatricalizing an untruth: in life such an accusation, however gracefully spoken, could be received cheerfully only by a proud deceiver or an idiot. This final act sends out bleak signals. The action has escaped from Venice, its commerce, and its law to bask in the magical realm of Belmont, where a rich monarch oracularly, if posthumously, awards his daughter the princess the poverty-stricken, leadstruck contender whom she desires and will be able to govern with her hereditary wealth. But the enchanting precincts of Belmont in act 5 dimly reflect the fury and disappointments of the earlier acts.

For no matter how devoutly we believe that the play was originally looked on and classified as a comedy, and no matter how generously we define words like *comedy* and *comic,* this play cannot take on and sustain an upbeat tone in performance without becoming distorted. A "comedy," technically speaking, has felt out and then overlapped the limits of the genre. Compare the two big "choice" scenes, Bassanio's selection of the lead casket to which he is "led" by a soothing background song and the trial that takes up almost the entire act 4: the morality implicit in the latter makes the moralizing in the former look trivial. The astute painting of the casket scene by Frederick Barth, which once hung, and possibly still does, in London's National Gallery, has a swooning, lyrical look to it, although a pink-gowned Portia with tresses of pure gold has a hand to her mouth to denote anxiety. Precisely the second half of act 4 (before the rings intervene) and the whole of act 5 comprise the play's dominant innovation: comedy that is heart-breaking without sliding into sentimentality. In her pioneering treatment of the changing interpretations of Shylock, Toby Lelyveld writes:

> It is largely a matter of guesswork as to whether it was Richard Burbage or Will Kempe who first played Shylock. There are ample grounds for suspecting that either actor could have played the role to the complete satisfaction of an Elizabethan audience. But since Kempe played comedy, and there is no evidence that Shylock was played as a comic character in Shakespeare's day, the probability is considerable that Burbage played the part. Whether or not Shylock was played seriously, there can be no doubt that whoever essayed the role gave it the unsympathetic reading that the sixteenth-century playgoer had come to expect. (1961, 7)

The comic mode of playing may validly return to this play, if ever, only well after this half of this century, in some distant future that has no record of the world's goings-on—at a time when the religions of the past two thousand years and their warring sects have expired. What happens in the action to Shylock bears no comparison with the Holocaust and can hardly be looked on as a symbol of it, a minimal metonym. All the same, by taking Shylock all the way to the brink of a disgusting, literally disheartening murder, and immediately after, ruining him with the loss of his daughter, savings, religion, and shaky standing in the community, Shakespeare composed a sub-tragedy that overwhelms the comic roundup in act 5. Shylock brings a tragic disaster on himself to an extent by his tenacious greed for revenge apparently legalized by the bond. The outcome is also partly tragic for Antonio, who grants Bassanio the loan in conditions of self-endangerment.

Because the sub-tragic tone disturbs an audience much more than do the endings of the other comedies, in which young rednecks, opportunists, and simpletons take home sensitive women, this is the most freighted of the plays in the comic canon. I am contending that if the texts of the play today, with their minor variations, correspond closely to the one Shakespeare wrote, Shylock can never have been either a purely melodramatic villain like the medieval Vice on stage, as is sometimes claimed; nor can he have looked convincing as a figure of fun—and especially not as a clown—except by distortion. We can compare him with a Pantalone, the predecessor whom, as a Venetian resident and a tightwad of a businessman, he slightly resembles. But the plotting, the spate of Venetian encounters, does unfold plentiful melodrama and that in turn provides a series of clues to enacting and responding to Shylock, because, as I have suggested, he is responsible for his own downfall, if *only to an extent*. Retrospectively, seen from the end of act 4, the villain has all the time been a victim.

The first decision in the main plot, to borrow, falls to Bassanio, when he tells his dear friend ("O my Antonio") he needs "to get clear of all the debts I owe" (1.1.34) and Antonio assures him that "My purse, my person, my extremest means Lie all unlocked to your occasions" (1.1.138–39). Unluckily, "all my fortunes are at sea. . . . Therefore go forth. Try what my credit can in Venice do" (177; 179–80). It may be that Bassanio tries every other moneylender on the Rialto before approaching Shylock; if not, he can be considered an imbecile for not reckoning with Antonio's hatred, which, as Antonio's intimate—or even if he had been only a member of the outer circle—he must have heard repeatedly expressed. The hatred inevitably would be reciprocated:

SHYLOCK [Antonio] hates our sacred nation, and he rails
Even there where merchants most do congregate,
On me, my bargains, and my well-won thrift
Which he calls interest. (1.3.45–48)

Bassanio goes to, or ends up with, the worst creditor he could have picked, and it is astonishing that Antonio assents to this particular loan. Astonishing but therefore dramatic—as we remind ourselves when we psychologize about a role, it does not choose to arrive at decisions: it is chosen. Shakespeare has to open the action somewhere; Bassanio and his plight provide a tensile springboard. To Shylock, the normally modest-mannered Antonio looks "like a fawning publican," but now, as their initial encounter in the action gets under way, Shylock reminds himself that he hates the man, first for being a Christian, and second for lowering "the rate of usance" in Venice. Then follows the couplet that starts to shift the initiative from the borrower and his guarantor to the lender—about catching Antonio once upon the hip and "feed[ing] fat the ancient grudge." But the big (and naturally, insoluble) dilemma of the play forces us to ask: If Shylock's malice aforethought did extend to a determination to murder Antonio legally, how could he know that all Antonio's argosies would vanish—for long enough to allow his claim to Antonio's flesh? Is this anything more than a wish he expects to be granted as if by magic? As he says, "Antonio is a good man," meaning "sufficient," but though "there be land rats and water rats and water thieves and land thieves" (1.3.12, 17, 22–23), Antonio's loss of everything within the appointed three months would be too much to hope for, unless Shylock, like a number of critics, believes he is living a fairy tale.

As we learn in retrospect, the wish came true only temporarily. At the point in the play when the loan is agreed upon, it may be enough for Shylock that he has some (admittedly theoretical) power over his tormentor and has forced the latter to come to him so that he, Shylock, becomes the benefactor of the usury Antonio has often condemned. If

Shylock does not marvelously foresee that Antonio might be wiped out, another possibility offers itself: that these Christians might accept him as an equal. Does the play slip into irony or lies? He urges:

> I would be friends with you and have your love,
> Forget the shames that you have stained me with,
> Supply your present wants, and take no doit
> Of usance for my moneys, and you'll not hear me.
> This is kind I offer. (1.3.136–40)

Bassanio admits, "This were kind," and then Antonio, Shylock's most zealous reviler and saboteur of his trade, bids him good-bye with, "Hie thee, gentle [gentile?] Jew." Irony seems out of place, although the scene ends with Antonio mollified and Bassanio suspicious, a swapping of attitudes.

ANTONIO The Hebrew will turn Christian; he grows kind.

BASSANIO I like not fair terms and a villain's mind.

ANTONIO Come on. In this there can be no dismay;
My ships come home a month before the day. (1.3.177–80)

Later, in the trial scene, Shylock will say he took an oath to heaven to have the pound of flesh, but I contend that in the scene in which the three men strike the bargain, Shylock's friendliness and Antonio's satisfaction should register at face value, for the sake of dramatic impact.

One can trace the birth and growth of Shylock's revenge motive in the action by examining the sequence of events that follows this scene and leads up to the trial. Bassanio invites Shylock to dine. He declines. Whether he does so openly is a matter of interpretation. Most twentieth-century editors read Shylock's speech at l.3.31–35 (including the words, "but I will not eat with you, drink with you, nor pray with you") as a direct retort; but some view the speech as an aside, up to "What news on the Rialto?" (35–36), on the grounds that Shylock, despite his grudges, would not speak aloud bluntly enough to sabotage the deal. But once the bond has been agreed upon, he accepts with distaste, telling Jessica that he will "go in hate, to feed upon the prodigal Christian" (2.6.15–16)—in other words, at the expense of the impecunious nobleman who is possibly using Shylock's money to pay for the dinner. That night there will also be a masque. But in the evening Antonio tells Gratiano, "No masque tonight. The wind is come about; Bassanio presently will go aboard" (2.6.65–66). Since the host is leaving aboard a boat, the dinner, like the masque, must be called off. But who tells Shylock? When he returns home unfed, in the story, not the action, his daughter and savings are gone. Lorenzo has stolen Jessica, who in her turn has stolen not just a cash box but a reminiscence of the gold, silver, and lead receptacles at Belmont: a casket. The play doesn't specify that Antonio and Bassanio lured Shylock out of his house so that Lorenzo could plunder it. Lorenzo, however, is a known friend of theirs. Launcelot Gobbo, who doesn't shape up as anybody's ideal servant but must know the run of Shylock's house—when he enters and leaves—has just gone over to a new employer, Bassanio—grounds for suspicion.

Even if Antonio and Bassanio have nothing whatsoever to do with the double theft, Shylock, surveying the evidence, is bound to conclude that the invitation to leave his house fits together too neatly with the burglary, followed by the flight to Belmont of Bassanio (and Gratiano), to be the melodramatic coincidence it probably is. He might well construct his own scenario. He loaned them a large sum. The insolvent pair plotted to inveigle him from his home (out of what he might consider Christian gratitude—a sort of "Do anything that hurts a Jew"), while their accomplice robbed him of his treasures, of which they will now take their share: his daughter, who eloped with a Christian and will (at best) shamelessly "marry out," his gold ducats, and his two jewels. *But he has no proof.* And here we can trace one reason why, in the court sequence, he eludes an answer to the question put by the Duke, Portia, and others about his motives. Mark Van Doren writes:

> Nor is he disposed to justify his conduct by a show of reason. If he knows the language of reason he does not use it; if he knows his motives, he will not name them (in Wilders 1970, 97)

I argue here that he has reason to *feel* he knows his motives—that he wanted to be friendly, that the "friends" took ruthless advantage of him, and that he was entitled to revenge, whether or not he subscribed to the tenets of the Old Testament. Melodramatic coincidences and misunderstandings of this sort crowd the historical landscape of international drama.

But what about Shylock's indisputable, inhumane parsimony? He himself does not speak the cry usually ascribed to him, "My daughter and my ducats" or "My ducats and my daughter," the latter supposed to mock his priorities. It comes from a report by Solanio (2.8.12–22), who refers to Shylock as "the villain Jew," "the dog Jew" (in the same scene), and "the devil . . . in the likeness of a Jew" (3.1.19–21)." Shylock does say to Tubal, "I would my daughter were dead at my foot, and the jewels in her ear! Would she were hearsed at my foot, and the ducats in her coffin!" (3.1.83–85). The repetition of "at my foot" suggests not so much recovery of the stolen jewels and money as a desire for her death in preference to the further disgrace she will bring upon him and his faith. As for the two missing jewels, taken by some critics to be the equivalent of a castration, the loss of Shylock's "rocks," he seems less to want them back than to see them in Jessica's ear, an expunged memory, when she is buried.

Ellis Rabb's version of *The Merchant* converted the Vivian Beaumont stage into a sybaritic Venice of 1973, the year of the production. Rabb drew on Bassanio's and Antonio's "bosom love," as well as other hints in the play to portray the six Venetian Christians as a fellowship of gay men. They frolicked on and off a pleasure vessel anchored in the port of Venice. The 1970s were a time when directors discovered that many baffling situations in classics lost their ambiguity when boosted with a homosexual heave: the anguish of, say, Medea or Hedda Gabler or Vivie Warren was cleared up by making them lesbians. Rabb, however, could justifiably read into the action, without twisting the text, Portia's feeling of a rivalry with Antonio for the love of Bassanio. Her game with the rings, for example, displays a fear that her only hold on her new husband is her money. To Nerissa she says, "We shall have old swearing That they did give the rings away to men" (4.1.15–16); and in Rabb's production Portia, played with a memorable mixture of ferocity and winsomeness by Rosemary Harris, hit the word *men* unusually hard. Besides, Portia and Nerissa win the favors from the Venetians while dressed as men, just as Jessica, before she elopes, feels afraid that, if she holds a torch while in drag, she "should be obscured." Lorenzo, playing upon the word *should* as Shakespeare's roles occasionally do, replies, "So are you, sweet, Even in the lovely garnish of a boy" (2.6.45–46). Rabb, it seems to me, was on to something here. Antonio refers to himself as "a tainted wether of the flock" (4.1.114), and one might put varied constructions and misconstructions upon the words *tainted* and *wether*. The play does deal with what today we call gay-bashing, much as it deals with Jew-trashing. But the two prejudices are what the play *exposes,* among other matters, not what it supports, much less promotes. Despite the wealth of critical literature given over to descriptions of chaste friendship among men in Shakespeare's day and of friendship's superiority in Elizabethan minds to heterosexual love, the scenes between Antonio and Bassanio cannot help striking today's audiences as instances of homosexual affection and accepted as such by Portia and the Venetians. Antonio's standing in the mercantile community of Venice, as we see in the trial scene, improves his status as an accepted insider. Only at the end do the male antagonists, the outsiders, Jew and homosexual, moneylender and merchant, both Venetian citizens, resemble one another.

Like the stolen jewels, the stones, the word *rings* and the objects it signifies have long had a bawdy connotation: a woman's sexual organ or a man's anal opening or a woman's. Portia might well fear other women's charms less than loss of her husband to a male rival.

The Rabb production spiffed up Sydney Walker to a gloss under which Shylock looked unrecognizable, a certifiable Wall Street bigwig who goes home to a realtor's dream house on the Connecticut shoreline. This was not the first contemporary setting for the play, nor the first occasion on which Shylock was presented as a responsible, clean-living father of the girl next door. Shortly before, Jonathan Miller had tugged the play forward three centuries to the 1880s or thereabouts and into a prototype of a Pall Mall club, a male preserve from which the London Venetians in their swallow-tailed jackets snubbed Laurence Olivier's Shylock. Olivier sported a scholarly pince-nez, besides a formal getup as impeccable as the Savile Row outfits of the others, those stuffy Victorian Protestants. He acquired some curious, twanging vocal mannerisms, followed the pattern of an unfairly reviled Shylock set by Edmund Kean and Henry Irving, and overpowered the rest of the cast.[4] During his altercation with Salerio and Solanio, Olivier raged enough to send storm waves along the canals.

But his fervor had earlier been exceeded by the most unleashed Shylock I have seen, Frederick Valk's, as directed by Tyrone Guthrie at Stratford, Ontario, in the 1950s. A bear of a man with a roar of a voice; a gigantically proud citizen of the world who considered it an honor for others to secure loans from him, this Shylock scorned any effort to moderate his demands or accommodate himself to the Venetians. Unhampered by a mid-European accent, Valk smashed his way into Shakespeare's prose and verse, looking not at all apologetically soaped for easy general consumption.

Gratifying though it may be to witness a Shylock who incarnates all the finest qualities of a Jew, *of a human being*, differentiated from other good men only by the faith he was born into—a Dustin Hoffman in the West End and on Broadway, a Mike Nussbaum in Hartford, Connecticut, I find the distortion regrettable. Shylock, the last of the principal roles to enter the action, fluctuates in his desires, his will, his loquacity. At one moment he wants to turn himself into a divine sword of vengeance against his foe. Then he wants the tormentor to like him, act toward him in a friendly fashion, to admire him as "kind"—Hamlet might say, as "kin." Then he suspects Antonio of conspiring to rob him of daughter and wealth. Then he delights in the loss of Antonio's first cargo due home. Then, meeting Antonio in the street, escorted by a jailer, he behaves as though Antonio had willfully lost the argosy in order to swindle him (3.3). He is probably an intolerable father, like many fathers of daughters: too worried, too protective, too eager to lay out the course of her life for her, and too anxious that she uphold the faith. On the Rialto, in front of investors, other merchants, usurers, and hangers-around, Antonio has often "voided rheum" upon Shylock's gaberdine and beard and kicked him

like a dog (1.3)—charges Antonio confirms. Shylock bore the offenses "with a patient shrug, For sufferance is the badge of all our tribe"
(107–08). But no longer.

As is almost always the case, when we meet a role for the first
time in a play's action he or she is behaving abnormally, has turned
into a different role from the one before the action begins. Was he
ever a devil or, as Launcelot calls him, "a kind of devil" (2.2)? In this
play one or another devil is in many mouths. The one who springs
from Gobbo's during a soliloquy somehow corresponds to the Gobbo conscience, which pleads with him not to leave his master,
whereas "the fiend," the "devil himself," tempts Launcelot to run
away. But the play's clown is not the author's mouthpiece: if he
were, Launcelot himself could not be called (by Jessica) "a merry
devil" (2.3.2). And if "the fiend" or "the devil himself" is tempting
Launcelot to run away to Bassanio, while his conscience opposes the
devil's temptings, his musings are pretty mixed-up—as they are
probably intended to be; Halio compares the soliloquy with the self-
debates in a medieval morality play. In 1.3, when Shylock is retailing the story of Laban, Jacob, and "the woolly breeders," Antonio
exclaims, "Mark you this, Bassanio, The devil can cite Scripture for
his purpose" (95–96). In 3.1 Solanio, noting the arrival of Tubal, says,
"Here comes another of the tribe. A third cannot be matched, unless
the devil himself turn Jew" (73–74). Now, for the first time, Shylock
finds himself in a position to expostulate freely. He is needed; his capital is needed. He does not have to dress or speak to match the finery
or accent of anyone who, like Antonio, behaves as Shylock's enemy
and superior. The miracle of Shylock is that his protests pour out of
a man dressed in shabby, spat-upon gaberdine in an era well before
drycleaning. This does not require that he look dirty and repellent,
like the Shylock of Maurice Moskovich seventy-five years ago.
(Moskovich looks, by contrast, quite dapper as Mr. Jaeckel in Chaplin's *The Great Dictator.*) But the role's eloquence and conviction are
more astonishing because of their source. He disgorges them as if
they are propelled by the fervor of a rabbinical student steeped in the
Torah, Talmud, and Midrash, who has engaged in the same disputa-
tions as generations of Hebrew scholars. In the BBC TV version, directed by Jack Gold, Warren Mitchell bestowed on Shylock an East
European accent of the sort that became familiar to Britons after the
Polish and Russian pogroms and Hitler. A shabby little foreigner who
spoke in ripe Yiddish intonations, he offered a startling contrast to
the Antonio, John Franklyn-Robbins, a tall and distinguished Brit of
noble voice, garb, and mien. Mitchell offered a persuasive portrait of
a Jew in Britain today or yesterday—but the connection with Venice
went unheeded.

The drama of Shylock's role resides in his being a great polemicist whose mien gives no clue to his verbal skills but actually belies them. I argue this on the strength of Shakespeare's perennial theme: appearances deceive (in hate as in love). If directors and actors do justice to the false impression of Shylock, the trial scene will startle spectators even more than it normally does, for they will expect, after his humanitarian pleas in his own defense, that he will apply them to others, to Antonio—that he will reform by giving play to the mercy that Portia urges upon him. If, though, immediately after her mercy speech he tries to rush to judgment by gabbling, "My deeds upon my head! I crave the law, The penalty and forfeit of my bond" (4.1.204–05), he grows slight, predictable. Should we not see a moment of indecision before he answers—not to palliate his cruelty but to give him a chance to look for weaknesses in his case? He will not plunge forward like a chess player who cries "Checkmate!" as he ruins his game with a reckless move. Despite his wavering, Shylock remains true to his vindictive first impulses: he takes refuge in the oath he says he swore. Whereupon Portia teaches him a lesson—which I will shortly return to.

Shylock hoodwinks himself because he believes *he* is counter-teaching a lesson—to Antonio, and through Antonio to Venice, and through Venice to Christianity. "The villainy you teach me I will execute, and it shall go hard but I will better the instruction" (3.1.67–69). He will evade responsibility for his own conduct (note the word *you*, implying that everybody else is to blame), much as Caliban will do ("You taught me language, and my profit on't Is I know how to curse" [*Tempest*, 1.2.366–67],)—or as the singer insists in the famous old vaudeville song "The Curse of an Aching Heart": "You made me what I am today. I hope you're satisfied . . ." Or perhaps anticipating the Naturalists of the past century and a quarter in deducing good and bad conduct from social environments (effects I personally believe in), Shylock's spite has grown so ingrained that it has rotted his moral fiber.

But his is far from being the only embittered role. When we look at one dominant feature of the dialogue, we cannot help noticing that in scene after scene the roles engage in baiting or teasing one another. And the succession of "needle points" in the action takes the place of more obvious and less malicious comedy: an additional reason why, apart from some structural resemblances to other, more clearcut comedies, *The Merchant* seems hardly comic at all in its texture, only in its ambiguous close.

In the first of these scenes Salerio and Solanio mock Antonio as they review some likely causes of his sadness. Next, Nerissa and Portia mock the impudence of her suitors in daring to compete for her hand (1.2); in the Jonathan Miller production, they scoffed at lantern slide portraits. Shylock provokes Bassanio with his exasperating, noncommittal "Well," as he affects a deliberative manner, inciting Bassanio to ask bluntly, "May you stead me? Will you pleasure me? Shall I know your answer?" (1.3.7–8); and in the same scene Shylock, reminding Antonio of his past contempt, asks sarcastically, "Should I not say, 'Hath a dog money? Is it possible A cur can lend three thousand ducats?'" (118–19). Two scenes later, Old Gobbo holds back until his son has completed his big number, his soliloquy, before entering to ask for directions to "master Jew's," where he can locate that same son, who points out to the audience that "this is my true begotten father, who, being more than sand blind, high gravel blind, Knows me not" (2.2.32-35). He proceeds to torture the old man by telling him that "the very staff" of his age," the "very prop" of his life, has gone to heaven.

Scene 3.1 splits into two parts; in the first Salerio and Solanio taunt Shylock with the loss of his daughter and ducats; in the second part Tubal arrives just before the Christians go and puts Shylock on a stock-market graph—alternately into high delight as he recounts Antonio's probable losses and then into the doldrums as he reports on the absent Jessica's spendthrift behavior with Shylock's money and precious stones—this probably constitutes the first alternation of "the good news is . . . and the bad news is . . ." Launcelot, Jessica, and Lorenzo bandy words in 3.5 that seem like the sort of thrusts and parries exchanged between Berowne and Rosaline or Beatrice and Benedick; they have spiteful edges, especially the question of whether Launcelot has got a black woman in the household pregnant: in production, as a rule these lines are either cut or spoken with a chop-chop delivery and much false laughter that renders them unintelligible.

The entire fourth act, taken up with the trial, presents Shylock juggling with the feelings of the onlookers who cannot understand why the venerated Antonio should be so misused. But Antonio goes on to revile Shylock (lines 70 ff.), after which Portia toys with Shylock, telling him, apropos of the pound of flesh, that "the court awards it, and the law doth give it," and then that "the law allows it, and the court awards it" . . . until, with Shylock's cutting implement—sometimes a huge axelike knife—poised inches from Antonio's chest, she commands, "Tarry a little; there is something else . . ."

A second "tarry" command from Portia flatly contradicts an earlier statement, which no one else in the courtroom appears to notice. In introducing herself to Shylock, she says,

> Of a strange nature is the suit you follow,
> Yet in such rule that the Venetian law
> Cannot impugn you as you do proceed. (4.1.175–77)

Yet after "Tarry, Jew," by which time Shylock sees himself trapped by lack of permission to shed blood, she says,

> The law hath yet another hold on you.
> It is enacted in the laws of Venice,
> If it be proved against an alien,
> That by direct or indirect attempts
> He seek the life of any citizen,
> The party 'gainst the which he doth contrive
> Shall seize one half his goods; the other half
> Comes to the privy coffer of the state
> And the offender's life lies at the mercy
> Of the Duke only, 'gainst all other voice. (345–54)

By encouraging Shylock to go ahead with what she confirms as a legitimate case, Portia hides the penalty: half his property and the chance of capital punishment.

The spite and needling continue. Once she has turned the tables on Shylock, Gratiano hits him repeatedly with Shylock's own boomeranging words of praise for Portia, "a learnèd judge" and "a Daniel." The second time she tells Shylock to tarry, as he is about to leave, she reveals the law's other hold on him, forfeiture of his possessions. Only the Duke's mercy lies between him and execution. We go forward to Portia and Nerissa, in their legal outfits, as they implore their husbands to part with the rings and, in the following act, berate them for doing so. In that final act, Jessica and Lorenzo exchange their "in such a night" sentiments, summoning the ghosts of celebrated pairs of lovers, all of whom came to disastrous ends, and concluding with their own.

> JESSICA . . . In such a night
> Did young Lorenzo swear he loved her well,
> Stealing her soul with many vows of faith,
> And ne'er a true one. (5.1.17–20)

As this act proceeds, Portia contrives in the most innocent manner to induce Antonio to swear he will withdraw from Bassanio's life and, like an elementary schoolteacher, she gives him a "gold star" for good conduct by passing along the letter with the cheerful tidings about his argosies.

If it appears from this rundown of needling that Portia lets drip more spite than anyone else in the plotting, we can remember that she in her turn has been subjected to the spite of her dead father who set up a situation in which every suitor's attempt at the three caskets puts her too on trial. Portia can be cutting (or worse) and also insincere. When Morocco asks her not to mislike him for his complexion, she reassures him that, were it not for her father's denial of "the right of voluntary choosing . . . Yourself, renownèd Prince, then stood as fair As any comer I have looked on yet For my affection" (2.1.1, 16, 20–22), *fair* being the operative pun here. After he unlocks the golden casket and finds "a carrion death" and the advice that "all that glisters is not gold," Portia tells Nerissa, "Let all of his complexion choose me so" (2.7.79). More than one editor defends Portia from the charge of racism by noting that "complexion" refers to sensibility, not only to skin color; they may be right, but they forget, perhaps, Morocco's introductory line about not misliking him for his complexion.

The masks Portia wears, moment by moment, reveal her as one of Shakespeare's shrewder heroines whom a spectator ought to pity for their poor taste in husbands. But before putting Portia through the tests devised for her swains, her father evidently felt she was more than able to take care of herself. Perhaps one grows disappointed in this youngish woman with the wondrous virtues to which Bassanio pays tribute (1.1.163), virtues fleshed out by her beauty and gilded by her wealth, the "golden fleece"—because in the trial scene especially we expect a figure who rises above ordinary virtues and her evident high order of intelligence in dealing with Shylock, who goes down into the depths of cruelty. Despite her oratorical skills, she only punishes him; she does not persuade him.

Granville Barker, in signaling the multiplicity of her role, says that

> the figure built up for us of the heiress and great lady of Belmont is seen to be a mere child, too, who lives remote in her enchanted world. Set beside this the Portia of resource and command, who sends Bassanio post haste to his friend, and beside that the schoolgirl laughing with Nerissa over the trick they are to play on their new lords and masters. Know them all for one Portia, a wise and gallant spirit so virginally enshrined; and we see to what profit Shakespeare turned his disabilities. There is, in this play, a twofold artistry in the achievement. Unlikelihood of plot redeemed by veracity of character; while the artifice of the medium, the verse and its convention, and the stylized acting of boy as woman, re-reconciles us to the fantasy of the plot. (1995)

Barker's preface serves as a salutary reminder that the play can be regarded as a "fairy tale"—at least in part. I am unsure whether Barker means us to regard Portia as actually young—which I assume she is not—to be an international love prize, even if played by a boy, or that a "second" girlishness comes bubbling back on occasion to her late-twenty-something surface.

In my view Portia and Nerissa have been waiting around for years for Lord Right and Mr. Right Servant to rescue them from the casket curse. The attribution of fantasy to the text becomes desirable if we are not to look too closely at the casket inscriptions. The gold and silver make literal sense if we apply them to Portia and the suitors, Morocco or Aragon: "Who chooseth me shall get what many men desire" and "Who chooseth me shall get as much as he deserves" (2.7.5 and 7); but the lead teaser, "Who chooseth me must give and hazard all he

hath," makes no sense vis-à-vis Portia and Bassanio, for this impecunious wooer gives and hazards only what Antonio "hath." He will be
a kept man, but he will promote his wife into nobility by way of compensation. Selecting the lead casket shows him to have a weak talent
for discrimination. Since he makes what is logically the wrong choice,
higher powers must have intervened: God, Portia's parent (the other
heavenly father), fluke, or a magic spell induced by listening to the
incidental music about the origin of "fancy."

The Merchant of Venice has repeatedly been called a play about love
versus money or justice versus mercy. In certain limited respects, it is
both. But money is a technical dramatic device. Shylock refuses triple
the repayment of the debt when he thinks he is winning the case. This,
like Hamlet, is a revenge play. Shylock doesn't care after a time what
name the revenge will get him among the Christians. He has faced
abuse too often in the past. But the thirst for revenge goes out of control when he mistakenly thinks that Antonio conspires to rob him of
the three things that uphold his identity: his usury (the one occupation
open to him, and that by default), his only child, and his religion. A
Jew, segregated and despised in Italy or anywhere else, could put only
one meaning on a child who marries out: she betrays what he has
taught and what he learned, as well as the future of Jewry. At the end,
as if to make the pill he must swallow all the more bitter, Antonio, the
Venetian who grants him the favor of restoring half his wealth until he
dies, concedes the allowance only for so long as Shylock reneges on his
religious beliefs. His renunciation, the ultimate degradation, is necessary to the play: it demonstrates the cruelty that underlies the poor
quality of mercy granted by the law and, by implication, the community. Thus, the nearest approach to magnanimity comes from Antonio,
who asks "to quit the fine for one half of his goods"—but almost immediately compromises the gesture by the proviso "that for this favor He
presently become a Christian" (4.1.379, 385).

The fifth act, that dropping away, tells us that the Christians have
nearly everything going for them in the end. Bassanio, after investing
his own and Antonio's money on the Belmont gamble, is punished by
marrying a rich heiress. Antonio may lose Bassanio, but he gains three
of his ships back, by the grace of Portia, the weather, and luck. Portia
and Nerissa have, for the moment, tamed two degrees of fortune hunters, aristocrat and commoner. The future of Jessica and Lorenzo, even
under a sunset, doesn't look rosy. Still, they will inherit Shylock's
house (in the ghetto?) and his money; meanwhile, they already occupy a wing of the Belmont home. Shylock, who had to amass his own
money by the only means available to him, other than becoming a rab-
bi (if rabbis were paid then), thought he had one sure prop to lean on,
the law. Then Portia teaches him a lesson as she snatches that prop out

from under him. She turns the familiar law against him and invokes a new law, a secret law that neither he nor the Venetian court was aware of. No wonder all he can say is, "I am content," and then, "I am not well" as he walks out of the courtroom and into history's insults.

Nobody can gainsay that the role of Shylock was and remains Jewish. But it is broader than Jewishness. One could argue in its favor that it might have helped to temper impressions left by that caricature, Barabas from Marlowe's *Jew of Malta*. But more than any of the multitudinous procession of Jewish roles that have followed, Shylock, as a central figure, turned *The Merchant* into a landmark play. Not all his successors proved as wise and compassionate as Lessing's Nathan, as pitiable as Chekhov's Anna Petrovna Ivanova (born Sarah Abramson), as romantically dippy as Shaw's Mendoza, as driven as Galsworthy's Ferdinand de Levis, as compassionate and wonder-struck as the families of Odets, or as oratorical as Chaplin's Jewish barber. By the second decade of the twentieth century, the floodgates had begun to open in Eastern Europe (and on New York's lower East Side). By the end of the century Jewish plays had entered repertories everywhere, but Shylock had continued to outgrow those later figurations, and himself. By now critical writings about *The Merchant* can no longer restrict themselves to disputes over Shylock's Jewishness: he has become the most powerful stage image of a human quarry, hounded by prejudices, who turns and tries to bite back.

Because the word *Shylock* has repeatedly served as an instrument for anti-Semites to wield, numbers of Jews and others have regretted, deplored, or condemned showings of the play; many continue to do so. For these well-meaning, protective souls, it matters little that the predecessors of this fictitious pound-of-flesh demander go back to a thousand or more years before Shylock and were gentiles. His literary birth, they insist, like Fagin's, does not excuse the author's part in giving Jew-baiters a name and faith to fasten to an image of a miser. But there is no reason to confuse Shylock with Fagin. Dickens created an unmistakably unflattering role: a criminal who makes no attempt to justify his trade or defend his religion.

But wouldn't anti-Semitism, like racism or sexism, exist without Shakespeare's help? Does it not rely on psychic fuel that drives certain temperaments—a combustible, varying mix that derives from such ingredients as envy, easily aroused rage, and yes, self-contempt? A leading question for a society that wishes to remain civilized has always been how intolerance can be subdued, or better, dissolved, rather than whether *The Merchant* should be banned or restricted to spectators who have passed a love-thy-neighbor test. Shylock, much as we may dislike his approximation of a personality when enacted, so long as it is not enshrouded in a benign disguise, is more true to life than the dramatist's

would-be censors give him credit for. For one thing, his speech, sometimes said (erroneously) to be Hebraic in its intonations and even more,
its repetitions, is, rather, Shakespeare's most successful attempt to find
polemic, even oratory, in relatively colloquial talk.

I claim that Shylock is Shakespeare's first successful plain rhetori-
cian, as opposed to a manipulator of rolling periods, because, unlike
his nearest rival in this respect, Mark Antony, he is not a politician;
nor is he a colloquial clown like Launcelot Gobbo or Bottom or the
Launce of *Two Gentlemen*. His speech about Jacob, Laban, and the
"streaked and pied" sheep (1.3.69–88) could serve as a model for our
financial sages who instruct the gullible, would-be "woolly breeders"
how to make the most of their savings. Jacob's profit-building incorporates both manufacturing and investment. Antonio's business consists of investment only but in its two successive phases, supplying
capital and taking risks. Shylock, even before the infamous deal with
Bassanio and Antonio, does practice usury. But so does every investor
these days, large or small, active or passive—as, say, a contributor to a
retirement fund. Antonio the benevolent lender could never survive
in a mercantile economy, especially not today's, if he opposed usury
under one of its euphemistic names like smart buying or selling, pac-
ing the market or staying ahead of its leaps, loops and other gyrations.
Today's Antonio can no longer afford to make loans gratis. He has lost
at least some of his scruples and haughty hatred, for he has melted
into today's Shylock; the merchant and usurer have joined forces.

But mercy on us all!—does a modern merchant-usurer claim a
pound of flesh?[5] Well, what else is a C.E.O up to when he hurls thousands upon thousands of pounds of flesh off the payroll and onto what
is left of the public purse? And bribes the firm's friends and doubles in
Federal and State legislatures to reduce that purse to its most shrunk-
en state? And combs the world's labor markets for the poorest, most
tractable, unprotected, and therefore most punishable workers? And
caps his soaring fortunes by basking in the applause from brokerage
"analysts" that sends his stock's prices to dizzying new heights?

Notes

1. The probable sources for the main plot and subplots cited in most scholarly editions of the plays are: a story from *Il Pecorone* (1558) by Giovanni
Fiorentino; *The Jew of Malta* (circa 1589) by Christopher Marlowe; "The Ballad
of Gernutus" and *The Jew*, two anonymous writings; *The Three Ladies of London*
(circa 1581) by Robert Wilson. A surprising quantity of the plot material
comes directly or indirectly from these sources. Shylock's forced conversion
does not. A number of writings compare the plot materials of these sources

with Shakespeare's reworking of them. For a summary see M. M. Mahood (1987, 1–8), or Jay L. Halio (World's Classics edition, (1993, 1994, 13–29).

2. James Shapiro has recently published a methodically researched book about Jews in Shakespeare's England, *Shakespeare and the Jews* (1996).

3. The name Salerino (Salerio with an inserted *n*) or Salarino, which crops up in a few editions and productions, sometimes for an additional role, sometimes as a composite of two roles, sometimes as a substitute for one of them, may have come into being from a printer's error or from the interference of an unidentified editor. See Dover Wilson's elucidation, (100–04), of what he called the three "Sallies," also Mahood's section on textual analysis (1987, 179–83), or Halio's (1994; 1962, 87).

4. The production, filmed for television, is on videotape. Besides Olivier, the cast includes Joan Plowright as Portia, Anthony Nicholls as Antonio, Jeremy Brett as Bassanio, and Michael Jayston as Gratiano. The acting is mostly of high caliber, despite a pair of campy caricatures of Morocco and Aragon, although the text is severely cut, omitting Launcelot Gobbo and his father. Among Olivier's vocal mannerisms are the omission of the *g*'s on the end of "ing" words, with a slapping emphasis on the now-final *n*, much as some of the titled figures practice "ing's" in P.G. Wodehouse, also some unorthodox pronunciations, such as *Bassaynio*. Other novelties in the production: a small, intimate courtroom for the trial scene, with no audience; but after Shylock is assisted offstage—he really does look "not well"—we hear him weeping. Outside, he lets out a howl like a wolf's: the noise stuns the Venetians left in the courtroom.

5. *"That for this favor, He presently become a Christian,* the Merchant of Venice insisted in his moment of victory over Shylock, showing only a limited understanding of the quality of mercy; and the Duke agreed, *He shall do this, or else I do recant The pardon that I late pronounced here . . ."* Thus Salman Rushdie in *The Moor's Last Sigh* (1995, 89). Rushdie's multistrand, international, interfaith novel keeps adverting to *The Merchant* and its roles; its references to the play show critically adept leaps of understanding. A few reviews and letters to sundry editors accused the author of being willfully anti-Semitic, a jab as misplaced as the charges against Shakespeare.

Measure for Measure

In the BBC television film, a faithful and lucid exposition of *Measure* directed by Desmond Davis and circulated in 1978, a highly charged moment supervenes almost at the end: the straightenings-out reach a dramatic high point as *character* suddenly parts from *role*. Duke Vincentio (Kenneth Colley) holds out his hand to Isabella (Kate Nelligan):

> I have a motion much imports your good,
> Whereto if you'll a willing ear incline,
> What's mine is yours and what is yours is mine. (5.1.546–48)

In the play Isabella conveys no answer—by word or movement. In the BBC version Nelligan waits for at least fifteen seconds before accepting his clasp. Clearly mistrustful, she cannot tell whether his curt but not-quite-explicit proposal of marriage amounts to another of his deceptions. He prefaces it with "Dear Isabel"—did he offer it in all sincerity?" Is she, for her part, ready to give up her novitiate and go secular? Does she want to marry at all? Can she accept him for a husband? And as a citizen of Vienna can she turn down its ruler? In the pioneering production directed in 1950 by Peter Brook at Stratford-upon-Avon, Barbara Jefford as Isabella took an even longer pause than Nelligan's at an earlier point in the text, as though sickened by the prospect of pleading for Angelo (John Gielgud) to be spared execution—but she went on to kneel to the Duke (Harry Andrews), because of Mariana's entreaty (5.1.451). If all the roles live at the mercy of the Duke, his character (and Isabella's fate) in any given production live at the mercy of the director because of the action's successive hairpin bends. As is often the way with Shakespeare's act 5s, the text favors a range of alternative readings for virtually every moment. John Barton, in his staging of the play in 1970, kept Isabella onstage at the end, after the

166

rest of the cast had trooped off. Did she feel rebellious? Uncertain? Had she refused the proposal, if it was a proposal? A 1996 production by Barry Kyle for the Theatre for a New Audience kept the closing moments ambivalent and respected Isabella's failure to respond vocally to the Duke's invitation by emptying the stage of everyone but the two actors and giving her (Jacqueline Kim) a lengthy pause, perhaps to take account of the moment's privacy, after which she walked pensively across to one of the two ornate chairs that served as thrones; seated herself; turned her head slowly to the Duke (Bill Camp), who had sat in the matching chair; and conferred on him a Mona Lisa smile. Enigma. Slow blackout.

The closing act has just emerged from a bewildering swirl of events. Having relied on the ducal guidance to extricate her from the treacheries of Angelo—Isabella said earlier, "I am directed by you" (4.3.136)—she hardly believes she can now take back possession of her own destiny and steer it. The middle acts of the play have passed like a nightmare: she may feel giddy from his gyrating instructions, as though a speeded-up Hitchcock merry-go-round she was riding on had braked to a hard halt.

The dramatic progression has grown so twisted, doubling back on itself, switching into reverse, overrun with entrances and exits—altogether a dreamlike dance—that she has ample reason to wait—and wait—before arriving at a wordless decision. If Duke Vincentio was a man and not a creature of the stage, he would heave a gasp of relief at having skated over a vast acreage of thin ice. The plotting—the playwright's disposition of the roles—has become more tortured than the climax of *Hamlet*. It is hard to say what those roles amount to any more. Analyzing them as psychological homogeneities by heaping together their conflicting characteristics and trying to unify them by means of a word, a sentence, even a paragraph, would prove unrewarding to actors and unconvincing to spectators.

This act 5 keeps turning on itself as though to rewrite the play. By my count some twenty contrary sequels crowd into it, almost all of them at the behest of the Duke. Shakespeare uses that role as an idea and a percussion instrument to dictate the cadences through a run of shape-changing events. Despite the advantage we enjoy from our lofty superiority over the roles, we feel no more sure than Isabella does of what precisely is going on: whether the Duke is serious or fooling, an angel of mercy or of murder. She undergoes ridicule from Angelo and from the Duke, who calls her a lunatic, a "fond wretch," and says she was "set on" by somebody to make her accusations against Angelo, who receives the opportunity to judge her and punish her as well to "your height of pleasure." The Duke then goes out on a casual exit line, "I for a while Will leave you," after he has ordered Escalus to question Friar Lodowick. Shortly after departing, he reappears under a cowl *as* Friar Lodowick and is, in his turn, ridiculed by Lucio, who keeps butting into the proceedings, tossing in his counterfeit ten groats' worth. The Duke uncowls himself. The trial turns against Angelo. Mariana begs that he be spared . . .

The action staggers forward with the gait of a helpless drunk. The Duke marries Angelo off to Mariana; condemns Angelo to death; pardons him after Isabella's plea; fires, then re-engages and promotes the Provost; threatens Lucio with a public whipping, then commutes the sentence when he marries Lucio off to the "punk" who has borne his child; thanks most of the roles on stage; murmurs his share-and-share-alike offer to Isaella, which goes unanswered in words. N. W. Bawcutt argues that the Duke's remark is not an offer of marriage but a promise of one, which does not *require* a reply (1994, 62–63). But as onstage drama it does call for a reaction; on film it cries out for a reaction shot of Isabella. The Duke concludes on a businesslike note as he suggests they all start out for the palace, where he will fill in the missing details, the bits of offstage story. He says nothing about formal or informal celebrating, nor does anybody speak an epilogue. Only the last two couplets of his speech, in rhyme, mark a scene ending.

With more than eight hundred lines to speak, Duke Vincentio has by far the longest role in Shakespeare's comedies (including the romances), markedly longer than those of Prospero, Leontes, or Rosalind, longer even than several of the large tragic roles (Lear, Timon, Antony, Coriolanus). And yet he remains a role of a thousand faces—of characterological overlaps that cancel each other out until he becomes a transparent figure, identifiable, if at all, only by reckoning up all the faces and phases. Critics have nonetheless persistently sought quick or summary identifications for him. He is providential, a god; he is diabolical, a tempter; he is a scourge, a torturer, a social conscience, an inspiration, a joker; he is a playwright within the play, a stage manager, a stunt man. Some of his preliminary announcements, instead of lending consistency to his late appearances, make him even more difficult to sum up. He says, for example,

> I will keep her [Isabella] ignorant of her good,
> To make her heavenly comforts of despair
> When it is least expected (4.3.109–11)

and so assures us that he will not mean it if he appears to treat her no better than a rag doll. But when an actor plays the later moments for all they are worth, as he should while condemning her, he makes his audience believe that he is not merely gainsaying his previous "comforts" but also abandoning his previous, honorable aims. In act 3, while he plays Friar Lodowick, he rebuts Lucio's gossip about affairs with women by saying, "I never heard the absent Duke much detected for women. He was not inclined that way" (3.2.118–19); but in act 5 he abruptly wants Isabella as his consort. Through the course of the action he behaves at one moment or another like a brute to all the other roles he talks to, including Escalus—and Isabella. In a good cause? Or in a selfish cause—say, for the sake of a game he wishes to play?

Can we accept this chameleon as the hero of a comedy? We do not even hear his age mentioned, unless we refer to a line of Lucio's that mentions "your beggar of fifty" and seems to allude to the Duke. After the Duke's words, "not inclined that way," the scene continues:

LUCIO O, sir, you are deceived.

DUKE 'Tis not possible.

LUCIO Who? Not the Duke? Yes, your beggar of fifty; and his use was to put a ducat in her clack-dish. (3.2.120–23)

It is Lucio, too, who calls Vincentio "the *old*, fantastical Duke of dark corners"—(italics added). It proves nothing, but the only other Vincentio in Shakespeare is an old man, the verbally abused father of Lucentio in *Shrew*.

Shakespeare has taken comedy's bridegroom-to-be to assorted limits of unsuitability. Afterward, he will scatter selections from the Duke's characteristics as a leading role into the new patterns of Leontes and Prospero. But we cannot help wondering about a comic ending in which only one of four marriages, impending or achieved (that of Julietta and Claudio), looks well-arranged, while the others look inauspicious: the ones between Isabella and the Duke; Lucio and his pregnant "punk" named Kate Keepdown; Mariana and Angelo, the man who failed to uphold a recognized marriage contract.[1]

Members of the public—academic critics, professional reviewers, and other lovers of theatre—often emerge from this play, whether read or performed, baffled by Duke Vincentio's instability as a role. They leave with stronger impressions of three other leading roles—Isabella, Angelo, and Lucio—as well as the farcical Pompey Bum and Elbow. The impressions are likely to have arisen from affection or distaste, which have at least as much to do with emotional predispositions of the impressed as with anything written into the roles themselves. Isabella can be summed up as a paragon, or as bloodless; Angelo as a different sort of paragon, rectitude gone rotten (as soon as sorely tested); Lucio as a prescient Shakespearean fool, a foppish slave to fashion, a witty liar. But when reconsidered, these roles each amount to bundled contradictions that also decline to fit themselves to I.D. tags. Over the five acts, in one scene or another, every principal role will become more than different, its own opposite, sometimes a plural number of its opposites. And the language: its halts and qualifying statements make the listener stop listening for a couple of seconds, trying to recast them and not always managing to. The skilled use of word stresses and the elegant choice of content for the lines enable them to lead independent lives as quotations—Isabella's famous "O, it is excellent To have a giant's strength, but it is tyrannous To use it like a giant" (2.2.112–14), or Lucio's attempt at dispelling resistance: "Our doubts are traitors, And makes us lose the good we oft might win By fearing to attempt" (1.4.77–79).

What happens to the Isabella who appears to Lucio at first like a vision of a saint in the raw, one of the rare examples of purity amid Vienna's stews, of which we hear much but witness little? Her halo remains firmly in position through her early scenes and is brightened, turned up a few kilowatts, by our indignation at Angelo's bargain. But even before the oscillations of her prison scene with Claudio, the halo quivers when she says to herself, "More than our brother is our chastity" (2.4.186); and it goes askew when she tells him she quakes,

> Lest thou a feverous life should entertain,
> And six or seven winters more respect,
> Than a perpetual honor. (3.1.74–76)

This reference to six or seven winters goes unnoticed by the editors I consulted, some of whom explain unnecessarily that "respect" means "value." After allowances for poetic licence, the line implies either that a youth of Claudio's age has, in noncriminal circumstances, what today's insurance carriers call a life expectancy of fewer than ten more years, or else that Isabella, in her rage, demeans the prospect of a full life by making it seem worth no more than a half a dozen additional years denuded of the more hospitable seasons. To some eyes, the halo vanishes altogether after Claudio begs, "Sweet sister, let me live" (135), whereupon she spits out vituperation at him and drops insinuations about their mother:

> O you beast!
> O faithless coward! O dishonest wretch!
> Wilt thou be made a man out of my vice?
> Is't not a kind of incest to take life
> From thine own sister's shame? What should I think?
> Heaven shield my mother played my father fair!
> For such a warpèd slip of wilderness
> Ne'er issued from his blood. Take my defiance,
> Die, perish! (138–46)

But having shown an obverse side of the role, Isabella will come to seem less prudish when she consents to take part in a plot enabling

Mariana to share Angelo's bed; and she cleanses a soul badly sullied by her outburst to her brother when she at last kneels to plead on Mariana's behalf for Angelo's pardon. Whether she altogether renovates her role's reputation depends, once again, on who is responding to the play or performance. Some people detest any woman (or any part) with a "chastity hangup." Others automatically suspect her motives.

A. P. Rossiter argues that in the prison scene she screams abuse at Claudio because she is fearful of being violated, as he is fearful of being executed (in Story 1961). The fear is not at all a bad motive for the actress. For the role it means introducing a consistency that the play doesn't support without strain. But events whirl past Isabella so tempestuously that the action itself remains hostile to her after no provocation on her part, threatening her sanity and eliciting from her, at her moments of partial self-control, at best a defensive and brave confusion. The final torture of Duke Vincentio's charges and twistings comes after not only the danger from which she yearns to free her brother honorably but also the trap Angelo has set.

ISABELLA I will proclaim thee, Angelo, look for't!
Sign me a present pardon for my brother,
Or with an outstretched throat I'll tell the world aloud
What man thou art.

ANGELO   Who will believe thee, Isabel?
My unsoiled name, the austereness of my life,
My vouch against you, and my place i' the state
Will so your accusation overweigh
That you shall stifle in your own report
And smell of calumny . . . (2.4.152–60)

To which she must despairingly agree: "To whom should I complain? Did I tell this, Who would believe me?" (172–73).

According to an Associated Press report datelined Aberdeen, Maryland, April 17, 1997, "A soldier testified today that after her drill sergeant raped her, he threatened to kill her if she told about it but boasted that nobody would believe her if she did." Art may imitate life, but life doesn't wholly imitate art. Life, though, sometimes *follows* art and works variations on it.

A role such as Angelo's, even before an actor's characterization fattens or diets it, serves more than adequately for stage mimicry of a personality. We call it *he* and *him*, just as we speak of the Isabella role as *she* and *her*, but Angelo need not evoke exact and recent or even worn and distant memories of a prim ruler we have known or known of; he need not add up to a plausible, psychological whole. Most of us have known of real rulers, and real non-rulers,whose personalities— as much as we can learn about them—do not amount to plausible wholes. The Angelo aspects in different scenes stretch toward new areas of plausibility. Thus, Angelo should not appear a hypocrite in the play's first scene or in his encounter with Elbow, Froth, and Pompey (2.1) or during the bulk of his first exchange with Isabella (2.2.6–146). Even in the substantial tail of that scene, especially in his closing monologue (169–94), we see him struggling with unaccustomed sensations and self-condemnation, because "Most dangerous Is that temptation that doth goad us on To sin in loving virtue" (188–90). Two scenes further on, he reminds us of Claudius at prayer and of "My words fly up, my thoughts remain below" (*Hamlet*, 3.3.97):

> When I would pray and think, I think and pray
> To several subjects. Heaven hath my empty words,
> Whilst my invention, hearing not my tongue,
> Anchors on Isabel. (2.4.1–4)

Presenting Angelo early on as innately venal is jumping the gun. At the end of the play, he has become its villain. Hardly anybody will spare any admiration for his former punctiliousness. Nor does he redeem himself when he asks to be executed.

But because he shifts his ground, as the other roles do, the middle segments of the action leave open to the performers and to the public the choices that shape the role's meanings in varied ways. How, for instance, did he behave when, in the story, he gave his order to go forward with Claudio's execution? We see only a messenger arrive with a paper (4.2.102–06). Do we take the order as treachery after he believes he has had his tryst with Isabella? Or does he confirm his original death sentence when his lawyer's conscience prompts in him a twinge of absolute justice? Does he hope to violate Isabella's vows, not only her body, to undermine her Christian zeal, which he envies? That is, does he hope to penetrate her spiritual armor, to degrade her so that she becomes a fitting subject for his attentions? Or is he excited by her coldness toward him, although he was unmoved, and still is, by the warmth of Mariana's love?

As for Claudio, he undergoes a turnaround as extreme as his sister's: he even seems responsible for hers. The section of the prison colloquy that leaves them in private (except for the Duke's eavesdropping in his Friar Lodowick cowl) calls for acting reciprocity of a most sensitive caliber; this is the opposite of a love scene: a quarrel building to a hate scene on her part and, on his, terror that pours out but then crystallizes into poetry. At first, he brushes aside her equivocations with terse questions and statements that express his determination to find out whether he can take advantage of any loophole in the law and his sentence: "Is there no remedy? (3.1.59) . . . But in what nature? (69) . . . Let me know the point" (72). So unwomaned is she by the possibility that Claudio will not make the ultimate sacrifice to preserve her chastity—how could he think it less precious than she does?—that she doesn't heed the urgency in his voice and goes on to misunderstand him. When he says, "If I must die, I will encounter darkness as a bride And hug it in mine arms" (83-85), he means only if he *must* die. But she hears a more elevated sentiment, because that is what she wants to hear: an assurance that he will die, if he must, to rescue her from the intolerable bargain. She forgets she has not yet made the terms of the bargain explicit. And so she answers him with one of her unintendedly most callous exclamations:

> There spake my brother! There my father's grave
> Did utter forth a voice. Yes, thou must die.
> Thou art too noble to conserve a life
> In base appliances. (86–89)

"There spake my brother!" could mean that Claudio lives up to their father's worth, but she did not say, "There spake my father's son!" She seems, rather, to mean that Claudio lives up to *her* worth—he is a legitimate brother, not in any sense a bastard. Not until she spells out the Angelo offer does he first recoil in shock, then weigh the bargain, then think of getting around it, then meditate on the awfulness of dying and its aftermath:

> This sensible warm motion to become
> A kneaded clod, and the delighted spirit
> To bathe in fiery floods, or to reside
> In thrilling region of thick-ribbèd ice . . . .
> The weariest and most loathèd worldly life
> That age, ache, penury, and imprisonment
> Can lay on nature is a paradise
> To what we fear of death. (121–24, 130–33)

After that she hardly grants him a chance to speak, even after he pleads, "Nay, hear me, Isabel" and "O hear me, Isabella!" (150, 154), whereupon the disguised Duke steps out of hiding. When she has left, he lies to Claudio:

> Angelo never had the purpose to corrupt her; only he hath made an assay of her virtue . . . She . . . hath made him that gracious denial which he is most glad to receive. I am confessor to Angelo and I know this to be true; therefore prepare yourself to death. (164–70)

At this point Claudio is unsettled, if not overcharged. Instead of wondering why Angelo didn't inform Isabella that he was "most glad to receive" her refusal and why he, Claudio, also had to endure a test, he regrets that he didn't realize (but how could he?) that the offer was a ploy; he could not have saved her even if he'd agreed to: "Let me ask my sister pardon. I am so out of love with life that I will sue to be rid of it" (173–74).

The scene has sucked him and Isabella through harrowing feelings, but it is not yet complete. As its coda, the Duke, having worked on Claudio, turns his attention to Isabella and instructs her how to play the bed trick so that Mariana may substitute for her in the darkness and sheets. Whether the plan appeals to her because it seems just or because it consists of revenge masquerading as justice, Isabella does take part, with thanks to the disguised Duke "for this comfort," in a plan based on out-of-wedlock sex, the "sin" for which she reprehended Claudio a few minutes before. She and her brother have each traveled across vast emotional ranges. In Davis's television version a beautiful moment in the prison had Isabella and Claudio, both kneeling and both dressed in white, faced at right angles, rather than at one another, so that their gazes crossed, rather than met at odds, as each evidently weighed his or her fate against the sibling's.

Comparable changes overtake three other prominent roles. Lucio, at first a mildly sarcastic friend to Claudio and a means of inducing Isabella to plead on behalf of the condemned man, turns into a gossipy meddler. In act 5 he supports Isabella again, then undercuts her by vilifying Friar Lodowick. He goes from being the play's mouth for high comedy to its only outlet for reciting the Duke's shortcomings—some of them imaginary, some difficult to overlook. Escalus, the smooth functionary trusted by the Duke and Angelo alike to take over responsible duties, turns into a perplexed pawn. Pompey, the pompous pimp, recasts himself with no evident strain as an associate hangman, but still among friends.

> I am as well acquainted here as I was in our house of profession. One would think it were Mistress Overdone's own house, for here be many of her old customers. (4.3.1–4)

Pompey, referred to in the First Folio as "Clown," is no word slouch like some of his clownish predecessors (from Costard to Bottom and, in this play, Elbow). He combines fastidious speech ("One would think" in the previous citation) with lower than low-class work. In the last two acts when Lucio abandons high-comedy to become the Duke's irritant, his full-time thorn in the glove, Pompey effortlessly fills the breach with grisly humor.

ABHORSON Sirrah, bring Barnadine hither.

POMPEY Master Barnadine! You must rise and be hanged, Master Barnadine!

ABHORSON What ho, Barnadine!

BARNADINE [*Within*] A pox o' your throats! Who makes that noise there? What are you?

POMPEY Your friends, sir, the hangman: You must be so good, sir, to rise and be put to death.

BARNADINE [*Within*] Away, you rogue, away! I am sleepy.

ABHORSON Tell him he must awake, and that quickly, too.

POMPEY Pray, Master Barnadine, awake till you are executed, and sleep afterwards. (4.3.20–33)

He predates today's informers and other professional malefactors bribed by police to join forces with the guardians of sacred law and order, making it hardly possible to differentiate between the criminal and the crime-buster. I am reminded of the lines of Joe Keller ("killer"?) in act 1 of *All My Sons*:

> When I got home from the penitentiary the kids got very interested in me. You know kids. I was [*Laughs*] like the expert on the jail situation. And as time passed they got it confused and . . . I ended up a detective. [*Laughs*.]

Critics, both those who admire *Measure* and those who reprove it, discuss the inconsistency of roles in this infinitely discussable drama more intently than any other aspect of the play, even more than morals that can be tasted to the tasters' spiritual profit. In 1874 Walter Pater found a "tendency to dwell on mixed motives" not only in the text but also in one of its sources, "Whetstone's old story." Do the Duke, Angelo, and Isabella in particular constitute an experiment in creating roles? Or are they, as Clifford Leech (1950, 66–73) speculates in a careful reading of the play, examples of Shakespeare's carelessness? Do their contradictions go back to the author's corrupt "foul papers," to insufficient time or little inclination to revise and unify? Is he indulging in deliberate mystification, not to say obfuscation? Although the last cause seems unlikely in a playwright who appears to write with a fine consciousness of likely audience reactions, the other causes appear too probable to be dismissed. If the strange ending hastily straightens out most plot complexities (the nature and motives of the roles), it does so by encouraging us to concentrate on textual complications, but these are not grave enough to compromise the play's overall integrity.

Integrity, not integration. Admiring writers awed by the work's comic and other ambitions may feel unable to reconcile them. Shakespeare has taken his experiments further than before. His mode of harsh or bitter comedy, capped by the forced, final matches, was not a new risk for him, only a more pronounced one than in, say, *Two Gentlemen, As You Like It, Twelfth Night*, and other, earlier plays.

As for this play's integrity, some critics have succeeded in integrating its elements, in finding, or inventing for it, a coherent vision. I will look briefly at three of these attempts: a morality defense by R. W. Chambers, Knight's making a Christian document of the play (the

Chambers and the Knight overlap on some theological-cum-ethical issues), and William Empson's view of it as almost wholly ironic.

Chambers takes issue with critics who, mostly in the interwar
years, found the play unnecessarily violent or cruel. He points out
how tempered it is in comparison with one source. Shakespeare

> treats [Whetstone's] barbarous old story of Promos and Cassandra
> [by] removing its morbid details, harmonizing its crudities, giving
> humanity and humor to its low characters, turning it into a consis-
> tent tale of intercession for sin, repentance from and forgiveness of
> crime. (1937)

Chambers vehemently justifies the behavior of the three principal
roles and the manner in which the author has plotted them. He concludes with Isabella's forgiving of Angelo and the introduction of Mariana to avoiding imposing the unsavory Angelo on his heroine in front
of the audience. While, for Chambers, the "Duke is shown to us as a
governor perplexed about justice, puzzled in his search for righteous-
ness, seeking above all things to know himself," Isabella "stands for
mercy" and her "marvelous and impassioned pleadings" are "unsur-
passed anywhere in Shakespeare." Her ordeal makes of the play

> an expression of "the greatest discovery ever made in the moral
> world" [a citation from A. E. Housman]: the highly unpleasant dis-
> covery that there are things more important, for oneself and for oth-
> ers, than avoiding death and pain.

Knight descries more than a generalized adherence to Christian
doctrines: "a clear relation between the play and the Gospels, for the
play's theme is [from Matthew] 'Judge not, that ye be not judged.'"

> The play tends towards allegory or symbolism . . . The persons of the
> play tend to illustrate certain human qualities chosen with careful
> reference to the main theme. Thus Isabella stands for sainted purity,
> Angelo for Pharisaical righteousness, the Duke for a psychologically
> sound and enlightened ethic. Lucio represents indecent wit, Pompey
> and Mistress Overdone professional immorality. Barnadine is hard-
> headed, criminal insensitiveness. (1930, 158)

In this synopsis Knight defines the roles as if they belonged not to a
play by Shakespeare but to a medieval morality, Everyman or The Castle of Perseverance. But after granting them an allegorical shading, actors
will see (and wish to perform) more in them than Knight's two- or
three-word descriptions imply. The play could undoubtedly be staged
like a morality, in a church setting[2] or a mock-up of one with disciplined, even formalized movement and speech; the stage effect might
prove static, as with Murder in the Cathedral, but if Knight is correct, the
result might offer a sacred interpretation that dissolved most or all of

the questions that arise. The drama would then become a sermon, not strictly to its disadvantage, for "the play must be read [*must* overstates the argument], not as a picture of normal human affairs, but as a parable, like the parables of Jesus." Knight's Christian interpretation has found acceptance among a number of probably predisposed critics; but although the play deals respectfully with Friar Thomas and Friar Peter, one can't help noticing that when the Duke puts on his friar's robe and turns into Father Lodowick, some of his more sententious speeches support some unintended self-derision, most conspicuous in his 43-line dose of cold comfort for condemned Claudio, beginning with "Be absolute for death" and ending with:

> What's yet in this
> That bears the name of life? Yet in this life
> Lie hid more thousand deaths; yet death we fear
> That makes these odds all even (3.1.1 and 38–41)

to which Claudio replies (a wickedly comical touch), "I humbly thank you." Neither self-abnegation nor the Church itself escapes mockery in this play.

Empson's chapter investigates meanings and ambiguities of the word "sense" as it appears and reappears in the play; but his explorations lead him to

> wonder what Shakespeare thought [of the roles he adapted from Whetstone], and whether he cannot sometimes be found grumbling to himself about the plots that he was using, in a way that the audience was not expected to notice.

Empson himself expresses unease with the behaviorism of some American critics of Shakespeare, which dictates that they should claim their work is "objective." If we give *objective* its full potential, to "wonder what Shakespeare thought about it" becomes a disgraceful self-indulgence: a critic should limit himself to rigid proofs, like the scientist that he is. Perhaps "social scientist," rather than "scientist" *tout court*, is what Empson means, especially at the time when he was writing, the late 1940s, when objectivity had become faddish and criticism sociological, a condition from which it has never recovered. At any rate, Shakespeare "was not in the mood to write comedies," but "the old real situation of the Sonnets, however irrelevant, was a source of energy"; and he saw

> the wicked deputy as one of the Cold People of Sonnet 94, the lilies that fester and smell worse than weeds; he christened him Angel; after that he found the plot interesting.

According to Empson, because Shakespeare did not give Claudio the chance to sacrifice himself for Isabella, as in the source, and denied him "so much dignity," Shakespeare has provided "good evidence that he found the behaviour of Claudio disgusting," while the Duke treats "his subjects as puppets for the fun of making them twitch" . . . Further, "Isabella turns out not to care a rap about Claudio." All in all, concludes Empson, "there was room for Shakespeare to put in mixed feelings of his own."

In this delicate strain, Empson ridicules the roles, suggesting that it was their author who willfully made them ridiculous, but for the benefit of only whoever had the acuity to perceive what he was up to, because he went about it "in a way that the audience was not expected to notice." Thus, Shakespeare laughed at the old plot, what he had made of it, and what he had done to the comic genre. The joke, though, is on him because nobody (until Empson) spotted the irony as being so pervasive. Empson's claim is not unique. Knight also found some melodramatic lines ironic and amusing. Of Isabella's line, "More than our brother is our chastity" Knight says, "When Shakespeare chooses to load his dice like this,—which is seldom indeed—he does it mercilessly" (1930, 181).

As he makes fun of the play and makes the play fun, Empson, jiggling the word *sense* through a selection of meanings, attributes the "problem" of the comedy to that irony the dramatist purportedly summoned to keep his boredom at a distance. Empson achieves several trim results with this contention. He takes courteous jabs at individual names among his older contemporaries, and also at different types of criticism then and still current: biographical, socially scientific, political, and linguistic. His word games with *sense*, especially as Angelo uses it—in, for instance, his aside, "She speaks, and 'tis such sense That my sense breeds with it" (2.2.147–48)—remind us that it is Isabella's intelligence, eloquence, conviction, and ferocious purity, as well as her looks, that fire the deputy's blood. The actress need not have the beauty of Kate Nelligan to besot him, although scarcely a spectator would gripe about that beauty, but she does need a stage instinct and skills akin to Nelligan's.

I have never heard of an actor who made a reputation from playing either Angelo or the Duke, but several have done it with Isabella: the role brought to startled public and critical notice the performances of Barbara Jefford (1950), Judi Dench (1962), and Juliet Stevenson (1983), and many others have played it with distinction. Brian Gibbons says Mrs. Cibber, Mrs. Yates, and Mrs. Siddons all performed the role repeatedly and to acclaim (1991). The attraction she draws from Angelo comes about as instantaneously as that of Romeo, Juliet, Rosalind, Orlando, or Proteus, but from the beginning, unlike the others', it has sinister undertones, not tragic or fatalistic but oppressive, unhealthy, swampish.

No site in *Measure* corresponds to a transforming green world. Act 5 takes place in the open, at the gates of Vienna, and thus provides for a crowd scene, if not a spectacle, with its sizable onstage audience. But the earlier acts alternate mostly between official, cold, bright appointment rooms and the dismal exterior and interiors of the prison, the green world's shadowy counterpart overhung with death sentences. In its gloomy precincts, thanks to "the old, fastastical Duke of dark corners" (4.3.156–57), Isabella's and Claudio's hopes for reprieve expire, to be replaced by resignation, hurried plots, and breathless reassurances, all of which they must work through, if only to satisfy comedy's formal demands.

Young male students of recent vintage often grow vexed or skeptical over Isabella's aggressive defense of her chastity, Angelo's mix of stern justice for others and lax morality for himself, and the scurrying make-work and reversals of the Duke. These students regret being unable to appreciate what must have been an acceptable dramatic dividend for a seventeenth-century theatre public. But was it? Shakespeare surely introduced these role peculiarities to startle his own audiences, much as they startle us; in other words, from the beginning these peculiarities had dramatic punch and substance because for many spectators they defied belief.

Who learns a lesson? Escalus, for one. He says,

> I am sorry one so learnèd and so wise
> As you, Lord Angelo, have still appeared,
> Should slip so grossly, both in the heat of blood
> And lack of tempered judgment afterward (5.1.581–84)

implying a misjudgment of Angelo—who picks up his opening words and speaks a matching refrain, but to voice not a mere personal correction but a general apology to all present and an error not of perception but contrition:

> I am sorry that such sorrow I procure,
> And so deep sticks it in my penitent heart
> That I crave death more willingly than mercy.
> 'Tis my deserving, and I do entreat it. (485–88)

If Lucio regrets having aspersed the Duke, he doesn't apologize or absorb any lesson, merely gives the ruler a princely title and begs a big favor:

> I beseech Your Highness, do not marry me to a whore. Your Highness
> said even now I made you a duke; good my lord do not recompense
> me in making me a cuckold. (5.1.525–28)

Claudio may learn at last the lesson that there is a God of mercy—who is not of a divine or even supernatural stripe—but, then, we have no clue to what the act 5 Claudio thinks or feels: before and after the Provost removes his muffle, he speaks not one word. Nor does Isabella during the ninety-odd lines that conclude the play, once she has knelt to the "most bounteous sir" and pleaded on behalf of Angelo—or, more probably, of his new, instant wife, Mariana. We can note that Mariana's fate was determined in the given circumstances preceding the action, as Isabella's is *in* the action, by what happened to her brother; here we find echoes of Viola and Olivia.

The Duke, a special case, evidently set out to teach *himself* something. What he actually learned from his frenetic, often countervailing spurts of activity may have disproved what he expected to learn. Beginning with a belief that criminal punishment in Vienna has gone tepid, if not torpid, under his rule, and that it needs much more rigor if the city's moral fiber is to be fortified, he takes on a second pre-Brechtian role. Almost like Shen Te, the softhearted heroine of *The Good Woman of Setzuan*, who, to protect herself from parasites, assumes the guise of an invented, ruthless male cousin whom she calls Shui Ta, the Duke feels unable, as himself and by himself, to take on the corruption of Vienna, and so he creates another self to serve as his ally.[3] But in contrast to the heroine of *The Good Woman*, Duke Vincentio in *Measure for Measure* creates a second persona who for a time resembles the first, because they both come across as scrupulous. But when we look back to the first, he has started to fade out of sight. Even as the play opens, he is changing as he bids his counselors (and his usual self) good-bye. He will hide beneath the cowl of an observer. Angelo's brand of justice, he knows, will be harsh. Will it be just? If so, it will supply him with the answer he evidently hopes for: that Vienna ought to live under penalties that are fast, sure, and fair. He gives Angelo his charge:

> In our remove be thou at full ourself.
> Mortality and mercy in Vienna
> Live in thy tongue and heart. (1.1.44–46)

The question of whether *at that moment* he takes into account Angelo's past deceit with Mariana remains open. It does not come up for consideration until well into act 3. Was it an afterthought? Perhaps, but if it had arisen earlier it would have taken some sting out of Angelo's purposed bargain with Isabella, which seems to represent for a time his first fall from chilly honor. The Deputy himself banks on his reputation, on the disbelief of Vienna should Isabella publicize his duplicity. As with real-life case histories, people would speak of him like friends of today's serial killers, terrorists, and child-slayers: "He'd never have done that . . . One of the most honest guys I ever met . . . He couldn't kill a bug, let alone his own kids."

In act 5, after the Duke goes through his twenty or so forswearings and turnarounds, he ends up dispensing limited pardons to everyone, even Lucio. Was he finally testing his leadership, reveling in the exercise of power? Or has he learned his lesson for himself—to put up with the weaknesses of others, as well as his own, and even with personal insults, when he tells Lucio, "Thy slanders I forgive" (530)? Callousness, he has discovered, also has grave flaws, more forthrightly harmful ones than liberal governance. And "the properties" of government are announced in act 1's (and the Duke's) opening line to be the play's topic. As governmental attributes, mercy contends with justice. Therefore, in all the cases he ends up judging, he makes use of a string of conspiratorial devices; he cruelly puts Isabella, Mariana, Claudio, and Angelo on the racks of grief or uncertainty, but his resolutions live up to the mercy that Portia merely preached: he returns to an enlightened version of his original role—or so we take it—and refrains from seeking justice through severity.[4] The conspiracies have also drawn both Angelo and Isabella away from their ruthless moral extremes, leading the one to repent as the other forgives.

Suppose that at the end a director does not let Isabella accept the Duke; let us say she turns away or doesn't smile in silent acquiescence or goes so far as to grimace in distaste—as happened in John Barton's and other celebrated twentieth-century productions—is the play still a comedy? I would say so. The Duke has rescued the endangered Claudio, Juliet, Barnadine, and Mariana, as well as endowed a temporary respectability on the "punk" who bore Lucio's child; he has rescued Isabella herself from Angelo and Angelo from disgrace and execution. Three marriages take place. Even if Isabella goes back to the convent she finds herself no worse off than at the start of the action. But does it matter, anyway, which slot we drop the play into, when much of it already falls under the rubric of melodrama? Hardly at all. Most anthologies nowadays include it with the Comedies for the sake of convenience. But the dramatist's accidental or deliberate restraint in act 5 in withholding Isabella's consent or her rebuff strikes me as preferable to more assertive endings for this continually astounding drama.

Notes

1. For a helpful account of contractual arrangements for marriages in Shakespeare's time—that is, engagements and the equivalent of breach of promise—see Bawcutt (1994, 6–8).

2. The Barry Kyle production did take place in a church playhouse, St. Clement's Episcopal on West 46th Street in Manhattan.

3. Brecht has several Januslike leading figures in his plays. Others beside Shen Te include Galy Gay in *Man Is Man*, a civilian transformed into a brutal

warrior named Jeriah Jip, and Herr Puntila, who turns generous when drunk and incapacitated—the opposite of his mean, sober self. One might argue that "something inside" the sober, antisocial Puntila makes him seek drunkenness in order to liberate his withheld good traits, as does the role Puntila is modeled on, the millionaire in Chaplin's *City Lights*.

4. I cannot accept, without more abundant proof than has been offered, that Duke Vincentio in some way satirizes or resembles King James, any more than I could accept the Queen of the Fairies, played by Mistress Quickly, to be a skit on Elizabeth I.

LOVE, TRUE AND FALSE

T his rubric might apply to several of the comedies not included in the grouping, most pertinently to *Much Ado*. But in these four the true and the false co-exist, either in two different plots or in one role. In *Two Gentlemen* Proteus, true to his name but not to his friendship and love, is rescued by the friend he doubly betrayed in a rounding-off that gravely offends some viewers but does bring the play back under the comic shelter. Falstaff in *I Henry IV*, in addition to being the principal cause of the comic and farcical impetus, stoutly embodies a never-to-be solved enigma. One can determine roughly how Prince Hal feels about the old knight. But does Falstaff love the Prince as dearly as he professes? Whatever *Part II* says about the rejection, and whatever *Henry V* says about Falstaff's heartbreak before his death, these are other plays, tainted evidence. The reborn (or preborn?) Falstaff of *Merry Wives* shows no love for Mistress Page or Mistress Ford, only for their assets. But Ford—does he love his wife? Another open question. More questionable loves include those of Slender and Dr. Caius for Nan Page, although we can hardly doubt that Fenton loves her—for at least the duration of the action. *As You Like It* supplies a selection of four pairings, from the dubious (Audrey-Touchstone) and the resigned (Phoebe with Silvius) and the suddenly miraculous (Celia-Oliver) to the deferred but madly impassioned (Rosalind-Orlando). One-sided love, that aching experience, sometimes poetically verges on the exhilaration of love that is mutual.

The Two Gentlemen of Verona

In Shakespeare's third comedy, if it *is* his third, we find for the first time planning with malicious intent—intrigue, which leads to an infusion of melodrama in the course of which at least one role tries to defeat or capture at least one other role. In calling on melodrama, I do not restrict its application to 19th-century melodrama but to roughly what the French call *un drame sérieux,* distinct in its form from tragedy. If a tragedy has a leading role responsible for his or her own downfall, a melodrama in this sense has a leading figure whose downfall is plotted by some other role or roles—not always successfully. The intrigue determines both the main plot and some of the tissue of sub-plots. In the main plot, which takes in the adventures of four young victims of love, the intrigue requires deceit. Valentine tries to deceive the Duke of Milan to win Silvia, the Duke's daughter, away from the favored suitor, Sir Thurio. Proteus, in order to win Silvia in turn away from his recent friend, Valentine, is willing to deceive that friend and his recent beloved, Julia, as well as the Duke, Sir Thurio, and Silvia herself. She deceives her father to run off in pursuit of Valentine, who has been exiled from Milan. Julia, with a similar motive—to get close to the man she loves—deceives Proteus by disguising herself as his page. It might even be said that Valentine deceives *himself* when he amazingly offers Silvia to Proteus, who has just threatened to ravish her. But after bouts of contrition and pardon, the four young folk are paired off, as though they had become two ideal matches.

Because some of the deceit, as well as the contrition and pardoning, seems unconvincing to many commentators, for them the play has become a source of embarrassment, pique, apology. Certain of them believe it could be Shakespeare's earliest juvenile writing rescued from a lower drawer or a previous draft.

Much of the disquiet arises from not only Valentine's pardoning Proteus and being ready to drop Silvia into his hands, but also from the sudden unfairness of the proposal. It should come about as a result of more lines, more deliberation, more argument on both sides; it should not be simply a collapse of Valentine's indignation, blatantly decreed by the dramatist. Worse yet, it should not proceed without reference to the feelings and some protestations from Silvia, who remains silent through the wrenching of the action, and Julia, who momentarily passes out.

Kenneth Muir, among others, calls this Shakespeare's first romantic comedy, implying that tolerance for a beginner is in order. But he finds "halting verse" and "forced rhymes" in the scene of renunciation (1979, 30–31). Has some interloping editor or playwright been at work? The text was printed late; some material may have been lost and restored by other hands before it reached the Folio's printer. Clifford Leech (1969 xiii) outlines a range of textual difficulties, oddities, and incongruities in the play, such as whether certain scenes are laid in Milan, Mantua, Verona, Padua, or Naples; the questionable delivery of letters; whether the Duke is indeed a duke—or an emperor; whether it matters if the scenes that feature Launce were inserted after the rest of the play was drafted (xv-xxi). Muir believes the ending is sardonic; pointing to the alternating ferocity and humility of the outlaws who elect Valentine their leader, the feeble rivalry embodied in Sir Thurio, and the baffling conduct of Sir Eglamour, who boldly escorts Silvia but runs away without explanation when the outlaws capture her. The appearance of two Sir Eglamours in the play suggests hasty editing of the text but may also allude to what M. C. Bradbrook calls "a popular romantic drama from the middle of the fifteenth century onwards . . . such as the play of Sir Eglamour performed at St Albans," perhaps still a known quantity to Elizabethan audiences (1963, 25–26).

And Valentine? "His behavior is absurd," writes Muir, "and Shakespeare meant us to think it absurd." Muir proposes that the presence in the play of Launce and Speed, the comic valets, projects an ironic tone; so does Julia's swoon. Still, to turn the logic of an ending around and call it ironic has often served as a defense of the indefensibly under-thought-out. Shakespeare mixes moods continually and serves up more impudence and more reward for the spectator than most other playwrights do. Consistency of quality is as unhelpful as an implement for analyzing his theatre as any other sort of consistency.

Bertrand Evans claims that, with this play, the author adapted "the materials, themes, and conventions of meandering narrative romance (or lyric verse) to dramatic form" (1964, xxv). According to Evans, Valentine's failure to realize that Silvia employs him to write endearments from her to himself (2.2.100–130) shows him up as the "true prototype of heroes and secondary heroes of the comedies to come, of Orlando, Orsino, Claudio, Bassanio, some better, some worse, but all essentially obtuse, less aware than the heroines." Evans's theory in *Shakespeare's Comedies* (1960) convincingly proposes an imaginary landscape of mountains, hills, knolls, and other "heights" of advantage that some roles (here, the heroines) enjoy over others (the heroes) in understanding the deceptions being played out.

Almost everyone who has written about *Two Gentlemen* finds in it a contest between love and friendship. Does friendship win out, as many writers suggest, when Valentine in that often-cited couplet shows himself ready to sacrifice Silvia as a reward for Proteus's penitence?

> . . . That my love may appear plain and free,
> All that was mine in Silvia I give thee. (5.4.82–83)

Or does Shakespeare exalt love over friendship, since the two men at last gain the women they seemed destined for? Or do love and friendship fight each other to a standoff? Will love and friendship both prove unstable, liable to evaporate or grow warped at a whim? Does the author revere both types of relationship or gently revile them as fraudulent? MacCary posits a theory of the progression in Shakespeare's comedies:

> I have suggested that Shakespeare distinguishes four types of object-choice and presents these in a continuum suggesting development. A young man is first obsessed with a mirror image of himself; the melancholy of Antipholus of Syracuse as he seeks his lost twin represents this case in its extreme. He then enjoys the companionship of another young man, and thinks that only in such company can he come to know himself and make a place for himself in the world. A transitional stage from this dependence upon a male friend to a dependence upon a female lover occurs when he becomes attached to a young woman transvestized as a young man. When he first begins to love a woman, he might either idealize her or debase her, in both cases projecting upon her preconceived notions of the nature of women. Finally he recognizes in the young woman a being of great complexity and novelty, an independent and constantly changing creature who contradicts all his expectations and leads him to new discoveries about himself and the world.
>
> This opening up of a young man's heart to variety in erotic experience is shown by Shakespeare to stimulate an awakening of his mind." (1985, 110)

In this interpretation, Proteus is not so much in desperate love with Silvia, for whom he appears to fall with a suppressed crash, as determined (unconsciously?) to steal somebody precious to his friend and virtual lover. According to this view, for Proteus Silvia is a substitute for Valentine. When Proteus betrays Valentine to the Duke, we could strain

to put a favorable construction on his treachery by imagining that he
starts out hoping to teach Valentine a lesson for bragging in excessive
praise of Silvia (2.4.146–62) at the expense of Julia or at the expense of
him, Proteus. The play neither supports nor foils this interpretation, but
it could hardly make much difference in production. All the same, even
when allotted a motive that is not really vindictive, Proteus has not
considered how severe a penalty the Duke may exact from a man who
plans to elope with his daughter: Proteus could be sentencing his friend
to death. Since the two young men behaved affectionately toward each
other in the opening scene, with Proteus lamenting their separation, we
might choose to look upon the betrayal as an aberration, to view Proteus as the prey of the abstract monster Lust. Yet, in a soliloquy spoken
before he approaches the Duke, he reasons his way methodically to the
conclusion that friendship and other serious considerations should be
subordinated to self-interest (2.6. 1–6 and 17–24), because "I to myself
am dearer than a friend, For love is still most precious in itself" (2.6.23–
24). If we discount hypocrisy here, a coverup for lust (a big "if"), love
has for the moment vanquished friendship.

Those historians who claim that, in line with Lyly's drama,
Shakespeare and most of his audience believed in friendship over love
face retorts from later critics who contend that by the time *Two Gentlemen* was written, the belief was obsolete. Kurt Schlueter takes the position that friendship has to do with the model behavior of a
gentleman (hence the word *gentlemen* in the title), according to the tenets set forth in *The Courtier* by Castiglione, which, after its translation
into English, had much influence in the sixteenth and seventeenth
centuries and which meant that gentlemen served as models of behavior for one another, so that Valentine offers his beloved to Proteus as
an example of socially admirable selflessness (1990, 3–6). Schlueter
finds fault with productions that, in his view, miss the point about the
exemplary nature of friendship.[1] We lack opinion polls from the author's time to help or confound us. I beg the fascinating question by
saying that this play puts Valentine's love in conflict with that of Proteus; that it puts their friendship in conflict with both loves; that a
sympathy between the two women verges on another friendship,
which conflicts with the other elements; and that the conflicts may be
resolved in any number of ways by loaded performing.

In three of the four young leads the first two acts of the play rush
through one inconsistency of role after another. Valentine, before
leaving Verona, gently ribs Proteus for being love's dupe:

> Love is your master, for he masters you;
> And he that is so yokèd by a fool
> Methinks should not be chronicled for wise. (1.1.40–42)

In Milan, near the start of the next act, this same love-scorner is confessing to his servant that he has loved Silvia "ever since I saw her" (2.1.63). Meanwhile Proteus, living "dully sluggardiz'd at home," doesn't wish to obey his father's command to educate himself by travel if it means giving up Julia (1.3). But once in Milan, rejoining Valentine and meeting Silvia, he finds her driving out his love for Julia (2.4), and, although slightly troubled by the new attraction, he cannot resist it. No dramatic change is evident in Silvia, but in Julia, the other marker point on the play's moral compass, the action toys with several role changes before she settles into a steady resolution. Like Portia, with one suitor for each casket, Julia and Silvia each have three. Julia's suitor named Sir Eglamour is evidently not the same Eglamour who will escort Silvia away from Mantua. At first (1.2), Julia asks Lucetta's advice as to which of her suitors she should marry. When the maid favors Proteus, Julia declares, "Why he of all the rest hath never moved me," and Lucetta answers, "Yet he of all the rest I think best loves ye" (1.2.27–28). Julia ponders: "I would I knew his mind," upon which Lucetta produces a letter addressed "To Julia," and "sent, I think, from Proteus" (vv. 33 and 38). Julia, insisting on her pose of haughty, heart-whole lady, gives back the letter unread and dismisses the servant. Alone, she reproaches herself.

> How churlishly I chid Lucetta hence,
> When willingly I would have had her here!
> How angerly I taught my brow to frown,
> When inward joy enforced my heart to smile!
> My penance is to call Lucetta back . . . (1.2.60–64)

Lucetta, having returned, drops the letter as if by accident. After some banter over whom it might belong to, Julia tears it up. Seconds after Lucetta has left her to herself again, Julia slips into rapturous apologies addressed to the absent Proteus. She takes up the bits of paper with Proteus's name and her name on them and stuffs them into her bosom: "Thus will I fold them one upon another. Now kiss, embrace, contend, do what you will" (1.2.129–130). She leaves the remaining scraps for Lucetta to pick up and pretends she still does not care about the letter.

Three scenes on, she and Proteus are exchanging vows, rings, and farewells, before he departs for Mantua. And five scenes further along, immediately after we see Proteus argue himself into a preference for Silvia, we meet Julia again, this time being sweet to Lucetta because she wants advice. She is thinking of taking off in pursuit of Proteus and in drag. The advice comes back repeatedly: Don't go! She goes. In a 1994 production in Central Park, the director, Adrian Hall, telescoped two scenes. He kept Proteus on stage, immobile and seated on a bench, after the soliloquy in which he declares his love for Silvia and

his renunciation of Julia. Julia (Nance Williamson) and Lucetta (Cam-
ryn Manheim) played the following scene around him as if Proteus
(Malcolm Gets) were not there to witness Julia's determination to follow him. This blocking sharpened the irony of Julia's devotion to a
man who has just resolved to give her up.

In summary, then, over the procession of the five acts the two
gentlemen turn into their opposites, Valentine from a bachelor who
slights love into a love-impelled swain, and Proteus from a loyal friend
and devoted lover into a repudiator of altruistic motives in favor of
self-interest. Silvia changes from a vivacious beauty whom "all our
swains commend" to a silent mystery; Julia goes from being a coy lady,
a fetching leftover from the age of chivalry, to the first in a succession
of Shakespeare's adventuresses in doublets and hose.

If we exclude servants and musicians, *Two Gentlemen* incorporates
twelve identified secondary roles, including three outlaws, and they
populate ten or more subplots. Most of them serve the action's melodrama, sometimes with comic results: Lucetta, Sir Eglamour, the Duke
(Silvia's father), Antonio (Valentine's father), Antonio's servant Panthi-
no, the Host of the inn where Julia stays en route and hears her rival
serenaded by Proteus. The two male servants function otherwise. They
are both described as being "clownish," but Valentine's man, Speed, is
more of a would-be wit, probably an adolescent like Moth, drunk on
words and assonances. Speed descends from the servant of Plautine
comedy and farce, as well as commedia dell'arte, and his line continues through Molière and Beaumarchais. Speed is speedier on the uptake than his master, as when he spots that Silvia, in getting Valentine
to write a letter to a "secret, nameless friend," "woos you by a figure."

VALENTINE What figure?
SPEED By a letter, I should say.
VALENTINE Why, she hath not writ to me.
SPEED What need she, when she hath made you write to yourself? (2.2.144–49)

The master becomes the servant's stooge, the feed of Speed. And the
servant makes the master look like a dummy, much as the ventrilo-
quist's doll generally does with his handler. (In some performances I
have seen, Speed's sense of superiority, indulged too blatantly, grew
insufferable.)

Proteus's servant, Launce, is a different bag of tricks. He radiates not
wit, but humor. Speed's airs irritate him. When Launce plays a trick on
Speed he looks forward to rejoicing "in the boy's correction." Launce
anticipates by four centuries the guest on late-night television and the
solo performance artist on stage who specialize in self-deprecation and

yarns about their crazy families. He goes nowhere without his "sour" dog, Crab. He is so fond of Crab that he gives him away—in place of a tiny "squirrel" of a lapdog intended as a present to Silvia from Proteus. That gentleman has described himself (but only to himself) as being "spaniel-like," because "the more [Silvia] spurns my love, The more it grows and fawneth on her still" (4.2.14–15). But his gift goes awry. When the lapdog is stolen by some boys, Launce tells his master, he replaced it with Crab, "who is a dog as big as ten of yours" (4.4.55–56). Crab, size notwithstanding, is a mutt with an undisciplined bladder. Sylvia spurns him. Crab loses Launce his employment. Although Launce hurls a rhetorical question at his hound, "When didst thou see me heave up my leg and make water against a gentlewoman's farthingale?" (4.4.37), this servant who is a dog's master will go on taking the blame for Crab's indiscretions on other people's floors. Crab's sourness implies that he's named after a crab apple, as most editions note; but the word is also close to crap—if the word was in usage then—an apt name for a dog who, like any dog, is a carefree bowel-emptier. Launce's offering the pooch to Silvia in a subplot may comically refract the main plot—a satirical preview of Valentine ready to hand Silvia over to Proteus.[2]

Valentine's peculiar generosity in offering his friend his sweetheart, which over the centuries has provoked thousands of words of opprobrium, was taken up by Inga-Stina Ewbank in a celebrated essay. She tells how George Eliot confided to her diary that on a rereading, the offer disgusted her "more than ever;" Ewbank believes there may have been some personal perturbation on Eliot's part—doubts about the fidelity of G. H. Lewes, her lover—that caused her to feel enraged over the batting around of two women between two men. (Not that one need be in Eliot's situation to find the offer repellent.) Ewbank says, "Elizabethan audiences would have seen Valentine's lines as a noble and universally valid climax to the action" (1972, 31). Anne Barton also writes:

> Most Elizabethans would have seconded the opinion of Francis Bacon in his *Essays* that friendship is a serious matter and passion a far more dangerous and ephemeral kind of commitment. Although it might seem less promising as a dramatic subject than love, friendship was in fact celebrated in a number of Elizabethan plays. (1974, 144)

Ewbank aligns the friendship-love competition with some of the sonnets, especially number 40, and concludes that in *Two Gentlemen* Shakespeare "produced a work which is ultimately less dramatic than many of his sonnets." She cites the shortage of physical action in the comedy, its dependence on words to appeal to the ear rather than the eye, and its use of letters, rather than answerable lines of dialogue. She contends that Valentine is obtuse. He all too often is—a bit of a

Bertie Wooster to Speed's juvenile Jeeves. But not throughout. Once again, a Shakespeare role defies consistency, refuses to behave "in character." She dismisses proposals that the end of the play is ironic, but notes that "there is a theoretical pressure on the scene which is not practically realized." By "pressure," I would guess she means the auditorium's thirst for comeuppance, which must be slaked. If it were, the alternative to what we have would be a punishment imposed on Proteus by Valentine or by the Duke or, somehow, by the women, one or both, or else some form of voluntary penance, such as exile or suicide. In either case Julia would go unpartnered and her heroism unrewarded; Valentine would feel dismal; and the play would turn bluntly into something apart from comedy, yet still without the pleasing pathos of *Love's Labor's Lost* in its closing moments. As the work stands we may have a novelty: a cold reconciliation, a pardon that doesn't blot out Proteus's offenses, a final celebration that remains, at best, brave. The marriage to come between the largest male role and the largest female role still looks shaky, not more likely to crumble than those in *Twelfth Night, Dream, All's Well,* and other comedies; but *apparently*, as John Wilders puts it, "Shakespeare has written himself into a situation which admits of no really satisfactory outcome" (1984, 17).[3] Once we take account, however, of the play as an occasion for a performance, rather than as reading material only, varied opportunities offer themselves.

Even if the play *were* less dramatic than the sonnet Ewbank alludes to, number 40—"Take all my loves, my love, yea, take them all . . . Lascivious grace, in whom all ill well shows, Kill me with spites; yet we must not be foes"—with which it certainly has striking affinities, a director and actors would have all sorts of resources for feeding in as much movement and bodily opposition as are desired for the roles that "are left to stand about, forgotten, in uncomfortable silence."[4]

Further, Ewbank says that only a few lines elapse between Valentine's accusation and his forgiveness. So they do. But to edify people who insist on a due parade of realistic motivation, the actor doing Valentine can always walk around communing with himself, tensely oblivious to his onstage spectators and how much is at stake for them. He can almost visibly wrestle with the role's worst instincts before scotching them, by clutching his head, holding up his hands, punching his other palm, instead of Proteus's teeth, and resorting to similar make-it-all-clear gestures. He can take note of Proteus kneeling before him. Receive looks from Julia that say, "For my sake, spare him, please!" Glimpse Silvia, whose moist-eyed expression tells him, "You know what I love most about you? Your merciful nature." He *can*. The gap between accusation and forgiveness might be spun out into a tortured, prolonged but suspenseful change of heart, mind, postures.

Muir and others believe that the lines in the last scenes are not Shakespeare's. Leech proposed that he wrote them in a hurry at a later time, in preparation for a performance. A part or a whole of the original text may have been lost, replaced, trimmed, or jeopardized by the efforts of a collaborator: we now see Shakespeare's intention, whatever it was, stripped of his poetry, which might have made good on the promises or "pressures" of the play. Close to the other end of Shakespeare's career, John Fletcher as collaborator gets the blame for most of the deficiencies of a play that has sometimes been regarded as a counterpart of *Two Gentlemen: The Two Noble Kinsmen.* The lines do fail to rank, generally speaking, with Shakespeare's most memorable poetry, although some surprise us with their beauty and aptness. But I would not come down too hard on the dramatic content. If Valentine makes his sacrificial offer in the name of friendship, he imitates Julia's example in forgiving Proteus. Are we, then, to picture Valentine and Julia, the two forgivers, as self-lacerating victims of love, like the real or imaginary person in the sonnet who urges his "love" to "take all my loves"? Are we to spank these roles verbally for not behaving in their own best interests? The most irrational feature of the play is not, in truth, Valentine's stupid, perversely noble yielding up of Silvia but Julia's pursuit of Proteus. Such pursuits do happen. Admirable women stand by contemptible men. When they do, their plight seems more pitiful than that of an admirable man who chases after or upholds a contemptible woman.

Critical discomfort is twofold, not so much with friendship-versus-love as with implausibility and insufficient dramatic fiber. I am arguing that Valentine's and Julia's forgiveness resembles what happens in life when one person dotes on another (Julia: "His looks are my soul's food" [2.7.15]). But to return to our theme, if roles are as unpredictable as personalities, straining for plausibility may lead to realism that is overstated, crass.

Dramatic insufficiency is another matter. Roles dumped onstage without enough functions—lines to speak, activities to perform—can only mean that the dramatist has plotted the work badly. It may be worth recalling, all the same, that this very "fault" crops up in *Hamlet* (the continual, unexploited presence of Horatio) and in other respected plays, particularly those in which royal figures are accompanied by retinues of the nondescript. Today's directors often compensate for "flawed" (meaning nonfunctional) plotting. With underused roles they can introduce plastic human bodies into the lifeless scenic design to their hearts' content.[5]

If we scrutinize the play's supposed weaknesses, we might also pay attention to some of its strengths. Paring down much of the plotting to soliloquies and two-character scenes can make for dramatic concentration and point up the play's forensic nature. (Wilders observes that

the play is not only a romance but "also a debate—or rather a series
of debates—on travel and education, on loyalty to friends and parents,
but mostly . . . on the absorbing and paradoxical sensations of love"
(BBC TV edition, 1984, 12). I will cite one sequence that Shakespeare
has realized as subtly as anything in his comedy: it deals with Proteus's
request for Silvia's portrait, leading into Julia's encounter with Silvia.
Proteus tells Silvia that his former sweetheart and his former friend
are both dead; then he pleads:

> Madam, if your heart be so obdurate,
> Vouchsafe me yet your picture for my love,
> The picture that is hanging in your chamber.
> To that I'll speak, to that I'll sigh and weep;
> For since the substance of your perfect self
> Is else devoted, I am but a shadow,
> And to your shadow will I make true love. (4.2.116–22)

In his infatuation he has led himself to believe that the thought of his
making "true love" to her "shadow" will arouse her jealousy.[6]

Two scenes later, the action rides on our blinking at two improba-
bilities. First, Julia's disguise does not come into question when she
visits Silvia as Proteus's envoy—a woman would be more likely to see
through it. And second, Silvia does part with the picture; her reason
for so doing might be that she takes a liking to this "Sebastian," although not so powerful a liking as Olivia's for the other "Sebastian,"
Viola as Cesario, who will come wooing on Orsino's behalf. It could
also be that since she has already made plans with Eglamour to pursue the exiled Valentine, Silvia believes Proteus's suit is hopeless. But
if she detests him and his lying ("Thou subtle, perjured, false, disloyal
man!"[4.2.92]), why would she oblige him by handing over the portrait? Because it makes for good theatre. Comic theatre. The scene between her and Julia seethes below the surface with Julia's feelings of
being betrayed and at the same time betraying (she has already told
herself, "Because he loves her, he despiseth me. Because I love him, I
must pity him"[4.4.94–95]), while she keeps a polite front. As they
converse, she makes implicit comparisons between herself and Proteus's new love, the portrait in its frame proving useful as a property,
a point of reference during the encounter, as Julia studies the rival and
her image. In the soliloquy that follows the encounter Julia can say
openly to the picture what she could not to the person, "A virtuous
gentlewoman, mild and beautiful!" The thought arouses her indignation and also draws our attention to this first of Shakespeare's comic
appositions between a blonde and a brunette:

> . . . And yet the painter flattered her a little,
> Unless I flatter with myself too much.

Her hair is auburn, mine is perfect yellow;
If that be all the difference in his love,
I'll get me such a colored periwig. (4.4.186–90)

No critic has more fun with the shortcomings of *Two Gentlemen*
than does H. B. Charlton, who, fortunately for the art of the pointed
putdown, is one of the most entertaining critics of Shakespeare's comedies. Charlton, taking an approach later refuted by successors, blames
the flaws on Shakespeare's use and misuse of holdovers from romance
literature and its absurd traditions. These should not have been grafted onto comedies. Whereas Bertrand Evans rejoices in the birth of a
new genre, Charlton, some thirty years earlier, laments the survival of
dramatic features that should, in his view, have been allowed to die
off. The upshot in the play is lashings of comedy that are unmeant,
scenes and roles that are ridiculous. What? Proteus doesn't see in the
pageboy he hires the woman with whom, not long before, he was
madly in love? Were her face and form such a blur at that time that he
no longer recognizes them? The true heroes of romance, says Charlton, were supermen; he cites the example of

> Jacques de Lalaing, the bon chevalier, the mirror of knighthood who
> adorned the Burgundian court in the middle of the fifteenth century
> [and] who had become the pattern of chivalry for all Europe. (1938, 34)[7]

Valentine the inept is anything but this sort of a knight, errant or sta-
tionary, but as soon as the three outlaws spot him they want to make
him their captain, even their king, so vividly do his deportment and
other evidence of superiority impress them. (Eventually they settle for
making him a captain.) Sir Thurio, who refuses to fight with Valentine
for Silvia, is called by Charlton "the one person in the play with a mo-
dicum of worldly wisdom" for declining to risk his skin. But even if one
disagrees with Charlton, Sir Thurio is nowhere near being a person. He
is a role whose cowardice exists to highlight the valor of Valentine.

Charlton further writes of the regrettable absence from French romance of "women with the forcefulness of a distinct personality."
"Substantial beings." And "distinct personality." He is too astute a critic
to ask for more verisimilitude in Elizabethan comedy, but in his account of how he believes the offscourings of romance undo this play
he seeks more truth-to-life in the roles. He also singles out improba-
bilities that happen to resemble the ones we find sprinkled freely
through the comedies accounted Shakespeare's "best" or "greatest" or
"masterpieces"—*Twelfth Night, As You Like it, Dream,* and *Much Ado.* But
is Proteus not equally with Julia and Launce—or more—a "substantial
being" of this stripe? Charlton either overlooked his substantiality (the
role with the most lines in the play) or rejected him for being insub-
stantial because the critic doesn't admire him.

There has always been a tendency in criticism to find likable
roles—even some cloddish ones—more persuasive, richer inventions,
better family types than one-dimensional villains. Critics have a way
of forgiving likeable dummies their faults. They may serve as correc-
tives, according to the antique definitions of comedy, for our misdeeds
and murky thoughts. A spectator, asked which role is the villain and
which the hero of this play, would very likely elect Proteus the villain—at any rate the principal villain, although not, as we see, an ir-
recoverable villain (some audience members would point to Silvia's
father as a secondary villain), because even though he does not keep
faith with his friend, Proteus will have to bring himself up to snuff to
be worthy of Julia. A thoughtful theatregoer might well hesitate before fastening onto a hero, but the bumbling Valentine seems like an
inevitable choice, in part because the play instructs us that he only,
among the suitors in Mantua, managed to secure the unshaken affection of Silvia the gorgeous; in part because he is the only possible candidate; and in larger part precisely because he makes the heroic,
unselfish, appalling offer in act 5. Proteus the "villain" may, like Iago,
have a larger role than the hero, but he is no Iago, only a comic wa-
verer. He does what is required of his role; so does Valentine.

Silvia, as it turns out, remains silent not only during the sacrifice
scene but through to the play's end. Perhaps she has been robbed of
speech by Proteus's "What is in Silvia's face, but I may spy More fresh
in Julia's with a constant eye?"—a neat compliment to Julia, who deserved some encouragement after her trials, but to Silvia an almost literal slap in the face. Through most of the play she has been a mystery.
"Who is Silvia?" the famous song asks, "what is she, That all our
swains commend her?" And answers itself evasively, " . . . Silvia is ex-
celling; She excels each mortal thing Upon the dull earth dwelling."
Silvia, whose name we associate with the sylvan setting of the last
scenes, is a radiant prize of love. Explain her unwitting power? Go
explain magnetism or Marilyn Monroe . . .

Whether on purpose or not, Shakespeare did not unfurl the action
as a sample of sensible motives. The patterns of logic in the conduct of
the main roles are abnormal. The outlaws are abnormal in their sudden acceptance of Valentine and their equally sudden eagerness to re-
enter respectable society. The setting is abnormal, if we take this play
to be the first in which the green realm heals: henceforth for Shakespeare's comedies it will not be abnormal but customary. Most of the
roles are gathered finally in the natural arboretum, a place for transformations. It has them under its beneficent influence. We can read
this effect quite literally without encroaching on the metaphorical
hints. Each main role, as well as each secondary role present, does
undergo a change of fortune, taken to an extreme by the events just

past, as though every one had come into the penumbra of a hostile, then a friendly star. In that final scene only one of the three fathers in the play's action or story is present. Valentine must be an orphan. No mothers are mentioned; mothers are scarce in classic comedy: we find few in Molière's theatre as well.

Silvia, in danger of defilement by a man she dislikes, even though she gave his envoy her picture, is restored to her lover. To smooth out another wrinkle, her treacherous father now approves of the match. Julia swoons at the prospect of losing Proteus to Silvia but returns to consciousness, like an awakening princess, to find herself in the perfect situation for shedding her "Sebastian" identity, comparing rings with Proteus as a token of love and a pledge and a sexual contract, and regaining him.[8] Proteus himself slumps into his worst moments in the play: his promise to woo Silvia "like a soldier, at arms' end . . . and force ye" (5.4.57–58), the shock of Valentine's intervention, and the shame of having Valentine show him up. But as consolation, here is Julia, even better-looking than he remembered, loyal as ever and on hand. As for Valentine, earlier, in the forest, the fugitive was caught by bloodthirsty bandits: Outlaw Number 2 has stabbed a man "to the heart"; Number 3 has committed "suchlike petty crimes"; Number 1 warns, "If thou scorn our courtesy, thou diest" (4.1.51, 52, and 68). They turn out to be gentlemen, like their prisoner who becomes their captain, and whom they admire because he is a linguist. (Is he also good at origami, knots, amateur cuisine?) They may have lied about their past but no more shamelessly than Valentine does when he boasts he slew a man, whose death he now regrets (4.1.26–29). Silvia, having trekked or galloped after him, catches up, and after a dip in fortune occasioned by his own mad magnanimity, is restored to him.

It will not do to posit a gay relationship between the "hero" and "villain" by saying that Valentine proves ultimately fonder of Proteus than of Silvia, and hence his gesture of renunciation. Despite his words of affection, he leaves Proteus twice without making plans to see him again. Perhaps what we need to do is make *dramatic* sense of that gesture. The downs and ups in the green realm, just described, bring the ending into line with a comic, five-act closure and also sharpen the suspense by deepening the dramatic valleys or raising the dramatic peaks. The audience experiences something very like the usual rush of expectation gratified. But it does so after a shocking decision by Valentine. The young Shakespeare (or the not-so-young Shakespeare, if we are dealing with a text he revised) displays disdain for the neat wrap-up, as we will notice again in act 5 of *The Merchant*, *Dream*, and other comedies. In almost every instance he will unveil a fresh kind of act 5, in which there is one or more surprises, or where the play will veer offtrack, even in a new direction that steers right away from what went before. If theatre practitioners can bring themselves to give this effect the benefit of the doubt by taking it for a deliberate move by the playwright, an additional Shakespeare signature, they may then cope with it as a contravention of aging traditions.

Two Gentlemen is not difficult for a reader or critic to put down but difficult to appreciate. For some, it may be a problem play. But I remain allergic to the word *problem*. The performance history was a sparse record for its first two hundred years. It went without a revival in Shakespeare's life, so far as is known. But in the late nineteenth and early twentieth centuries such pioneers as Granville Barker and Poel tackled it, and since then, so have B. Iden Payne, Michael Langham, and Peter Hall. In 1972 John Guare adapted it as a rock musical for the New York Shakespeare Festival, directed by Mel Shapiro: it went out of Central Park and into a Broadway run.

Today, I would venture, one of its most attractive features to a director would be exactly that astonishing but theatrical *and highly comic* gesture of Valentine's, which lifts the last act away from its trim conclusion and into a realm of speculation. If plausibility must be served, show the character helplessly torn between impatience to recover Silvia and a refusal to take advantage of Proteus's abjectness, until he settles on an I-give-up answer, which will be funny—because nonsensical—to watch, and also funny because Valentine is, or should be, a comic role. When Proteus informs Silvia's father that his former friend means to elope with her, Valentine traps himself into explaining how to manage an elopement with the aid of a rope ladder like this one under his cloak. In a play that relies largely in acts 1–4 on scheming by the four young principals, Valentine's offer represents a moment of late improvisation or, if you like, inspiration.

One staging scenario, not by far the only possible one, might follow through in the comic spirit and make sense of the offer—or rather match its nonsense—by showing that Valentine cannot quite credit the glaring fact of a betrayal by Proteus. He watches the attempted rape of Silvia until almost too late. Has he perhaps overlooked or forgotten or simply failed to understand something, as happened with the letter he wrote himself on behalf of Silvia, when Speed had to explain what she was up to? He no longer has a Speed with him in the forest to supply enlightenment: even before Launce leaves the play (scene 4.4), Speed, who went with Valentine into exile, was plotted out of the action after scene 4.1. Unhappy Valentine. What did he do wrong this time? He scratches his scalp. Pulls his earlobe. For the moment he has turned into practically as farcical a role as Launce was. Just in case he has somehow provoked his friend, how can he rectify the error or omission? He will perform an act of apology! Not only will he set his friend a gentlemanly example, he will also repair the breach by giving up what is most precious to him. Silvia. (Whose name might be construed as the way through the woods.) Valentine is not so much dimwitted as fearful of appearing a dimwit. But his offer is ridiculous, as well as being in line with his role and at least as much a betrayal of Silvia as Proteus's betrayal of him and Julia.

Strangest of all: audiences accept this moment, however it is presented to them, when critics often cannot. The spectators I have sat among hardly seemed to notice the Valentine gesture or, if they did, they kept their indignation to themselves. The comic and theatrical coup exploded by the gesture doesn't need to be ironic. Valentine and Proteus both come across as mock-heroic roles. What they *are* is more absurd than what they think or do as they earnestly strike futile, comic poses. To say this is not to disagree with Don Taylor's remark, apropos of his BBC TV version, that "in act 5 we are within a few lines of a tragic outcome" (BBC TV edition of the play, 34)—but those few lines will not be traversed.

Holman Hunt's nineteenth-century painting of the scene[9] misses that comedy. Proteus kneels, his head lowered, left hand at the back of his neck as though swatting a wasp. A bearded Valentine, looking older, takes possession of his friend's right hand with, "Come, come, a hand from either" (5.4.116), as he lets his own right hand drape around the neck of Silvia, who also kneels. Julia leans against a tree recovering from her faint. In the background the Duke, Thurio, and the outlaws await their cue to enter four lines further along. Hunt may well have read Valentine's line with nineteenth-century melodramatic relish. Most recent productions and editions of the play see the line as a needed moment of reconciliation between not only Proteus and Valentine but also between Julia the sorrowful and Proteus the penitent.

At this point the spectators have unspoken demands. They are looking forward to a resolution, a smoothing-out. They know the play is supposed to make its impact as a comedy: almost everything about it has repeatedly affirmed the humorous tone, and not least the encounters with the gentlemen-outlaws, a farcical bunch who call to mind a Gilbert & Sullivan chorus, the mix of left-wing protesters in *Man and Superman*, act 4, or, as Don Taylor remarks, "the Red Shadow and his gang from *Desert Song*," (ibid., 26). Valentine's offer is merely another of those obstacles to a neatly cut and chamfered ending—a handicap that must be brushed aside in time for a joyous curtain. Audiences don't blink at it. That doesn't make the offer negligible: besides being comic, it is also a Shakespearean act of mercy, and we have to soar to the far end of the dramatist's oeuvre for the comparable gesture by Prospero (5.1.25–30) when he forgives his enemies. Some members of each audience will very likely come back to the gesture during post-curtain discussions on the way home.

Notes

1. Schlueter also examines cuts and alterations made in versions rewritten for production by Benjamin Victor (1762), John Philip Kemble (1790 and later), and subsequent theatrical figures—changes often made to suit actors who had aged well beyond the plausible years of the roles.

2. When Proteus takes on Julia-Sebastian as his page to replace Launce the clown (or "lout"), the effect is reminiscent of the plotting of Cordelia. The latter disappears as if replaced as Lear's companion and child by the Fool. When she reappears, the Fool has gone. Perhaps it is not so much a question of replacement as of *dis*placement.

3. A history of the *BBC Television Plays* has been written by Susan William (1991). The director of this 1983 production, Don Taylor, wisely chose to stress—but lightly—the "theatricalizing" of certain settings, especially the forest with its regularly spaced, columnar trees.

4. Even when Ewbank published her article in the early 1970s, critics clearly needed to wag an admonitory finger now and then at directors who were feeding in so much embroidery, so many shticks to keep observers' eyeballs rotating in their sockets, that they distracted spectators from the plays without any compensatory payoff.

5. Productions of *Richard II* by John Barton (1974) and Steven Berkoff (1994), to seize on two examples I recall, have been unusually effective in their staging of groups of bodyguards and attendants whose presences are not mentioned or specified in the printed play but serve as disciplined choruses who constitute unspoken threats. Such invented characters performed in both the Ingmar Bergman stage version of *Hamlet*, when Fortinbras entered with violent shock troops, and in Kenneth Branagh's *Hamlet* film, when Fortinbras again led an assault on the Elsinore palace.

6. It may be that a woman's portrait, even a miniature that went into a locket, was once regarded as having talismanic properties. In Gozzi's *Turandot*, the portrait of the princess, even though "no painter has captured all her beauty," has "such power of fascination that young men who glimpse it rush blindly to their death" (1.1. *Turandot*, in *Carlo Gozzi: Five Tales for the Theatre*, [1989]).

7. I cannot help wondering whether one of the self-appointed supermen of our time, Jack Lalanne, borrowed and adapted the name of Jacques de Lalaing.

8. Rings also clinch *The Merchant* and *All's Well*.

9. Hunt's canvas possibly still resides in the Birmingham Art Gallery in England.

Henry IV, Part I

If Shylock swamps the main plot of *The Merchant*, Falstaff does very nearly the same by springing out of a subplot in *Henry IV, Part I* and taking command of the play. Aside from Shakespeare's tragic roles, these two are his most vivacious (and contrasting) male figures, almost autonomous as presences, so amply, so variously brought to new births by actors that one can imagine them in other given circumstances, as one does Hamlet or Iago. The extreme antithesis of parsimony against brazen self-indulgence (if without the ready wherewithal) precedes by three-quarters of a century Molière's invention and incarnation of Harpagon (1668) and then Monsieur Jourdain (1670). Assertive though Falstaff may be as a role, like Shylock he cannot help bending, as a character, into what an actor makes of him; the range of opportunities has swollen into an enormous body of interpretations, as have the chances for willful distortion. Much as directors, actors, and critics often wanted Shylock to appear clear and his motives justifiable, so they looked for a Falstaff who knows exactly what he is doing, where his bread-and-butter lies, and the flavor of jam he will daub on it; or they rhapsodize over him, more besotted by his charms than are the other figures in the play. But however we limn him in our minds, he can, like Shylock, perform that acrobatic feat of jumping off the page. Or, as M. M. Mahood gracefully puts it, "We recognise in the first words of Shylock and Falstaff the same new-found and boldly grasped power to individualise a character dramatically through the sounds, rhythms, idioms, and images of prose speech" (1957, 2).

Certain writers understandably argue that Part I of *Henry IV* should not be detached from Part II in performance or in criticism. But since this is a book about comedy and Part II does not have a comic structure—not quite; it has the resolution and form of a renunciation drama—Part I will be considered here as a self-contained unit, in which form it most often appears, despite the re-emergence in Part II of roles named Falstaff, Bardolph, Peto, Mistress Quickly, and others in that band of "irregular humorists" from the earlier play (enlarged by such newcomers as Doll Tearsheet, Justices Shallow and Silence, Pistol, and the country soldiers). I say some of these are *roles named* Falstaff, Bardolph, and so on because they do not amount to the same roles as in Part I, any more than the roles with the same names as those in *Merry Wives* and *Henry V* coincide with these as acting possibilities. Even the minor roles who impersonate dramatic types or commedia derivations, like Pistol the braggart or Bardolph the slow-witted, burgundy-nosed hanger-on, and may sound echoes of the earlier names, change their shapes from play to play.

In Part II, as he disowns and disavows Falstaff, the former Prince Hal, now Henry V, reminds him, "Presume not that I am the thing I was" (5.5). Orson Welles, not taking this statement to heart, reached into both parts of *Henry IV, Henry V,* and *Merry Wives* to create an amalgam of Falstaff and the other figures for his rich-textured film *Falstaff: Chimes at Midnight,* the screenplay of which had become a new, synthetic composition. It is safe to say that Welles constructed his film for the sake of incorporating much of the Falstaff-Prince Hal partnership from the first part of the *Henry IV* plays. The most startling change among the plays happens to Mistress Quickly: in Part I she runs the tavern, allows Falstaff quantities of credit, and is taken to be an attractive young woman with an unidentified husband; when Falstaff asks, "Is not my hostess of the tavern a most sweet wench?" Hal replies, "As the honey of Hybla" (1.2.39–41). In *Henry V* she has become the wife of Pistol and a nostalgic rememberer of Falstaff, but in *Merry Wives* she opposes Falstaff. In *Chimes at Midnight* Welles had her played—beautifully—throughout by Margaret Rutherford.

It is no longer a novelty to include *I Henry IV* in writings about the comedies, although by the most evident definition it also belongs with the histories. As in most of the histories and tragedies, men dominate the action in both parts of *Henry IV,* which offer constricted roles for women. Part I has snippets of scenes for Mistress Quickly, Lady Hotspur, and Lady Mortimer. The last two do behave in motherly fashion toward their spouses, and Quickly serves as a provider for Falstaff, but as in most of the comedies, the action includes no "technical" mothers' roles. The King has no consort; Prince Hal, despite his reputation as a lush and lowlife, will remain unentangled with female partners, either at court or in the tavern at Eastcheap; his transformed and promoted role in *Henry V* will, however, woo Princess Katherine of France, probably as much for reasons of state as for love. Therefore, the play's conclusion hardly resembles comic endings found elsewhere in Shakespeare, consisting of one or two happy marriages in process or in prospect. Hotspur and Mortimer, Earl of March, have already wedded their charming wives, but at the end of 3.1 Mortimer and his lady have left, not to reappear, and by 5.4 Hotspur, dead, has been borne away ignobly on Falstaff's back.

It's possible to strain quotation marks by saying that Falstaff has "wooed" Hal in the action, and Hal has "wooed" his father, while his father has at last reaffirmed his "marriage" to Britain, after his two sons smash the rebels and bring the civil war to a temporary end. In this case, *I Henry IV* would be another play that rounds itself off by matching up an *older* couple, not so much for the sake of fertility as for reconciliation.[1] Only in this sense does the play conform with the *structural* notion of comedy as it invokes "love" as a motif and concludes on an upbeat register.

But I follow the lead of scholars who have analyzed Shakespeare's comic output and concluded that the outcropping of Falstaff, that gigantic monadnock on this historical landscape, forces one to treat it as comedy, despite unorthodoxies of structure.[2] Here, then, I skimp on some broader perspectives of the play, including the political and historical background and foreground, and the personal wrangles, among them the King's distrust of the Prince and the Harry-vs.-Harry theme, which reflects the civil war. There are four Harrys in the play: the King, the Prince, Hotspur, and his father, the Earl of Northumberland. Because of the meticulous cross-cutting of plots, we see alternations of scenes with the two Harry sons, showing their differences as potential rulers, as well as the theme of fathers against sons. As the lines keep reverting to solar imagery, the play seems to keep asking which son will become the "sun." Regretfully putting most of this material aside, I will attempt to draw a bead on Falstaff and look at his impact on other leading figures in the drama, especially on Hal and on Hotspur, on the participants in the Boar's Head subplot, and, by way of his soliloquies, on himself.

For some time commentators have concluded that the main plot comprises Hal's brushing past a number of real and imaginary impediments to the throne, to end up as England's greatest warrior. Of the play's three principal groupings—the King and Court, the Eastcheap ne'er-do-wells, and the rebels (the representatives of the Percy family, Owen Glendower, and their allies, such as the Earl of Douglas and Archbishop Scroop)—Hal is aligned with the first two. He finally defeats the previously undefeatable Hotspur and Douglas from the third group, killing Hotspur and inducing King Henry to free Douglas. If we ask why Hal's starring, heroic rank hasn't always been acknowledged, the answer has connections with the scheming nature of Hal's role. He leaves hardly any moral impression as firm as those left by the three braggarts, Hotspur,

Glendower, and Falstaff. But if an actor plays Hal with Machiavellian undertones, he will not pay tribute to the role's callous heroism. In the BBC TV production the Prince of Wales's lines and later Henry V's were played for sympathetic responses by David Gwillim (a Welsh name). Gwillim's "I know you all" soliloquy had warmth and an affectionate tone, which the speech calls for. As his father, Jon Finch interpreted the King with a frozen realism that never falsified his scenes but let the playwright's ironies glint through the elegantly enunciated lines. Anthony Quayle gave an agreeable enough Falstaff in this television version, a picture of ruptured innocence and bewilderment, lovable but insufficiently relishing the crooked character his acting had carved out of the role.

A comparison of *Henry IV* with selections from the best known source documents, the *Chronicles* of Holinshed (1587), Samuel Daniel's verse drama on the civil wars between the houses of York and Lancaster (1595), and the play (or plays) *The Famous Victories of Henry the Fifth*, printed in 1598 and of uncertain authorship, reveals Shakespeare's toning down of Prince Hal's escapades. David Bevington writes,

> Many of Shakespeare's reshapings of material in *Famous Victories* take the form of transferring qualities from the Prince to his companions, and most of all to Falstaff [1994, 22], Bevington supplies some material on *Famous Victories*, [17–23], and provides further sources on the evolution of Falstaff as a role [see especially the footnote on 23], as well as Falstaff's "biblical guise." (32–33)

But this is the youth Falstaff has chosen to fasten onto as he entertains grandiose hopes. In their give-and-take scenes they enact some of the most spirited conflict and mock-conflict that the playwright wrote. The principal deduction from the name Falstaff relates to the Prince: taken literally, it gives the knight the character of being, despite his bulk, a false staff of life, a thin reed to lean on, a phony father. (The true father, however, is morally repugnant, a conniver who deserves the epithet *false* more than Falstaff does.) The first syllable of the name also suggests the fall of man, even a tenuous link with the fallen archangel, with whom several parts of the text compare him, for the edification of those of us who scrutinize names for denotations. The surname Falstaff is Shakespeare's invention or *trouvaille*, often linked with or confused with the name of Sir John Fastolfe, a gallant Lollard soldier. Most critics writing about this play point out Sir John Oldcastle as the original name, mentioned in *The Famous Victories*, and also based on a historical personage whose influential family may have objected to the cracks about him in the plays. At the same time as his scenes give us a handle on Falstaff's slippery vitality—accomplished through some unholy bargain?—they help to pin down the foxy nature of the Prince. The opening conversation between these unalikes is worth quoting at length.

FALSTAFF Now, Hal, what time of day is it, lad?

PRINCE Thou art so fat-witted with drinking of old sack, and unbuttoning thee after supper, and sleeping upon benches after noon, that thou hast forgotten to demand that truly which thou wouldst truly know. What a devil hast thou to do with the time of the day? Unless hours were cups of sack, and minutes capons, and clocks the tongues of bawds, and dials the signs of leaping houses, and the blessed sun himself a fair hot wench in flame-colored taffeta, I see no reason why thou shouldst be so superfluous to demand the time of day.

FALSTAFF Indeed, you come near me now, Hal, for we that take purses go by the moon and the seven stars, and not by Phoebus, he, "that wandering knight so fair." And I prithee, sweet wag, when thou art king, as, God save Thy Grace—Majesty I should say, for grace thou wilt have none—

PRINCE What, none?

FALSTAFF No, by my troth, not so much as will serve to be prologue to an egg and butter.

PRINCE Well, how then? Come, roundly, roundly.

FALSTAFF Marry, then, sweet wag, when thou art king, let not us that are squires of the knight's body be called thieves of the day's beauty. Let us be Diana's foresters, gentlemen of the shade, minions of the moon; and let men say we be men of good government, being governed, as the sea is, by our noble and chaste mistress the moon, under whose countenance we steal.

PRINCE Thou sayest well, and it holds well too, for the fortune of us that are the moon's men doth ebb and flow like the sea, being governed, as the sea is, by the moon. As, for proof, now: a purse of gold most resolutely snatched on Monday night and most dissolutely spent on Tuesday morning, got with swearing "Lay by" and spent with crying "Bring in," now in as low an ebb as the foot of the ladder and by and by in as high a flow as the ridge of the gallows.

FALSTAFF By the Lord, thou sayest true, lad. And is not my hostess of the tavern a most sweet wench?

PRINCE As the honey of Hybla, my old lad of the castle. (1.2.1–41)

With "my old lad of the castle" Shakespeare cannot refrain from some word play on the role's original name.

Falstaff's innocent query about the time calls forth a lengthy and, in its literal language, a stream of picturesque abuse from Hal. A director will as a rule open the scene with Falstaff snoring as though he had dropped off in the middle of talking, while the Prince studies him with bemused contempt, or alternatively, as though Hal had just entered his private suite in the palace to find "that gray Iniquity, that father ruffian, that vanity in years" (2.4.448–49) taking a breathy snooze on expensive upholstery in the middle of the day. But beyond the scorn and the expository material about thieves by night, which drops hints about a scene and offstage events to come, these two clearly revel in improvising witticisms in the fashionable balanced rhetoric of the time ("we that take purses go by the moon and the seven stars, and not by Phoebus, 'he, that wandering knight so fair, 's" or "a purse of gold most resolutely snatched on Monday night and most dissolutely spent on Tuesday morning"), and in putting verbal spins on one another's meanings and improving one another's images. Some image-improvement in the same scene:

FALSTAFF 'Sblood, I am as melancholy as a gib cat or a lugged bear.

PRINCE Or an old lion, or a lover's lute.

FALSTAFF Yea, or the drone of a Lincolnshire bagpipe.

PRINCE What sayest thou to a hare, or the melancholy of Moorditch?

FALSTAFF Thou hast the most unsavory similes, and art indeed the most comparative, rascalliest, sweet young prince.

If Hal, who is probably seventeen or eighteen, passed his days in the company of his father or Sir Walter Blunt, the Earl of Westmorland or some other courtier, or even with retainers, he'd listen to laments about upholding the royal family's reputation and sustaining his standing in the realm—pre-eminent but for his father's. With Falstaff he has a relaxed time practicing oral deftness without the drag of formal instructions. By resorting to a steady flow of taunts, he can maintain a convenient distance (to his own satisfaction) between the knight and himself. These two are used to one another; a certain affection trickles out of Falstaff; perhaps it is gratitude for Hal's allowing him to say lad or *sweet wag*, instead of *Your Highness*, and to address him in the second-person singular and even drop an insult about Hal's lack of grace.

The conversation twinkles along, apparently effortless banter, but it carries assorted meanings. Falstaff tries to sound out Hal about his own prospects when the Prince will ascend the throne, but always in a joshing tone; he hints at the dishonesty behind the criminal system extant, governed by "the rusty curb of old father Antic the law," while he looks hopefully for hints of favoritism toward himself and his cronies. Will there be hanging? Will the Prince appoint him a judge? Hal replies with matching casualness that Falstaff may become (the words are cleverly ambiguous) a hangman or a hanged man. Whereupon Falstaff proclaims himself ready to reform: "I must give over this life, and I will give it over. By the Lord, an I do not I am a villain." Hal immediately asks, "Where shall we take a purse tomorrow, Jack?" Without hesitating, Falstaff responds, "Zounds, where thou wilt, lad" (94–95, 97–98). The sudden changes of resolution—to live up to a Christian ideal, then to lift purses—serve as preparation for Hal's big speech of the scene, and of the early part of the play; but the arrival of Ned Poins cuts into the dramatic flow.

Poins is a conundrum. He evidently has an education, but no title. Because he is seldom seen out of the Prince's company, either in this play or its successor, and because neither of them has any truck with women, he is taken sometimes to be Hal's lover.[3] If so, he will be thrown over, together with Hal's other drinking and roistering buddies. In this scene, Poins proposes to rob Falstaff, Bardolph, Peto, and Gadshill (named after the site of the robbery in Kent, to the southeast of London) of the proceeds of *their* highway robberies, and Hal agrees to join him. But left alone on the boards, Hal will now clarify his motives to the audience—and himself.

His twenty-three-line soliloquy that follows announces his intention to "be more wondered at" by "redeeming time"; it strikes some critics as a sign of the Prince's stepping outside his role as he becomes the narrator of his own reformation. And every critic I have read who has anything to say about the speech finds it displays the role's hypocrisy. But it seems to me that, if delivered as a dispassionate and calculating statement, it not only lets the catch out of the bag too soon but also fades in momentum. I see it, rather, as a speech in which Hal talks himself into the need to accept the burdens of future kingship—and finds his present position better as a springboard than if he'd been a good boy, a conforming Prince of Wales. The spectators see his satisfaction grow as the speech gathers conviction. They might also notice a resemblance between his extemporaneous sentiments here and the free-wheeling back-and-forth of his earlier exchanges with Falstaff, when a prince and a knight speak prose, not verse, and Hal's guard appears to be down but never all the way. In that earlier dialogue, a dignified Sir John says,

> Thou hast done much harm upon me, Hal, God forgive thee for it.
> Before I knew thee, Hal, I knew nothing; and now am I, if a man
> should speak truly, little better than one of the wicked. (1.2.90–93)

In other words, "You're the tempter, not I." Falstaff then makes up his mind to reform—before reversing himself several times, for, after all, reform is a rash act if it impedes a thief in his sincere vocation of lifting purses. Hal is now making up *his* mind to reform. Earlier, he appeared to be Falstaff's corrupter: "Where shall we take a purse tomorrow, Jack?" Not *shall we* but *where* shall we?—and *tomorrow*. Will he truly reform or only seem to? Falstaff wants to look like, not the instigator but the pupil.

Whether or not Hal and Poins are lovers—and I see no hard evidence in the play to support the supposition, only one or two sugary endearments from Poins that could amount to no more than conventional flattery (for example: "my good sweet honey lord" [1.2.156])— a number of commentators have wondered whether *Falstaff* loves Hal.

Here again are two unattached males. Hal is a cool enough friend to have said something like Diaghilev's request to Cocteau, *"Étonne-moi, Jean!"* ("Keep me entertained, John!" i.e., "Show me something amazing!"). And this Jack of all shadowy trades delights in obliging. But because he loves the Prince? Only, I'd speculate, in the manner one might love an adoptive son who could set the royal seal on a lucrative appointment or a cushy pension. Fat Jack looks out for himself, lives for tomorrow's dawn, takes joy in the boldness of his hints about its imminence. But love as an unspoken, unsigned pact between consenting adults or between an infatuated senior and a chilly junior? I believe it could be justified (weakly) only as part of the trilogy setup, leading to a contrasting, teary-eyed payoff in Henry V, 2.1 and 2.3, scenes about the knight's death—not faked this time—that the author tints in exquisitely cool colors, courtesy of a slow-talking Quickly.

The next scene, 2.2, begins to resolve Poins' deception. Falstaff and his confederates rob three travelers; the disguised Prince and Poins steal the proceeds. The double theft constitutes one of Falstaff's controversial turns because on our interpretations of it depend the dispute over whether he is a coward. Flat assertions that he is or is not have arisen from writers who dislike or admire the old knight in an instinctive fashion, some of them without convincing evidence either way. In some cases it's assumed that, because he delights in exaggerating the odds against him in numbers of enemies, he must be cowardly. During the robbery, he urges on Bardolph, Peto, and Gadshill with hilarious whoops of encouragement meant to disguise or deny or mock his age ("They hate us youth" [2.2.86] and "young men must live" [90]). He may stand further back than the others, but he is keeping an eye out for Hal and Poins, who seem to be missing. Besides, he is old, immense in the gut, half-blind in the dark, winded, accustomed to military formations from his training, and feeling lost without his horse. Then, after Hal and Poins descend on him and the others, seize their cash, and chase them away, "Falstaff sweats to death," says Hal, "And lards the lean earth as he walks along" (107–08). "Walks": weighty, bone-tired, and surely too arthritic to run.

The surprise assault from behind will later (2.4) give Falstaff a good excuse (in his own mind) to elaborate on the swelling number of "rogues in buckram" or "misbegotten knaves in kendal green" who attacked him personally. Reconstructing the double robbery back in the Eastcheap tavern leads to Falstaff's most breathtaking self-defense. Two aspects of this scene help clarify the relationship between ruler-to-be and subject. First, the scene opens while Hal and Poins are awaiting the return of the robbed robbers. Hal boasts to Poins that he is already "the king of courtesy" among the "loggerheads" or dimwits who work in the

Boar's Head; he wins them over with his (pretended) modesty toward them. As one might say in twentieth-century working-class Britain, this nob doesn't put on side. Hal and Poins then proceed to tease Francis, one of the loggerheads, by summoning him from different seats in the tavern, earning him a reproach from his supervisor, the Vintner. Second, when the Prince and Poins challenge Falstaff's hyperboles, when they believe they have him trapped in a corner of his unintended choosing, he trounces them verbally, twice, by slipping away through oratorical orifices they could not have foreseen, while he arouses a big laugh—almost of relief—on the part of everybody onstage and off. At this moment he must realize, if he did not do so before, that Hal's friendship is a form of rivalry and hatred. From the auditorium we cannot help noticing that the Prince treats him with the same sort of ill-concealed disgust he has just shown for Francis. The scene is also remarkable in that its low-life setting comfortably embraces some of the most astonishing high comedy ever written, as Falstaff first claims that he will not admit his lies or do anything else "under compulsion" (a line reminiscent of some American politicos' insistence that they would never make peace "under duress"), and then that he "knew ye as well as he that made ye . . . Was it for me to kill the heir apparent?. . . Why, thou knowest I am as valiant as Hercules, but beware instinct. The lion will not touch the true prince" (264–69). And by the way, he is "glad you have the money." The comparison with Hercules and the image of Falstaff as a lion, if read with the mischievous tenor of the lines, reveal a Falstaff with a tremendous sense of humor about himself and his own limitations, and make arguments about his cowardice appear irrelevant and irresoluble.

The same scene, 2.4, which runs to nearly 550 lines, forges on. Some inconsequential exits and entrances—mostly inserted, I would guess, to allow the Falstaff actor time for a second wind—give way to the celebrated farce-within-a-play episodes in which Falstaff plays King Henry and Hal plays himself, followed by a reversal of the adopted roles. Once again the gravamen of the two sets of lines differs despite the similarity in their rhetorical devices, subtle alliteration, balanced clause arrangements, and lists. Falstaff's charges in his role of King are comically good-natured as he pretends the King knows his "pleasing eye [whatever that is], and a most noble carriage," as well as "virtue in his looks," (418–19, 422-23), a distinction from Hal's other cronies. The Prince, evidently irritated by this spirited self-justification, then asks to swap roles in order to unload a vehemently ill-natured paragraph about Falstaff. As Hal "becomes" the King his speech goes from a trot to a canter to a flat-out gallop, and contains some of the choicest, most anally fussy epithets directed at Falstaff.

> Why dost thou converse with that trunk of humors, that bolting-
> hutch of beastliness, that swollen parcel of dropsies, that huge bom-
> bard of sack, that stuffed cloak-bag of guts, that roasted Manningtree
> ox with the pudding in his belly, that reverend Vice, that gray Iniq-
> uity, that father ruffian, that vanity in years? Wherein is he good but
> to taste sack and drink it? Wherein neat and cleanly but to carve a
> capon and eat it? Wherein cunning but in craft? Wherein crafty but
> in villainy? wherein villainous but in all things? Wherein worthy but
> in nothing? (444–54)

The opprobrium is generally greeted in the theatre, or even in a reading, with storms of laughter, a volley of home truths aimed at the
round clown; yet Prince Hal doesn't as a rule benefit much from it and
enjoy repute as one of the two wittiest roles in the play, nor even as
an orator who can match Hotspur. Shakespeare has made him not
only a practical joker but also an accuser, most of whose lines—other
than those explaining his intentions to reform—serve to enlarge and
brighten . . . *the role of Falstaff,* which becomes so gargantuan and varied that its ramifications grow almost impossible to take in.

Falstaff's most ardent plea on his own behalf leads to the retort
from Hal that is almost always taken to be another foretaste of his
break with Falstaff. The knight, as the Prince, pleads with the Prince,
as the King:

FALSTAFF . . . No, my good lord, banish Peto, banish Bardolph, banish Poins;
but for sweet Jack Falstaff, kind Jack Falstaff, true Jack Falstaff, valiant Jack
Falstaff, and therefore more valiant being as he is old Jack Falstaff, banish not
him thy Harry's company, banish not him thy Harry's company—banish
plump Jack, and banish all the world.

PRINCE I do, I will. (2.4.468–476)

Once again—as the Prince without warning becomes himself—if Hal
lets out his four words ominously, anticipating the rejection in *Part II*
and the death scene in *Henry V,* rather than with a humorous and self-
satisfied tone that matches Falstaff's comic insolence and even caps
him on both accounts, the actor is cheating as he plays out of the moment. He must remain in the comedy, not settle on one intention, not
give the game away. For without knowing what follows, we should
trust Hal's promises to Falstaff and even, perhaps, trust the ones made
to his father. ("I shall hereafter, my thrice gracious lord, Be more myself" [3.3.92–93]).

The play's most piercing scene closes when the "Sheriff with a most
monstrous watch" enters the tavern in pursuit of Falstaff and others who
have been followed by "a hue and cry" since the robbery. Before lumbering off to hide behind an arras (without the peril that would later attend

Polonius in such a trap), Falstaff speaks some advice: "Dost thou hear, Hal? Never call a true piece of gold a counterfeit. Thou art essentially *mad* [or *made*] without seeming so" (486–87). The italicized words remain in critical contention. Falstaff first affirms himself as a shining example of authenticity, as thief, father, trainer, counselor; and in all of these, he is too valuable to throw away by being handed over to the Sheriff—the genuine, once-and-forever Falstaff. But that follow-up sentence about Hal is as much of a teaser as are some of Hal's lines. Aside from the tricky question of whether a key word is *mad* or *made* (and the manuscript of the Folio is hopelessly indeterminate; it can read as either), it could imply, You cannot go against your own nature as royalty or as a member of this [crazy] circle. But if Falstaff has suddenly donned a prophetic mantle, he could be reminding Hal that, despite the latter's insults, he, the Prince, is as much of an impostor as anybody, and could himself be detected someday. An interpretation here has to be tentative. The prefatory words, "Dost thou hear, Hal?" strike some critics as Falstaff's attempt to make himself heard above the uproar occasioned by the Sheriff's arrival. Too stagy. I read them as a preface, saying that, for once, Falstaff wants Hal to listen seriously. Perhaps the advice-plea works. Hal does not give him away, whether (a) he is moved by Falstaff's words or (b) doesn't want to lose face as a snitch in front of the "loggerheads" or (c) gives in to a generous impulse.

By the time the Sheriff is politely reassured and dismissed, Falstaff is "fast asleep behind the arras, and snorting like a horse" (523–24). Hal orders Peto to go through his pockets. They marvel at some receipts for Falstaff's alimentary intake, especially the gallons of sack. What did Hal expect to find? Sequestered proceeds from the robbery? New, incriminating items? Grounds for future challenges and mockery? He decrees that the stolen money shall be repaid: magnanimity or caution? Does he remind himself that, as king, he might be remembered for *all* his actions as a prince?

Falstaff has earlier brought "villainous news" about the rebels, who are now gathering a head. Hal decides to "procure this fat rogue a charge of foot," because "we must all to the wars," even though he noticed how hard the septuagenarian (or older?) "fetches breath." The scene gives way to a contrasting confrontation (3.1), which gives way to a pact between Hotspur and Glendower, which in turn marks the end of the peace in England. The rivalry between Glendower the magician and Hotspur, who says he favors plain speaking, proves to be as comical, if suitably staged, as some Falstaff scenes. The two warriors squabble over nationality, over territory before they possess it, and over who is the more extravagant braggart:

GLENDOWER

> ... At my birth
> The frame and huge foundation of the earth
> Shaked like a coward.

HOTSPUR   Why, so it would have done

> At the same season, if your mother's cat
> Had but kittened, though yourself had never been born....

GLENDOWER

> The heavens were all on fire; the earth did tremble.

HOTSPUR

> O then the earth shook to see the heavens on fire
> And not in fear of your nativity. (3.1.15–18, 22–24)

Hotspur's difficulties in coming to terms with the Welshman might be said to anticipate his slaying by the Prince of *Wales* or, as Hotspur addresses him, Harry Monmouth, Monmouth being situated in southeast Wales.

Before Falstaff meets up with his charge of foot (which he wishes were a charge of horse), he realizes that somebody went through his pockets. He accuses the Hostess or one of her guests of robbing him of "three or four bonds of forty pound apiece and a seal ring" that belonged to his grandfather and was "worth forty mark" (3.3.102–04 and 83). This diversionary tactic saves him from acknowledging that he owes heavy sums to the Hostess for food and especially liquor and loans. The Prince walks into the tavern in time to hear Falstaff reviling him. While eliciting some information about the theft, Hal accidentally gives away his knowledge of the contents of Falstaff's pockets whereupon Falstaff drops the accusations. He plays prudent when the Prince is present; he does not feel assured about the latter's goodwill.

With his retinue of ragged, strung-out soldiers, rounded up from among the poorest, oldest, weakest, unhealthiest, least costly recruits he can find, Falstaff, accompanied by Bardolph, briefly meets Hal and the Earl of Westmorland on the way to the battleground at Shrewsbury (4.2). A last parley takes place before the hostilities get under way (5.1). After the parley, Worcester declines to tell Hotspur, his nephew, of "the liberal and kind offer of the King" (5.2.2). The civil war breaks out in this very scene. The King offers forgiveness to the rebels, even at this late time, if they will disband. A terse exchange follows between the Prince and Falstaff, who contrived to attend the meeting. Hal's animosity has become irrepressible:

FALSTAFF Hal, if thou see me down in the battle and bestride me, so: 'tis a point of friendship.

PRINCE Nothing but a colossus can do thee that friendship. Say thy prayers and farewell.

FALSTAFF I would 'twere bedtime, Hal, and all well.

PRINCE Why, thou owest God a death. [*Exit.*] (5.1.121–26)

As the alarums sound and warrior after warrior strides across the stage, we glimpse Douglas or Hotspur looking for the enemy while Falstaff looks for an inconspicuous spot on the Shrewsbury battlefield to take a snooze. Hal finds him and tries to borrow his sword. Falstaff will not part with it, though he swears he has already done for Percy; he counteroffers his pistol, but the holster harbors only a bottle of sack. The Prince, no longer appreciating the old man's jesting, hurls the bottle at him before racing off to find a sword to despatch more rebels with. (If Falstaff's sword is the one he wielded during the Gad's Hill robbery, it would have been of limited use to Hal, because, as Peto told Hal earlier, "he hacked it with his dagger, and said he would swear truth out of England, but he would make you believe it was done in fight" [2.4.302–04].)

The penultimate scene played between Falstaff and Hal, also on Shrewsbury Plain, follows the single combat between Hal and Hotspur. Hotspur's death onstage is unparalleled in the plays identifiable as comedies. Mamillius and Antigonus die offstage, as does the Princess of France's father, who figures in the story but not the action. Hero and Hermione die symbolically and recover. But Marjorie Garber observes (see introduction to this book) that we are repeatedly reminded in the comedies of the presence of death (1980, 121–26). Hal pays tribute to the dead man's valor, then spots Falstaff lying close by.

> What, old acquaintance, could not all this flesh
> Keep in a little life? Poor Jack, farewell! . . . .
> Emboweled will I see thee by and by.
> Till then in blood by noble Percy lie. (5.4.102–03, 109–10)

The stage directions tell us that Hal goes off and "Falstaff riseth up," speaks his last soliloquy, thinking he will claim the credit for Hotspur's death, and "takes up the dead Hotspur on his back," after putting a signature of a sort on Hotspur's corpse by adding a wound to one thigh. The battle is now over. Hal returns to the scene with his brother, bewildered to find Falstaff alive and claiming to have "fought a long hour [with Hotspur] by Shrewsbury clock" (146) after Hal left. The two princes do not believe him, but Hal says he will let Falstaff brag that he beat Hotspur, "if a lie may do thee grace" (155). Falstaff picks up the body again, and promising to reform, for the fifth or sixth time in the action, he hauls Hotspur's corpse away, hoping for promotion and good results from becoming abstemious: "If I do grow great, I'll grow less; for I'll purge, and leave sack, and live cleanly as a nobleman should do" (161–63). In John Burrell's cherished Old Vic production in the late years of World War II, Falstaff (Ralph Richardson) bore the body of Hotspur (Laurence Olivier) by letting it hang down his back with the knees coming forward over his shoulders, holding it in place, as if it were a cape, by folding his arms over Hotspur's ankles. Olivier liked to punish himself; when Falstaff is supposed to throw the body to the ground to illustrate his disgust with the two princes for refusing to believe him, Richardson merely unfolded his arms. Olivier, after having hung upside down for some minutes, crashed on his head—with two such descents on matinee days.

Falstaff has brisk and amusing scenes and sub-scenes with Bardolph, Poins, the Hostess, and other denizens of the Boar's Head. He appears onstage only once in the presence of the King and utters one sarcastic line apropos of Worcester's leadership of the insurgents ("Rebellion lay in his way and he found it" [5.1.28]), which Hal quickly squelches. Although he does impersonate the King as stern parent and in some productions caricatures the gravity and vocal mannerisms of the actor playing the King, between the two father figures we find nothing of the reciprocity of his scenes with Hal. With Hotspur's remains he has only a one-sided conversation: as Harold C. Goddard points out, he doesn't stake an utterly false claim when he says he killed Hotspur (1951). If honor was the guiding star of Hotspur's actions, Falstaff, in the speech that shudders away from (and demystifies) honor, made the gallant hothead's motives look medieval, bypassed by time.

In that honor speech and others, Falstaff does give voice to some of his, and his author's, most enshrined remarks. As with Hal's soliloquies, Falstaff's are not mere pause points, rest areas off the narrative highway; they lean forward actively; they denote decisions. Most strikingly, they represent the real rebellion in the play. Hotspur and his undependable allies, including his father the defaulter, rebel to compete for territory, glory, and other rewards—to garner the recompense promised the Percy family by the then-uncrowned Bolingbroke once his "infant fortune" came of age. Falstaff, although he reveals an unappeasable hunger for material—especially edible—self-aggrandizement, and though he deludes himself into the hope of an earldom or dukedom (5.4.141), persistently rebels against conventional ideas. Audiences still gasp at his audacity, even when he merely confides in himself. He is the master of non-Jewish *chutzpah*.

By the time he concludes his first soliloquy, Falstaff has already broached two matters he will revert to: the injustice of the law, and casting off his insalubrious habits and companions to be a new man. That soliloquy pictures him during the night robbery feeling unhorsed, inadequate, and betrayed: "A plague upon it when thieves cannot be true one to another!" (2.2.26–27). Between soliloquies again, he complains to Bardolph about the decline in the times: he has "fallen away vilely"; he bates, he dwindles:

> my skin hangs about me like an old lady's loose gown; I am withered like an old applejohn. Well, I'll repent, and that suddenly . . . . An I have not forgotten what the inside of a church is made of, I am a peppercorn, a brewer's horse. The inside of a church! Company, villainous company, hath been the spoil of me. (3.3.1–10)

He thinks back to his earlier existence and it seems to him that he was

> as virtuously given as a gentleman need to be . . . swore little, diced not above seven times—a week, went to a bawdy house not above once in a quarter—of an hour, paid money that I borrowed—three or four times. (14–18)

Even in the dumps, Falstaff remains a supreme entertainer as he makes over his past and present selves. If Hal happens not to be on hand, he will fence with Bardolph or any other foil. When he keeps on at Bardolph about his crimson nose, the poor man at last bursts out, "'Sblood! I would my face were in your belly!" to which Falstaff, joyful at having provoked him, retorts, "God-a-mercy! So should I be sure to be heartburned" (3.3.49–51).

Falstaff, who would drop any of his pals with even less ceremony than Hal's in snubbing him ("banish Peto, banish Bardolph, banish Poins," etc.), trades shamelessly on their good natures and ignorance. On the march with his "slaves as ragged as Lazarus in the painted cloth, where the glutton's dogs licked his sores," he sends Bardolph on ahead into Coventry to buy a supply of sack and verbally tricks him out of the payment. Meanwhile, he has made a tidy sum by conscripting rich men for his "charge" and excusing them on payment of bribes. To produce a following of some sort, he "had the most of [his company] out of prison," and since they look as shabby as scarecrows, "they'll find linen enough on every hedge," that is, steal laundry set out to dry along their route (4.2.13–47). Those enraptured with Falstaff as admirable, even romantic, misconstrue the comic swaggering of the role: he is not a super-hero but the super-antihero. He will swindle his benefactors and anybody else who crosses his path. But he physically ill-treats no one. He has a more contagious sense of humosr than Iago's or Richard III's but is devoid of their brutality. Yes, he is the biggest "heavy," but not the medieval Vice, even with a Roman parasite grafted on. He models the charmer absolute. Magic spells spill out of his brain. But he is a crook through and through, a relentless sponger. A number of critics have chosen, as Falstaff's nearest equivalent in our times, W. C. Fields, in the misanthropic persona he created: baby- and child-hater, audience-lover, distruster of good actions, and literal juggler.

If we look at prevailing attitudes to honor among the leaders of the three groups in the play, we find King Henry pays it lip service in so far as honor gives him excuses to avoid honest government and settle debts of alliance (to the Percy family most of all) by promising crusades to the holy land and "the sepulchre of Christ—Whose soldier now, under whose blessèd cross We are impressèd and engaged to fight" (1.1.19–21). He'd lead them if only these confounded rebels would give over with their demands. In short, the King owes no obligations or influence whatever to honor.

As the impeccable cross-cutting proceeds between the subplots, we notice that for Hotspur, by contrast, honor is the guiding principle of life:

> Send danger from the east unto the west,
> So honor cross it from the north to south,
> And let them grapple . . . .
> By heaven, methinks it were an easy leap
> To pluck bright honor from the pale-faced moon,
> Or dive into the bottom of the deep
> Where fathom line could never touch the ground,
> And pluck up drownèd honor by the locks,
> So he that doth redeem her thence [Hotspur himself] might wear
> Without corrival all her dignities . . . . (l.3.195–97, 201–07)

Despite his allegiance to honor, Hotspur reveals an enviable sense of humor in scene after scene, starting with his first monologue, before the rebellion, when he denies denying the King some Scottish prisoners. He re-creates the effete envoy who came onto the battlefield to demand those prisoners.

> . . . A certain lord, neat and trimly dressed,
> Fresh as a bridegroom, and his chin new reaped
> Showed like a stubble land at harvest home.
> He was perfumèd like a milliner,
> And twixt his finger and his thumb he held
> A pouncet box, which ever and anon
> He gave to his nose and took't away again . . . .
> And as the soldiers bore dead bodies by
> He called them untaught knaves, unmannerly,
> To bring a slovenly unhandsome corpse
> Betwixt the wind and his nobility . . . .

The entire forty-line speech (1.3.30–69), in which Hotspur gives the King his malicious and insulting impersonation of the envoy (who, after all, was the royal representative), swings between satire and rage. The role goes on alternating through Hotspur's later scenes between comic mockery, the glorification of honor, and spasms of anger in dealing with his father, uncle, and allies. In his squabble with Glendower over who will control what territory, Hotspur, with an impudence that equals Falstaff's, wants to turn the "smug and silver" River Trent into a new course that will give him an additional arc of fertile land. But Hotspur's end, not at all comic, comes almost self-willed—as death chokes off his loquacity in mid-sentence.

> I better brook the loss of brittle life
> Than those proud titles thou hast won of me.
> They wound my thoughts worse than thy sword my flesh.
> . . . . No Percy, thou art dust
> And food for—(5.4.78–80, 85–86)

Looking over the King's regrets that Hotspur, the other young Harry, would have made a more desirable son and heir than Hal (1.1.77–89), and his wishes that "some night-tripping fairy" had exchanged the two when they were in their cradles, some critics believe that the King has a grudging affection for the fiery Hotspur.[4] A production could hint at such fondness, but it might be misplaced. The King, with his respect for appearances over actuality, seems to yearn less for Hotspur as a son than for his own son to earn something like "the praise" won by Hotspur. The King says in the opening scene that he feels

> envy that my lord Northumberland
> Should be the father to so blest a son—
> A son who is the theme of honor's tongue,
> Amongst a grove the very straightest plant,
> Who is sweet Fortune's minion and her pride,
> Whilst I, by looking on the praise of him,
> See riot and dishonor stain the brow
> Of my young Harry . . . O, that it could be proved
> That some night-tripping fairy had exchanged
> In cradle clothes our children where they lay,
> And called mine Percy, his Plantagenet!
> Then would I have his Harry, and he mine. (1.1.78–89)

But when Hotspur, soon after, confronts Henry (1.3), the latter speaks warningly, with no hint of warmth. At the end when he learns from Hal that Hotspur died in the battle ("the noble Percy slain" [5.5.19]), he doesn't so much as remark on it. I prefer to interpret Henry's speech as a willful shock aimed at his court listeners as he almost disowns the Prince of Wales by comparing him unfavorably with the most blatant threat to the throne.

Falstaff, in his penultimate soliloquy, may be foreseeing Hotspur's end, shortly to come, as he brings a comic curse to bear on honor as a justification for dying, after Hal tells him he owes God a death:

> 'Tis not due yet. I would be loath to pay him before his day. What
> need I be so forward with him that calls not on me? Well, 'tis no mat-
> ter; honor pricks me on. Yea, but how if honor prick me off when I
> come on? How then? Can honor set to a leg? No. Or an arm? No. Or
> take away the grief of a wound? No. Honor hath no skill in surgery,
> then? No. What is honor? A word. What is in that word "honor?"
> What is that "honor?" Air. A trim reckoning! Who hath it? He that
> died o' Wednesday. Doth he feel it? No. Doth he hear it? No. 'Tis in-
> sensible, then? Yea, to the dead. But will it not live with the living?
> No. Why? Detraction will not suffer it. Therefore I'll none of it. Honor
> is a mere scutcheon. And so ends my catechism. (5.1.127–40)

Scrambling the word *prick*, even with an innocent meaning (but
bawdy intention, if honor is nothing more than a stiff, fired-up member), into sentences about repaying God for life, *and doing it twice for
emphasis,* while slamming the revered notion of honor to justify supposedly virile, warlike activity, makes for a combustible mixture.[4]

Did Shakespeare succeed in squashing honor by ridiculing it?
Only, regrettably, to those who heard and those who still hear the
speech, and then no more than temporarily. Less than seventy years
later in France, where gross, Spanish-affected slavishness toward hon-
or persisted and fomented duels, despite a royal ban, Molière blasted
the notion and the appeal of honor in several plays, most fiercely (and
comically) in *Don Juan* and *Sganarelle, or The Imaginary Cuckold.* It persisted, not only among the military in every country, but also—as a
perversion of soldierly beliefs—among hoodlums. Warped, suicidal
honor remains at the disciplinary core of terrorist sects, as well as of
street gangs in every American metropolis, to whom the words "Your
mother!" are a challenge to fight.

Soon after Falstaff comes back into sight, in a scene that cries out
for brutal, cinematic verism, the corpulent old half-drunk rolls and
stumbles across a field of corpses, having not three of his 150 ragamuf-
fins left alive. He spots the corpse of a friend of the King, and resumes
the honor theme:

> Soft, who are you? Sir Walter Blunt. There's honor for you. Here's no
> vanity. I am as hot as molten lead, and as heavy too. God keep lead
> out of me. I need no more weight than mine own bowels (5.3.31–35)

"Here's no vanity." He's not too proud to avoid being slaughtered—if
he has the option. On his next appearance, he puts this modesty into
practice when he happens on the encounter between the two young
Harrys, and cheers Hal on, drawing the attention of mighty Douglas,
who killed Sir Walter and now assails him. Before there is any chance
for Falstaff to take a wound, he drops to the ground as if dead, and he
remains recumbent until after Hal has outfought Hotspur, spoken a

tribute, and moved on. Hal's promise to embowel Falstaff (gut him and prepare him for embalming) draws this response from Falstaff, "If thou embowel me today, I'll give you leave to powder me and eat me tomorrow." As this last soliloquy continues, Falstaff announces his fear of "this gunpowder Percy, though he be dead" (121–22). Or what if Percy, like him, was shamming? Here Falstaff rationalizes his adding a wound, dishonoring the corpse, and then claiming a reward from the royal family. Yet if the actor and director respect the text, the soliloquy should not be treated as a prefigured plea but as a sequence of ideas that emerge from Falstaff's teeming brain the moment he taps it. His line about being powdered and eaten is quoted by J. I. M. Stewart in support of Falstaff as a sacrificial steer:

> Falstaff, in fact, is the "sweet beef," "the roasted Manningtree ox with the pudding in his belly," who reigns supreme on the board of the Boar's Head in Eastcheap—a London tavern . . . almost certainly even better known for good food than for good drink. There is thus from the first a symbolical side to his vast and genuine individuality; and again and again the imagery in which he is described likens him to a whole larder of "fat meat." (1949, 138)

One would have to swirl together all four plays that deal with Falstaff and/or Hal to reach the conclusion that the former is consumed in effigy. But is Falstaff in fact, as Stewart claims, the sweet beef and other hefty delicacies?

In this play, which contains much richer a Falstaff role than do the others, he cuts a very different figure from a pitiful sacrificial victim. By cunning and impudence he survives the battle of Shrewsbury, which took a welter of lives. He marches off the bloodied landscape bearing the prize to which he is not entitled, Hotspur, the role who *does* resemble a sacrificial—well, certainly not a lamb; perhaps a tiger. Until the following scene (5.5), the play's last, goes into its quiescent, not to say tepid, unFalstaffed windup featuring King Henry's self-satisfied prophecy ("Rebellion in this land shall lose his sway" [5.5.41]), we have witnessed in action the most ingratiating con artist that fiction holds out to us.

Notes

1. The endings of *Comedy of Errors* and *Winter's Tale,* are two more notable examples of elders reconciled.

2. In a 1964 critical anthology, four of the fourteen reprinted essays on Shakespeare's ten history plays have Falstaff's name in their titles and others deal with him as a striking figure in the play's fabric (in Dorius 1964). A later

compilation devoted to the one play Harold Bloom (1987), gives over four out of its nine reprints, plus the editor's introduction, to Falstaff.

3. If MacCary (1985), had dealt with *Henry IV* in his book and had treated it as part of a trilogy that advanced into *Henry V,* he might have seen Poins as one of those second young men MacCary discerns in the comedies as a male lover, one step on the hero's progress to heterosexual love. But it is Falstaff, not Hal, who makes sexually suggestive remarks about Poins: "I am bewitched with the rogue's company. If the rascal have not given me medicines to love him, I'll be hanged; it could not be else—I have drunk medicines" (2.2.16–19). Gus Van Sant took the gay relationship for granted, and then took it further in his film *My Own Private Idaho* (1991), the story of young male hustlers in the northwest corner of the United States. The Poins figure, a narcoleptic hauntedly searching for his mother and played by River Phoenix, becomes the principal role. The Hal figure (Keanu Reeves), the disreputable heir of an industrial magnate, is his lover-protector and the former lover of Bob Pigeon, a not particularly fat man referred to as "the fat man" (William Pichert). Van Sant's screenplay stiffens when it quotes from and paraphrases Shakespeare (or Orson Welles' *Chimes at Midnight?*) in and among the American vernacular of the hustlers; but a late scene that contrasts the decorous funeral of the stand-in for Henry IV with the wild informality of the funeral for the "Falstaff" dramatically catches the essence of Hal's pull between the true and false fathers.

4. This particular attack by Shakespeare on the notion of honor, or sacred obligations to oneself, is nearly matched in play after play by Ibsen in which some figures talk slightingly about *duty*, regarded in the nineteenth century as a nexus of sacred obligations, borne especially by women, to men, including dead ancestors.

The Merry Wives of Windsor

"Shakespeare in the Bronx!" A circular announcing five showings in February 1995 of *It All Comes out in the Wash* called the performance an "exciting and hilarious adaptation" taken from "one of Shakespeare's masterpieces," *The Merry Wives of Windsor,* and "based on Giuseppe Verdi's *Falstaff."* The play has long had its carefree adapters, as well as its outright detractors, some of them masked as friends who take pity on the work as they address its weaknesses and dress its wounds. In 1702 came a durable challenge from John Dennis: his note to the effect that Shakespeare had had to whack out the comedy-farce in fourteen days at the behest of Queen Elizabeth, who commanded the playwright to produce a work featuring Falstaff in love. The order for one script (or full staging?) in two weeks still gets passed along by some modern textbooks without counter-challenges—such as, was Dennis boosting his own chances? That same year he concocted and staged his reworking of *Merry Wives.* It did not win much applause or a lengthy life. Entitled and now entombed as *The Comical Gallant,* it is concisely summarized by H. J. Oliver (1971, xi–xii). Dennis did not adduce any evidence for his assertion of a two-week deadline or of the Queen's specifying a command performance. And, for all we know, this play— or an earlier draft—*preceded* the two parts of *Henry IV.*

In any case, comparisons are otiose. The Falstaff of *Merry Wives* is not the same role as either of the Falstaffs of the *Henry IV* plays—nor, come to that, is it the same as the Falstaff whose death is disconsolately reported in *Henry V.* In *Merry Wives* the Falstaffian novelties, of which there are plenty, start from the differences in his relations with his acolytes, Nym, Bardolph, and Pistol, elsewhere his followers, now unwanted companions being cast aside to become a tapster (Bardolph), or rejecting rejection and turning traitorous (Nym and Pistol).

Mistress Quickly also takes on a new role in this play: neither Falstaff's
adorer and financial savior nor the hostess of the Boar's Head tavern
in Cheapside, an incidental part in the Henry plays. Here, as the
housekeeper to Dr. Caius ("in the manner of his nurse, or his dry
nurse, or his cook, or his laundry, his washer, and his wringer," according to Parson Evans [1.2.3–4]), she plays a prime mover in the
action. Justice Shallow, instead of being Falstaff's former schoolmate
and sharer of memories, as in *II Henry IV,* declares himself in the opening scene the legal foe of Falstaff, who, he says, has trespassed and
poached on the Shallow estate, "beaten my men, killed my deer, and
broke open my lodge" (1.1.105–06).

Merry Wives departs from the Shakespearean pattern of at least two
pairs of young lovers. Falstaff pursues the Mistresses Ford and Page,
who, added to the antics of Ford, take the place of a secondary, comic
couple. As a further departure, the ration of verse is low: though the
third lengthiest of the twelve plays strictly defined as comedies, this
one has a much higher proportion of prose (almost 87 percent) than
the others.[1]

The assorted geographically separated locations in the Henry IV
plays—London, the metropolis, the "wen" (from the Palace, at the ze-
nith of the social scale, to what is roughly today the East End),
Shrewsbury, Kent, Gloucestershire, Wales, and elsewhere—and the
international, mostly French flavor of *Henry V* differ from the scenic
surrounds of the *Merry Wives.* These, circumscribed by the limits of the
rural town or sizable village of Windsor, some forty miles west of London today, do not include the royal castle. A sketch of Windsor as it
was just before and after 1600 appears in William Green's critical work
(1962) and in T. W. Craik (1990, 2). In the homogeneous, respectably
middle-class enclaves everybody knows everybody. Two outsiders, the
French physician and the Welsh minister, have been absorbed into the
community; even the ambience of the Garter Inn seems overwhelmingly bourgeois. As a result, although the scene sequence of criss-
crossing plots adheres to the chronicle or epic pattern of Shakespeare,
the air of enclosure and neighborliness makes the action seem more
structurally "dramatic" (self-contained and modern) than that of any
other Shakespeare play except *Comedy of Errors.* And just as *Errors*
builds into a situation that disrupts the city of Ephesus (and as *Shrew*
grows into a disturbance of the peace of Padua), so *Merry Wives* upends
for a time Windsor's settled community.

Once again Shakespeare uses the last act to work against an expected comic ending. Even if editorial hands have wrought the breakdown
into acts and scenes we accept today, the final segment of the play,
whether we call it act 5 or otherwise delimit it, rounds off the structure
and provides a principal reason for calling the work a comedy. Since

comedies work by wit and willpower, the roles seek certain ends and reach them, not always as expected. In farces, chance, serendipity, or some higher power takes over: the roles propose; the playwright disposes.

The main plot, a double one, recruits an unusually large number of the roles. It begins when Falstaff tells his companions that Mistress Ford and Mistress Page are intoxicated with him. He will capitalize on their infatuation and con money out of them. He assumes they control their homes' finances. That paunchy old Jack can play the lounge lizard and kept lover is, at best, a hopeless wager and at the same time prime material for knockabout capers. Whether or not the wives ever handle their families' income (unlikely), they do snatch control of the main plot. That plot then swerves into the games they concoct to humble him. Three times, after snatching the initiative from him, they lure him, instead of his tempting them. They teach him three lessons in a row before he wakes up to the overriding one, familiar to everybody: experience teaches us that we do not learn from our mistakes, but fall prey to the same ones again and again.

Craik points out that "Shakespeare gives most of the principal characters more than one function in the play's multiple action" (1990, 16). That action has seven subplots, which draw on roles from the main plot.

1. Nym and Pistol, to whom Falstaff confides his plans, blab about them to involved parties. Having steered this subplot into the main plot, after 2.2, Pistol returns only once, at night in the guise of a hobgoblin, to speak five lines (5.5.41–45), while Nym vanishes altogether after 1.3. Even Bardolph, resurrected as a tapster, gets to utter no more than four curt lines, which add up to sixteen words. The trio of layabouts will probably take on more visual activity in performance than the measly ration of lines implies.

2. Master Ford, to check up on whether Falstaff is indeed paying court to Mistress Ford, takes on the name of Brook and the role of a rich idler hopelessly enamored of Mistress Ford. He will bribe Falstaff to secure him a favorable wooing position, but nobody else must know about the deception: the brook must flow beneath the ford. Most of all he longs masochistically to catch Falstaff in action seducing his wife.

3. Dr. Caius and Abraham Slender compete for the dainty hand of Anne (or Nan) Page, Slender supported by Justice Shallow and Master Page, the doctor supported by the Mistresses Page and Quickly, so that Mistress Page becomes the only mother in Shakespeare's comedies to attempt to dictate her daughter's choice of a husband. (If Shakespeare really had meant to write about

Falstaff in love—out of his emotional element—he could have lined up Falstaff as a fourth suitor for Anne; but in Shakespeare no young woman is enticing or unlucky enough to draw more than three suitors.)

4. The third suitor, Fenton, a "gentleman" reported as a former crony of Prince Hal and Poins, although he doesn't materialize in the "Henriad," has the support only of Anne herself and Quickly (again), who is as responsive as Falstaff to bribes. But Fenton needs no further backing in order to trick both Page parents out of their daughter.

5. The Host of the Garter Inn mischievously tells Caius and Evans to meet in different places for the duel they are intent on waging. They pay him back by having his horses temporarily stolen—or do *they* steal them? The theft goes unresolved.

6. Quickly, the go-between who earns her name more vigorously than the Quicklys who appear in other plays, looks out for herself, keeping her pockets stuffed as she sprays out promises to various suitors. The greater aptness of Quickly's name in *Merry Wives* than in the other plays where it appears supports the notion that this play could have been written before the other Falstaff plays. In act 5 she turns into the Queen of the Revels, a transformation that has led one or two critics to take her portrayal for a satire on Queen Elizabeth, perhaps conceived as a penalty for having commanded the play, if the Queen truly did so. If she did, and if the author tried to satirize her by means of Quickly, he went pretty wide of the mark, appearing to have targeted instead one of her confidant(e)s with a hand outstretched for political alms. It is astonishing how much critical effort has been squandered over the centuries in attempting to link Shakespeare's roles with historical models—some of the models celebrated, like the Queen, others suddenly exhumed from oblivion. As yet I have not discovered one such linkage that contributed to a play's theatrical life, although here and there one gets caught up in a story that is engagingly told and worth reading, even if it has no likely application to a staging.

7. Master Shallow's plans to report Falstaff—these evaporate in act 1.[2]

Apart from this abandoned underplot and one or two other bits of unfinished business, by the end of act 5 Shakespeare has satisfied the desiderata of comedy posited by critics since his death. The semi-scapegoated transgressor has been punished, but so, to one degree or another, has almost everybody else; the events have brought the community together for a celebratory ritual that precedes a marriage. The sylvan setting, "the park at midnight" as Page calls it (4.4.17–18), the green realm, asserts its healing nature. The mood even complies with Coleridge's rough distinction between the probable of comedy and the possible, the less likely, of farce, for most of the play does fall unmistakably into probability. The laundry basket, the beatings, and most of all the unconscious self-revelation of roles by means of humor and humors have added their farcical touches, without encroaching on the action's overall believability.

And Falstaff? The role as depicted in this play has found valiant defenders, among them H. J. Oliver, who guides our attention to the poetic bravura and comic substance in the Falstaff scenes. These do not amount to letdowns, even when measured against the Falstaffian counterparts in *I Henry IV.* His perorations of grumbling about his mistreatment and, in the play's culminating scene, when he wears the disguise of Herne the hunter (*Horne* the hunter in the first quarto edition), his midnight appeals, as "a Windsor stag, and the fattest, I think, i' the forest," to Jove (5.5.1–15), followed by his ecstasy at landing between the two wives—"Divide me like a bribed buck, each a haunch"—are utterances we'd receive gratefully from any author. If a Falstaff role does not sparkle with quite the same impertinence in Windsor as it does elsewhere, if this one writhes out of tight corners by being helped and hindered, rather than by its own verbal dexterity, one can think of a good reason for the relative modesty.

Not that I noticed the reason before seeing the BBC television version. In that production, directed by David Jones—one of the most thoughtful, as well as inventive, artists to have come out of the seethe of talent at the Royal Shakespeare Company—the Falstaff (Richard Griffiths) looked restrained, more of a youngish bumbler than a superannuated heartthrob. He made no pretense of being smitten by the two hectic housewives, not even when he insolently kissed Mrs. Ford with a "by your leave" that she had no time to contest. Here Jones and Griffiths remained loyal to the play. Falstaff doesn't tell his acolytes that he loves or will love. He will *"make* love to Ford's wife," because "I spy entertainment in her. She discourses, she carves, she gives the leer of invitation" (1.3.41–43). Similarly, he goes on,

> Page's wife, who even now gave me good eyes too, examined my parts with most judicious oeillades. Sometimes the beam of her view gilded my foot, sometimes my portly belly.
>
> PISTOL *[To Nym]* Then did the sun on dunghill shine.
>
> NYM *[To Pistol]* I thank thee for that humor.
>
> FALSTAFF O, she did so course o'er my exteriors, with a greedy intention that the appetite of her eye did seem to scorch me up like a burning glass! . . . . She bears the purse too; she is a region in Guiana,

> all gold and bounty. I will be cheaters to them both, and they shall
> be exchequers to me. They shall be my East and West Indies, and I
> will trade to them both." (1.3.57–70)

Thus he either believes that the women are mad about him or else he
believes he can delude Pistol and Nym into believing the fiction, so that
"we will thrive, lads, we will thrive" (72), in the tempting first-person
plural. We can note that at this beginning of the strictly mercenary
venture, Falstaff refers to both ladies not as themselves but as the wives
of Ford and Page. He evidently looks forward to the thrill of bilking the
two men out of their spouses' affections, as well as their money. He
may have the reputation of an old and incapacitated lecher, but lechery is not his motive for trying to board a ford and turn a page.

Much of the dialogue in Jones's production was played for laughs
at regional accents and mistaken words; but the idiosyncratic language
does pay rewards. In the maelstrom of happenings, Falstaff, in spite of
his extravagant boasts, appeared as a fairly still center, meditating sad-
ly over his misfortunes between the bouts of frenzied activity. Falstaff
claqueurs will grow disappointed if they look forward to more quibbles, semantics, and oral weaseling out of predicaments, such as the
celebrated "Was it for me to kill the heir apparent?"

A new play presupposes a new role: the Falstaff of the second part
of *Henry IV* demonstrates this truism. Extending the cherished Falstaff
persona of the Henry plays into *Merry Wives* forges a spurious figure.
The true one here may have more lines to speak than any of the other roles do; the play, though, is not named for him but for the two
merry wives and for Windsor. In addition to him and the three mistresses, Quickly included, the cast offers a motley bundle of clowns.
Jones fastened onto this extreme instance of what Shakespeare did
less spectacularly in other comedies: he let those minor parts explode—not only into the speech eccentricities of Pistol and Nym,
Shallow's repetitions and Slender's hesitations, the ripe accents of the
Welshman and the Frenchman, Quickly's crippled and misapplied
words, and the Host's hearty, flattering greetings and welcomes. And
explode not only in language but also in contradictory characteristics:
the combative, even combustible, manners of Caius and Evans (anything but a typically soothing doctor and a conciliatory parson),
Quickly's venality and saucy lies, liberal helpings of spite and sarcasm
from the Host. So do impotent old Shallow's retailing his feats as a
youthful swordsman. He boasts: "I have seen the time, with my long
sword, I would have made you four tall fellows skip like rats"
(2.1.211–13). "Though I be now old and of the peace, if I see a sword
out, my finger itches to make one. . . . We have some salt of our
youth in us" (2.3.40–44). Leslie Hotson links this bluster to Gardiner's

having "been fined for drawing blood in a fight" when he was young (1931, 103).[2]

All those wild roles coming at spectators in the opening scenes, in succession or together, are liable to leave them more confused than amused. Hence the holding back or toning down of Falstaff, who in the Jones version didn't resemble the galloping Gargantua we expect. His recounting of his imprisonment in the buck basket amid the filthy, stinking clothes was rueful or wry, rather than uproarious with indignation, as it is generally played, or overplayed. In this interpretation Falstaff became a pathetic figure of fun, the victimized loser, the offender who has been sufficiently punished and is eventually forgiven. He differed from the other roles in being less crazy, not more. He underwent his ordeal as an outsider, much as Egeon, the outsider in *Errors*, almost loses his life because of the trade war between Ephesus and Syracuse, with its hostile treaty, which contains a most-unfavored-nation clause. Mrs. Ford wonders, "What tempest, I trow, threw this whale, with so many tuns of oil in his belly, ashore at Windsor?" (2.1.60–62). We never do learn what brought the strange "whale" to Windsor in the first place. Scholars have amassed evidence that points to a connection with conferring of the Order of the Garter, a ceremony customarily held in Windsor castle. A real Garter Inn, named after the award, may have existed in the town at that time. But what would attract Falstaff to the ceremony is food for speculation. Such speculation may color the play's story but doesn't really affect its action.

To compensate for Falstaff's reticence, then, the second, third, and fourth longest roles, as well as the minor parts, needed to take on more dramatic freight. Jones's casting of Prunella Scales as Mrs. Page, Ben Kingsley as Ford-Brook, and Elizabeth Spriggs as Quickly, plus other bold character studies, created a cluster of dazzling luminaries, instead of second-rate fill-ins.[3] All of a sudden the play became rife with acting prodigies. The two housewives, baffled at first by Falstaff's letters (Mrs. Page: "What, have I scaped love letters in the holiday time of my beauty, and am I now a subject for them?"[2.1.1–3]), swiftly recast themselves as temptresses. Quickly's manner flitted back and forth between confidential and conspiratorial as she dropped revelations and ushered visitors in and out, showing off a rare array of Spriggs's facial contortions. Although Mrs. Ford calls her "that foolish carrion" (3.3.176), suggesting that she is a rotting old bawd, Quickly must have some attractions. Pistol, in an aside, takes a fancy to her and metaphors her into a galleon to be boarded.

> This punk is one of Cupid's carriers.
> Clap on more sails! Pursue! Up with your fights!
> Give fire! She is my prize, or ocean whelm them all. (2.2.128–30)

But Shakespeare pursues that pursuit no further. In *Henry V* we find a different Quickly and Pistol married—and Pistol and Nym at logger-heads.

William Green writes, "The most complete humors portrait in *The Merry Wives* is that of Ford." At the same time, "the entire handling of Ford's character is one-dimensional and makes an interesting contrast with the deeper study of jealousy found in *Othello*" (1965, xxxi). There is some truth in this, even if we remain wary of claims of relative di-mension and depth. But Othello's jealousy swells gradually under the nurturing of Iago (particularly in 3.3); and Othello's is not a comic, theatricalist role, even though several times he seems abstracted, not in command of himself, ready to fall prey to the epilepsy that takes possession of him once. Ford, however, starts out jealous and keeps uncovering confirmation for his suspicions and then humiliations at being wildly, obviously wrong. He trembles at the prospect of becom-ing a *cornuto*, and yet appears almost unmoved by the Falstaff revela-tions when he plays Brook, as though that role were an instrument he had practiced on all his life. Kingsley demonstrated that Ford, al-though no Othello (or Leontes either), can blossom under the warmth and pressure of intensified acting. Like George Dandin and also one of Molière's seven Sganarelles, this study of a man who imagines himself a cuckold (and in Dandin's case is) combined delight at hearing his fears come true with horror at the imminent sprouting of horns.[4] In scene after scene one saw the hilarious anguish on Kingsley's face, the rictus that became now a smile, now a signal that he was dying inside.

One simultaneously laughed at Brook and grieved for Ford. I would not swear that the role is as "deep" as Othello's; but whereas Othello becomes driven into a murder, Ford drives himself into ridicule. And although what he does to his wife doesn't begin to compare with what Othello does to his, Ford plays the more malicious of the two.

> Our revolted wives share damnation together. Well, I will take
> [Falstaff], then torture my wife, pluck the borrowed veil of modesty
> from the so-seeming Mistress Page, divulge Page himself for a secure
> and willful Actaeon; and to these violent proceedings all my neigh-
> bors shall cry aim. (3.2.30–39).

Entrusted to Kingsley, the role's passion grew immense yet meticu-lously delineated. It reminded me of once seeing a Plautus farce done in France with dancing to accompanying flute and drum music, a matching of potent feelings and disciplined comic rhythms. The role of Ford offers enough artistic latitude to have attracted actors, long be-fore the matchless Kingsley, of the caliber of Kemble and Kean. Ac-cording to Oliver, "Kemble (at first) and Kean preferred to play Ford" to playing Falstaff (1990, xii).

The wives in this play are not merely merry; they also triumph over the men. Mrs. Page doesn't secure the groom she wants for Anne—Dr. Caius, an absurd choice, as is her husband's preference for Slender—but she has declared she will not oppose Fenton's bid for her daughter, as Page himself has firmly done, and the outcome doesn't displease her. She seconds Mrs. Ford in crushing the plans of both Falstaff and Frank Ford. Falstaff has not discriminated between the wives; it was they and Ford who determined to have him concentrate his efforts on Alice Ford. The two women are not strongly differentiated, except as we see them in colloquies with family members: Mrs. Ford has no daughter or son (in the action) and we do not see her in conversation with (and affected by) offspring. Mrs. Page's husband is not jealous—is, indeed a bit lumpish, so we do not see her assailed by a ranting mate. From the start, they are both cheerful, not bewildered but bemused by Falstaff's impassioned correspondence; for a change, these are two sizable roles that hardly change, though they do grow in intensity. Directors like to cast them for contrast, almost reflexively, like the pairs of heroine-lovers in the earlier comedies, and to confer on them unlike manners. But there might be some advantage (and exploratory novelty) in having the two roles look and behave like twin sisters; the effect would nudge the action away from comedy and toward farce, but it would not infringe on the roles as written and might bolster the atmosphere of bustle and fluster. "Letter for letter," says Mrs. Page early on, apropos of Falstaff's identical messages to the two wives (2.1.66–67), "but that the name of Page and Ford differs!" Did Shakespeare mean to imply a similarity, even a symbiosis, between the wives?

Once again, role depends on function, while character depends also on acting qualities, physique, manner. For some commentators it has not been enough that these two women's roles outwit the men's: they have done nothing more than prove themselves obedient bourgeoises. (See, for two examples, Anne Parten's "Falstaff's Horns" [1985], and Marilyn French's *Shakespeare's Division of Experience*, [1981].) When Mrs. Page affirms that "wives may be merry and yet honest too" (4.2.97), she means subservient; she clearly shares men's common prejudices about women. Or does she? Interpreting that line and presuming that an author (Shakespeare not escaping) ought to create female roles that any woman could wholly approve of strains the play out of recognition; it chooses to ignore the wives' signs of disobedience, such as Mrs. Page's dispute with her husband over a son-in-law and Mrs. Ford's "I know not which pleases me better—that my husband is deceived, or Sir John" (3.3.161–62).

Of the other two women of consequence, "sweet Nan" Page gains the husband she desires; and Mistress Quickly, who has garnered purses

from nearly all the contenders, could not fail to come out a winner. But
the female roles do not quite end there. *Merry Wives* brings on several
males in drag: not only Falstaff as the fat woman of Brentford but also
the pair of lads who are taken for Anne by Slender ("I came yonder at
Eton to marry Mistress Anne Page, and she's a great lubberly boy"
[5.5.180–81]) and by Caius ("I ha' married *un garçon,* a boy; *un paysan,*
by gar" [5.5.200–01]).

In the preceding chapters, I have talked about multiple roles within each role as an alternative way of looking at roles that are called
inconsistent. But how far can we stretch this multiplicity? Can we, for
instance, extend it from Ford's secondary performance as Brook to the
playing in other roles of some lines that are clearly *insincere?* In talking to Falstaff either Mistress Page or Mistress Ford would condemn
the play to a sudden end if she told him how she feels about his advances. She must pretend to welcome them, to maintain the fiction
created by him. But intervening lines and scenes let her drop asides, if
not entire soliloquies, devoted to her true sentiments. She can also indulge in confidential chitchat with others to reveal her disgust with
Falstaff and disbelief at his goatish pretensions. In scene 4.2, Mrs. Ford
twice calls him "sweet Sir John" (7, 73); then, as soon as he flees up-
stairs, at her suggestion, to dress as the "witch" of Brentford she tells
Mrs. Page, "I would my husband would meet him in this shape. He
cannot abide the old woman of Brentford . . . forbade her my house,
and hath threatened to beat her" (77–80).

Falstaff himself waxes graphic in his amorous outpourings to the
wives, but his insincerity differs from theirs. Quite possibly he grows
so eloquent and so addled by his assumed ardor that he half-believes
what he proposes. On a slight sign of trouble, though, he will snap out
of the self-induced spell. When Mrs. Ford tells Mrs. Page that Falstaff
is too big for the buck basket, he rushes out of hiding and pleads with
them to let him get in it. Mrs. Page expresses surprise to find him at
the Fords'—she knew he was there all along, but affects to feel competitive about his love, and hurt. Falstaff murmurs, "I love thee." And
then, "Help me away. Let me creep in here" (3.3.123–30). The "I love
thee," to make its intended effect, is neither rushed nor matter-of-fact:
it is rapturous—till he sobers up and recalls what she owes him by way
of compensation for his love: "Help me away."

Mistress Quickly will assure all three of Anne's suitors—and Falstaff—of her fidelity to their cause. We have no way of gauging one of
the fascinating aspects of this role, whether she means anything she says.
Her moral consciousness stays fluid. Even as she races around, she floats.

Charming Anne, who might seem like another of those mentally
spayed young lovers, has to keep up a pretense of interest in Slender,
out of respect for her father, and to make allowances for whether the

ninny will commit himself to any statement that implies he is wooing her. (He will not.) When confronting her mother over the possibility of marrying "yond fool," Dr. Caius, Anne concocts one of the play's wildest images: "I had rather be set quick i' the earth And bowled to death with turnips!" (3.4.86–87). In the final scenes she has promised her mother to dress in green and go off with Caius; has promised her father to dress in white and go off with Slender; and then scampers away to marry Fenton. She leaves her defense to him, a clever variation on the plea for understanding delivered in a comedy by the bridegroom who has defied his bride's parents' wishes—only this time the plea is not a plea; drained of apology, it becomes a defiant instruction that rescues its speaker from the shallows of naiveté. Telling the Pages, "You would have married her most shamefully Where there was no proportion held in love," he berates them.

> Th' offense is holy that she hath committed,
> And this deceit loses the name of craft,
> Of disobedience, or unduteous title,
> Since therein she doth evitate and shun
> A thousand irreligious cursèd hours
> Which forcèd marriage would have brought upon her.
> (5.5.215–16, 219–25)

Here we have yet another fifth-act innovation for comedy: reproaches from a new son-in-law. Not even Petruchio ventures so far.

The bully-boy salutations emitted by the Host as he flatters patrons with the names of heroic and mythical and sometimes misattributed forebears ("Hector of Greece") betrays a bogus friendliness; he comes on too strong, too eager to please. But when Bardolph, his new tapster, reports that some Germans who booked space in his inn want to rent three of his horses, he snarls, "They shall have my horses, but I'll make them pay; I'll sauce them. They have had my house a week at command. I have turned away my other guests. They must come off. I'll sauce them" (4.3.8–11). When he addresses a servant like Simple, his bluff manner with patrons gives way to brusque rudeness: "What wouldst thou have, boor? What, thickskin? Speak, breathe, discuss; brief, short, quick, snap" (4.5.1–2).

Pointing to these multiplicities and duplicities within single roles is merely another way of saying that, like living persons, roles transpose according as they speak to other roles who have different effects on them and draw from them shy or knowing or hostile or other reactions, the set of variables being colored by the situations and places they find themselves in. It seems unnecessary to belabor the similarity or the far greater breadth of choices the actors can reach for as they convert their roles into characters.

A leading issue faced by a director of this play is whether to try to get inside Falstaff's ordeals. Does he deserve the triple comeuppance? Should the audience be made to rejoice in it and to feel like applauding the other roles when they crow over his plight? I can't help feeling that the times have changed our perception of the role. For him to give us pure buffoonery, to turn into an instrument of *relaxing entertainment*, deprives us of his intelligence; it may enhance the farce motifs but Falstaff is no fool, not even a true clown. He ages. His ambitions flourish as ever, while his capacities wane. The name, with its play on *false staff*, emphasizes his inabilities, his impotence. (In *Two Gentlemen* the word *staff* is a play on stick and phallus).[5] In the final scene, as Herne (or Horne) he wears the buck's horns, prefigured when he escaped from the Ford house in a "buck basket."

But in spite of the cracks about cuckoldry, Falstaff is neither a cuckold nor a wittol (a passive accepter of a wife's infidelities or, as an old edition of Shakespeare neatly puts it, "a contented cuckold") because, so far as we know, he has no wife for philanderers to pursue. The spread of antlers on his head mocks the very notion of his cuckolding Ford or anyone else. The scene in which the children got up as fairies pinch him and sing at him has its element of cruelty, which cannot be too freely indulged without damaging the balance at the close; that same scene includes a miniature trial by fire. But the scene mutates through the song of exorcism ("Fie on sinful fantasy! Fie on lust and luxury! Lust is but a bloody fire Kindled with unchaste desire"—[5.5.93–96]) into a ceremony of healing and purification. In this "green scene" Pistol plays a goblin, Parson Evans a satyr, and Mistress Quickly, as queen of the fairies, gives the children their instructions. Mrs. Page announces, "My Nan shall be the queen of all the fairies, Finely attirèd in a robe of white" (4.4.70–71). But in the event the role is taken over by Quickly, without explanation. Her speeches, delivered in all seriousness and with impeccable poetic diction, open up the role and allow the scene to comment on her managerial presence in the previous acts. Perhaps we are meant to think Mrs. Page changed her mind about the white robe when she determined to dress Anne in green for Caius; or perhaps somebody mentioned that it would be inappropriate for the fairy queen to vanish before the ceremony was over. According to W. W. Greg's 1910 Oxford edition of the play, the confusion arose originally because of the casting with boys and possible doubling of roles (89). Craik supports this interpretation (40n). The ceremony recruits a goodly sample of the Windsor community to enforce the last vision of middle-class togetherness.

There are two other little slices of the play that give many critics pause and, when excised, allow directors to shorten the performance, but not much. One is the Latin lesson that Pastor Evans conducts with young William Page (4.1). The other, the apparently incomplete plot having to do with the Host's horses and the German visitors, has come in for a number of detailed critical treatments, some of which refer the play to a real event in which a German nobleman, Duke Friedrich of Württemberg, eagerly sought the British order of the garter. But the two brief sequences that refer to "the Germans" (4.3 and 4.5.60–87) and have only one link to one subplot of the comedy can act as brakes or wedges, providing delays for the sake of suspense. They might be compared with Touchstone's long interruptions in 5.4 of *As You Like It* concerning the "quarrel on the seventh cause," which Jaques relishes—useful for Rosalind to spend convincing time to put on bridal gear and get into step with Hymen, but demanding on the audience.

About the Latin lesson's function in the plotting more or less the same can be said. Not all its wordplay on the part of Mistress Quickly, who overhears the Latin and tries to make her peculiar brand of sense out of it in English assonances, is intelligible today or worth listening hard to. But the word-antics of Evans and Quickly, those two oddities, become virtually visual, a peephole of sorts into sixteenth-century education. As Craik remarks, the scene "has plenty of verbal humour—more, in fact, than Catherine's English lesson in Henry V" (51n). I don't go along with that "in fact," although the point is well taken and, as always, each performance makes its own determination of the scene's quality. The teaching takes place out in the street. We learn from an incidental remark thrown out by Evans that Slender, of all unsuitable figures, is the school's headmaster: "Master Slender is let the boys leave to play." Another incidental remark expresses Mrs. Page's disappointment about the school's closing for the day, for she will now have young William on her hands (is he named for young Shakespeare, who tersely recalls his own Latin classes?); but she groans a line that sums up the comedy: "Tis a playing day, I see."

Notes

1. *Much Ado* has the second highest percentage of prose, 78 percent. The figures then drop abruptly to 61 percent in *Twelfth Night* and on down to 19 percent in *Dream* and 11 percent in *Errors*.

2. This subplot fades out or is pushed aside by the weight and stress of other dramatic material, or it may belong to a string of satirical allusions. Leslie Hotson connects Shallow in both *The Merry Wives* and *II Henry IV* with a predatory Justice Gardiner in Southwark, with whom Shakespeare, among many others, tangled legally. Hotson sees Slender as Gardiner's stepson, a figuring forth of "one William Wayte, a certain loose person of no reckoning or value, being wholly under the commandment of the said Gardiner." Hotson

is here quoting from a 1590 legal "letter of administration." Recent scholars do not take a full account of Hotson's book, *Shakespeare versus Shallow* (1931, 101). It includes his research report—270 pages of it in the book—which, with characteristically challenging interpretations, remains fascinating, like a once-reigning, "elegant" theory. (See, for example, Craik's comments in the Oxford edition on Hotson's thesis, [1990, 7–8].)[2]

3. Other inspired assignments by Jones included Alan Bennett as Shallow, Michael Graham Cox as Mine Host of the Garter Inn, Judy Davis as Mrs. Ford, Ron Cook as Simple, Michael Bryant as Dr. Caius, Bryan Marshall as Mr. Page.

4. The Sganarelle referred to is the principal role in *The Imaginary Cuckold*. When he suspects his spouse of infidelity with a neighbor, he proclaims, "I will stir up new strife And tell the world he's sleeping with my wife."

5. Lance and Speed are speaking of Proteus's parting from Julia.

> LANCE Marry, thus: when it stands well with him, it stands well with her.
>
> SPEED What an ass art thou! I understand thee not.
>
> LANCE What a block art thou, that thou canst not! My staff understands me.
>
> SPEED What thou sayst?
>
> LANCE Ay, and what I do too. Look thee, I'll but lean, and my staff understands me.
>
> SPEED It stands under thee indeed. (2.5.20–28)

As You Like It

The monologue by Jaques, the Seven Ages of Man (2.7.138–65), could supply an epigraph for this book: "One man in his time plays many parts," which rings true in our rushed world, and truer when we substitute *person* for *man* and *a single day* for *his time*. Other lines and phrases from that speech—and from the rest of the play—have engraved themselves in texts on political science, sociology, and psychology, as well as on literature, the arts, and the common wisdom. As an explicit, metaphysical comedy, *As You Like It* yields up scores of quotable sentiments about existence, love, identity (sometimes inflated to *personhood*), government, acting, and other forms of duplicity. But two less familiar lines could have served equally effectively for the play's epigraphs: Celia's tricky "*Was* is not *is*" (3.4.29) and Oliver's "'Twas I, but 'tis not I" (4.3.136). In no other Shakespeare play do we find such an assortment of unstable roles—Oliver being a wondrous example—who undergo glaring revision, a possible reason why no record exists of a production during or soon after Shakespeare's lifetime. Most of the action unrolls in the Forest of Arden, a green world brimming over with potential transformations. A schoolgirl, Brigid Nugent from P.S. 115 in New York City, who attended a production of *As You Like It* at The Theatre for a New Audience, wrote to the producer, Jeffrey Horowitz:

> The Forest of Arden has magical powers. At first, Oliver was mean, but when he was in the Forest of Arden he started to become forgiving. That was because when you're in the Forest of Arden, you can fall in love, be happy and be forgiving and act as you like it!

The forest itself consists of a theatre of many-purpose settings. Anything but mere clumps of trees and intervening clearings, it contains tracts of jungle, enclosed fields, and open meadows where sheep may safely graze and justify the environment's description, at least in part, as actually pastoral. For the 1993 staging in Central Park by Adrian Hall, Eugene Lee's design abolished much of the regular stage and drew on the advantages of the real hill, the lake, and al fresco views in front of the audience. Troupes in London's Regent's Park, in the Berkshires ("Shakespeare and Company"), and elsewhere have similarly exploited the outdoors, weather concurring. The Hall-Lee setting displayed occasionally noisy, but talented, chickens and other farm animals under a little lean-to. There is nothing like a live animal or two, even a humble cat, dog, or bird, for keeping human actors on the alert.

Stan Wojewodski directed an overtly indoor production at the Yale Repertory in the spring of 1994, designed by Dawn Robyn Petrlik, calling on abstract sliding screens of framed gauze, like a cross between Italianate slotted wings and the "traveling curtains" employed by Orson Welles. But most directors like to work this story out of doors if they can.

In Arden's many-branched woodland with its fluid or elastic inhabitants, anything, it might seem, can happen. And get out of hand. But Shakespeare governs the exposition with assurance. The three rapid scenes of act 1 lay out conflicts between two pairs of brothers, Duke Senior and Duke Frederick, Oliver and Orlando; they account concisely for the flight of four of the main roles into Arden's variegated depths, plus Duke Senior's earlier retreat there with his retinue. The next three acts—the play's extended middle—unwind with all deliberate speed, inspecting and commenting on their content as they hold off the resolution. Finally, act 5 bursts into four weddings, not the usual allotment of two for comedies, and the god Hymen flies in to bless the unions. In an all-male Cheek by Jowl production that came to the United States in 1994 from London, the Hymen is solicited and picked up by a gay Jaques, who has not yet gone off to live with Duke Frederick as a hermit, Hymen being a role sometimes played these days as a hermaphrodite by a woman or a lipsticked lad. Several recent all-male performances of *As You Like It* preceded the Cheek by Jowl effort. There have also been all-woman versions. Of the marriages, two appear to have questionable futures, but those belong to the segment of the story beyond the action, about which we can speculate with no profit beyond intellectual elation. The four marriages, however, supply one more of Shakespeare's act-5 innovations, as does the epilogue spoken by a female role, Rosalind.

Even for spectators who do not come to the play demanding out-and-out realism, several circumstances in the action prove hard to swallow. They relate to Rosalind; in her Ganymede outfit, she goes unrecognized by her father, Duke Senior, his exiled courtiers, and her beloved Orlando, all of whose male gazes must have noticed, if not scrutinized, her features and build. The father and lover remark, rather late in the game, on Ganymede's resemblance to Rosalind, during the time while she is offstage, converting herself into a bride. Duke Senior says, "I do remember in this shepherd boy Some lively touches of my daughter's favor." Orlando comes back with, "My lord, the first time that I ever saw him Methought he was a brother to your daughter" (5.4.26–29). In some stage imitations of hard-edged reality, either or both lines have been spoken tongue in cheek when the speaker(s) had already noticed that Ganymede is Rosalind—from her hand, her reactions, a catch in her voice, or some other giveaway. Earlier comic heroines, Julia and Portia, plus Nerissa, have already hidden their everyday selves in drag, and Viola and Imogen will too. They went or will go undetected as women, so why not Rosalind? Admittedly, she has the most expansive and at the same time elusively quicksilver female role in Shakespeare, and therefore one of the most difficult and sought after. Among celebrities alone, the roster of English-speaking Rosalinds includes Maude Adams, Peggy Ashcroft, Eileen Atkins, Edith Evans, Helen Faucit, Katharine Hepburn, Barbara Jefford, Margaret Leighton, Julia Marlowe, Helen Mirren, Kate Nelligan, Gwyneth Paltrow, Vanessa Redgrave, Ada Rehan, Athene Seyler, Fiona Shaw, Sarah Siddons, Maggie Smith, Juliet Stevenson, Janet Suzman, and Peg Woffington. But I can think of no reason for Rosalind's disguise to let her down, other than weak acting, like that of the German actress Elisabeth Bergner, who played with Laurence Olivier in the 1932 movie directed by her husband and had little sense of the inflection of her lines. So long as the other roles attribute to Ganymede "his" traits, the character remains secure.

Another misgiving about Rosalind lies in her delay, which vaguely recalls Hamlet's, structurally speaking, in that she defers, rather than defers *to*, audience expectations. Anne Barton writes that Rosalind is "as central and dominating a figure in her fashion as Hamlet is in his own, very different play" (Riverside edition, 366). She will not discard her masculine persona, to revert to womanhood and resume her full role as Orlando's "white goddess" until halfway through act 5, scene 4, though she has repeatedly met Orlando and, qua Ganymede, received promises of love and fidelity from him on behalf of Rosalind. René Girard suggests that in the pastoral world (as elsewhere) it is better not to be too much on hand for your lover or he/she may grow bored with you. Hence, he posits, Rosalind's keeping to the disguise. If she

> consented to be wooed openly, in her own name, by her own lover, her constant availability would rapidly squander the metaphysical capital that has accumulated during the phase of separation. Under her masculine disguise, Rosalind can enjoy her lover's presence without losing the benefit of absence. She makes herself accessible, yet keeps reaping the fruit of inaccessibility. She can have her mimetic cake and eat it, too. (1991 Introduction)

But reaping the fruit (reaping *fruit*?) and eating the mimetic cake of inaccessibility bring a lover restricted satisfactions. Girard goes on to say that pastoral literature "devises the most artificial tricks to postpone gratification as long as possible."

Here we have a believable explanation (based, it is true, on a pathetic fallacy) for Rosalind's reluctance to literally redress herself; better yet, it corresponds to what countless critics beforehand had hypothesized. But as an explanation I cannot accept it as a full one. There may be more to this delay, which is quite peculiar in view of her instant attraction to Orlando before she even marvels to see him hurl the wrestler Charles into unconsciousness and before she hands him the chain from around her neck. It is not as though she needs, from what we can see and hear, further reassurance that she is in love with him or he with her. Does she mistrust her love? Is she waiting for nothing less than timeproof reciprocity, which it looks as if she already has? To Celia, who gently teases her and so draws forth a confession, she admits,

> O coz, coz, coz, my pretty little coz, that thou didst know how many fathom deep I am in love! But it cannot be sounded: my affection hath an unknown bottom, like the Bay of Portugal . . . I cannot be out of the sight of Orlando. I'll go find a shadow and sigh till he come." (4.1.197–200, 207–09)

Anne Barton argues that

> Rosalind clings to the part of Ganymede because of the freedom it allows her. In her boy's disguise, she escapes (for a time) the limitations of being a woman . . . the conscious object of Orlando's love. She learns a great deal about herself, about Orlando, and about love itself which she could not have done within the normal conventions of society. (1974, 366)

John Doebler looks at what Rosalind teaches, rather than learns. She

> wants Orlando to know that women are not goddesses but frail human beings who can be giddy, jealous, infatuated with novelty, irritatingly talkative, peremptory and hysterical (4.1.142–49), though she is circumspect as to whether women can also be unfaithful. Orlando must be taught that love is a madness (3.2.390), and he must be cured, not of loving Rosalind, but of worshiping her with unrealistic expectations that can lead only to disillusionment. Rosalind teases him, as Portia does Bassanio . . . but she does not seriously threaten him with wantonness. . . [He] can learn to love "Ganymede" as a friend and then make the transition to heterosexual union in his blessed discovery that the friend is also the lover. (1992, 291).

Here we have a commonsensical approach to the question and the relationship. But Doebler continues:

> When Orlando has been sufficiently tested as to patience, loyalty, and understanding, she unmasks herself to him and simultaneously unravels the plot of ridiculous love we have come to associate with Silvius and Phoebe. [The] innocent titillation, found also in Shakespeare's source, is not meant to hint at homosexual attraction as we understand it. (291)

Doebler's postulates, then, fit into the idea that the comedies exemplify lessons, persuasion, and wish-fulfillment. Rosalind instructs not only Orlando and herself but also Silvius and Phoebe, and even offers lessons about life to Jaques (4.1), though her wit rescues her from pedantry. But these explanations have not moved beyond realism. I believe we have to take account of the play's infusion of magic in the last scene with the irruption of Hymen, and assume the workings of miraculous power. Certain of Shakespeare's plays deal openly with magic: supernatural moments supervene in, say, *Hamlet, Macbeth, A Midsummer Night's Dream, Richard III, Julius Caesar,* and *The Tempest*; they feature the instant stardom of gods and ghosts.[1] We are talking about the author's fiat, of course. We look into his borrowings from Christian heaven, the heights of mythical Mount Olympus, and as-yet-unfound territories, much as we do at a Greek tragedy. Arden enchants.

Rosalind may want to reveal herself over and over to Orlando. She fights back the temptation, not knowing why. Arden's spell works upon her. She thinks her will prevails, but it may serve forces she is unaware of.

ROSALIND I can do strange things. I have, since I was three years old, conversed with a magician, most profound in his art and not yet damnable. . . .

ORLANDO Speak'st thou in sober meanings?

ROSALIND By my life, I do, which I tender dearly, though I say I am a magician. (5.2.58–60, 67–69)

She affirms this power before she returns in act 5 as a bride and again in the epilogue when she tells the audience, "My way is to conjure you." Brissenden footnotes the word *conjure*: "(a) make a solemn appeal (b) affect you by magic (referring to Ganymede's alleged magical powers" (1994, 227, n. 11). But magician or not, she too is entrapped. In much the same fashion, it can be ensorcelation (the author again) that accounts for Duke Senior's and Orlando's inability to recognize her, rather as they cannot recognize her magical gifts. We may choose to believe that Rosalind's claims to be a magician are not the truth, or that she puts Orlando (and others present, if they listen) into an incantatory mood for the round in which she, Orlando, Phoebe, and Silvius take part.

SILVIUS [To love] is to be all made of sighs and tears;
And so am I for Phoebe.

PHOEBE And I for Ganymede.

ORLANDO And I for Rosalind.

ROSALIND And I for no woman, etc. (5.2.80–84)

But before long, she complains, the echoes are "like the howling of Irish wolves against the moon" (106–07). The audiences, offstage and on, are also being softened up by her sudden other-worldliness and by the incantation for her exit, Hymen's apparition, and with him, Rosalind re-entering. She appears transformed by her wedding dress, as though she plays Hymen's ethereal partner. Possibly she is herself bewildered to some extent by what has happened and is happening to her. Rosalind's confidence in herself and in her sense of belonging fluctuates, as does that of most roles in all plays. Anything but a fixed or stiffened stage entity, the part can grow tiresome if the performer enacts the lines with no imaginative stretching.

The magic does not quite end with Hymen and Rosalind. After he makes pronouncements about the four couples to be married and introduces a "wedlock hymn," another novelty walks in. This is the brother of Oliver and Orlando, the second son of Sir Rowland de Boys, even if his name does not begin, like his brothers' names, with an *O*.[2] Where did he spring from? He identifies himself as a second Jaques. Orlando mentioned him early in the action (1.1.5–6), at school. But he, Orlando, had to labor on the property. Oliver allowed him no reward or wages or initiative, only kept him "rustically at home" (1.1.7), where he had to win an education for himself however he could. Thus, in act 5 all three sons appear together. Jaques de Boys is mortal, not a supernatural being; but his materializing is almost as strange as Hymen's. Furthermore, this unfamiliar figure helps wind up the action by relaying the good tidings about Duke Frederick's renouncing his dukedom and converting to a hermit's existence. We hear no account of how Jaques de Boys reached Duke Senior's encampment, if that is what it is. Magic evidently remains at work. *De Boys* means "of the woods," and in case the French name suddenly seems misplaced, we can recall that Le Beau appeared in act 1, and that, although Warwickshire had its own Forest of Arden, the name is an anglicization of the Celtic word for the Ardennes, the wooded uplands in France, Belgium, and Luxembourg.

What are the properties of this vast and multiform den of nature? Girard is skeptical about Arden as a paradise. If it is so paradisiacal, why do all the courtiers but Jaques troop back to the court? His question, though, should be aimed more at certain Romantic critics than at the roles themselves, who do not see the forest as an unalloyed paradise, despite the verbal neighborliness of Arden to Eden. Anne Barton writes:

Arden is a place set apart from the ordinary world. It is emphatically not a paradise. Winter, cold winds and rain, the penalty incurred by the Old Testament Adam, come to it. Some of its native inhabitants are churlish and stupid. Yet the forest is essentially a good place, not because it possesses limitless wealth or supernatural power, but simply because in Arden fortune does not oppress and stifle nature. (Riverside edition, 366)

In the famous speech by Duke Senior that opens act 2, he tries to comfort himself and his circle by saying that Arden proffers certain consolations, compared with the court life of "painted pomp," but he doesn't omit mention of the forest's "icy fang" and the "churlish chiding of the winter's wind," which makes him "shrink with cold." The former courtiers' new

> life, exempt from public haunt,
> Finds tongues in trees, books in the running brooks,
> Sermons in stones, and good in everything. (2.1.6–17)

These benefits must be sought, however: an operative word is *finds*. In cool fact, the courtiers do not troop back to the court *in the action* or go anywhere but into the final dance. Ralph M. Sargent says:

> all the exiled characters who have gone through their period of reformation in the forest will not stay in it but are now to return to court, there to play their part in civilized life. As Jaques says to the restored Duke:
> You to your former honor I bequeath;
> Your patience and your virtue well deserves it." (1969, 245)

But the Duke has not returned, at least, not yet; and the "former honor" that Jaques has no ability to "bequeath," except as a joke, is Senior's active resumption of his prerogatives as Duke. Duke Senior's only mental foray into the future is to declare that "every of this happy number . . . Shall share the good of our returnèd fortune According to the measure of their states" (5.4.171–74). He doesn't specify when. They might (who can say?) stay in the forest for a while. Or take later vacations there. Or otherwise split their time between the play's two settings: the court, where all is formal and predictable, and the forest, which can erupt into spontaneous magic.

Critics have offered thorough descriptions and analysis of the pastoral ideal, the Age of Gold, as well as Shakespeare's toying with the pastoral's forms and traditions. Doebler writes:

> Whereas [Thomas] Lodge [in *Rosalynde: Euphues' Golden Legacy*, a principal source of *As You Like It*] cheerfully accepts the pastoral conventions of his day, Shakespeare exposes those conventions to some criticism and considerable irony. Alongside the mannered and literary

Silvius and Phoebe, he places William and Audrey, as peasantlike a
couple as ever drew milk from a cow's teat. (Bevington 1992, 289)[3]

As McFarland suggests, the literature devoted to the unspoiled
Age of Gold and its Golden People harks back to dream images concocted—perhaps unconsciously—from true and false memories, that
is, nostalgia, beliefs in the possibility of an untroubled childhood and
a Garden of Eden, tied to hopes of eternal youth. In Shakespeare's
comedies, McFarland adds, a "reciprocity of social and religious con-
cern" underlies "ideas of hope, joy, and sacred community" (1972).
Born in the early Renaissance, the pastoral may have arisen from the
notion of planned gardens on estates and around chateaux, often
called "orchards," where marvels come to pass. Shakespeare does not
maim the pastoral; he implies that one pays a price for attaining to
even a fraction of this ideal.

As You Like It has five notable references to cuckoldry, all in the second
half. The first is uttered by Touchstone during his mockery of Corin.

CORIN The greatest of my pride is to see my ewes graze and my lambs suck.

TOUCHSTONE That is another simple sin in you, to bring the ewes and the
rams together and to offer to get your living by the copulation of cattle; to be
bawd to a bellwether, and to betray a she-lamb of a twelvemonth to a crook-
ed-pated old cuckoldly ram, out of all reasonable match . . . (3.2.74–81)

Most editors gloss *cuckoldly* as a synonym for *horned*; but here Touchstone also uses the word to make believe that the old ram has himself
been cuckolded, while cuckolding his earlier partners by being cou-
pled with a young, virginal lamb. Like many of Touchstone's lines,
these are playfully perverse, an assertion of his superiority when it
comes to argument.

The sequential scene expands on Touchstone's view of horns as
not unfortunate but acceptable, necessary, "precious." He could be
toying with words here, or better, fooling around with ideas.

. . . Here we have no temple but the wood, no assembly but horn-
beasts. But what though? Courage! As horns are odious, they are
necessary. It is said, "Many a man knows no end of his goods." Right!
Many a man has good horns and knows no end of them. Well, that
is the dowry of his wife; 'tis none of his own getting. Horns? Even so.
Poor men alone? No, no, the noblest deer hath them as huge as the
rascal. Is the single man therefore blessed? No. As a walled town is
more worthier than a village, so is the forehead of a married man
more honorable than the bare brow of a bachelor; and by how much
defense is better than no skill, by so much is a horn more precious
than to want. (3.3.46–59)

The catechistic format resembles Falstaff's on honor, and the content reminds us of Lavatch's speech praising cuckoldry (*All's Well*, 1.5, 41–55). This is not quite a soliloquy, so far as we can tell, because it is delivered in front of the uncomprehending Audrey, while Jaques secretly listens in and relishes the knots and wrinkles in Touchstone's reasoning. If Audrey understood him, what might she make of providing horns as her dowry?

The next example is spoken by Rosalind. Here, and on a number of other occasions, she steps outside her role as innocent and sounds like a cynic; and as in the previous instance, she mocks her opposite number in the colloquy. She speaks as Ganymede, substituting for Rosalind: "An you be so tardy, come no more in my sight. I had as lief be wooed of a snail."

ORLANDO Of a snail?

ROSALIND Ay, of a snail; for though he comes slowly, he carries his house on his head—a better jointure, I think, than you make a woman. Besides, he brings his destiny with him.

ORLANDO What's that?

ROSALIND Why, horns, which such as you are fain to be beholding to your wives for. But he comes armed in his fortune and prevents the slander of his wife. (4.1.48–58)

Here we have Rosalind openly playing a Touchstone: fanciful, challenging to the point of discourtesy, vulgar in moderation. We have to ply our imagination during this little exchange, for while she seems to laugh with a light heart at Orlando, she feels nettled by his lateness: he pleads that he has "come within an hour of [his] promise" (40–41), but she will tell Celia in the coming act that she "cannot [bear to] be out of the sight of Orlando" and the audience must recognize that he has dashed her satisfaction.

The brief song-scene that follows, "What shall he have that killed the deer?" sung by an unnamed Second Lord (although in performance it is usually assigned to Amiens, the play's minstrel), confers on the killer the deer's "leather skin and horns to wear." The second part of the little song changes direction and addresses itself to the killer:

> Take thou no scorn to wear the horn;
> It was a crest ere thou wast born
> Thy father's father wore it,
> And thy father bore it.
> The horn, the horn, the lusty horn
> Is not a thing to laugh to scorn (4.2.14–19)

These lines punish the hunter with mockery, questioning the legitimacy of his birth. They conclude that even a deer-slayer, proud of his

prowess, is not exempt from being cuckolded, any more than his forebears were. A sketch of a costume "designed by Salvador Dali for a
1948 production of *As You Like It*" has a ragged coronet of twigs and
leaves, a compromise between a sunburst and a simulation of horns;
but from the crotch of the wearer, who is described as a *vanneur*, a win-
nower, there protrudes in place of a codpiece or "athletic supporter" or
pouch a miniature stag's head with pointed antlers growing out of it.[4]

Act 4 seems to be the "horniest" of the five, for another—and the
last—reference crops up briefly in the scene after Rosalind reads aloud
the love poem to her from Phoebe, delivered by the hapless Silvius,
Phoebe's admirer. As the messenger of his own ruin, the young man
stands by, bewildered. His plight draws a compassionate cry from Celia, "Alas, poor shepherd!" Whereupon Rosalind grumbles,

> No, he deserves no pity.—[*To Silvius*] Wilt thou love such a woman?
> What, to make thee an instrument and play false strains upon thee?
> Not to be endured! (4.3.66–70)

Professor Latham compares this remark to Hamlet's made to Rosen-
crantz and Guildenstern about being played on like a recorder (1975, n.
107). While the locution is not dissimilar, Hamlet detects a lie being
practiced upon him by men, but Rosalind's words connote a husband's
betrayal by an unloving wife, much like her earlier allusion to the snail.

What do the reminders about cuckoldry signify? Apart from inviting
titters from the knowing ones in the auditorium, they act astringently
on a comic ending as they let us *almost* in on the trials of the long-term
alliance known as marriage that might possibly arrive after act 5.

No hammer blows are needed to strike home the changes, some of
them drastic, undergone by the roles in this play, even the secondary
ones. There are some exceptions: Duke Senior; his speaking and non-
speaking lords, Amiens included; Dennis, who is Oliver's servant and
gets to utter two lines; Silvius, the lovesick young shepherd; Corin, the
stoic old shepherd; Audrey, slow and pliable; and William, who courts
her in opposition to Touchstone. After being threatened by Touchstone
with "a hundred and fifty ways" of death, William should recoil in terror of this self-styled assassin, but instead cheerfully bids him, "God
rest you merry, sir," and takes his leave (5.1.45–58). The line could be
(and surely has been) played against its meaning—to sacrifice an
amusing, unexpected reaction for a trite, obvious one. Le Beau, who
comes and goes twice only in a single scene (1.2), unbends as he alters from a stately courtier "with his mouth full of news" (89) to a
friendly acquaintance and admirer of Orlando. Charles the wrestler, in
his first scene with Oliver, also has a mouth full of news; he must be

privy to a pipeline to the goings-on at court. A bit later his mouth is full of threats, before the wrestling bout that leaves him unconscious. The Charles of 1.1, who rashly promises to mangle Orlando, turns reasonable when he serves as a guide to the court of Frederick. From him we learn of Duke Senior's exile with his followers. He also supplies information about Rosalind before we have met her, in reply to a question by Oliver. As one more contradictory character, Charles is well-spoken, grammatical, apparently accurate in his reporting; he doesn't deserve the epithet "thug" dropped on him by Ruth Nevo (1980). According to Arthur Colby Sprague, in reply to Frederick's inquiry, "How dost thou, Charles?" a line spoken by Le Beau, "He cannot speak, my lord," was "appropriated" in the late eighteenth century by the actor doing Touchstone and enlarged to: "He says he cannot speak, my lord" (*Shakespeare and the Actors,* London: 1944, reprinted in part in Signet Classic edition, 192).

We are not privy to the change in Duke Frederick, the tartar who had hoped to "take His brother here and put him to the sword," because his conversion "both from his enterprise and from the world" reaches us at second hand (5.4.157–161). Upon entering the forest, he must have come under its wholesome spell. Oliver, once a tyrant who hates Orlando, comes to feel as shamed as Frederick and amazed by his brother's courage in saving his life. He exudes love for Celia and becomes a contented outdoorsman who decides that

> my father's house and all the revenue that was old Sir Rowland's will
> I estate upon you [Orlando], and here live and die a shepherd.
> (5.2.10–12)

Orlando, the resentful sibling and wrestling whiz of act 1, has by the final curtain become a fierce protector of old Adam, as well as a poet and graffiti artist, self-trained and adapting easily to the forest, where he carves helpless trees. A welcomed but unofficial official among Duke Senior's woodsy retinue, and a wondering, unpunctual swain, he collapses emotionally, lovestruck, early in the action, as a result of his first encounter with Rosalind (1.2) and an augury of his infatuation. One of the two poems attributed to him—they are read by Rosalind and Celia—may end in a whimper ("And I to live and die her slave"), but its opening lines have charm and substance:

> Why should this a desert be?
> For it is unpeopled? No.
> Tongues I'll hang on every tree . . . (3.2.123–25)

Further along, as he chronicles his beloved's peerless combination of the best qualities of heroines of antiquity and myth, he sums her up by praising Rosalind's (and his) author's labors as something like the product of a choir of cherubim:

> Thus Rosalind of many parts
> By heavenly synod was devised. (147–48)

One woman, it seems, as well as one man, plays "many parts" in her time. Orlando also shares with Jaques a comic scene of mild, mutual dislike.

JAQUES God b' wi' ye. Let's meet as little as we can.

ORLANDO I do desire we may be better strangers . . . .

JAQUES Rosalind is your love's name?

ORLANDO Yes, just.

JAQUES I do not like her name.

ORLANDO There was no thought of pleasing you when she was christened.

JAQUES What stature is she of?

ORLANDO Just as high as my heart. (3.2.254–66)

The flexibility of Celia's role, less dramatic than Orlando's, involves her disguise. She changes from being an adornment of Duke Frederick's court and his presumptive heir (he has no named or mentioned sons) and the more assertive of the two young women to being a shepherdess whose accent, like her "brother's," is solidly upper-class British—"something finer," says Orlando to Ganymede, "than you could purchase in so removed a dwelling" as their cottage (3.2.334–35). Celia is the one who first proposes exile in the woods to join her uncle. Latham writes, "Critics tend to greet a good Celia with surprise, as though Shakespeare had not written a good part for her" (1975, lxxxvii). Celia has been blessed with some of the most telling lines, whether teasing or affectionate, in her colloquies with Rosalind. Hers is not only a rewarding role for an actor to embody and spectators to take in but also a demanding one. She remains onstage for much of the play and serves as a spirited partner for Rosalind (in 1.2, 1.3, 3.2, 3.4, 4.1, and 4.3), not a mere sidekick. The relationship cools off toward the end as though Celia fears she is losing Rosalind or has already lost her; and the part dwindles in act 5. But earlier, Rosalind should not overwhelm her.

Touchstone and Jaques have come in for much scrutiny. Helen Gardner contrasts these "two commentators of the play": "Touchstone is the parodist, Jaques the cynic."

> Touchstone sustains many different roles . . . . He becomes the maudlin lover of Jane Smile; with the simple shepherd Corin he becomes the cynical and worldly-wise man of the court; with Jaques he is a melancholy moralist, musing on the power of time and the decay of

all things; with the pages [who sing "It Was a Lover and His Lass"] he acts the lordly amateur of the arts, patronizing his musicians. It is right that he should parody the rest of the cast, and join in the procession into Noah's Ark with his Audrey. (1959; in Signet Classic edition, 212–30; see especially 227)

But so does Jaques "sustain many different roles." Neither part conforms to type or expectation. In some places they almost exchange roles. Brissenden writes a thorough comparison and contrast of Touchstone with Jaques (1994, 25–35); but although he supplies some good reading and recognizes the many-sidedness of both parts, he ends up dealing with them as something like fixed psychological entities.

By marrying Audrey, not without serious misgivings, Touchstone sets himself apart from the usual clowns in Shakespeare and elsewhere. As a "commentator" the clown generally remains outside the story; he exists primarily to comment, rather than participate. Feste twice ventures partway into the action when he taunts Malvolio, but in doing so the first time he assumes the fictitious guise of Sir Topas. Touchstone, who declines to let Martext, the bumbling clergyman, marry him to Audrey, does let himself be married to her, thereby becoming a participant in the action. He differs from the clown-fools who propagate wisdom, sometimes reproachfully. His personal comments boil down to offense, sarcasm, and mockery, often bitter.

Gardner, Latham, and other critics have pointed out that his contribution to the famous dispute with Corin over the relative virtues of town and country (3.2) seems to consist of a series of idle distinctions, an entertaining misuse of words, puffed up with false, would-be philosophical dignity by the repetition of "in respect of"—in a word (Gardner's), cynicism. Yet looked at line by line, the speech expresses Touchstone's simultaneous attraction to and dislike of "this shepherd's life," which Corin had asked him about. Touchstone fled into these precincts willingly, partly to keep the two young women company, partly because the court had become a perilous place for any remnants of Duke Senior's entourage, and perhaps partly because the Forest of Arden drew him toward adventure, toward risks (with its lioness and serpent, as a later scene reveals), even a turning around of his life, a particularly appealing prospect if Touchstone is sliding into middle age. But arrived in this peculiar diversity of a forest, he finds the shepherd's life constraining, a handicap. For safety he swapped intellectual and other stimulation. He misses the glitter of the court, to which (until busy act 5) he will not be able to return without likely penalties, even death. Hence his soured wit. In the scene with Corin his bile flows as he pronounces the dignified old man "in a parlous state" (3.2.41–42), shallow, sinful, and damned. Having verbally defeated Corin, who

pleads, "You have too courtly a wit for me. I'll rest" (67), he proceeds
to have words with Rosalind over the quality of the verses Orlando
has written about her. On stage Touchstone often appears to be a benevolent presence; one sees his chiding and carping as unmeant, even
apologetic, a habit left over from playing the truth-telling fool at court.
Besides, directors, like critics, want him to act as the opposite of Jaques
the melancholic. Touchstone, however, speaks acerbically most of the
time, even when he talks to himself. Contemplating his marriage-to-
be with Audrey, and urged by Jaques not to let Martext marry him, "a
man of your breeding . . . under a bush like a beggar," he meditates:

> I am not in the mind but I were better to be married of him than of
> another, for he is not like to marry me well; and not being well mar-
> ried, it will be a good excuse for me hereafter to leave my wife.
> (3.3.82–86)

Does he mean it? Is he speaking aloud? Even a maiden as dense as
Audrey would have to take umbrage at words so bluntly cruel. Perhaps he is once again improvising variations on ideas, for he then
rhymes, "Come, sweet Audrey. We must be married, or we must live
in bawdry" (88–89).

In marriage, as in other affairs, opposites may attract, the union
between Audrey and Touchstone supplying an instance. But is Jaques
really the opposite of Touchstone? Laurel to Touchstone's Hardy? After he first runs into Touchstone (offstage, in the story), he hurries
back to Duke Senior, who greets him with, "What, you look merrily"—an unusual look for Jaques, who exclaims in excitement:

> A fool, a fool! I met a fool i' the forest.
> A motley fool. A miserable world!
> As I do live by food, I met a fool,
> Who laid him down and basked him in the sun,
> And railed on Lady Fortune in good terms,
> In good set terms, and yet a motley fool. (2.7.11–17)

Perhaps Jaques's reputation as a despondent figure, among critics as
well as among the other roles in the play, is not wholly deserved. Pin-
ning to his name a single adjective that means sad or depressed or pes-
simistic inhibits other roles from displaying comparable characteristics
and tries to settle him in a mold. The one Jaques I have seen who
hinted at a multiformed character on stage[1] was Richard Pasco's, the
outstanding performance in that particular version of the play, the
BBC TV movie (1978), although he had played the role on stage not
long before under the direction of Buzz Goodbody at the Royal
Shakespeare Company. Pasco did "look merrily" at the right moment,
and at other moments that he made *appear* right. He rejoiced in the

notion of wisdom from the lips of a "fool." He suffered from (and re-joiced in) fool envy. Like Touchstone, he did not feel at ease in the for-est: he was restless, looking for a way out, not from the forest but from a personal dilemma.

Jaques, whose name with the C missing is not French, like Le Beau's, but a scatological British assonance for *jakes* or outdoor toilet, dwells in a mind apart from those of his fellow courtiers, possibly be-cause he occasionally laments over a sobbing deer (2.1.66) or a fouled-up past, which Duke Senior calls, without being contradicted, "as sensual as the brutish sting itself," the result having been assorted dis-eases (2.7.66-67). In the end, when Jaques announces that he will join Duke Frederick, he commits his future to an eremitic existence and becomes the play's third penitent. But before that, we see his pity for the wounded deer, which, like him, has parted from "the flux of com-pany" (2.1.52), one of the "native burghers of this desert city" (2.1.23), as Duke Senior puts it. We also observe his eagerness to help Touch-stone in his marriage, and his learnedness, which matches Touch-stone's. When Touchstone tells Audrey, "I am here with thee and thy goats, as the most capricious poet, honest Ovid, was among the Goths," Jaques, who is in hiding, mutters "O knowledge ill-inhabited, worse than love in a thatched house!" (3.3.5–9). Contemporary spectators who have not read the play beforehand and studied the footnotes, or who are not as learned as Touchstone and Jaques, will not make much of the pun on *goats* and *Goths*, and less still from Jaques's reply.

This role, too, plays many parts during his time onstage. His speech about the seven ages of man clangs in the memory of one who did school homework on the play and then had to recite its sustained gloom in bright oratorical cadences, those familiar bells, some of which may sound out of tune. The ages do not need to sound down-beat so much as comically regretful about the end to which we all come, but only if we live long enough to repudiate the remaining tat-ters of our immortal longings. Those ages, declining as they advance, could be narrated with some zest, some pleasure in the utterance, as though Jaques relishes working his improvisatory powers to the full and making discoveries. The part may not have attracted as many first-class talents as Rosalind's has done, but it is a favorite among old-er leading men and younger ones appropriately aged.

Rosalind has often been considered the playwright within the play. She is, but to a limited extent, although at the end, thanks to the magic of her promises and her own floatingly happy unreality, she does give the impression of being in control. Her delivery of the epi-logue strengthens this godly effect. As she says in her opening sen-tence, "It is not the fashion to see the lady the epilogue; but it is no more unhandsome than to see the lord the prologue." She adds, "Yet . . .

good plays prove the better by the help of good epilogues," an irrefut-able claim. Despite its prose, her monologue is as felicitous as any in Shakespeare. The magic sequence and Jaques de Boys's plot-squaring observations, which preface the epilogue, help to enforce the view of Rosalind as, not the play's conductor, but a commanding image.

Like Touchstone, she is a great talker who can be cruel—to Orlan-do as well as to Phoebe. At the same time, she radiates sexuality—not carnality or concupiscence, nothing that smacks of greed, but an allure that counteracts her portrayal of Ganymede, so that she never surren-ders all her femininity and thus Orlando and others are justified in addressing her by such salutations as "pretty youth." People who know her well, like Celia, or slightly, like Orlando in act 1, go beyond cherishing her. They idolize her. She acquires powers that consort with those of the Forest of Arden, not supernatural ones, perhaps, but powers that exceed a high human average and noticeably grow in the course of the action.

At first, when her early mood—or condition?—resembles Anto-nio's or Portia's in *The Merchant* or Orsino's or Olivia's in *Twelfth Night*, she could, like them, complain, "I know not why I am so sad" or "My little body is aweary of this great world" or "That strain again; it had a dying fall." She attributes her depression to her father's banishment. When Celia begs her to "be merry," she asks, "What think you of fall-ing in love?" (1.2.22) but she follows up, after meeting Orlando, with an excessive tribute to his father: "My father loved Sir Rowland as his soul And all the world was of my father's mind" (214). She primed herself for her next encounter with an eligible man, then knew what to say when she met him. As Orlando plays heroic young David to Charles the wrestler's Goliath, he turns into the embodiment of Rosal-ind's wish expressed as a question.

The other, larger question, silently posed, then becomes, If this is only act 1, scene 2, how will Shakespeare hold off the fulfillment? With love rivals? Parental obstacles thrown up? With second thoughts on the part of the two lovers? He scorns such devices, electing instead to make Rosalind put Orlando through a series of tests that do not check out his courage (she has already witnessed that) but his intel-lect, imagination, and fidelity, as well as his overall suitability. A mere splinter, a flake, a whisper of caution in her makeup, fortified by the enchantment of Arden, holds her impatience to win him in check for most of four acts. She doesn't embark on a cross-country pursuit, as Julia and Helena do; she doesn't bide her time, as Viola-Cesario does; nor does she rescue anyone from death, as Portia does. She simply (simply!) plays at make-believe: You be you; I'll be a stranger. The game ends when the forest's powers tell her to round it off neatly.

Once in Arden and her new, masculine guise, her tongue finds a new edge, whether she addresses Celia, Orlando, Touchstone, or Jaques—with the last two she engages in cutting duels of disparagement—or Phoebe, whose infatuation thrives on Ganymede's affronts. The most famous and often-quoted of those affronts illustrates the simple language in which Rosalind couches her wit, when she hands Phoebe some investment advice: "I must tell you friendly in your ear, Sell while you can. You are not for all markets" (3.5.59–60). The reason for her more cutting remarks may lie in a couple of sentences spoken late in the game by Touchstone, probably by way of explanation: "We that have good wits have much to answer for. We shall be flouting; we cannot hold" (5.1.11–12). And as most editorial glosses tell us, *we cannot hold* means "we cannot hold back" or "cannot hold it in." Wit comes into being when it shows itself and shows itself off. It is not latent. And those—roles as well as people—endowed with its skills must exercise them. As is sometimes said of another sort of potency, Use it or lose it.

Now, wit is almost always exercised at the expense of others. True, some contemporary stand-up comics and monologuists like to skewer themselves. And when Rosalind emerges from a bout of wit and finds herself companion to a confidante like Celia, she may speak of herself with disapproval. And uncertainty. Or she may fly into anxiety, as when she hears from Celia that Orlando is nearby.

> What shall I do with my doublet and hose? What did he when thou sawst him? What said he? How looked he? Wherein went he? What makes he here? Did he ask for me? Where remains he? How parted he with thee? And when shalt thou see him again? Answer me in one word. (3.2.217–21)

But she puts on a brave front by quelling her yearnings and dropping into the species of dramatic irony that Shakespeare employs during impersonations, a device picked up by Molière and generations of farceurs.

ORLANDO Fair youth, I would I could make thee believe I love.

ROSALIND Me believe it? You may as soon make her that you love believe it, which I warrant she is apter to do than to confess she does. That is one of the points in the which women still give the lie to their consciences. (375–81)

Some commentators believe that Rosalind likes her temporary androgyny, if not glories in it. (See, for example, Ruth Nevo, [1980], one of the most eloquent partisans of "this trickster heroine.") In absolute contrast, Janet Suzman, who played the part with great distinction and teaches it, writes that at "the glowing centre" of the comedy "is a

smitten Rosalind telling herself that no one ever died for love, all the
while dying for love herself" (1995, 111). An actor can make sheer
enjoyment of the role, as many have done; but it is likely to become
more self-satisfied than the action warrants. She does exploit the masculine opportunities, but mostly as a ribber—who suffers occasional
pangs of dread, of detection. I have seen more than one performer
overplay the confidence and undercut the wit, turning the role into
Lady Snoot.

As You Like It is not exactly a songfest, but it does incorporate five
songs: "Under the greenwood tree" in three stanzas (2.5); "Blow, blow,
thou winter wind" in two stanzas (2.7); "What shall he have that
killed the deer?" in one stanza (4.2); "It was a lover and his lass" in
four stanzas, with a repeated chorus (5.3); and "Wedding is great
Juno's crown" in one stanza of six lines (5.4). In some productions,
the single verse of eight lines, "Then is there mirth in heaven" (also
5.4), is sung, not recited, by Hymen—or by Amiens while Hymen
mouths the words. Latham points out that the songs have at least two
functions, other than being there for their own worth: they help denote the passage of time while they are sung, like the lines sung by a
Greek chorus; and they tackle themes and ideas not dealt with in the
dialogue (1975, xxiii-xxvi). Some musical settings for the songs are
reproduced in Brissenden's Oxford edition as Appendix B ibid., 233–
38. Because of the comedy's indebtedness in certain of its structural
features and setting to the pastoral, some directors like to add incidental mood music, like that of Mendelssohn and other composers for
Dream, or the orchestration one resents in movies when it is designed
to "back up" (that is, drown) chunks of dialogue. The songs are more
cheerful on the surface than most of those in other Shakespeare; none
has anything like the gravity of say, "Willow, willow." The third stanza of "Under the greenwood tree," however, whether sung, spoken, or
croaked by Jaques, is a comic condemnation of himself and the other
courtiers for "leaving [their] wealth and ease"—a sentiment that becomes ironic when reviewed from his act-5 decision to join Duke Frederick and shun "dancing measures." And "Blow, blow" with its
chorus of "Then heigh-ho the holly! This life is most jolly" actually laments "man's ingratitude" and his betrayals of friends, adding, "Most
friendship is feigning, most loving mere folly." "What shall he have
that killed the deer?" as observed earlier, says that the deer-slayer
should earn the dead animal's horns to wear and become a public
spectacle. "It was a lover and his lass," rendered by two pages who are
not mentioned elsewhere in the text, hints that spring is the time for
making love in the "green cornfield." The tone is lyrical, even innocent, in keeping with the age of the singers; but in the BBC TV production the two boys in question had been drilled to trill their r's so

aggressively and the song was so slow and seemed so repetitious, like some repeated choruses in songs by Brecht, that the number began to sound like a boozy British pub ditty. In a version imported from London by the Theatre for a New Audience in 1993 and directed by Mark Rylance, who also played Touchstone—as a slow-talking, cud-chewing country boy, a young Corin—he gave himself this "hey, ding a ding, ding" song to deliver; it became the outstanding sequence in the play and proved a relief from a constricted staging.

The final songs, and perhaps one or two earlier ones, belong to modest masques. A masque's function resembles a song's. It can denote the passage of time, establish themes and ideas not present or merely hinted at in the dialogue, and in other ways remove the play from reality, draw attention to its artificiality, its fantastic touches, much as happens in *Dream* when the fairies take over the palace of Theseus.

Notes

1. Some plays also incorporate quasi-miraculous happenings that are treated in a realistic fashion, such as Henry V's defeat of the French army at Agincourt and Helena's curing of the French King's fistula, ascribed to skills taught her by her father; these "wonders" are understood to have been wrought by human agency.

2. We also find two Olivers in the comedy, the brother and the clergyman, Martext.

3. A surprising quantity of the substance of *As You Like It* appears in Lodge's *Rosalynde*, including some of the names, much of the story line, and the matches of Celia and Rosalind with the brothers.

4. The illustration of the Dali costume is reproduced in the Epilogue to S. Schoenbaum's *Shakespeare: the Globe and the World* (1979. 193). The dramatis personae of the play include no "winnowers." Dali was in all likelihood portraying a participant in the hymeneal celebrations of act 5, who might appear elsewhere in the play as a rustic presence.

TRANSFORMATIONS

Transformations of human roles are the ultimate in inconsistency. Shakespeare doesn't follow Ovid's lead in metamorphoses between human beings and other animate matter, except to flirt lightly with the idea when Falstaff wears antlers in *Merry Wives* and Bottom receives the head of an ass. Still, in the three plays subsumed here the transformations do come about through the properties of that unrivaled agency, magic, such that the first impressions registered by the roles should, as always, be mistrusted. Unlike most of today's drugs, taken orally or by injection, the love-in-idleness of *A Midsummer Night's Dream* enters a spirit (rather than a body) by way of the eyelids. So does its antidote. But how much of those juices remains in the spirits of the four young lovers and Titania when the night frolics end? Or *do* they end as the action dips into another night, the fairy realm takes over, and Bottom and his fellow artisan-actors troop back to workaday Athens? When time as chorus butts into *The Winter's Tale* right after act 3, not long before the play's halfway point, sixteen years have slipped by. An array of transformations begins. These affect almost all the main characters, but especially the two adolescent lovers, their parents, and the stalwart "middlewoman," Paulina. Prospero, who rules *The Tempest* as well as his unidentified island, uses his "art" to summon a party of his ancient foes and bring about transformations among them. In so doing he transforms his daughter and himself by intention.

A Midsummer Night's Dream

Disharmony erupts in both the natural and supernatural worlds of *Dream*. Could the clash of the "shaping fantasies" account in part for the comedy's unpopularity, except in crippled forms, among critics and audiences for at least a couple of hundred years after Shakespeare's death? Even then, did the rare productions melt two worlds convincingly together? Pepys thought the play "insipid"; Hazlitt found it "unmanageable" for the stage. In the nineteenth and earlier twentieth centuries it recovered from amputations, graftings of music, and illustrative ballet, to rebecome itself, the dramatic comedy with farcical streaks we are familiar with today. But it had to make its rites of passage through the imagination of such partisans as Samuel Phelps, Augustin Daly, with his strengths and weaknesses for spectacle; and, most devotedly, Granville Barker. Early in the twentieth century, Max Reinhardt brought forward gauzy and comic versions; he would eventually collaborate on a movie with William Dieterle (1934), which still pops up on late-night television, owing to the pulling power of James Cagney as Bottom and the youthful Mickey Rooney as Puck.

After the success of the film, which did not quite assure Hollywood that Shakespeare was not poison at the box office, versions of what was becoming a staple Shakespeare on stage stayed for a time in the ornamental vein. An influential critic in the 1930s concluded: "*A Midsummer Night's Dream* is barely more than a delicate, tenuous piece of decoration" (Traversi 1938). After World War II, open-air productions like the ones I saw as a youngster in Regent's Park in London would win commendation for being entrancing, enchanting, and other adjectives of delight that were not meant as literally as they should have been.

Jan Kott dealt a blow to the cheerful interpretations when he posited *Dream* as a nightmare (1966, 213–36). Kott treated *Dream* and *The*

Tempest as the palimpsests of a jaundiced vision, "Shakespeare's bitter Arcadia," corresponding to war, holocaust, and other horrors of the twentieth century, in which they did not originate. A welter of revisionary articles and stagings followed as part of the shift away from beaming (and beaming at) the play as fairy-tale entertainment for arousing a child's wonder in each spectator.

To cite merely two examples of shift to "darker" viewpoints: "The Darker Purpose of *A Midsummer Night's Dream*" by Michael Taylor (1963), and "'But We Are Spirits of Another Sort': The Dark Side of Love and Magic in *A Midsummer Night's Dream*" by David Bevington (1978). Stage "darkenings" in England by Peter Hall and Peter Brook and in the United States by John Hancock, Alvin Epstein, and Liviu Ciulei, among others, influenced countless college and high school productions. (As a useful reference, Sylvan Barnet, editor of the Signet Classic edition, added a synopsis of the play's history "on stage and screen" in the expanded edition, [1986, 191–202].)

By late 1993, at a talk given at the Graduate Center of CUNY, Jill Dolan spoke of a college production of *Dream* in which all the characters were gay. The discontinuity in the roles could stand up even in such an interpretation. The post-Kott years have disclosed that the work is neither murky without relief nor shadowlessly sunny—nor a compromise, either—but dappled like the woodland in which its three middle acts take place by moonlight. The play's overall effect, though, is subversion of the comic form, especially in the reconciliations and restoration of order. Even as a fantasy, *Dream* cannot help being more of a comedy (with flashes of farce) than it is anything else; at the same time, its fifth act in particular lets out strong hints of a new and, for some purposes, improved comic ending. A preliminary to the more sardonic plays (*Measure*, *All's Well*, and *Troilus*) had arrived, and was shortly succeeded by more comical dissimilarities, among them, *Merchant of Venice* and *Much Ado*.

The exertion of magic in *A Midsummer Night's Dream* exceeds that in *Hamlet*, *Macbeth*, *Julius Caesar*, *Richard III*, and even *The Tempest*. The play also invokes cosmic disturbances, "prodigies" that result from conflict between sprites, in this case Titania and Oberon, as against conflict between mortal roles of the sort that occurs in *Caesar* (1.3, 2.2,) and *Lear* (2.4, 3.1, 3.2). Magic, more than any other dramatic ingredient, militates against a psychological elaboration of roles. Bottom may appear to become an exception as he stubbornly hews to his role after his crowning as an ass and the award of Titania as his provisional mate; but ass-headed Bottom has become a gracious dispenser of gentle greetings, in contrast to his earlier and later self as a stage glutton, a greedy appropriator of others' lines and parts. Instead of expanding the roles, the playwright makes his manager of magic, Puck, with the encouragement of the supervisor, Oberon, create an environment that grows more playful, hostile, hopeful, or deceptively enticing: for Titania and her fairy contingent a spiritual battlefield; for Helena, a strange realm where she may gain the gratitude and regain the sincere affection of Demetrius; for Hermia and Lysander, a lose-the-way station en route to his "widow aunt," the dowager "of great revenue" (1.1.157–58); for the "mechanicals," a tranquil, outdoor rehearsal area—for a time; and for Theseus and Hippolyta, hunting grounds that distract them from a four-day wait for their wedding night.

Like strings of strangers who later find themselves thrown together aboard a steamer outward bound, in an elevator, on a train, in a grand hotel or some other tower, huddled in a lifeboat, on an island in a little hut, the four young love-victims endure a night of frustration and exhaustion in the forest. Peter Holland notes that the play

> contains only one description of something that may unequivocally be taken to be a dream, one "real" dream, Hermia's dream of the serpent [2.2.151-56]. . . . Everything else that is recounted by mortals or fairies as having been part of a dream is not a dream at all. The experiences have been turned into dream, experienced as if they were dream—but they were not. (1994, 4)

One could make a case that the word *dream*, used evocatively rather than literally, refers to a collective dream by each audience exposed to the play.

The youthful quartet is one of five species of roles that meet in the action. Although nominally Athenians, the four youngsters, together with Hermia's father, Egeus, have British upper-middle-class manners. They play romantic, amusing leads of a sort, but two roughly equal pairs instead of one dominant and one subsidiary pair. There is nothing distinctively Greek about them except one of the names. Two of the other names, Helena and Hermia, however, have mythical overtones as they recall Helen of Sparta and her daughter, Hermione; while the fourth name, Lysander, of ambiguous origin, sounds like an English corruption of Alexander (of Macedon?). Kott and other critics say one can hardly distinguish the two men, or the two women. These four do indeed form the principal source of perplexities during the three middle acts, their muddles shared at times (depending on the pace of the action) by the audience and by Puck, who is not infallible. Still, the playwright took some care to contrast the women by physique and temperament and put the men into differentiated situations, which allot them dissimilar tasks and, therefore, roles. In the very first scene, an alliance between Egeus and Demetrius (firmer than that between Baptista Minola and Petruchio) makes Demetrius look mercenary, just as his switch in affection from Helena to Hermia makes him look unreliable as a wooer. Lysander comes out of the scene looking honorable, sincere, ready to risk all for love—the very pattern of a romance-struck swain.

Those, including the audience, who look on the quartet's sonata of varied adventures in the forest as farcical are on the right woodland track, but the farce arises from anxieties, growing into fears, growing into criss-crossing of the four roles. For them the nightmare consists of having lost will power. Without being drugged and before going into the forest and falling under its puckish spells, Hermia shows herself ready to defy her father, lose the dowry she is entitled to, and face death or the inside of a nunnery for life. She displays a more positive front (although not less drive) than does Helena, who starts out as a literal follower. She pleads:

> I am your spaniel, and, Demetrius,
> The more you beat me I will fawn on you.
> Use me but as your spaniel, spurn me, strike me,
> Neglect me, lose me; only give me leave
> Unworthy as I am, to follow you.
> What worser place can I beg in your love—
> And yet a place of high respect with me—
> Than to be usèd as you use your dog? (2.1.203–10)

The verb *use*, used three times, together with the request to be spurned, struck, neglected, lost, mark her as Shakespeare's most abject heroine, and one of the funniest.[1] Spectators hearing the exchange between her and her beloved laugh with a frisson of horror at her audacious self-loathing as they also recognize one of the saddest spectacles one can encounter in life: a woman making a fool of herself over a man, and worse, an unworthy man.

After being drugged, however, the men declare their passions with an unwonted abandon. With all this load of woe upon her, Helena is, still, a role actresses crave to play: a taller, more gawky, less fierce, and generally more humorous part than Hermia's. The two drugged men are no less fervent in their quarrel. For love of Helena they will put swords through each other if Puck lets them. It makes little theatrical sense to think of them as fixed entities, cast-iron characters: their roles dictate verbal, physical, and psychological flexibility. Adrian Noble's production for the Royal Shakespeare Company, which visited the United States in 1996, brought out corresponding but differentiated qualities in the two young pairs, to make each figure quickly identifiable. The two men wore leisure jackets, but Demetrius's was solid blue and Lysander's solid green; the women wore matching summer frocks, but Hermia's was solid purple and Helena's solid orange. The costumes, like the sets, were designed by Anthony Ward, who also came up with a simplified method of doubling the costumes of Theseus (gold cloak) and Oberon (purple cloak), both played by Alex Jennings, and of Titania (in red) and Hippolyta (adding a white outer garment), both played by Lindsay Duncan. Barry Lynch put on a wild wig and bared his chest for Puck; for Philostrate he added a yellow tunic to Puck's yellow pants. (The mechanicals wore modern working-men's clothes. Quince had a bicycle.)

Much of the dialogue among the quartet is in rhyme, which drops its additional spell over roles and audience, creating an atmosphere more artificial—quasi-ritualistic—than if the lines were blank verse or prose. (*Dream* has a higher incidence of rhyme than any other Shakespeare play.) The bulk of the verse, including most of the *Pyramus and Thisbe* skit, is cast in the usual iambic pentameters, but the spell-like, act-5 speeches of Titania, Oberon, and Puck move into trochaic tetrameters, the same meter as the speeches of the "weyerd sisters" in *Macbeth*; some parts of *Pyramus and Thisbe* fall into an irregular medieval dimeter ("Asleep, my love? What, dead, my dove? O Pyramus, arise . . ." [5.1.318–20]). The number and rapidity of exits and entrances also connote a loss of control that intensifies the atmosphere of stylized farce. Thus the two men, as Puck's prey, prey on the two women and almost drive them to desperation, Hermia by neglect, Helena by a surfeit of compliments. In Elijah Moshinsky's BBC TV version, when Lysander and Demetrius both find themselves in love with Helena, they enjoy her speech about the betrayal by her best friend, Hermia (2.2.129–40). But soon after they fall to weeping at her misfortune. Moshinsky's film presented a forest that looked like a swamp in which the young quartet had to drag themselves through mud mazes, while Oberon dunked Puck's head in groundwater for placing love-in-idleness on the wrong eyelids.

But after the four lovers awaken from the nightmare and sit with Theseus and Hippolyta wherever act 5 happens—very likely back in Athens at the ducal palace—as they watch the performance by Bottom and the other artisans, their liberation from the enchantment of the green realm and from the torments of Morpheus and Puck affects them strangely. Upon the two young women, the release has the effect of utter silence; neither of them says one word during this last act. Are they subdued by their dream experiences? Afraid to upset the now-perfect balance of men and maids? Overawed by the presence of the Duke and his bride? They were bright, colorful talkers who have gone dry. Upon the two men the release has had the opposite result. They watch the performance of *Pyramus and Thisbe* and seems too free with their mockery: super-confident, brash, objectionable.

The second species of roles is the pair of revenants from myth, Theseus and Hippolyta. Here we have an anglicizing of the cousin of Hercules, a hero who performed his own twelve labors and even visited the underworld, again in imitation of his cousin, to do a favor for a friend. Now he no longer governs Troezen in addition to Athens, as the Theseus does in *Phaedra* or *Hippolytus,* or he may be too diffident to mention it. He says he wooed the great Amazon warrior with his sword and won her love doing her injuries (1.1.16–17). In Theseus' speech, "doing thee injuries" may mean that he wounded her during their single combat or took over some of her land or in some other way jeopardized her rule; it could even mean that she fell for him after he called her uncomplimentary names. The phrase seems designed to cover many possibilities and to let the playwright swiftly out of the myth and into the action of this play. She doesn't deny that he won her love, not merely her person. Directors who depict her as unwilling or resentful or militantly feminist take her for an actual woman, instead of a name and a bit of a role borrowed from Greek story-telling; they fear giving offense to fierce women in the auditorium. Disputes notwithstanding over whether Hippolyta is, mythically speaking, the same figure as Penthesilea in Kleist's and other writings and/or the same as Antiope, who supposedly was the mother of Hippolytus, according to some critical writings she has acquired an unexpected dramatic function in the fifth act when, almost incidentally, she defends the wholeness of this apparently piecemeal play (5.1.23–27). Theseus comes at us today, as he may have come at the author, from several directions. In the accounts of his exploits he trades on the love of women. In Ovid, Theseus abandoned Ariadne, the most celebrated victim of his ingratitude, the beautiful daughter of King Minos of Crete, on the island of Naxos after she helped him thread his way out of the maze that concealed the Minotaur (*Metamorphoses*, Book VIII). For helping him Theseus rewarded Ariadne by raping her. He dropped her on the isle of Naxos and eloped with her younger sister, Phaedra. In *Dream*, however, a politically correct distortion becomes as out of place as any other distortion. The playwright offers only one hint, after the role's early confession and determination to reform, that this Theseus belongs to other myths. That hint is the presence of a role named Egeus, the name in myth of Theseus's earthly father, also his forebear as ruler of Athens.

> O O O O that Shakespeherian Rag—
> It's so elegant
> So intelligent . . .

Shakespeare's new interpretation of Theseus sets up a sobersided and settled pragmatist, a judge as well as a duke, less glamorous for an exbattler like Hippolyta to contemplate as a husband than she might wish. Athens itself has no particular character in the play: it serves as little more than a contrast with—and in act 5, a refuge from—the "green" setting of the middle three acts. (It could, of course, have implied something like the genesis of theatre in the west of Europe, since this is Shakespeare's most wholeheartedly "theatricalized" play. I mention this as a highly unlikely possibility. A similar unlikelihood arises from the names Thisbe and Theseus, which could be taken to remind us of Thespis. Hippolyta is a hunter, like the goddess Diana (Artemis), and so is Theseus, like the Theseus drawn in "The Knight's Tale" of Chaucer. One of Diana's aspects is as the goddess of the moon—talk of the moon passes between Hippolyta and her bridegroom in the opening lines. Theseus complains:

> Four happy days bring in
> Another moon; but, O, methinks, how slow
> This old moon wanes! She lingers my desires . . .

To which Hippolyta soothingly replies,

> Four days will quickly steep themselves in night;
> Four nights will quickly dream away the time;
> And then the moon, like to a silver bow
> New bent in heaven, shall behold the night
> Of our solemnities. (1.1.2–4 and 7–11)

The play has started to live up to the word *Night's* in its title and to its nocturnal advance when she predicts that days will steep themselves in night. But her image of the silver bow in heaven as the new crescent moon also predicts the intervention of that brash and suspect bow-bender, Cupid. No conflict has persisted between these two presumably older lovers, older for sure in their origins than the youthful Athenian quartet. Theseus seems at first to play the rigid keeper of what Lysander will shortly call "the sharp Athenian law" (1.1.162); he gives Hermia four days to deliberate, and

By the next new moon [swollen from the crescent sliver referred to earlier]

> . . . . either prepare to die
> For disobedience to your father's will,
> Or else to wed Demetrius, as he would,
> Or on Diana's altar to protest
> For aye austerity and single life. (83, 86–90)

Diana is now alluded to in a third aspect; as well as being the goddess of hunting and the moon, she is the goddess of virgins. And, the most peculiar of her aspects, the goddess of crossroads. Yet, toward the play's end, finding the quartet of young lovers asleep and Demetrius now affirming that "the object and the pleasure of mine eye Is now Helena," Theseus relents, rejecting the importunity of Egeus, who begs "the law, the law, upon [Lysander's] head." The Duke answers, "I will overbear your will" (4.1.169–70, 154; 178). Once again, as in the forgiveness granted Egeon by Duke Solinus at the close of *Errors*, Shakespeare's drama doesn't support those critics who insist he is a traditionalist and an exponent of law and order above all else. Here he shows that men, who make laws, can unmake them.

To the playwright's ancient and (for his time) modern Athenians he adds a third distinct species, working-class artisans, would-be artists nervous about their performance but not seriously at odds to begin with. They have come upon a "green plot" for their stage and a convenient hawthorn brake for their "tiring house." Bottom's grandiloquence, much admired by the others, and his yearning to play all the parts and direct the show mean that Quince has to rein him in. Later his ass-headed apparition terrifies the others (3.1.98 ff.), who believe him dead or "transported." Alas, Bottom has fled somewhere and "the play goes not forward" for "not a man in all Athens [is] able to discharge Pyramus but he" (4.2.5 and 7–8). Flute's little elegy, his moment, so to speak, in the moon, works as a choice specimen of emphatic oratory:

> O sweet bully Bottom! Thus hath he lost sixpence a day during his life;
> he could not have scaped sixpence a day. An the Duke had not given
> him sixpence a day for playing Pyramus, I'll be hanged. He would
> have deserved it. Sixpence a day in Pyramus, or nothing. (19–24)

The speech also immediately precedes the reappearance of Bottom and their capers of joy that spring out of the gloom when the other five see him wearing his original head. Bottom, functioning as a solo turn, brings the central portion of the play into collusion with the stories of the lovers' quartet. The actor has the largest and favorite, most broadly and persistently farcical role in the play as a nonstop performer, constantly grabbing the initiative.

In his scenes with Titania and the fairy detachment, though, he becomes more restrained, altogether at home as a guest in these novel surroundings and excessively courteous to his fairy courtiers, one dainty "mounsieur" after the next, as he accepts their "apricocks and dewberries," their "purple grapes, green figs, and mulberries" (3.1.161–62), and other oblations. Here he becomes an opposing counter-role to that of Helena. She doesn't know how to respond when two infatuated men woo her; in her self-deprecating way she hasn't earned their love; they must be making fun of her; she is being put upon. Bottom, by way of contrast, accepts Titania's endearments and body as though his translation into ass-over-head and partnership with beauty were the most natural happening. His gregarious nature, reversals, and overblown speech let this commoner glide into majesty without any sign of strain, while he unconsciously exploits the not-frightening or otherwise likable qualities and demeanor (despite its obstinacy) of the ass as a mini-horse. But why the ass? To start, the notion of an *ass* for a *head* itself implies a world turned upside-down, as well as the word's having become an epithet of stupidity. During Medieval years the Feast of the Ass or Festum Asinorum was unofficially celebrated in many churches by an inversion of authority: junior clergy took over from the seniors and pitilessly mocked the conventional service, braying and hooting. Bottom is sometimes bumptious but not really stupid, although we laugh at him as though he were, in what may be a conditioned response.

The ass, in its deliberate way, is also believed by many people to have exceptional virility. The belief may have originated with folk legends or, more likely and specifically, with Apuleius' The Golden Ass, the tale of the man who was turned into a donkey and acquired tremendous prowess as a sexual partner, or with the mythical donkeyfication of Midas (Midass?). Kott interprets the union of Titania with Bottom as signifying that Titania longs to make love with a bestially endowed man—this pale and almost insatiable female (not unlike Alfred Hitchcock's opinion of blondes) pretends to Oberon that she underwent a nightmare when the episode, Kott argues, actually represented a wish fulfilled. Unlikely, because the playwright tells us that only Bottom's head undergoes the animal transformation, not his trunk and sexual equipment. Besides, the farcical overtones of a woman matched with an ass register more strongly than does any grim sexual business, and so do the overlapping of two groups or types of being.

Titania's love and solicitude for the ass, if portrayed as in, say, Landseer's illustration of her lines, "Sleep thou, and I will wind thee in my arms. Fairies, begone, and be all ways away" (4.1.39–40), consort with the tenderly sentimental mid-nineteenth-century view of the play. But for modern audiences the sight of this pair of lovers cannot help but come across as zanily incongruous. Peter Brook declared at the time of his production that Oberon gives his wife to "the crudest sex-machine he can find." But Bottom does not happen in Titania's way by Oberon's *design*. Oberon doesn't know what will be "the next thing she then waking looks upon." His speculations are wrong: "Be it lion, bear, or wolf, or bull, On meddling monkey, or on busy ape" (2.1.179–81). And when he later sees Bottom enwrapped in Titania's arms Oberon exclaims, "This falls out better than I could devise" (3.2.35). To split a meager hair even further, is it correct to call Titania Oberon's *wife*? He is listed as the King of the Fairies, she as the Queen, but whether fairies marry is as open a question as how many can fit on the tip of a pine needle. Nor do they appear to live what looks like a domestic relationship. Besides, Puck, not Oberon, eavesdrops on the mechanicals and assifies the weaver. And Bottom, even as a partial ass, hardly conforms with anyone's idea of a sex-machine, crude or subtle. In the Brook production Titania and Bottom were hauled aloft aboard a couch into the flies and a dream of the ideal sex act. The couch was reminiscent of the one in Douanier Rousseau's "The Dream," painted in 1910 and now lodged in New York's Museum of Modern Art. On that couch lies a naked female figure, living in the lush jungle life (including two staring lions) amid the spectacular setting. Did Rousseau have the Shakespeare comedy in mind?

As Bottom goes from ham to ass, to genteel lover, to friend and patron of fairies, and back to ham, so Flute, Snout, Starveling, and Snug travel through worry over the coming performance to fear, to their moments of inept glory—though the anxiety doesn't let up for the producer-director-prompter Quince until Pyramus and Thisbe are finally dispatched.

The fourth species or ingredient stirred into this farcical brew of middle-class youths, working-class summer stock enthusiasts, and royal mythicals is the fairy troupe, split into two divisions or "trains," like the double chorus in *Lysistrata* or *The Bacchae*, and led respectively by Titania and Oberon, although not divided up according to sex. When the leaders first meet, the action (2.1) does not stipulate any size for the accompanying "fairy trains." In an amateur or some other production without cost restrictions, ambitious parents of small, dressed-up children seize the opportunities to swell the trains to stage-filling numbers. R. A. Foakes offers some convincing speculation about the numbers of participants in the trains in Shakespeare's time, and during the past two centuries (1984, 4 and illustrations 3 and 4 of Charles Kean's (1856) and Granville Barker's 1914 productions). Peter Holland has a section on fairies in *Dream* and other literature, and he adverts to most of the points of discussion about them in the accumulated commentary (1994, 21–34).

In a preceding sequence Puck encounters a lone fairy, usually played by a grown actress; and in a scene (2.2) soon after the royal encounter, Titania's train sings and dances to lull "our lovely lady" to sleep. Apart from the scene (3.1) in which Bottom addresses a few favored Titania followers—Peaseblossom, Cobweb, Moth, Mustardseed—neither train reappears until close to the end of the play when Oberon and Titania, "with all their train," gently invade "this house" (5.1.397), presumably the palace in Athens, and bless "the owner of it" (414). For most of Oberon's time on stage—in some portions of it he is allegedly invisible—he appears minus his train, handing out instructions and reproaches to Puck; Titania's activity nearly all takes place under the eyes of her train, which acts as a security team. Two brief exceptions are the few lines before she and Bottom sleep together,

> Fairies, begone, and be all ways away.
> *[Exeunt Fairies.]*
> So doth the woodbine the sweet honeysuckle
> Gently entwist; the female ivy so
> Enrings the barky fingers of the elm.
> O, how I love thee! How I dote on thee! (4.1.40-44)

and her awakening in the continuation of the same scene, after Oberon relents and applies "Dian's bud" (a desexing agent, named for the goddess in her chaste aspect) to negate the effect of "Cupid's flower" or love-in-idleness.

The ordinary fairies, then, are drones who have little to do in the action other than creating "atmosphere," the nearness of magic.[2] But their king and queen tie threads into other main strands of the play: Oberon into the lovers' quartet mostly by way of Puck; Titania into the mechanicals by way of Bottom. They each accuse the other of prior love affairs: he with Hippolyta ("the Amazon, Your buskined mistress and your warrior love" [2.1.70–71]), she with Theseus, stolen "from Perigouna, whom he ravished." Theseus also broke faith "with fair Aegles," Ariadne, and Antiopa (78–80).

The quarrel between the king and queen illustrates Shakespeare's combination, as a craftsman, of delicacy and might. Their opening encounter tells us that they are squabbling, not over their infidelities with mortal partners but over possession of the Indian boy, the changeling son of Titania's deceased "vot'ress." Because of Oberon's jealousy and "brawls," and because he is determined to have that child from her, says Titania,

> The winds, piping to us in vain,
> As in revenge have suck'd up from the sea
> Contagious fogs; which, falling in the land,
> Hath every pelting river made so proud
> That they have overborne their continents. (2.1.88–92)

The crops have rotted, flocks have died and "fatted" crows, "rheumatic diseases do abound," and the seasons grow confused:

> . . . the spring, the summer,
> The childing autumn, angry winter, change
> Their wonted liveries; and the mazèd world
> By their increase, now knows not which is which. (2.1.111–14)

Have these catastrophes happened in Athens, all of Greece, Britain (she mentions the nine-men's-morris game), India (from which she has come), or the entire world? She says they result from the tiff between her and Oberon, but not that fairy magic is responsible. The overflow of rivers and drenching of continents represent the type of global or cosmic disorder consequent upon acts of wrongdoing committed in Seneca's plays.[3] If the quarrel, started and inflamed by Oberon, launches such vast reprisals from El Niño and La Niña, or the great super-magician in the sky, Oberon's desire to take the changeling boy either makes him look like one of today's "chicken hawks," a child-molester who has "gone off" his spouse, or a profligate who had sex with the child's mother, Titania's "vot'ress," and is therefore the boy's father. He consigns his queen to the first wild creature that passes and releases her from the spell only after he has

> . . . at my pleasure taunted her
> And she in mild terms begg'd my patience,
> I then did ask of her her changeling child;
> Which straight she gave me, and her fairy sent
> To bear him to my bower in fairy land.
> And now I have the boy, I will undo
> This hateful imperfection of her eyes. (4.1.56–62)

But this vindictive monarch can seem reborn: he will pity Helena's plight, rectify Puck's mistake by tipping the potent potion on the lids of Demetrius, and anointing Lysander with Dian's bud, (identified as *artemisia* or *chaste plant*) to reunite him with Hermia. Here is inconsistency of role reaching out to some of its kindest bounds.

There remains to discuss the fifth type of role, of which the play provides one example. Some commentators have taken Puck as a version of Cupid, and he does say, after teasing and exhausting Lysander and Demetrius and seeing Helena and Hermia worn out and bedraggled,

> Cupid is a knavish lad
> Thus to make poor females mad. (3.2.440–41)

But Puck has made the two males mad, not the females—at least, not *directly*; nor does he carry Cupid's trademark, the bow and arrows. He must either be speaking of the "real" Cupid or talking metaphorically or excusing himself from causing upsets by shoving the blame onto the son of Aphrodite. But when, on Oberon's orders, he spills the love potion on Lysander's eyes, he serves a Cupid-like function, unintentionally creating havoc among the relationships in the quartet. Kott and other critics prefer to see Puck as diabolical. Kott writes:

> The philologists long ago discovered the devilish origin of Puck. Puck is simply one of the names for the devil. His name was invoked to frighten women and children, together with the ogre and the incubus. (1966, 213)

The entry under *Puck* in an etymological dictionary says:

> AS. *puca*, cogn. with ON, *puki*, mischievous demon. In ME. synon.
> with devil and from 16 cent. with Robin Goodfellow. See *pug*. Also
> used in dial. of the nightjar or goatsucker, a bird regarded with su-
> perstitious dread.

The entry under *pug* embellishes the other definition only slightly:

> As in pug-dog, pug-nose. App. in some cases for *puck*, devil, later
> applied to an ape. (Weekley 1967)

The lower-case *p* here suggests that a puck became a generic term for a
mischievous demon or imp, rather than a synonym for Satan, more of
a trickster in most interpretations than a diabolical creature. But what
did *Shakespeare* imply by the name? Puck's first appearance, his encounter with the unnamed Fairy, marks him as a breed distinct from an
echt member of the fairy battalions, more of a weekend conscript or
flextime employee. Two speeches specify a number of his misdoings,
both in what the Fairy has heard about him and what he brags of:

FAIRY Either I mistake your shape and making quite,
Or else you are that shrewd and knavish sprite
Call'd Robin Goodfellow. Are you not he
That frights the maidens of the villagery. . .?
Skim milk, and sometimes labor in the quern
And bootless make the breathless housewife churn,
And sometime make the drink to bear no barm,
Mislead night-wanderers, laughing at their harm?
Those that "Hobgoblin" call you, and "sweet Puck,"
You do their work, and they shall have good luck.
Are not you he?
PUCK   Thou speak'st aright:
I am that merry wanderer of the night. (2.1.32–42)

He goes on to tell how he makes Oberon smile with his jests, fools
a horse by neighing like a filly, pretends to be an elusive, uneatable
crab apple or a three-legged stool that moves out from under an old
woman, and makes those around laugh at her. Brooks (1985) calls attention to a similarity of the Fairy/Puck encounter to the one in Lyly's
Gallathea (1.2), "a dialogue where, to further the exposition, Lyly has
Cupid (a mischief-maker like Puck) interrogate a 'Nimph of Diana'
about herself and her mistress, who, she indicates, is at odds with his
mother Venus." The role conceals the motives of a prankster behind a
pleasing, even benevolent exterior. His practicality allows him to call
on atypical powers by which he can magically change form, size, and
voice. As a "sweet" Puck who can bring good luck, as well as knavish
oppression, he mixes loyalty as Oberon's factotum with mimicry and

mockery of others: he refers more than once to Bottom as a fool, as "the shallowest thick-skin of that barren sport," and to the mechanicals in general as "rude" and "patches" and "hempen homespuns" (3.1.73). But we find in his activities nothing like the sheer malice we expect of a devil (or of an Iago or Richard III or Don John)—or of an Oberon. The Pucks who preceded a blue-faced Ian Holm in Peter Hall's filmed production and the ones who followed—on stilts in the Peter Brook version—good-natured athletes who let the more tangy lines speak for themselves, strike me as having been close to what the action requires. A bitter-talking, evil-looking Puck is bound to prove a disappointment: the play will not sustain the actor, especially in his genial, applause-shilling epilogue.

In George Devine's production (Stratford, England, 1954) Puck and Oberon were costumed in birdlike garments, feathered—or fishlike scaled?—built by the team of three designers who called themselves Motley. The identity of the costumes made the roles look like the same species (illustration 7 in Foakes [1984], and illustration 2 in Holland [1994]. Holland devotes a substantial segment of his introduction [35–49], to Puck as Robin Goodfellow and other manifestations).

Thus five disparate types of roles recruited from myth, a variety of times and places, the mundane and the magical, become interdependent, interwoven, one might say—the biggest role is that of a weaver. The following diagram illustrates the author's pulling together of this complex of connections, as he cross-cuts between the groups and interrelates them. The two fairy trains are omitted, but they can be envisaged in the blank spaces below Oberon and Titania respectively. This is one play in which the main plot—the mix-ups among the quartet—loses ground when two of the subplots (the Titania-Oberon quarrel and the Pyramus-Thisbe rehearsals) join forces and, like two merged corporations, threaten their rival's competitive edge. Theseus and Hippolyta frame the play, with Puck's assistance at the end, but the mechanicals, qua actors, claim the center of attention through most of the last act.

The quantity of "story," background information or exposition, varies from group to group and among the individuals in each group. The action in the opening scene subtends into the past the dispute between Hermia and her father. Hermia relates early on the closeness of the two young heroines in their childhood and adolescence (1.1.214–216), and Helena embroiders upon the profound friendship (3.2.198–214): they were "like two artificial gods" or "Like to a double cherry, seeming parted, But yet an union in partition . . . Two of the first, like coats in heraldry, Due but to one and crownèd with one crest . . ."

We learn much less about Lysander and Demetrius and do not know whether they were friends before the latter's affection shifted

A Network: Five Pairs of Lovers, Multiple Love Relationships

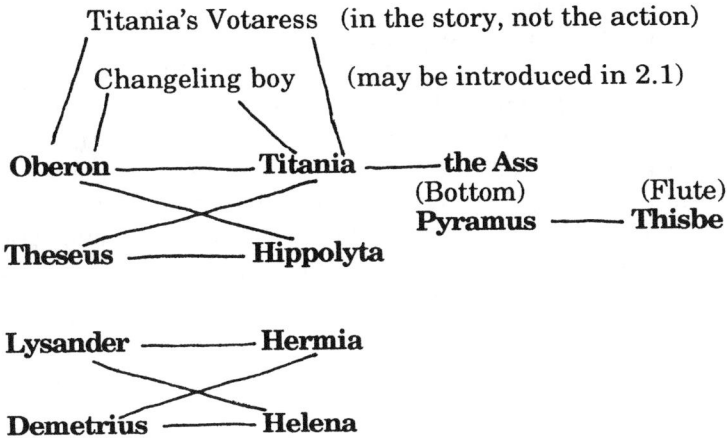

Titania's Votaress (in the story, not the action)

Changeling boy (may be introduced in 2.1)

Oberon———**Titania**———**the Ass**
(Bottom)　　　　(Flute)
Pyramus ——— **Thisbe**

Theseus ——— **Hippolyta**

Lysander ——— **Hermia**

Demetrius ——— **Helena**

from Helena to Hermia. The only background given for the mechanicals is their trades, although their names have some implications. Of the mythic derivations of Theseus and Hippolyta, including accounts from Plutarch, as translated by North, Chaucer, and Spenser, the playwright feeds into the text only sparing references to their lives; and although Titania and Oberon have Asian connections, and the break between them has brought damage to the universe, directors can make them into more or less what they wish. Granville Barker and much later Peter Brook and later still Adrian Noble doubled the roles of the fairy rulers and the mythical pair; Brook doubled several other roles. Doing this opens up performance opportunities for two actors and possibly cuts expenses on wages, costumes, and perhaps fringe benefits, but I don't see how it illuminates the play; it may even confound the audience unprofitably.

The play, then, splits into separate plots; and though they merge in act 5, I am not at all sure that they grow, as a number of critics believe, into Hippolyta's "something of great constancy; But howsoever, strange and admirable" (5.1.26–27). Rather, they clash. Their very disinclination to mix into a smooth theatrical paste seems to me the point of the last act and one of the play's contributions to the art of comedy.

The imagery is another matter. Anybody who thinks thematic material and figurative language can varnish over cracks, whether willful or accidental, in a dramatic composition—say, by means of scenic or costume design—doesn't err but skates on the play's surface, glossing over its other theatrical properties. The text is riddled with

allusions to animals, flowers, and insects, to their bestiality, pitiless nature, beauty or loathsome looks, and these have undergone exhaus-
tive critical inspection, but they often fall into or soar out of lists and
are not really figurative but plainly descriptive. The images of love,
sight, perception, deception and illusion, night, sleep, dreams, fantasy
(or "fancy"), and the moon, however, cling together or, more dynam-
ically, rotate in a coherent constellation. "This old moon wanes" in line
4 of the play but the topic of the moon has already risen, a line earlier. By lines 7 and 8, night has introduced itself, and the moon takes
another bow in lines 11 to 12. By line 30 Egeus is accusing Lysander
of having sung to Hermia "by moonlight at her window." Soon after,
when Theseus urges her to go with "your father's choice," eyes con-
spicuously enter the action.

HERMIA
    I would my father looked but with my eyes.
THESEUS
    Rather your eyes must with his judgment look. (56–57)

Theseus will give her until "the next new moon" to make up her
mind.

    By the end of the scene, Helena has fired off her soliloquy, which
turns the tone of the play around from melodrama to farce. The
speech drops more oft-quoted remarks than any speech in the play
other than that of Theseus on the imagination in act 5. She asserts that

Love looks not with the eyes, but with the mind,
And therefore is winged Cupid painted blind;
Nor hath Love's mind of any judgment taste . . .
Wings and no eyes figure unheedy haste. (234–37)

The playwright's studied irony here in relation to eyes makes Helena's
belief about love sound reasoned, if not mildly inspired; but the rest of
the play will contradict her: love really does look with the awakening
eyes, those deceivers, not with the mind.[4] The spells are laid on the
lovers and on Titania while they have their eyes closed. Love-in-idleness—identified as the unpretentious, not uncommon pansy, even if
Puck has to travel far and fast to collect it—gets squeezed only on eyelids. Oberon says he will release, not Titania, but her "charmèd eye"
(3.2.376). The mental aphrodisiac admittedly enters the head, and
thence the mind, where it takes effect—but not till after the subject
awakes and sets eyes on the first comer of the opposite sex. (Its neu-
tralizer, Dian's bud, equally does its job by absorption through eyelids.) If the product of love-in-idleness is love, its by-product, and that
of Dian's bud, is hatred of former or rival loves, evident from Lysander's vicious affronts to Hermia, which directors sometimes overplay in

performance by supplementing it with physical abuse, and also from Titania's disgust when she wakes after her night with Bottom. Don't trust your eyes, the play says repeatedly. Eyesight engenders fickle love. Such love is feigning, for what you see, isn't. ("Most love is mere folly," sings Amiens in *As You Like It*, 2.7, as part of the chorus of "Blow, blow, thou winter wind.") You look into the eyes of an adored one and seem to see a reciprocal yearning. Helena again:

> So the boy Love is perjured everywhere;
> For, ere Demetrius looked on Hermia's eyne,
> He hailed down oaths that he was only mine;
> And when this hail some heat from Hermia felt,
> So he dissolved and showers of oaths did melt. (1.1.241–45)

Demetrius may have felt "some heat from Hermia," but she did not make an effort to radiate any. He looked into her eyes and his sight misled him. Sleep, with its attendant "blindness," is sought as a restorative for waking stresses, love included—the First Witch puts the negative case when she lays a curse upon an innocent sailor whose wife offended her: "Sleep shall neither night nor day, Hang upon his penthouse lid" (*Macbeth*, 1.3.19–20). But a sleeping subject, unguarded by the waking senses, is vulnerable to attacks in the dark by unpredictable potions, nightmares, and other harm, "the fierce vexation of a dream" (4.1.68), not a dream's healing release, only those nightmares that issue from dramatized, possibly repressed, fears.

> HERMIA *[Awaking]*
> Help me, Lysander, help me! Do thy best
> To pluck this crawling serpent from my breast!
> Ay me, for pity! What a dream was here! . . .
> Methought a serpent ate my heart away. (2.2.151–53, 155)

In a television interview ("The Charlie Rose Show," May 27, 1996) Carl Sagan credited awakening eyes—after a nightmare—with the likely responsibility for sightings of flying saucers and other space phenomena. The susceptibility to night's dangers is enhanced in this play by the spell of Midsummer, a mayday festival reminiscent of the one celebrated almost three hundred years later in *Miss Julie* (1887), especially in the interlude. In Alf Sjöberg's dazzling film version of that play (1950), the frenzy of lovemaking, much more explicit than in Strindberg's text, comes as introductory material to the action, as men and women couple on hay in barns and out in the fields, much as evidently happened in many countries during May, Whitsun, and other summer holidays. Holland (1994, 104) quotes from *The Anatomy of Abuses* (1583) by Phillip Stubbes: "I have heard it credibly reported (and that *viva voce*) by men of great gravity and reputation, that of forty, three-score, or a hundred maids going to the wood over night, there have scarcely the third part of them returned home again undefiled." This is a time—a brief season, even—of abandon. Shakespeare hardly hints at any erotic goings-on, except when Titania temporarily worships Bottom. Hermia will not let Lysander sleep beside her; taking account, possibly, of the season and its festivities, she asks him to "lie further off . . . So far be distant" (2.2.63, 66). The action fastens on love frustrated, not consummated, up to act 5 and Pyramus and Thisbe.

That last act, in one scene, breaks more forcefully out of comic molds than do any of the scenes that precede it. Why, as a first point of inquiry, does act 5 exist? The action is smoothed out by the end of act 4. Anne Barton: "Shakespeare constructs a fifth act which seems, in effect, to take place beyond the normal plot-defined boundaries of comedy" (in Evans 1974, 219). Harold F. Brooks: "The plot is completed (except for Theseus' decision to 'hear that play') before the start of act 5. The romantic comedy of threat is over; the human and fairy couples are each at one in reciprocated love; and the comedy that mocks absurdities has ceased to touch any of them, though it continues, hilariously in 'Pyramus and Thisbe'" 1983, xcix). Peter Holland: "Act 5 is formally extraneous to the action of the drama, however essential it may be to the formal shaping of the structure" (New Cambridge, ibid., 10). The pairs have matched up in orderly fashion, as the earlier acts seemed to predetermine. Four nights have somehow gone by since act 1; it is hard to tell exactly when they vanished but the lapse hardly makes much difference. The couples, "three and three" (magic numbers), as Theseus puts it, ride the hours as endurably as possible until bedtime. But why bother? We will not witness the bedtime; this is no question of suspense (literally: dangling between a moment as expected and the moment fulfilled), and the experience of waiting is not an essential dramatic ingredient here, as it is in some plays.

As a rule act 5 constitutes either the climax of a play or the final convulsion(s) of a climax delivered in the previous act. But act 5 of *Dream* exists to play out a little melodrama, rehearsed and enacted as a farce, written as a skit on clumsy writing, playing with abandon, using medieval alliteration and metrics. *Pyramus and Thisbe* boldly states that theatre, like the human eye, like the moon, Diana's supposedly chaste orb, like a love promise, is feigning. Or like *Romeo and Juliet* it deals with a love that is star-crossed. A lion had chewed up Thisbe's garment, but not Thisbe. Pyramus kills himself under a delusion and the moon.

Here the author presents an uproarious, tragic upshot of going by appearances. It would be impossible for just about anyone but a chronically depressed soul to reckon seriously with the playlet. And the two young men laugh and joke, making malicious cracks about the performers. They take no heed of the lesson the playlet subjects them to, a lesson dramatized through the preceding three acts, that love is delusory, dangerous. But as with Silvia's silence during the last 114 momentous lines of *Two Gentlemen*, we are bound to wonder what the silence of Hermia and Helena portends during the 433 lines of act 5. Perhaps they digest the lesson their grooms-to-be ignore. As the mechanicals conclude their show with a bergomask dance and receive their reward in plaudits and cash, a clock speaks out. Theseus says,

> The iron tongue of midnight hath told twelve.
> Lovers, to bed, 'tis almost fairy time. (5.1.358–59).

He yields the building to the rule of night.

The previous act ended as a release from night, from sleeping, magic, love and its nightmares. Now an "iron tongue" urges the sextet back into night and its ordeals. In a moment they are gone. Before Titania and Oberon and "all their train" invade the house and take it over, Puck, alone on stage, characterizes the night:

> Now it is the time of night
> That the graves, all gaping wide,
> Every one lets forth his sprite,
> In the church-way paths to glide.
> And we fairies, that do run
> By the triple Hecate's team
> From the presence of the sun,
> Following darkness like a dream,
> Now are frolic . . . (373–82)

The lion's roar, the wolf's howl, the moon, the screech owl, the woeful wretch, the shroud, the gaping graves and their escaping ghosts, the triple Hecate (an aspect of Artemis-Diana associated with witchcraft and Hades)—these ominous night visions come from the impish part of Puck. But then the jocular part of his part takes over and allays his harshness.

> . . . Not a mouse
> Shall disturb this hallowed house.
> I am sent with broom before,
> To sweep the dust behind the door. (382–85)

To brush away, with the broom he traditionally carries, the detritus of the night before or the menace of the night to come? As though to live up to such an undertaking, Oberon proposes:

> Now, until the break of day,
> Through this house each fairy stray.
> To the best bride-bed will we,
> Which by us shall blessèd be;

And the issue there create
Ever shall be fortunate.
So shall all the couples three
Ever true in loving be;
And the blots of Nature's hand
Shall not in their issue stand;
Never mole, harelip, nor scar
Nor mark prodigious, such as are
Despisèd in nativity,
Shall upon their children be. (396–409)

After he, Titania, and the fairies between them chant thirty-odd tetrameters, sing, dance, and depart, Puck reasserts himself: Don't be upset. "Think but this . . . That you have but slumbered here." Treat this performance as a dream—a reminder of not the sort of dream meant by a phrase like "the American dream," if people still work that phrase sincerely, but of the fears and confusions associated with night, the absence of light. If you remain unhappy with us, Puck concludes with all the earnestness of a car salesman, call me a liar when I say I'll make amends.

But make amends how? When?

The "three and three" have not heard the mollifying, ritualized promises from Oberon (5.1.396–417) that "all the couples three [Shall] ever true in loving be" and that their offspring shall not know "the blots of Nature's hand," such as a mole, harelip, scar, or other "mark prodigious." Before they leave, though, the trio of ladies whose names, like Hecate's, begin with *H*, a nominal unification, may reflect during their silences on what led up to this resolution, before their surrender to love and night.

- Lysander has called Hermia "thou cat, thou burr! Vile thing," and "tawny Tartar," "loathed medicine," and "hated potion," and later, dwarf, minimus, bead, acorn—nothing irreparable, although *dwarf* is a bit much—and he remains under *two* doses of drug. It is no wonder that "Methinks," Hermia has said, "I see these things with parted eye, When everything seems double" (4.2.188–89).

- Demetrius insulted Helena until he received the dose of love-in-idleness, which still governs him. Perhaps for this reason, Helena has said, "I have found Demetrius, like a jewel, Mine own and not mine own" (4.2.190–91).

- Theseus has admitted that he conquered Hippolyta, as his mythical counterpart conquered other women, whom he later abandoned.

- And if that other mate, Titania, chooses to forget the fight over the changeling, and also forgets how Oberon, through Puck, humiliated her with Bottom, how he "at [his] pleasure taunted her" after she awoke (4.1.56), whereupon "she in mild terms begged my patience" (57), so that he got the changeling away from her while she was recovering from the drug—if she forgets all this, the audience may not.

Mocking memories undercut the smoothing-out reserved for act 5. As if to emphasize whom the roles-within-roles of Pyramus and Thisbe apply to, Bottom as Pyramus and Flute as Thisbe have this exchange:

PYRAMUS
> I see a voice. Now will I to the chink,
> To spy an I can hear my Thisbe's face.
> Thisbe!

THISBE
> My love! Thou art my love, I think.

PYRAMUS
> Think what thou wilt, I am thy lover's grace,
> And like Limander am I trusty still.

THISBE
> And I like Helen, till the Fates me kill. (5.1.191–96)

The names Limander and Helen, analogies with such redoubtable figures as Alexander and Helen of Troy, or Leander and Hero, are also close to those of Lysander and Helena, one lover from each pair. The gags about seeing a voice and hearing a face and the afterthought in, "Thou art my love, I think," together with the riposte of Pyramus, arouse laughs that distract from the audience onstage; those six close-up spectators appear not to notice the defective name-dropping. As a further warning about the mood at the end, we can recall Puck's forecast in the final lines of Act 3:

> Jack shall have Jill;
> Naught shall go ill.
> The man shall have his mare again, and all shall be well.

Does "his mare" suggest that the women are nags—or to be treated no better?[5] Or is the word an abbreviation? The syllable *mare* in *nightmare*, like the *mar* in the French *cauchemar*, does not signify riding a mare, or any other animal, but being ridden by a demon, such as a succubus, during the state of self-betrayal we call sleep.

Thus the play can be read, like other Shakespeare comedies that have shadowed meanings, with an overall ending that is upbeat, all the minor endings neatly rounded out; or it can be played for an opposite effect: as the night overtakes the day. A wishful dream or a formidable nightmare? Peter Brook's influential production of the early 1970s, affected by Kott's views of the play, but by no means governed by them, took the play in a third direction, neither reassuring nor horrifying, but almost scientific in its detachment: into reflexive theatricality all the way through, not merely in act 5: some reviewers went further and saw the staging as a comment on a circus. Sally Jacobs's set, a sanitized white, like the interior of a bleached cube with the fourth wall removed, had a high, flat upper level on which actors not appearing in a given scene jeered at the ones unlucky enough to find themselves trapped in the space at stage level, unable to leave by the few narrow entrances that closed into blank walls, with hardly visible doorways. To simulate administering the love-in-idleness and Dian's bud, the actors carried disks that spun precariously on poles. Puck strode the stage on stilts, above and beyond the reach of Lysander and Demetrius when they pursued him. Titania fondled Bottom on an expansive sofa shaped like a feather—a convertible feather—which lifted into the flies with the two of them aboard in rising bliss. Ladders and acrobatics featured broadly in the activities. Brook had reconceived the play's place and events, abandoning the green world and all pretense of a setting in Athens or a wood, as the roles became alternately caught up in and freed from the nightmare of performing in front of mockers. The action became a series of acts, a tribute to Shakespeare's epic structure. If Brook went even further than the playwright in revising the comic form, seldom did his version lose touch with the play's continual bursting of comic bubbles.

Adrian Noble's production also happened in the interior of a cube, only a red one this time. The forest settings in acts 2, 3, and 4 used drops in dark green and brown. Two doors and their frames on elevators rode up and down for Puck and Oberon to perch on (above the action like the spectators in Brook's version). Other doors in Anthony Ward's settings behaved with the repeated openings and closings characteristic of nineteenth-century farce. Whereas Brook's actors spoke the language to convey conversational ease, Noble's reveled in the plentiful rhymes; they did not ride over them or otherwise try to conceal them; his was a much more lighthearted treatment than Brook's. But like Brook, he played games with the comedy's artificiality, lowering colored ribbons from the flies in a spirit of celebration during act 5, and lowering lit bulbs at varying heights so that the night sky seemed to descend and lay a cloak of stars over the earth.

Notes

1. Proteus, as he releases a loose or floating adjective, also prepares to play the pet puppy: "Yet, spaniel-like, the more she spurns my love, The more it grows and fawneth on her still" (*Two Gentlemen*, 4.2.14–15).

2. Many people have scratched their scalps more furiously than Bottom over the probable size of the fairies. There is little point in rehearsing the whole array of arguments once again. They can be Lilliputian only on film or by means of some other artificial diminution, so they must be adult or child actors, even if they do speak of "cowslips tall" and claim to hide in acorn cups. The difficulty arises because of restrictive thinking along naturalistic lines. This is a play about magic. The fairy squadrons can change their size and other characteristics whenever, and as often as, they wish, playing at human size when they are onstage, and at other times, practicing personal downsizing or other transformations.

3. Harold F. Brooks has helpful annotations to Titania's bravura speech (1983, 30–35).

4. A comparison suggests itself here with the closing lines of Molière's one-act farce in rhyme, *Sganarelle, or the Imaginary Cuckold: De cet exemple-ci res-souvenez-vous bien; Et, quand vous verriez tout, ne croyez jamais rien* ("When all the evidence as you receive it Adds up to one conclusion, don't believe it").

5. Brooks, 1983, says in a footnote on p. 85 that "'All is well and the man has his mare again'" was "recorded by Ray in 1678 [more than 80 years after the play was written] as proverbial," but that F. P. Wilson found a similar line from before 1548 in Copland's *Jyl of Brentford's Testament*: "The poore mare shall have his man agayn." This may be a source or it may [vide *his* man] be a coincidence. In any event, Shakespeare uses the words with what I take to be significance for his play.

The Winter's Tale

As a contrast to the dream of a midsummer night, the winter's tale that young Prince Mamillius announces never reaches the auditorium.

HERMIONE
> . . . Pray you, sit by us
> And tell's a tale.

MAMILLIUS   Merry or sad, shall't be?

HERMIONE
> As merry as you will.

MAMILLIUS
> A sad tale's best for winter. I have one
> Of sprites and goblins.

After some urging and interruptions, he goes on.

> There was a man . . . . Dwelt by a churchyard. I will tell it softly;
> Yond crickets shall not hear it.

HERMIONE Come on, then, and give't me in mine ear. (2.1.22–32)

It might have been a cheering story meant to counteract the temperatures of winter. The opening scene of George Peele's *The Old Wives' Tale* (ca. 1591) includes lines 78–79, which say that a "merry winter's tale would drive away the time trimly." But merry or sad, the tale dissolves. Mother's and son's exchanges grow inaudible, then give way to the noisy entrance of the father, who is trailed by Antigonus and some lords. A different and deplorable winter's tale has taken over. It is the main plot, the self-inflicted misery of Leontes, and will persist from the start of 2.1 until 4.2, by which time Hermione has apparently died of chagrin at having been condemned by her husband for adultery and of shock at the news of Mamillius's mysterious death—cause unknown. But the action shortly moves off in a fresh direction, sweeping the main plot almost out of consideration for a time. New plotting launches a cast of mostly new roles, dominated by Perdita, in a spring-into-summer tale, which dissolves like a balm into the sorrowful tale of winter and soothes some of its wounds without altogether healing them.

Magic in the form of supernatural and wildly unnatural happenings supersedes what we might think of as natural motives and behavior in the action of this play, despite the concentration in the immense fourth act on nature itself and its properties. To explain this feature another way, we could say that the plotting consists for the most part of bald-faced manipulation. In *The Winter's Tale* no one role grows as blatantly into the playwright-within-the-play as Duke Vincentio does or Prospero. Apollo may act as a puppeteer from an offstage Olympian height, but the energies of the play itself are released through four roles who, in their exertions and their influences on other roles, command the movements of the play.

Time, personified as the chorus in 4.1, the scene that becomes the play's turning point, is not one of those four roles. A number of persuasive critics, among them Inga-Stina Ewbank and Frank Kermode, suggest that this play and certain other works by Shakespeare deal with the ravages, transformations, and the drama (including the comedy) wrought by and over time.[1] So this "romance" does; but every play wears down time, just as it occupies space. Although the appearance of Time as a narrator may tempt us into extrapolating, time itself is an ingredient in the mix of every action and story. In Adrian Noble's Royal Shakespeare Company version, which visited the United States in 1994, the actor playing Camillo recited Time's speech (4.1) as an anonymous statement. Camillo and Polixenes then went forward into their decreed business. Ingmar Bergman's staging, which came to New York some six months later, cast a woman as Time. Earlier twentieth-century critics became so used to calling the role Father Time and noticing his hourglass that they would have goggled at a formally dressed, middle-aged lady who carried an old-fashioned ormolu alarm clock and wore a long gown that had a train like a broad, flat tail; and yet, Bergman may have thought of Iago's allusion to the "many events in the womb of time which will be delivered" (*Othello*, 1.3.371–72), and decided that a male Time has no organ as pregnant as a womb. The Swedish director also respected the play's series of repetitions and correspondences analyzed by a number of critics, because after the last scene and a song sung by Emilia, Mother Time briefly re-established her ascendance as she crossed the acting area slowly, from downstage to upstage, still holding her clock. As the lights went down, a tick-tock grew audible.

Despite the dramatic ubiquity of time, a director of this particular play will take into optical account the sixteen-year hiatus, as well as the new *and older* roles laid out in the second part for Paulina, Leontes, Polixenes, Camillo, Hermione, the old Shepherd, and his son, the Clown. For in the first three acts, Hermione, Leontes, and Polixenes might be at most thirty-plus; the addition of sixteen years will not age them much but will emphasize the novelty of their roles as parents of grown-up offspring. When Leontes sees Florizel for the first time, he thinks of being a youth again.

LEONTES . . . Were I but twenty-one,
Your father's image is so hit in you,
His very air, that I should call you brother,
As I did him, and speak of something wildly
By us performed before. (5.1.126–30)

Possibly his mind goes back to being unmarried again. Add nine or ten years for the life of Mamillius up to the end of act 3 and the arithmetic puts the two kings and one queen in their early to mid-forties in the second half.

A succession of miracles begins with the onset of Leontes's rage. This irrupts in the second scene, after dialogue in which Archidamus and Camillo have spoken glowingly of the friendship between Leontes and Polixenes (1.1). Leontes seemed to confirm the friendship by entreating his friend to stay on in Sicilia. Polixenes, who has already stayed there for nine months, has his own kingdom and business to attend to. But Hermione repeats the plea. This time it succeeds. Leontes is now all effusion: "Hermione, my dearest, thou never spok'st To better purpose" (1.2.88–89). Still, he recalls that it took "three crabbèd months" of courtship, which

. . . had soured themselves to death
Ere I could make thee open thy white hand
And clap thyself my love. Then didst thou utter,
"I am yours forever." (102–05)

What goes on between Polixenes and Hermione now abruptly seems

. . . too hot, too hot!
To mingle friendship far is mingling bloods.
I have tremor cordis on me. My heart dances,
But not for joy, not joy. (108–11)

But what *does* go on between them? They are dancing together but, we can confidently say, not clasping each other in a modern fashion. They would be decorously separated, early seventeenth-century style, joined only and perhaps intermittently by one hand each at a time. Now, any man seeing his wife and best friend making harmonious patterns together in space and time might entertain a suspicion or two; but it's un-likely, to say the least, that he would implode, then explode, as violently as Leontes when he describes his observations and feelings to Camillo.

He has become, in his own words, "too hot, too hot!" and too fast on the false uptake for devotees of realistic playmaking. If we wished to account realistically for the sudden onset of Leontes's rage, we could note the six words that preface his praise of Hermione. When she tells him Polixenes "will stay," his first reaction is, "At my request he would not," which could be taken as a warning of the jealousy to come, or in admiration that magnifies his praise. Or it may be that as he sees the couple dancing he notices Hermione's pregnancy and re-members that Polixenes has been his guest for "nine changes of the watery star"; but this damning little deduction, also arrived at by some commentators, would mean that Hermione conceived the baby just about as soon as Polixenes arrived in Sicilia. Hermione has her own suspicions—of external interference: "There's some ill planet reigns" (106). Perhaps the harmony, the pleasure taken by Hermione and Polixenes in each other's company, galls Leontes. Toulouse-Lautrec is reported to have said, "Why is it . . . that the happiness of others makes us feel as if we have been robbed?"[2]

As the next miracle, Apollo's oracle, sought by Leontes and brought by Dion and Cleomenes from an imagined Delphi (on an island), dismiss-es Leontes's suspicions and brings fearful punishment in its wake. The tearing anger of Leontes subsides, overtaken by regrets and self-torment but not until—in quick succession—Mamillius dies; Hermione swoons and is reported lifeless; and Antigonus, despatched to Bohemia with Her-mione's baby, is ripped to bits offstage by a bear while a storm does in the vessel on which he sailed. An old Shepherd discovers the baby in her swaddling clothes, with her identifying papers and articles in the cradle, and rescues her, much as a shepherd rescued the baby Oedipus.[3]

Baby Perdita grows up between scenes 1 and 3 and keeps her name, Perdita, although no one knew it but Antigonus, to whom it was confided by a dream figure of Hermione. The bear slew him, however, before he had a chance to pass the name along, even to the bear. Had Hermione or Antigonus written it down among the papers in the cra-dle or on a label? Antigonus's dream, or his interpretation of it, led him to two false assumptions: that "Hermione hath suffered death," and that

Apollo would, this being indeed the issue
Of King Polixenes, it should here be laid,
Either for life or death, upon the earth
Of its right father. (3.3.41–45)

He'd left Sicilia before the oracle arrived, believing Leontes, not Hermione. Long after this obtuseness, but perhaps because of it, Apollo convinced Leontes to reward Paulina with a more discerning husband, Camillo.

The flukes of fortune continue. We learn from Florizel that his falcon flew, not off at random, but across land belonging to the Shepherd, enabling the offspring of Leontes and Polixenes to meet and fall in love. (Florizel was born within a month of Mamillius, and will serve as a replacement son, not a son-in-law only, for Hermione and Leontes.) In 4.4 Polixenes flies into a rage that resembles that of Leontes, except that we see a provoking motive, namely his son's refusal, five times, to be open about his forthcoming marriage as a prince to a girl who appears to be a shepherd's daughter. Polixenes deserves the rejections for disguising himself in order to spy on his son; but his bad behavior thereafter seems wished upon him and is a prime example of role transformation. As the comedy's final miracle, Paulina somehow kept Hermione alive, salted away for sixteen years.

One can believe in all these miracles but the last, which, from most interpretations, is no more than an apparent miracle, not genuine magic. Hermione, stage-managed by Paulina, imitates a sculpture supposedly created by Julio Romano before becoming herself. Critics often complain that the attribution to Romano, "that rare Italian master" (5.2.98) who lived in the sixteenth century, amounts to another piece of careless writing, because the action of the play is assumed to unroll in pre-Christian times. But if it is not defending "bad Shakespeare" to say so, the dramatist appears to play deliberate games with time; and using the name of an actual artist implies to me an actual sculpture. Instead of making us imagine that Hermione imitates a stone statue, why should Paulina not, in this supernatural atmosphere and as a climax to the other miracles, transform an actual statue? Why not go all the way? The play then conforms more closely with the Pygmalion and Galatea myth, but instead of Venus's granting Pygmalion's wish that his artwork come alive, as in Ovid, the magic responsibility here falls on Apollo; and the husband, instead of the sculptor, yearns her back into humanity when he obeys Paulina's "It is required You do awake your faith" (5.3.94–95). For the purposes of the staging, Paulina, that vital lady, has acquired miraculous powers, as suddenly and uncharacteristically as Leontes and Polixenes fall into their rages. She turns Apollo's agent. Evidence that a real transformation takes place we might deduce from two additional statements by Leontes. As he leaves, grief-stricken after Hermione's collapse, he says to Paulina,

> . . . . Prithee, bring me
> To the dead bodies of my queen and son . . . .
>   Once a day I'll visit
> The chapel where they lie . . . . (3.2.234–35, 238–39)

Every day for sixteen years? He may not have lived up to the vow quite so conscientiously, but he does affirm after her regeneration that

> . . . . I saw her,
> As I thought, dead, and have in vain said many
> A prayer upon her grave. (5.3.141–43)

It is unlikely that he ever opened the coffin for a quick check, but a miracle here seems more credible *and* dramatically satisfying than sixteen years of concealment. Contriving a statue, which a living Hermione can replace, should present no difficulty for a trained designer with Julio Romanesque aspirations. It is "but newly fixed," the color "not dry" (5.3.47–48), before the Hermione actor supplants it. The scene already calls for a curtain (59, 68). With or without the aid of a blackout and/or flash of light, the curtain facilitates removal of the statue and Hermione's substitution. Played out this way, the miracle will be full-blooded, not a mere deception.

In the plotting of *The Winter's Tale*, secondary roles form clusters of support or opposition around four figures. During the first half the action springs mostly from the impulses and activities of Leontes. He baffles and horrifies courtiers with his crazy accusations; orders Camillo to kill Polixenes; bewilders Mamillius with possessive maneuvering; asks for, then rejects, the oracle; charges Antigonus "on thy soul's peril and thy body's torture" (2.3.181) to bear away baby Perdita, "this female bastard" (175),

> To some remote and desert place quite out
> Of our dominions, and that there thou leave it,
> Without more mercy, to its own protection
> And favor of the climate. (176–79)

Two operative figures take over the play's second half. Perdita, grown up, introduces a new generation of roles which invigorates the main plot and some of its branchings. Her flowering into a supremely nubile maiden eligible to play Queen of the May for the summer festival and capable of enchanting Florizel and onlookers at the celebration is mildly undercut by ignorance of her true status. She feels unworthy of a prince, no matter how madly he loves her. She incites the disguised Polixenes to justify the grafting of one stock onto another, which she calls unnatural and he calls natural because, he says, nature dictates everything that happens, if only by unacknowledged causation and tacit approval. Her obvious beauty, imagination, goodness, and intelligence don't suffice for her or Florizel to overlook her inferior rank and make her worthy of a prince's hand. But when she gets to Sicilia, she charms Leontes and his courtiers. Her birth tokens not only establish her identity but also bring about the end of Leontes's long repentance and the recognition scene of Hermione's return to life.

The range of influence exerted by Autolycus, the third operative figure, although more limited in breadth and depth, emphasizes the class differences that keep bubbling up to the play's surface. As Florizel's former servant in some unspecified capacity but now "out of service" and hoping to get back into it, not even a hanger-on, he plays a Shakespearean equivalent of the Plautine smart slave, while his principal mark, the Clown, plays something like his Plautine complement, the dense slave, as he submits unknowingly to Autolycus's greedy hands. Autolycus purloins bed sheets put out to dry (like Falstaff's beggarly troops who will "find linen enough on every hedge"), and he sells sheet music, which in Adrian Noble's production had titles like *Hot Hands* and *Fast Fingers*. This Autolycus (Mark Hadfield) kept snapping up unconsidered trifles from all over—handkerchiefs, scarves, umbrellas, a watch, purses. During a fertility dance with the two rustic maidens, Mopsa and Dorcas, his hands danced as spryly as his feet. The era conjured up by Noble approximated Edwardian, with hints of an eternal Ruritania, although the Clown rode a modern bicycle— which Autolycus stole. In Ingmar Bergman's production Autolycus entered the Arcadian setting on a motorbike with a deafening exhaust and a homemade cart attached to the back to carry his ribbons and rags and songs. Oh, ill-placed modernity . . . .

Autolycus lightens the melodrama that sometimes enriches, sometimes sabotages, a romance drama like this one. He also adds a necessary, tart presence to the long pastoral scene (4.4), reappearing in the final third of it after a splashy introduction in scene 2 (Tillyard [1938], reprinted in Muir [1970, 86]).[4] Autolycus leaves so firm a dramatic imprint on the play's complexion that one realizes with a start that he appears, not lengthily, in only three scenes, which crop up relatively late in the action. His late springing-forth may have given Brecht the idea of a delayed arrival onstage for Azdak, the good rogue who becomes a moving spirit in *The Caucasian Chalk Circle*, which, like *The Winter's Tale*, recharges itself and makes a new start in its second part.[5]

Autolycus could also have inspired the tinkers in the plays of Synge and others; in the BBC television version of the play the actor had an Irish brogue. We never discover whether he earns, wins, or steals his way back into Florizel's favor and service; but he does exchange his shabby clothes for Florizel's illustrious outfit and then enjoys himself with the Clown and the old Shepherd as he plays a courtier who can become their advocate to King Polixenes (4.4.717–833) in return for all the gold they have and "as much more" to come. Grateful that he will accept this bargain price, they confide to one another that they are "blessed in this man" who "was provided to do us good" (vv. 830, 833). Later, we learn that he brought them "aboard the Prince," rather than the King, and although they learn offstage of "all the faults I have committed," the Clown still feels beholden.

CLOWN [*To Autolycus*] Give me thy hand. I will swear to the Prince thou art as honest a true fellow as any is in Bohemia.

SHEPHERD You may say it, but not swear it.

CLOWN Not swear it, now I am a gentleman? Let boors and franklins say it; I'll swear it.

SHEPHERD How if it be false, son?

CLOWN If it be ne'er so false, a true gentleman may swear it in the behalf of his friend. (5.2.157–64)

In this last scene he takes part in, Autolycus has turned humble, "bowing and scraping," says G. Wilson Knight, "to his former gull" ("Great Creating Nature," from *The Crown of Life*, [1947], reprinted in Muir 1970, 150]). Is he being duplicitous, as usual? I don't believe so. In earlier lines he exulted over his accomplishments as a thief: his slickness, quickness, winning tongue. But by the end of act 4 he "means to do the Prince my master good, which who knows how that may turn back to my advancement?" (4.4.837–38). Hence his desire for a good report from his clients. We could take this change of face, this desire for a return to his former position, its promise of advancement, and other presumed benefits as an underlying motive all along: his vaunting about his thievery covers up his disappointment at being out of service. But playing the moment in his first song-and-soliloquy scene requires the actor not to give away the hidden motive (if it really is that) or he will put the comedy in the lines at risk. Better that he contrive the moments as they fall, one at a time, each with full acting concentration.

Disputes have arisen over the structure of *The Winter's Tale*: its breakdown into subdivisions and parts. Tillyard, in *Shakespeare's Last Plays* (1938), announces a resemblance to Dante's Inferno, Purgatorio, and Paradiso. While it may prove tempting to align one masterwork with an earlier one, I find the resemblance strained and in need of restrictive definitions. The play can be subdivided conceptually into two, three, four, five, or more parts, according to the predispositions and prejudices of the subdivider. Some instances: Time's scene (4.1) can be regarded as a separate part; so can Antigonus and the baby (3.2) or the statue-into-Hermione sequence in 5.3. I prefer the single split into two parts.

In the final scenes of them both, Paulina takes over as the fourth governing role, ruling the king and queen of Sicilia. She mellows from the waspish, fearless, young court dame to Apollo's instrument, the maker of magic, and the questionable comfort of Leontes. In the closing scene of the play, all eyes may rest on the Hermione statue, but Paulina calls the shots.

The rest of the leading roles introduced in the first part reappear reborn at one moment or another (some of them more than once) from fresh vantage points demanded by the action. Thanks to Time, they have all aged. In addition to acquiring a sprinkling of wrinkles, Hermione changes from, successively, an adoring and amusing wife, a gently hortative friend, a sad mother, a spirited legal defendant, and an object of sympathy to the courtiers, as well as the jailer; into an unstoned statue who speaks fewer than ten lines, addressed in wonder to the stranger who is her daughter. She does not speak to her husband or refer to him, only mentioning to Perdita the court of "your father," to which both women have returned. Directors may romanticize the ending if they show her and Leontes, bodies intertwined, lips sucking up love in a Jonsonian "Drink to me only" ecstasy, but the lines do not give us the first Hermione at the last, no matter what the comic ending may seem to require. As an opposed view of Hermione's few lines, Helen Faucit, one of the most celebrated Hermiones, wrote:

> It was such a comfort to me, as well as true to natural feeling, that Shakespeare gives no word to Hermione to say to Leontes, but leaves her to assure him of her joy and forgiveness by look and manner only, as in his arms she feels the old life, so long suspended, come back to her again." (*On Some of Shakespeare's Female Characters*, published in 1891: excerpt in Muir [1970, 49])[6]

Paulina graduates from Antigonus to Camillo, both of them mature advisers in the early acts, but not yet aged—probably in their thirties and no more than a few years older than Leontes and Polixenes—and neither of them a particularly distinctive role. The stage tradition of a senile Antigonus, like other traditions, dies hard. Directors and critics frequently assume that Antigonus is an older man, possibly because Leontes taunts him by calling him a henpecked "lozel," married to a "callet" or "gross hag" (2.3.109, 98, 108), that is, a cuckold, who has a "gray beard." The line about the beard runs, "'Tis [he means Perdita] a bastard So sure as this beard's gray" (2.3.161–62). But to whom does "this" gray beard belong? Perdita, anyway, is not a bastard. Antigonus may also seem old by way of contrast with the newborn Perdita, as when the Shepherd says to the Clown, "Thou mett'st with things dying, I with things newborn" (3.3.110–11). Antigonus *is* dying, if not already expired; but one can die young or middle-aged. Besides, the Clown refers to Antigonus as the gentleman or the poor gentleman; he doesn't say he was old. But Nevill Coghill, a penetrating reader, writes in his defense of Shakespeare's stagecraft that the bear carries off "an elderly man" and also says that the bear went "in pursuit of an old gentleman (especially one so tedious as Antigonus)" ("Six Points of Stage-Craft in *The Winter's Tale*" in *Shakespeare Survey* 8, reprinted in Muir anthology.). Coghill's point, though, is a valid one and corresponds to many recent stagings, such as Ingmar Bergman's, in which the bear's assault is comic, not unlike the scene in *The Gold Rush* when a grizzly follows Charlie the tramp-prospector along a mountain path.

The death of Antigonus at the paws of a bear has come in for disproportionate discussion in the criticism, as here, mostly because of the five-word stage direction that takes him off the stage of life. The BBC TV version, directed by David Jones, showed a huge creature, a bear puppet, sticking a head and part of a hirsute torso into sight. Ingmar Bergman's bear, an actor in an oversized polar fur, pursued Antigonus and, before they reached the exit, enveloped him. Bergman also introduced a brown bear earlier in the play; on both occasions the bear raised what were clearly intended laughs from the audience, as John Irving often does from readers of his novels that have guest appearances by bears. Adrian Noble's bear appeared in flashes of strobe lighting; so did a suspended Hermione in an image remembered from Antigonus's dream.

Polixenes himself, in his rounding on Florizel for not reporting his marriage plans, acquires some bite at last. In act 1 he played little more than the bland buddy; in act 4 he turns into a vengeful parent, a variation of traditional comedy's forbidding, petulant father. His yelling at his son echoes the outbursts of Leontes, even though he does not act as brutally in punishing Florizel as Leontes does Hermione.

But the echo has a curious consequence. It makes us think that a lover's jealousy may, with age, become transmuted into a father's possessiveness, which *is* a kind of jealousy, as he rails at the son. Polixenes may even be smitten himself by the bewitching Perdita. His dramatic passage through the green world of pastoral Bohemia inverts the usual result of such progress from ill to good fortune, from obtuseness to discernment. The regress of Polixenes takes him from mildness to an agreeable dispute with Perdita (a mixture of testing and flirtation), to a tantrum, and on into an affective maelstrom. His ranting supplies the echo (or mirror) pattern for the action and a device to mimic the suspense in act 5.[7] In the substantial exit speech of act 4 we observe that Polixenes begins and ends by directing his anger at Perdita: "I'll have thy beauty scratched with briers and made More homely than thy state" (4.4.427–28), on to:

> . . . . And you, enchantment,
> Worthy enough a herdsman—yea, him too,

> That makes himself, but for our honor therein,
> Unworthy thee—if ever henceforth thou
> These rural latches to his entrance open,
> Or hoop his body more with thy embraces
> I will devise a death as cruel for thee
> As thou art tender to't. (436–43)

The sexual imagery in these few lines ("enchantment . . . latches to his entrance open . . . hoop his body . . . embraces . . . tender") hint at the jealous springs of his fury. Polixenes mentions his wife only once (1.2.78); it is not she but his "affairs" that "drag [him] homeward" (23–24) to Bohemia. Leontes also mentions the unnamed wife once, when he compliments Florizel: "Your mother was most true to wedlock, Prince, For she did print your royal father off, Conceiving you" (5.1.124). Perhaps Polixenes's effusive compliments and salutations to Hermione ("O my most sacred lady," 1.2.76) help sketch in a foundation, if a flimsy one, for Leontes's suspicions. Coghill argues that Leontes has reason for his rage:

> [It] is clear that Leontes, as in the source-story which Shakespeare was following, has long since been jealous and is angling now (as he admits later) with his sardonic amphibologies, to catch Polixenes in the trap of the invitation to prolong his stay, before he can escape to Bohemia and be safe. (in Muir [1970, 102])

Is it "clear"? A lengthy jealousy on the part of Leontes can only be speculative, intended to soften the shock of his access of fury. Impulses—they fight off theories of consistency.

As for the "echoes" in the play's second part, I should add that they are more distortions than reproductions. The Sicilian court exerts different influences on its courtiers than the countrified Bohemia does on its peasants and princes. Frye says,

> The second part is a tragicomedy where, as in *Cymbeline* and *Measure for Measure*, there is frightening rather than actual hurting. Some of the frightening seems cruel and unnecessary, but the principle of "all's well that ends well" holds in comedy, however great nonsense it may be in life. (in Muir [1970, 184])

In the final moments, the action dispenses with frenzy. Leontes has grown as tame in his contrition as Polixenes was in his bewilderment during the opening act. The author has transposed into a mood in which the rage has burned out as two audiences, offstage and on, absorb the miracle of Hermione's restoration. Leontes has not suddenly reformed; he experiences the most drastic role change not when he tells himself that Hermione and Polixenes are dancing passionately together; not when he suspects that Hermione's imminent baby, and then even Mamillius, may not be his progeny. No, he undergoes that metamorphosis into monklike penance on seeing Hermione swoon at the news of her son's death. He grows abruptly aware that he has provoked a double penalty from Apollo for a double sin: he spurned the oracle's answer and behaved with inhuman ferocity. Barbara A. Mowat, appreciatively says Leontes is "neither an unsympathetic nor an unbelievable character" (in Bevington 1992, 1,484). But we cannot average Leontes out, as if taking the role's overall measure. Such a summing-up might come from a director trying to persuade a reluctant actor to audition, but it does not cope with the role's innate variety. In act 1 Leontes is utterly loathsome, if we take our likes and dislikes seriously in theatre; in act 5, he is pathetic.

The metamorphosis of Leontes has wrought a parallel change in Paulina. As soon as the unnamed Lord tells her, "You have made fault I' the boldness of your speech," she feels the need to apologize: "All faults I make, when I shall come to know them, I do repent" (3.2.217–20). As the King signals in his departing line, for the next sixteen years, she will be his closest adviser. "Come and lead me To these sorrows" (242–43). Like a president who takes on a brash White House chief of staff, he surrenders his leadership. And in the closing speech of the play Leontes, who seems to have acquired a taste for devolving leadership, adjures Paulina (not once but twice) to lead the way out. He has remained in awe of her—virtually in subjection—through the sixteen years of unenacted story. Shakespeare does not dwell on the radically quietened and reformed Leontes, although I would say that the emotional storm that overcomes him in the first part represents a drastic change in role from what he was in that part of the story that precedes the action. But since his later reformation would seem limp if played out, the playwright compresses sixteen years sparingly into a few emphatic lines. Cleomenes tells *us*, when he opens the play's return to Sicilia, as he addresses Leontes,

> Sir, you have done enough, and have performed
> A saintlike sorrow. No fault could you make
> Which you have not redeemed—indeed, paid down
> More penitence than done trespass . . . . Forget your evil
> . . . . Forgive yourself. (5.1.1–6)

Then, to establish the pain of the long penance without dramatizing it (and Leontes's role) to the point of tedium, the author gives Camillo these lines:

> Your sorrow was too sore laid on,
> Which sixteen winters cannot blow away,
> So many summers dry. Scarce any joy
> Did ever so long live; no sorrow
> But killed itself much sooner. (5.3.49–53)

Critics often compare the jealous Leontes, almost invariably to his disadvantage, with the jealous Othello, just as they do Frank Ford. But
the comparison doesn't hold up. Leontes, like Ford, is not misled by an
Iago. As M. M. Mahood suggests, he may appear more like an actor.
She cites his lines to Mamillius. "Go play, boy, play. Thy mother plays,
and I Play too" (1.2.187–88). He is "play-acting in his outburst," she
says and

> it is characteristic of such obsessions as his that the sufferer is deluded
> yet half knows he is under a delusion—as when we know we are in
> a nightmare but cannot wake from it. (in Muir [1970, 217–18])

When he denies the oracle and Apollo, then takes revenge for the
message from Delphi, Leontes does seem relieved to drop the role of
prosecuting attorney, before he sinks into blaming himself for his cruel folly. Did he condemn Hermione so heatedly because he doubted
his accusations? I read Professor Mahood's observation as a way for an
actor to temper the inconsistency of a ferocious outbreak of rage; if he
plays Leontes *consciously* playing, maintaining two levels of awareness,
the scene could become too brittle to hold conviction.

Of the remaining role brought over from the first part into the second, one can say little because as Camillo retires from Sicilia in act 1, so
he retires from definition in both acts When he advises Florizel and Perdita to seek refuge with Leontes, he shows himself for the second time
as a sympathizer with those in danger, but almost immediately after he
appears as a plotter and planner in a harmless cause: acute nostalgia.

> What I do next shall be to tell the King
> Of this escape and whither they are bound;
> Wherein my hope is I shall so prevail
> To force him after, in whose company
> I shall re-view Sicilia, for whose sight
> I have a woman's longing. (4.4.666-71)

When in the next act and in the final—and therefore unanswerable—
speech Leontes awards him Paulina, we assume that they both accept
the offer, but we have little idea of what exactly Paulina has acquired
in the way of a follow-up husband, save that Camillo has proved a
loyal minister to two monarchs. By the playwright's decree the fifth
act ends with a double marriage, or one marriage begun and another
renewed, but also with an innovation. Both men and both women are
at least middle-aged, not lovebirds in their teens-to-twenties or immature pursued and youthful pursuer. Shakespeare still pays homage to
the pattern of comedy's double knot but ties it with a new twist. (Perdita and Florizel have already settled on the third match, despite the
temporary obstacles raised by Polixenes.) If Camillo has changed in

the course of the play (except in his loyalties), we hardly notice it. Like Horatio and the confidants in French neoclassicism, he proves the exception to the roles.

But the principals who arise in the second part of the play undergo their own alterations. I have already alluded to the humbler version of Autolycus that evolves between act 4 and his final appearance in act 5, by which time he has ceased singing his friendly, bawdy songs. Perdita shifts ground from being an innocent shepherdess with lyrical gifts to a debater who maintains that art can corrupt nature and thence to a defiantly and then a fearfully class-conscious fiancée. Florizel, wrapped up at the start of 4.4 in his bride-to-be, eager to approve uxoriously of whatever she says, however she behaves, stubbornly holds out against telling his father openly about his forthcoming marriage, and by the end of the same protracted scene, he has turned into Polixenes's enemy and quarry. In the Ingmar Bergman production Leontes, during his tantrum, struck Hermione down—a moment that corresponded to one in Bergman's film *The Passion of Anna.* Polixenes likewise hit Perdita during the flowers-and-herbs scene, 4.4, whereupon Florizel hurled his father to the ground and repeatedly kicked the prone body, so that there need be no doubt about Polixenes's subsequent revenge motive.

As for the Shepherd and the Clown, they regard themselves as having risen from rubes to gentlemen, the adoptive father and brother of the crown princess. The Clown prince takes on airs as he recites to Autolycus proof positive of his new prominence.

> I was a gentleman born before my father; for the King's son took me by the hand and called me brother; and then the two kings called my father brother; and then the Prince my brother and the Princess my sister called my father father; and so we wept, and there was the first gentlemanlike tears that ever we shed . . . . Hark, the kings and the princes, our kindred, are going to see the Queen's picture. Come, follow us. We'll be thy good masters. (5.2.140–46 and 173–75)

One of the most vivid changes, however, alters the environment to reflect the new place, season, mood, roles, and in most productions, the colors in the costumes, sets, and lighting. In Adrian Noble's production the Sicilians wore black. John Nettles as Leontes had on a bearskin hat, a *chapska*; it made him look Russian, perhaps like his royal father-in-law: the effect was mournful. In Bohemia, the feverish color in the costumes, a yellow aggressively told of Apollo, sun, fertility. In this vein Phyllida Hancock as Perdita sported a headful of blossoms like a wedding trophy.

Some recent critics have wished to throw new light on the wrangling over the relative, Senecan merits of country and town or country and court, presented as dull, honest innocence versus colorful, duplicitous sophistication, like that embroidered on in Touchstone's willfully garbled responses to Corin. In Shakespeare's time the movement of rural folk, like today's, to the cities in search of work, income, amenities, closer communal ties, a better future for children and the generations to come created crises: at one end of the migration there was depopulation; at the other end, failure to absorb the people who flocked to cities like London ("the Wen," meaning tumor) with its overcrowding, filth, and plagues—conditions that persisted for hundreds of years in European civilization—that is, city living and dying. Shakespeare's presentation of the arguments, however poetic, must have borne a realistic freight. Most migrants had surely remained unaware of the disadvantages of life in the overgrown, underserved municipal "villages" until they arrived there and perhaps heard them mentioned in a playhouse. But if, in a staging, Bohemia resembles Sicilia, the liberating sensation of acts 4 and 5 will be enfeebled or ironic. Playing the moment extends beyond the acting to other elements in a performance. Bohemia's ruler may prove as brutal as Sicilia's and the second locale no more sublime than the first, but the play requires a fillip, a new start in act 4 so that audiences see for themselves, only *subsequently*, the results of corruption or contagion borne from one locale to the other.

The reformulations of comic technique displayed in this play, such as the mating and remating of two older couples and the personification of time, extend to some uncommon economies of means. These could be contrived only by a thoroughly practiced dramatist. Certain editors and critics, including Dover Wilson and "Q," took umbrage at Shakespeare's "alienation-effect" in 5.2, when the three Gentlemen describe Leontes's triple reconciliation: the reception of Perdita as his friend-enemy's daughter-in-law to be *and* his own recovered daughter, besides his meetings after more than a decade and a half with Camillo and Polixenes. These critics would have preferred to have the scene dramatized, perhaps without considering the repetitiveness that would have ensued: the sort of scene in numerous plays and movies when people go through an orgy of "How do you do, how are you, pleased to meet you, do you know so and so, we haven't seen each other for it must be . . ." Subsequently Coghill and Traversi, among others, praised the scene's ingenuity. It starts with the pretext of satisfying Autolycus's curiosity about the encounters to which he might, at one time, have been privy as a member of the Bohemian royal household. But even in Florizel's exchanged finery, he has no access to the inner circles of the Sicilian palace, and is lucky to find three talkative courtiers who report the occasion and their feelings about it. Traversi writes that the scene is one of those episodes, characteristic of Shakespeare's later manner, in which incidents apparently trivial, even seemingly marginal to the main story, are woven by the conscious elaboration of style into a developing symbolic fabric. Its grave and involved prose is seen, in fact, on closer reading, not to be mere decoration, but to belong to the spirit of the play, in forming which it plays its own distinctive part. (in Muir [1970, 173])

The scene's fairly cool narrative tone does not encroach on the climax to come, Hermione's rescue from the halls of Dis and her stone coating. Carol Thomas Neely likens her to Ceres, the Mother Nature figure who pursues her daughter Persephone and brings her back to the bountiful surface of the earth, and it is true that Hermione could be imagined to have emerged from the underground of evil suspicion and neglect (1985, 81). The restoration of Perdita to her parents resembles the opening and closing of a fairy tale, the lost and found. Hermione's fate similarly seems a version of Sleeping Beauty, an effect strengthened in Bergman's staging. Instead of standing on what is variously described in criticism as a plinth, platform, or pedestal, from which she steps down, she entered as a corpse laid out on a catafalque under a body-length veil, which served as the curtain mentioned twice in the lines. As she awoke, prompted by Paulina's staccato commands, she sat up and clasped her head, her eyes still closed. The entrance and the movement were a startling *trouvaille*, and relieved the actress of holding the upright pose for almost longer than is tolerable. She lay on her side, resting comfortably. Actresses from the past, such as Helen Faucit, who played opposite Macready, and Ellen Terry, who played opposite Irving, attest to the strain, to the endurance needed to maintain motionless verticality. The picture of Bergman's Hermione (Pernilla August) when she sat up from her horizontality, though, was less that of a queen stepping back into her rightful place than of a hangover after a wild night. Even so, the scene's beauty became ultimately indestructible.

As in the other comedies, the women have imparted lessons. Perdita taught Polixenes and Florizel: in his speech of tribute, the latter admits how he has learned from her the art of savoring the arts of nature; while to the former, for all his resentment, she has served as a hospitable model arising from modest circumstances, a hostess who, in a very different fashion, lives up to the ideals of the Shepherd's late wife (expounded in 4.4.55–70). Paulina in her staunch wisdom, fortified by Hermione's endurance, has taught Leontes to surmount sorrow and self-hatred. The women, in whatever pose the director elects, form a tableau of three graces.

In this longest of the comedies and romances we see at last that the winter's tale is of its own demise. Even in winter's bleakest depths, as Shelley reminded himself, can spring, signaled by a wind from the west, be far behind? Villon more than three hundred years before, famously wondered what had happened to the snows of yesteryear. Spring's comedy overtakes the tragedy of sorts, Leontes' self-inflicted wounds in the play's first part, prompted by Apollo's urgings that he has deceived himself ("I have drunk, and seen the spider" [2.1.39]). The cycle grinds forward; tragic winter majestically gives up.

Notes

1. Ewbank, "The Triumph of Time in *The Winter's Tale,*" in *A Review of English Literature,* April 1964, reprinted in Muir 1970, 98–115. Ewbank sounds a caution: "It would, needless to say, be wrong to think of *The Winter's Tale* as a treatise on time. The play does not state or prove anything. But through its action, its structure and its poetry, it communicates a constant awareness of the powers of time" (114). Kermode (later Sir Frank) edited the Classic Signet edition, (1963, xxi).

2. Lautrec may have said the line to "Mademoiselle Dieterle, a singer and dancer at the Théâtre des Variétés" (Julia Frey, *Toulouse-Lautrec: A Life,* [1994, 167]).

3. Did the playwright intend a connection with Oedipus, or know of Oedipus, when he named the baby's guardian after Oedipus' daughter?

4. Also reprinted in Muir: Donald Stauffer's essay on Autolycus (*Shakespeare's World of Images,* New York: 1949, 169–79).

5. Brecht had read his Shakespeare, and wrote very free adaptations of *Measure for Measure* and *Coriolanus,* as well as *The Resistible Rise of Arturo Ui* which has "studied parallels to Shakespeare's *Richard III*" (Martin Esslin, *Brecht: The Man and His Work,* [1960, 307]).

6. See also Oxford School edition(Gill 1996, 125–27).

7. Ernest Schanzer and subsequent critics have demonstrated the balance in the two parts of the play by means of recurrences. See Schanzer, reprinted in Muir (1970).

The Tempest

Does this play lack a conflict? The party of Prospero's enemies and one friend from Italy, including its two clowns, presents no real danger to the protagonist or his daughter. Nor does Caliban. From the start Prospero plays all-powerful, a divinity, who from his island retreat can raise a storm at sea with his magical remote control. But this comedy, sometimes thought of as a poem with dramatic incidentals, grows into the dramatist's most elemental conflict, one that depends more on an inner, psychological clash than does *Hamlet*. Prospero's war with himself resembles in small the ocean lashing itself far from coasts, causing, as a by-product of its tempests, possible suffering to the vessels that enter its territory and butt into its self-administered punishment.

In Ariel's second song ("Full fathom five thy father lies" [1.2.400–08]) five words crop up that commentators have repeatedly and rightly taken to be at the play's heart, if not in its blood:

> Nothing of him that doth fade
> But doth suffer a *sea change*
> Into something *rich and strange*

Rich and strange supplied a title for an early film by Hitchcock, released in 1932: a young couple embark on an around-the-world ocean voyage, which transforms them by means of what might be a "sea change" for real. Hitchcock made sure spectators would recognize the source of the title: he quoted it on the screen. "Sea change" went on to develop an independent life. Journalists today commonly use the words to denote a widespread or emphatic social or political upheaval, although it originally seemed to apply to a large change in some aspect of nature.

In the course of *The Tempest* all the roles undergo changes, most of them—in attitude and condition—occasioned by two tempests. The current one, raised by Prospero, opens the action; twelve years earlier, another tempest, raging without his prompting or assistance, pounded him and weeping little Miranda on their "rotten carcass of a butt, not rigged, Nor tackle, sail, nor mast" (1.2.146–47)—on which they left a fictitious Milan, situated somewhere on a coast, in order to reach this "uninhabited island." It did have inhabitants even then, if nonhuman and only partly human.

To the two meteorological tempests we might add the passage of time. "Tempest" comes from Latin for both storm and time, the time here being both the twelve years between the two tempests and the several hours into which the action is telescoped. More tempests yet buzz in the consciousness of this unorthodox comedy's roles. G. Wilson Knight paid tribute to the play's novelties but traced similarities to earlier plays, not all of them comedies: "Shakespeare is continually at work splitting up and recombining already used plots, persons, and themes, weaving something 'new and strange' from old materials" (*The Crown of Life* [1947, reprint, 1964, 203]).

In addition, the play's language is unusually *rich*, even for Shakespeare, lavish with images. Wolfgang Clemen, one of the two monarchs of imagerial analysis (the other being Caroline Spurgeon), points out that many of the

> passages of imagery . . . have one feature in common: they continually act upon our senses; our hearing, smelling, tasting, and feeling are being appealed to. This is one of the main differences to the imagery in Shakespeare's early comedies, where there was far less direct appeal to the senses. (1962, 191)

At the same time the atmosphere of the island is *strange*: unfamiliar, colored (or tainted) by magic emanating from Prospero and Ariel and possibly some remnants of spells and other magical business still drifting in the atmosphere from the days of Sycorax, whom Prospero calls a witch. Apropos of *strange*, Michael Goldman observes:

> The word has its dangers for the director, as the tradition of over-gorgeous and extravagantly spectacular productions attests, but if the play's own sense of the word is inquired after, the difficulties can be avoided. (137–38)

The landscape itself, from what we learn of it, sounds ordinary, not other-worldly. Jan Kott lists some of its waters, groves, bogs, plant and animal life, most of which could have been commonly sighted in Jacobean England (1966, 252–53). But the island harbors at least two exotic, questionably human creatures, a unisex bird-spirit named Ariel, which can fly fast enough or quiver at a sufficiently high rate of convulsion to become invisible to everybody's eyes but Prospero's; and

Caliban, who may have a roughly human shape but is compared several times with a fish in looks and odor. Caliban could resemble a sea mammal, a walrus, for example. Or a sea bird, like a penguin, which waddles instead of flying. What would we make of a penguin—or, come to that, a kiwi, a duck-billed platypus, a cockatoo—if we'd never seen one or an illustration? Unfamiliar animals or specimens of humanity, as described by Othello, stir amazement: in Desdemona's case, what the Elizabethans called admiration. There seems little doubt, anyway, that the playwright meant to have both roles played by human beings who display evident human characteristics, rather than by birds, insects, or mammals, and Miranda refers to Caliban indirectly as "the third man that e'er I saw" (1.2.449).

Shakespeare's death precedes by at least a couple of centuries the beginnings of modern geology. We now appreciate that a literal sea change invokes far more radical an alteration to a landscape than, say, a modification of a shoreline. Eons of accumulated material weathered by rivers subside. Immense alluvial plains founder to become seabeds until later, eons later, they are thrown up into mountain folds (and islands), to be gnawed away by erosion. Wind, water, and ice use the smashed surface as a tool against itself in a never-ending cycle. All this slow frenzy results over further eons in one of the most dramatic metamorphoses: from sediments, such as the "yellow sands" of which Ariel sings, back into solid rockscapes, carved away by the same elements.

Yet if Shakespeare has nothing to tell about continental drift and overlapping earth plates and erosion, he does try to implant in us boundless vistas of feeling. Prospero, the magus and playwright within the play, may at last give up his "rough magic," but immediately before doing so he exults in the powers he has held that could alter the earth, sea, and sky, and compel the last two to contend.

> . . . . I have bedimmed
> The noontide sun, called forth the mutinous winds,
> And 'twixt the green sea and the azured vault
> Set roaring war; to the dread rattling thunder
> Have I given fire, and rifted Jove's stout oak
> With his own bolt; the strong-based promontory
> Have I made shake, and by the spurs plucked up
> The pine and cedar . . . (5.1.41–48)[1]

Location? The text points to the Mediterranean, very likely between Italy and Algeria, or, from another allusion, a mid-Atlantic point, like Bermuda. The Tempest may strike some readers, directors, and spectators as fantasy (historical fiction, a utopia, a dystopia) while to others it seems a fantasia on abstract, lyrical themes, but its language so bristles with violence, with an anger barely reined in by discipline and muscular imaginings, that its freight of personal affront cannot go unnoticed, despite Prospero's final, lingering and—in places one would say—grudging and self-serving forgiveness.

Still, in the original Folio edition, *The Tempest* did lead off the comedies. Was it ever a comedy? Is it still? If so, how come all the solemn, not to say portentous, presentations when it reaches the stage? Why the droning of the longer speeches? The catches in the throat? The gargling exercises? Homage to Shakespeare's last will and testament? A recitation of his esthetics considered after twenty-plus years of his gifts to the theatre? Deference paid to the abundance of tropes, the assortment of allegorical nods, prods, and kicks? The extension from *Measure for Measure* of a sermon on blessed mercy and forgiveness from a severe ruler?

A comic structure, which this play has, doesn't demand laughs all the way through. But in lyrical, spectacular, testimonial performances, the farcical scenes with Trinculo, Stephano, and Caliban need not appear as irreverent intrusions, betrayals of chords from a cathedral organ.

Yet, why insist, in the face of so much resistance, that *The Tempest* really is a comedy, and beyond that assumption, that it is comic, funny, through and through? In truth, the assumption is long overdue. In 1954 Bernard Knox wrote that the classical precedent does its work the more efficiently because it is not intrusive. Below the surface of medieval magic and Renaissance travel tales, the initial situation, the nature and relationships of most of the characters, the development of the action and its final solution are all conjugations of the basic paradigms of classical comedy (Wimsatt, 1954, 52–73; reprinted in Signet Classic edition, 1964, 163–181). Knox likens the play's roles and ingredients to those in a typical comedy by Plautus: a crotchety, protective father and his lovely daughter; her young suitor, whom the father doesn't openly welcome; the pair of slaves, one clever and dutiful, the other surly, both of whom he threatens with punishment or actually punishes at the first sign of rebellion or plea for freedom—Ariel's, say, at 1.2.243–98, and Caliban's at 1.2.324–333.

In one of the subplots, "Caliban's meeting with Trinculo and Stephano is a servile parallel and parody of Miranda's meeting with Ferdinand" (Knox, Signet Classic ed., 178); and the final scene restores comic order. A happy, if not ecstatic, union between the puppet-like lovers seems ordained. So does a union of friendship between their fathers and between Milan and Naples. The action trowels a layer of contentment over events and the figures standing within Prospero's magic circle, with the exceptions of the two "heavies": inept Sebastian, the brother of Alonso; and the deposed, "unnatural" Antonio, Prospero's brother, who speaks only thirteen words during act 5—

a snide comment about Caliban—and does not ask pardon or promise to repent his misdeeds, as Alonso does (5.1.118–19). Caliban will presumably regain his rule of the island. A. D. Nuttall says that Caliban will go back to Milan with Prospero and reproaches Glynne Wickham for thinking that Caliban will remain on the island (in J. R. Brown and Bernard Harris 1972, 129). But no critic other than Nuttall that I have read has interpreted the end of the play in this manner, and I find no evidence for Caliban's departure. Prospero does call Caliban "this thing of darkness I Acknowledge mine," but does not declare he will keep him and take him back to a court environment to which he will be unsuited, for Prospero considers him "as disproportioned in his manners As in his shape." Prospero's words to Caliban, "Go, sirrah, to my cell; Take with you your companions. As you look To have my pardon, trim it handsomely," give no more hint that Caliban will accompany him than do his earlier words. In his reply, Caliban merely agrees to clean up the cell, in preparation for a dinner with the visitors, and he regrets having taken Stephano "for a god" and worshiped Trinculo, "this dull fool," whereupon Prospero orders him: "Go to. Away!" (5.1.294–302.)

Nuttall, however, among other valuable observations, suggests that Shakespearean comedy resembles (may have been influenced by) that of Euripides, from whom the so-called New Comedy derives. We could appreciate better the transitions from Euripides onward if we had more theatre by Menander, but Shakespeare's right-angled turns in the action and his comic climaxes, especially the recognitions, are recognizably Euripidean. Shakespeare's romances, Nuttall says, are to his tragedies what Euripides's tragedies and tragicomedies are to the tragedies of Aeschylus and perhaps Sophocles. As for a comic performance of Prospero, when Peter Hall invited Laurence Olivier to take on the role of Prospero, the actor wanted it comic: "Prospero should lecture his daughter in the first scene while shaving" and not "wear all those whiskers and wigs" (1983, 43). The experiment might have proved worthwhile, but Olivier did not attempt it.

Shedding his supernatural powers, Prospero will resume the political burdens of a duke of Milan, but probably with more resolve than before. He states that in Milan every third thought shall be of his grave, but if so, he can reserve first and second thoughts to bestow on less saddening topics—unless he really is a near-decrepit who solemnly looks forward to retirement and delights in contemplating his death. Stephen Orgel raises the question of Prospero's age (1987, 79–82), recalling that "several recent productions have presented Prospero as vigorously middle-aged, or even youthful. In both Derek Jacobi's performance for the RSC in 1983 and Michael Hordern's in the BBC version, the sudden claim of age and infirmity ['Bear with my weakness.

My old brain is troubled' (4.1.159)] came as a powerful surprise" (80). Orgel adds that at the Old Vic in 1930, John Gielgud, then aged twenty-six, "played the part beardless and modeled his appearance on Dante" (80–81). But Dante at what stage of life?

In view of the play's self-evident comic structure and windup, why do so *few* theoreticians and, worse, practitioners treat it as comedy? Shakespeare critics, even though they deserve as much as their Greek brethren the titles of scholars and gentlemen, prefer to play up, rather than down, every other aspect of the master's arts. Those who write favorably of *The Tempest*—an overwhelming majority—strive to pay it its weighty due; they want it to sing a song of social significance, but stripped of overt preaching. Even a born rebel among critics, Jan Kott, the most startling Shakespearean to appear since, well, Leslie Hotson, or perhaps Samuel Johnson, asks us to read the play as a history of the world:

> As usual with Shakespeare, every metaphor and every image has a double meaning. The island is the world, the world is a stage, and all the people in it are actors. Prospero has only staged a performance, brief and fleeting like life itself. (Kott 1966, 282)

Without dissenting from Kott's conclusions, I don't see why they cannot apply in a comic version of the play. Let me add hastily that he doesn't say they cannot, but he deals with the work implicitly as a grim metaphor of history, which I'd paraphrase as a reflection of history's dispossessions, actual and attempted, mostly by treacherous means. Antonio dispossessed Prospero in the story. Prospero dispossessed Caliban and returns the favor to Alonso in the last act. Alonso dispossesses himself twice, the first time surrendering his share of Milan when he announces, "Thy dukedom I resign" (5.1.118); shortly after, he gives up Naples, in a wish, when he says of Ferdinand and Miranda, whom he believes lost, "O heavens, that they were living both in Naples, The king and queen there!"

Kott thus aligns the play with Shakespeare's histories, which do portray successive seizures of state power. The difference is that Prospero says he "abjures" supernatural power, whether he will indeed do so and whether he feels confident that temporal power will serve as compensation. He has also tried to straighten out the future by virtually depositing it in the united hands of Miranda and Ferdinand, the youth, hope, and purpose team. Nonetheless:

> once again everything will begin from the beginning, only the characters are wiser by experience. But wisdom is just as fragile as everything else. If there is hope in *The Tempest*, it is bitter. (Kott 1966, 287–88)

Kott hears the note of bitterness in Prospero's epilogue. The stage has emptied, but for him—or perhaps he has conformed with the direction *exeunt omnes* and then returned but still in character. He says his own strength is now "most faint." He "must be here confined by you, Or sent to Naples" and asks his listeners to "release me from my bands With the help of your good hands." Meaning applause? Possibly not, for

.... my ending is despair
Unless I be relieved by prayer,
Which pierces so that it assaults
Mercy itself and frees all faults.

The words *despair* and *pierces* seem to clinch the case for exponents of the tragic ending. If the antecedent of a delayed *which* is not *prayer*, but *despair*, Prospero may regard despair as a valid reason for forgiveness. Editors who gloss the word *prayer* commonly call it Prospero's plea or petition to the audience: if he can get this "prayer" off his chest, like a confession, he deserves a reward akin to what he accorded his brother when he "pardoned the deceiver." But if the word constitutes an image and Kott is right in asserting that every Shakespeare image is double, Prospero could equally envision an auditorium of hands that are not clapping on his behalf but clasped.

If offering this "prayer" is enough to "pierce" so brutally that "it assaults mercy itself and frees all faults," why does he, in the play's last couplet, again entreat the audience?

As you for crimes would pardoned be,
Let your indulgence set me free.

Despair is a strong word, but so is *crimes*; something like *lapses* or *errors* might more accurately have described his bad temper toward his two slaves; his defective upbringing of Caliban, that devil's progeny (according to him), and his self-indulgence (but in a defensible cause) in exploiting Ariel's powers for the sake of (mild) revenge. Even if, to lean over into a popular alternative interpretation, this speech becomes the playwright's much too modest farewell, one can hardly imagine him asking to be forgiven for *crimes* without granting him almost boundless poetic latitude. But he talks here not of his own crimes; he imputes possible crimes to the audience: As *you* for crimes would pardoned be (would want to be pardoned) . . . Can he mean this? Hardly. Is he being jocular, affable? Much more likely. (Whatever evil you have done may be worse than my worst.)

At the end of this action and endowed with these lines, the actor playing Prospero falsifies the play if he chokes over a self-belittling cry of pain mingled with a lugubrious apology. The speech may not go as far as irony; it is a lighthearted leavetaking from whatever we conceive the island to have been—penance, prison (including his "cell"), refuge, laboratory. His words convey no tinge of regret, no taint of nostalgia over quitting the "bare island," his substitute kingdom for twelve years, to return to civilization's bustle and assume old burdens anew. The burdens will not, for once, include the worry that overwhelms almost every aging ruler: succession. That dilemma might well be what he refers to when he says every third thought shall be his grave.

But I see the epilogue as support for the cheerful tone of the latter part of the fifth act. Prospero carried out his end of the unwritten bargain when he "pardoned the deceiver" and renounced his magic powers. Without the latter, he can no longer function on the island. He set Caliban and Ariel, his "tricksy spirit," free; now he asks for the same treatment: "Release me from your bands." He is inviting spectators to let him conclude this relatively short play, so that he can venture into the subsequent story, for Milan hasn't appeared in the action; that dukedom acts as the usual, second, alternative Shakespearean environment—but kept out of sight—while the island itself has had uninterrupted effects in the action as this play's "green world." The epilogue, more even than the fifth act, depicts the "sea change" in Prospero, his condition and not only his temperament: from the almighty ruler of the island he turns into a dignified supplicant. But he rises above the punishment and humiliations forced on him. He gains or recovers a sense of humor. The tone of the play does not forgive dispossession but it tries to explain instances of it and its cause, ambition.

If I didn't feel hesitant about overworking the words, I'd add that Prospero's career in the theatre has also suffered a sea change, from almost three hundred years of betrayed old gent who becomes benevolent to the scheming imperialist many commentators discerned in this century.

George Wolfe's 1995 New York Shakespeare Festival production, which began in Central Park and moved on to Broadway, offered a theatrical facsimile of an island. It could have been called the Isle of Eclecticism. Boards like gangplanks leading in varied directions served for entrances and exits. One board led to Prospero's cell, below which was Caliban's cave, as though Prospero slept and worked his experiments above a garage. The planks could be withdrawn to keep the island islanded. The Ferdinand was so intimidated by his adoration of Miranda that at times he grew incoherent. A nimble and well-spoken Caliban had a fine comic sense and looked not at all menacing, nothing like as fierce as the female Ariel. At the end Prospero's cell folded up into a narrow profile, while the lighting put Prospero into a double circle, the inner of royal blue, the outer of crimson. Wolfe surrounded Prospero with a sand-and-band show. The circle of sand that constituted one main feature of the setting became roughed up during the first half but could be raked smooth during intermission. Percussive instrumentalists, nearly jazzy but not quite, overcame some of the dialogue. Patrick Stewart's resounding voice asserted itself as one property of a well-enunciated, rather featureless Prospero; while the Ariel danced much of the time, delivered her words with a suitably incantatory lilt, had New York trouble pronouncing her r's, and was evidently meant to be spooky: she wore huge clawlike hands for one sequence, which not only looked menacing but also cast impressively fearsome shadows. Wolfe's staging, though, emphasized the concerto effect, because the secondary roles do not naturally cohere, and he did not try to force coherence upon them. He did, however, bring abundant comedy to the lines and activities. The biggest surprise he provided was finding a witty Miranda in both voice and gesture: Carrie Preston converted what reads like a naive recipient of Prospero's words and orders into a play-stealing intelligence who will, at the very least, co-govern with Ferdinand.

Some commentators relish *The Tempest* as Shakespeare's supreme accomplishment, more emotionally stirring or intellectually teasing than the big tragedies. It receives praise from almost every critic of note for the richness of its language and its pliable and unforced metrics. Certain skilled appreciators of Shakespeare, troubled by that absence of external conflict, find it lacking equally in eventfulness. True, after the unfolding tempest at sea, all feverish movement and raised voices, the protasis of 1.2 slows the action as Prospero pours out 148 lines of expository story. They are well punctuated by Miranda's questions and sympathetic comments. If, at the end of them, she falls asleep she drifts off not from boredom but because Prospero puts her out so that he can question Ariel privately. Miranda does not press him closely on at least one issue that affects her identity: she accepts her father's total characterizing of her mother as "a piece of virtue" who "said thou wast my daughter."[2] But once again, if we take the play as a comedy and Prospero as a version of the tyrannical and insensitive father, not as a flawless and heroic prototype, his remarks and her reactions fall into place. Her failure to inquire further about her mother can be attributed to the astounding (to her) revelation in the same lines (56–59) that her father was once Duke of Milan and she herself his only heir. Nor does she seem offended by the word *piece*, which is generally glossed as *example* or a synonym, but which, then as now, was contemptuous slang for a woman.

The purported lack of suspense derives from Prospero's confident journeyings between exposition of story past and promises of story to come. He reassures Miranda that all shall be well; he will restore the ship and rescue its crew and passengers; he will cease to frown on those who trespassed against him; he will play the god of unstinting mercy and, although never partnered again for marital purposes, he might be said to be reconciled with his first political love, Milan, rather as divorced couples in Hollywood myth try out new lovers then return abashedly to the original wives and husbands. Robert Langbaum believes Prospero always had in mind a reconciliation with Alonso and Antonio (Signet Classic edition, ibid., xxxviii). But Prospero's promises and questionable beliefs cannot be counted on by spectators exposed to the play for the first time; and abundant suspense results from the delay in finding out whether he will prove as merciful as he proclaims himself.

Nor is there, for the first-time spectator, any guarantee that Ariel and Prospero, as a conjuring team on even a nearly cosmic (as opposed to a merely cosmetic) scale, will prove infallible. Besides, I believe that critics, and especially daily reviewers, become obsessed with a craving for conventional suspense when they know better than anyone else that once we look upon *The Tempest* as theatre, not pure literature, it can be gussied up by directors, actors, composers, designers, and other hands practiced at artifice by the insertion of pauses, emphases, sideways glances, variations in vocal projection, songs, mood-inducing music and "enhanced sound"—all those lessons rediscovered from the film industry—so that it seems natural for the text to suspend suspense.

As a lesson in self-sacrifice, though, the play can become a trial to sit through, as it equally can when condemned to a lyrical treatment assigned to quivering larynxes. Even without being heightened by usual and unusual stage effects, this is one work for the stage that doesn't need additional entertainment gimmicks to placate a restless modern audience. Not that modern audiences are more demanding in this than their forebears. Orgel points out that from the seventeenth to the early nineteenth century, thinned-down, musically embellished, or all-out operatic versions of the play, especially the one by Davenant and Dryden, supplanted Shakespeare (1987, 5–13).

John Russell Brown observes that *The Tempest* "has more cues for song and music than any other of Shakespeare's plays, and requires a *'quaint device'* so that a banquet can disappear as if by magic" (1969, 10). All the late plays, written after about 1608, were, according to Frances A. Yates, "contemporary with the masques at court designed by Inigo Jones"; they "have a masque-like quality and may have used scenic effects more elaborate than those which used to be seen at the Globe" (1975, 11–12). Sumptuosity—quite a lot—already resides in *The Tempest*.

The action of *The Tempest* relies on unities of time and of place after 1.1—the place being a few locales on the island as well as the omnipresence of Prospero looking down from his cave on most of the few scenes he doesn't take part in (and possibly the ones he does), and the potential omnipresence of Ariel. That action's compactness also comes about because it is Shakespeare's next shortest play to *The Comedy of Errors* and has fewer scenes, nine, than any of his others, one fewer even than *Errors*. The bulk of criticism affirms that Prospero's most serious antagonist is not his brother Antonio, a minute part, but Caliban; if so, the main plot might be summed up as the Master vs. the Monster. But the Monster has fewer lines than Ariel, whereas Prospero has a higher proportion of lines, 30 percent, than any other figure in the comedies and romances, including the so-called "problem plays," except for that other playwright-within-the-play role, that earlier failed ruler, Duke Vincentio in *Measure*.[3]

Because of Prospero's dominance, the main plot consists of his straightening out the damage done to other roles—as well as his own. The subplots will then consist of Sebastian and Antonio against Alonso and Gonzalo, or the failed murder of Alonso; Caliban's rivalry with Prospero and his adventures with Trinculo and Stephano, or the failed, never-stood-a-chance attempt to sabotage Prospero's rule; the love match between Miranda the wonderer and Ferdinand, the reborn prince from what Yeats might call Under Wave; and the magicianship of Ariel and his subordination to Prospero, which have their repercussions on all the roles but are known only to Prospero and him (her? it?). If the lineup then is Prospero against the rest, we should see him separated from them. It has always been assumed that Prospero's cave would occupy the "inner stage" of the Globe or other Elizabethan public playhouse or some variation of it, or else an upper level, with or without a balcony, or even a structure of sorts at the summit of a hill that it commands, like Aase's house in Peter Stein's Berlin production of *Peer Gynt*. Evert Sprinchorn's theory of a raised but open platform at the rear of the stage, already referred to, strikes me as plausible for the cave in Shakespeare's time and today; it has no recess and will not need lighting (or backlighting) as special and questionable as a walled-in or gauzed-in space would require; literal-minded believers in magic can assume that Prospero has made the rocky walls invisible.[4] Certainly he must keep himself removed from the others until the end of act 5, the renunciation consummated; then he could come forward to the thrust of the main stage and mingle with them as an equal or a first among equals. In the Epilogue he will face outward, standing where his guest-prisoners stood before and faced inward and slightly upward toward him, only now will he confront the audience. Or he might descend to orchestra level to put himself on a par with the public.

But blocking Prospero in relation to the others seems straightforward when compared with deciphering his role. In this century Sir

Arthur Quiller-Couch and John Dover Wilson in the New (Cambridge) Shakespeare edition of the play, Eliot, Auden, Frye, Kermode, and others visualized him as the artist or a personification of Art, very likely because he refers to his conjuring as his art. The detection of so many admirable qualities in the role was bound to stimulate a rejection. If we turn from these and others to the darker side of the popularity poll, John Russell Brown points out that the playwright kept the roles, "even the central figure . . . at a distance," a reference to the relative objectivity of comedy itself that would have baffled some early critics, as would Brown's observation that Prospero's rages make him unpredictable and unstable (1954, 42). The verdicts of revisionary critics who have pored over the text uncover selfishness, cynicism, and machinations on Prospero's part, not only in his obloquies toward Caliban and the clenched grip he keeps on Ariel but also in his using Miranda as a lure to hook Ferdinand and so perpetuate his dominion.[5] The strictures these and comparably minded critics level at Prospero, far from demeaning Shakespeare's artistry, mean that one can esteem him all the more for his insights into history, psychology, ethics, and Machiavellianism. The link that looked so strong a century ago between the creator as person and his creation as psychic construct has been snapped in so many spots that there may never be a total and convincing repair.

In the 1950s Kermode wrote, "The time is perhaps near when some critic will radically alter the assumptions upon which criticism of *The Tempest* is at present founded." At the time and in that place Kermode was himself taking polite but comprehensive issue with the preceding editor of the Arden editions. He seems to have felt intuitively that a new wave of Shakespeareanism was gathering and that it would break with especial strength over the late plays. He proved prophetic. Orgel, for one example, in his Oxford edition, rejects Kermode's own distinction between the play's white and black magic, or theurgy and goetism, if only on the grounds that we learn that Sycorax was a witch only from Prospero, who never met her but vilifies her. To my knowledge, few writers have yet lavished praise on *Pericles* or *Cymbeline*, but the other two romances, the questionable comedies, and the later tragedies had come in for some drastic re-examination and fresh judgments even before the appearance in Warsaw of Kott's *Shakespeare Our Contemporary* in the early 1960s.

The whirligigs of time bring in not only revenge but also unexpected pleasures in the way of rediscovery. While Prospero underwent analyses that made his faults glare, some writers tried, and are still trying, to amend the damage to his reputation. As of the 1660s the Dryden-Davenant musical adaptation displaced Shakespeare's *Tempest* until 1838, when Macready exhumed the latter for the stage. Similarly, a more agreeable Prospero has emerged lately in criticism, one who makes the difficult choice to accept his limitations as a human being by abandoning his magic and the assistance of spirits. Barbara Howard Traister reestablishes a connection between the role and author:

> In this play about a creative magician who works within the limits of his magic and his humanity, Shakespeare has undertaken to demonstrate that he, too, can work within limits traditionally prescribed for drama by classical theory. (in Bloom [1989, 113–130])

James P. Driscoll finds that forgiving and accepting Caliban and freeing Ariel turn him into "the wise old man archetype."

> To the extent that Ariel and Caliban are projections from Prospero's penumbral self or shadow, their liberation advances his search for inner freedom. The moment Prospero forgives Caliban and acknowledges him his own, he accepts his own darkest, most primitive side. The moment he frees Ariel, he frees himself from reliance on unintegrated powers and establishes the full spiritual harmony and self-dependence that wholeness bestows. (1983, 85–98)

Frances A. Yates puts the play's theme, as she sees it ("reconciliation through the younger generation"), its central character, and his type of magic in a positive light, a blessed aureole, taking that magic to be continuous with scholarship and especially healing, as she describes Prospero as a figuration of John Dee, a magician of the later Elizabethan and early Jacobean years.[6] She finds that

> Shakespeare shows us an infinitely wise and beneficent figure, working for moral goodness and reform, a marvellous evocation of the Renaissance magic in his full imaginative and creative power. (120)

But if, as Yates and others testify, some branches of science, which include medicine, proceed out of what was once called magic and others are still called the occult, "Doctor" Prospero's denunciations of Sycorax may well spring from longstanding attempts by the primitive medical profession (often organized in academies) to put midwives (who were unorganized but accused of being members of covens or equivalent, evil groups) out of business by defaming them as witches. As Orgel notes, Prospero is the only witness, an unrelievedly hostile one, that the author allows to take the stand. But the playwright is still doing the fair thing, because Prospero's hostility does not work all the time in his own interests. Besides, the resemblances between him and the Pantalone-papas of the earlier plays strongly hint that Prospero has a comic and therefore fallible role. No paragon, he, no matter how power-blessed. After all, on Olympus the uppermost gods quarreled continually, plotted and counterplotted against siblings and, in the partnership of Zeus and Hera, against spouses.

Instead, Prospero is an occasionally exploitative ruler, an occasionally insensitive father, although much less so than the fathers in the early comedies, and an undependable narrator. Reckoning with these and other shortcomings makes him a more rewarding role for an actor to tackle and sustain. To set him up as a rank villain will distort what the author has provided and necessitates turning his opponents, principally his brother and Stephano and Caliban, into something like resistance fighters. Whatever our view of the role's ethical fibers, Prospero remains one of the playwright's great poets. Does his name have anything to do with prospering? The action does move into the upgrade of his life. His farewell to his book, staff, and extended powers coincide with his career's honor-laden consummation. He is not a CEO being forced into early retirement while still at the height of his abilities, but more like an executive moving from a branch office to take over a company headquarters.

From his own account, we cannot be sure whether he has had a hard time on the island while he permitted Ariel and Caliban to slave on his behalf and studied magic and basked in the adoration of his daughter. But since she says he never behaved so irritably before, only if we insist on consistency must he have seethed privately, silently, with a resentment that charged his efforts to grow adept enough with his "art" to insure his restoration. He will go back to reclaim the duchy of Milan, with an even grander prize, the kingdom of Naples, thrown in as a bonus. What comes after the action, the post-play segments of the story, when he becomes a double threat on the Italian peninsula and in the world of Europe, making ready for the assumption of control by Ferdinand and Miranda, and spending every third thought on grave issues, is not our business, even if we choose to write a sequel; but we may notice that his humility in the epilogue strikes a new tone, whether sincere or otherwise, to the power-flexing that leads up to it.

Almost one-third of the single scene that makes up act 4 comprises the masque that Prospero summons into being through his instrument, Ariel. Some commentators believe the author inserted the masque after the play had been written and possibly even performed without it, adding it for the marriage of James's daughter to a German Elector. If so—but the belief is questionable—Shakespeare tucked it into place deftly. It opens directly after his finger-wagging at Ferdinand about not anticipating the wedding night, and Ferdinand's "warrant" that "the white cold virgin snow upon my heart Abates the ardor of my liver," a comic sentiment if there ever was one and a pointer that we are not to take this youngster too seriously. The masque, a tribute to fertility, an autumn encomium, stars two goddesses and one godly messenger who disclose their recitation and singing talents.

These are not the genuine Ceres, Juno, and Iris who place themselves at the disposition of a magus of Prospero's persuasiveness, but spirit-actors who specialize in heavenly impersonations. The stage directions do not say whether the three damsels preside over the "graceful dance" that follows, performed by "certain nymphs" and their partners, "certain reapers, properly habited," or whether they take part. But the masque, which shuts off after Prospero abruptly recalls "that foul conspiracy Of the beast Caliban and his confederates Against my life" (139–41), progresses from birth to death in some eighty lines. It leaves Ferdinand looking, observes Prospero, "in a movèd sort, As if you were dismayed." The bridegroom must truly have felt impressed, as was intended, by this extravaganza, which shows off Prospero's Olympic and theatrical connections and briefly transforms the island with the musical revels that "now are ended." Orgel explains how the masque fits integrally into the rest of the play, some of which, preceding material, serves as an anti-masque (1987, 47–50).

Like the other noble daughters of the late plays, Imogen, Perdita, and Marina, Prospero's has undergone two principal forms of appraisal. One is idolatry; she represents the chivalric (and nineteenth-century) ideal, the loyal beauty without one bad habit, only this time on an island instead of up a tower. A different type of appraisal compares her to Juliet and the charm-exuding, sometimes flirtatious, beached and breeched heroines of the earlier comedies and finds her wanting, if not mildly retarded. As an object of male and female curiosity alike (or, perhaps, not so alike), this woman who is not yet a woman and, in the same body and temperament, this child who is no longer a child provoke our interest mostly by reason of unsoiled puberty and innocence and few signs yet of the directions in which the mature personality will bend. Shakespeare does not "characterize" the Miranda role the way modern playwrights shape their adolescents—with the aid of behavioral quirks and preferences and teenage slang, like the 15-year-old heroine of the network series "My So-Called Life."

Miranda makes one think of a frame still from a movie or a case of arrested development or a miniature of a wingless angel. She could mean virtually nothing to a viewer unless animated. Miranda's father is her only deity, until a younger god arrives. If there were more to her one might say she plays up to his vanity with a subtlety that nobody gives her credit for. During his exposition, Prospero asks her three times whether she is listening attentively, and three times she assures him that she is, the third time with what might be a touch of asperity: "Your tale, sir, would cure deafness" (1.2.106). Has she fallen asleep during his narration? Or does he fear his audience offstage may do likewise? Is he even jogging them out of postprandial yawns and snoozes? Through this role the play creates the double experience of life that must be at the selfish roots of much religious practice: the sort that a person who is not devout might feel under the burden of being in Miranda's sandals: the sensation—she must share it with Caliban—of being unremittingly surveyed from above, of always being looked down on and judged by Prospero and possibly Ariel in their everywhereness—with hope that the surveyor remains genially disposed toward the surveyed.

The part calls for resources from the actor who inhabits it. She begins by pouring herself into an all-but-empty vessel. Not that we should designate Miranda a symbol or icon. Icons and symbols do not need acting, only statuesque poses, splendid physical attitudes. And yet, Miranda's nonspecificity has one acting advantage: like Silvia and Ariel, she remains a mystery. Youngsters begin to come of age at around fifteen. Freud's question of what a woman wants has been superseded in the past score of years by a resuscitation of the antique question of what the coming generation wants.

What makes these juveniles—male as well as female—act, dress, talk as they do? If Miranda tries to unveil the mystery, to whatever degree, her final astonishment at the brave new world that has such people in it seems either sarcastic, ruining Prospero's superbly tart response ("'Tis new to thee"), or disingenuous, making *him* appear naive and throwing a new and hardly defensible light on her and her love for Ferdinand. As things stand, Miranda nearly breaks out of the mystery in at least one uncharacteristic moment, when her exclamation, apropos of the chess game, "Sweet lord, you play me false" (5.1,173), seems like a harking back to act 5 of *The Merchant*, Jessica in disillusion; but Miranda swiftly retracts and gets back into line by telling Ferdinand that he could do much worse and she would still accept it as fair play.

Did Miranda serve as Caliban's teacher? Or did Prospero? How we answer depends on how we assign one twelve-line speech, keeping in mind the slightness and resulting mystery of Miranda's part. Allotting her the "Abhorrèd slave" speech, aimed or hissed at Caliban (1.2.354–65) violates the Renaissance call for decorum—here, the suitability of speeches to roles—but just as certainly Shakespeare often violates that decorum with daring and variety. He usually does so, however, with a fairly clear purpose. It is hard to find a *clear* purpose here without straining for it, saying, for instance, that the speech represents one time when Miranda becomes a chip off the old block and mimics her father's customary, abusive tone to Caliban or says what she knows Dad would like her to say. This last ploy, especially if he gazes at her suspiciously while she enunciates it, is at least comic, or could be. Most editors today follow the First Folio printing to give Miranda the twelve lines. I am tempted to support Dryden, who transferred the speech to Prospero, as did a number of subsequent editors, including Kittredge himself in his edition (New York: 1939, xvii). At the risk of subverting the principal objective of this book, I find the speech not only out of keeping with

Miranda's role but also utterly *in* keeping with Prospero's, who falls to ranting whenever he addresses or discusses Caliban. Miranda is allotted only eleven other words in this sequence (309–10). Those are relatively mild and they allude to Caliban before his entrance. If she is deprived of the "Abhorrèd slave" lines, she doesn't address him directly at all, as if to confirm that his attempt to ravish her makes her shun him.

The reason most editors continue to assign the lines to Miranda is that Caliban may be speaking of her when he says, "My mistress showed me thee [Stephano claiming to have once been the man in the moon], and thy dog, and thy bush" (139), a reference that is taken to relate back to Caliban's remark that "thou" had taught him how "to name the bigger light, and how the less, That burn by day and night," the "thou" being a familiar form of address (to his step-sibling, Miranda) as against the "you" used later in Caliban's same speech, presumably to address Prospero. But in fact Caliban uses *thee, thou, ye, you both,* and *you* fairly indiscriminately. During that same scene it is Prospero, not Miranda, who uses the word *abhorred* earlier, to qualify Caliban's mother Sycorax ("her earthy and abhorred commands" [275]), and establishes ownership rights to it. It could be claimed that Miranda is mimicking and truckling to her father by using one of his choice words, but this would be the only clear example of such mimicry. A sensitive director will want to consult the two actors, mediating between their desires to have the speech, and try to foresee the different effects likely to result.

About Ariel, the more said the better. Unluckily, the more I read and think about him the less I feel there is to say. Prospero's magic governs this spirit and works expeditiously with him. His lines and practices (if he is not really a she, as she once invariably was on stage and occasionally still is, as in the George Wolfe production) as an attendant or assistant, a daemon who plays intermediary between Prospero and what some writers call the "intelligible gods," make it unlikely that one can draw firm lines around the Ariel role and onstage activities. He behaves like less of a chortling trickster than Puck does but also has more initiative: he is called a slave but makes arrangements on his superior's behalf as diligently as a confidential secretary. He sucks—survives?—like a bee (or hummingbird) on floral nectar, lies on a cowslip's bell, flies on a bat's back. Does he need to hitch a ride from a bat or can he fly independently of wires and visibly too? Or will he vanish from one point and appear instantly at another? Does he look better with wings? Bird wings? Insect wings? How wide? Some Ariels sing and dance: should they all? If the other roles do not perceive him, should they show any awareness of his presence, as Stephano does when Ariel plays a tune on a tabor and pipe (*s.d.,* 3.1.122) or during "noises, Sounds, and sweet airs that give delight and hurt not"?

Here a director is up against the same kinds of questions that haunt the history of stage ghosts and fairies. David William in *"The Tempest* on the Stage" says that "Ariel is probably the most difficult part in the play to cast satisfactorily." He goes on to suggest a "triune relationship" to "enhance the extraordinarily powerful impression which the supernatural element in the play is capable of making," that relationship consisting of Ariel and Caliban as "externalized aspects of Prospero—the one of his spiritual, the other of his sensual appetencies." The aspectual resemblances or linkage would be "*assisted* [William's own emphasis] by discreet costuming as well as casting (in Brown and Harris [1960]; reprinted in Signet Classic edition, 206–217, especially, in this connection, 215–216). A lissom three-year-old female dancer who could do justice to Ariel's lines might fill the bill, but defectively, if such a prodigy agreed to audition; the disparity would remain between human size, even child size, and the dimensions mentioned in "Where the bee sucks."

Cut the song? Go for a split personality, an Ariel played by several actors, one speaking, one flying, another miming movement and dance? Go for unbridled laughs by presenting Ariel as a clunky servant, like Launce, who can't take off properly when he tries to fly? Or lands on top of Prospero? Or acts dopily, like Dogberry, getting his orders wrong and earning ironic compliments from his master? Or a snotty chatterbox, like Parolles, by turns arrogant and obsequious? Incensed spectators would bring the performance to a halt. By analogy with Plato's image in the *Phaedrus* of the human soul as a charioteer driving two steeds, G. Wilson Knight sees Ariel as "fiery and excitable," but Caliban is "sluggish and unwilling" (*The Crown of Life*, 228).

In these days and on these shores, when and where tradition has had to give way so frequently to commercial novelties and social protest, designers fearlessly call on moving light shapes in an infinity of colors, on holograms, huge back projections, and the older but modified personifying based on body masks, multifaced and multiheaded apparitions with diabolical squints, twitching mouths, corkscrew limbs, and jarringly warped proportions. Might not such technological fancies compete with the words? Possibly. The danger is not excessive. But since Ariel is air and most embodiments of him a coy embarrassment to players and watchers, I would leave him as undefined as atmosphere, that is, invisible, that is, nonexistent: a mere voice and purveyor of those "noises, sounds, and sweet airs," on a frequency modulation wholly apprehensible only to his master and to the public, only occasionally to the other roles. Restricting and refining the role to its vocal opportunities also brings out the changes in temper between Ariel's pride in description, cautious irritability when asked to do more tasks than he thinks fair, his singing and rejoicing. One or two explosions of color might burst to celebrate his visual freedom , but let him keep it, and the disembodiment. And let Prospero control the air *and* the air-waves, just as, through Ariel, he dictates to ocean waves.

In the lineup of secondary roles we notice few sea changes as the action sails forward, probably because those roles are relatively narrow. If Ariel's second song (1.2.400–08) seems to begin with Alonso and aim itself at Ferdinand during the latter's first scene ("Full fathom five *thy* father lies"), everything in that king "doth suffer a sea change." Alonso does turn on his own past when he says he repents his part in the ousting of Prospero, and believes, perhaps, that the presumed loss of his son has come about by way of divine punishment. But the Alonso we see and hear contrasts with the tale told by Prospero; it contrasts an actuality with an expectation, the play's action with its story. Alonso may always have been a worrier, a verbal fidgeter. As for doggedly cheerful old Gonzalo: not much, if any, sea change here; he corresponds closely to what we learned about him from Prospero. An actor might hope to benefit from characterization by giving him touches of the conventional Polonius and Justice Shallow—a bit too free with advice and rosy prospects—or the muddled loyalty of Britannus in *Caesar and Cleopatra*. Still, as has been often said, he did take part in the original deposing of Prospero, even if he relented by bringing supplies and books to the makeshift raft.

The two unmitigated villains, Antonio and Sebastian, might seem to work variations on Don John and Borachio of *Much Ado*, but they come across as being more openly contemptuous and sarcastic, keeping to themselves and at times giggling together like a couple of "blighters" from *Tom Brown's Schooldays*. They are hard parts to dress up without getting in the way of the other roles.

Ferdinand acts wonder-struck from start to finish, as pop-eyed as an unequipped diver rising from a nightmare—smack in the center of the love-paralyzed swain tradition of Valentine and Orlando, but without any pull from the rival attachment felt by Bassanio. Ferdinand is so neutral, so bland an entity that if one insists on making him stand in for his entire generation, or even a generation of heirs who will come to power, one can paste onto him just about any wished-for interpretation. For those who like to like or dislike roles, not enough of him is revealed to make him dislikable. As a willing recipient of cautions and threats over premarital sex from his father-in-law-to-be and as an eager stacker of logs, he is, to Prospero, a worker to hold up to Caliban, who grumbles about hauling wood (and who did desire Miranda but now thinks of her as a consort for Stephano). Ferdinand takes orders, acts respectful, serves as a yes-man pupil as against a continual troublemaker.

But is Caliban a *born* troublemaker? Or a learner who came to resent an inevitable condescension, born of *noblesse oblige*, on the part of his tutor? Is Caliban hard done by? Is he an ingrate? One does not have to subscribe to a diagnosis that *The Tempest* dramatizes or justifies or excuses the evils of the colonial mentality to become aware that even if the antipathy between him and Prospero has grown out of a determination by each to blame the other, the primary responsibility for what has gone wrong falls on Prospero. While he gives Caliban such titles as the beast, the freckled whelp, hag-born, the poisonous slave got by the devil himself, the filth, as disproportioned in his manners as in his shape, and similar choice epithets, he doesn't scruple to flay Ariel, that hard-working, miracle-sprouting sprite, with "dull thing" and "Thou liest, malignant thing!" when Ariel develops a faulty memory. Genius Prospero may have, and magus unrivaled and conscientious he may be, and a force for ultimate good he may prove, but he lacks the classroom techniques and interpersonal niceties of today's diligent, progressive teacher. Directors who look into backgrounds have no trouble envisaging Caliban as the end product of an orphaned, minority childhood, an intolerant guardian, and an inept education. Caliban, like Shylock, claims to have learned to vilify by sheer imitation. Is there any real analogy between those two roles who differ markedly from the rest of the cast in each case? Is it an accident that they both wear "gaberdine"—as Trinculo reminds us when he takes shelter under Caliban's "gaberdine" (2.2.38)?

In one respect or another he corresponds to a cluster of literary prototypes, some of whom made their way into film: Hugo's Hunchback of Notre Dame, Burroughs's Tarzan, and other figures isolated from, or scapegoated by, a community because of their origins, appearance, manners—including Peter Handke's Kaspar Hauser, the original of the "wild child" featured by Truffaut in his movie of that title. As a crude, psychological approximation, Caliban is the victim who learned to hate when he discovered how easy it was to turn his self-loathing outward. In a modern society many people—not necessarily anything like a majority—strain to understand those who have crossed the law, even the ones who confess to depraved crimes; and many of those who do not strive to understand pay handsomely to read about and otherwise remotely experience the depravities. A range of unbidden, often unconscious sympathies color men's and women's responses to Caliban: some of them the attractions of repulsion. If the actor plays for overt sympathy, however, rather than for comedy, he will land in the horse pond of mawkishness.

However he affects the public, Caliban must repel the other characters on stage. In his Folio role description he is a "salvage [savage] and deformed Slave," and in the play he is mistaken more than once for a fish, the deformation doubtless being the fishy quality. Costume and make-up artists may fishify him by making him scaly, as well as shaggy, slimy, and grimy, and even add a modest fin or two to his wardrobe or skin, but the play gives no evidence that he ever lived in—or emerged from—the sea, a lake, or a stream, and neither did his mother or his purported father, the devil. He might, of course, constitute a limited throwback, a throwback reminder, a sea change from creatures who crawled out of primeval teeming ooze. But possibly Shakespeare's repetition of the word *fish* has the subliminal effect of making spectators think of stale fish, rotting fish, reeking fish, a characteristic that would segregate Caliban on stage all the more obtrusively.

When it comes to viewing him as the personification of Nature, vis-à-vis Prospero as the personification of Art, I am skeptical, and not only out of resistance to matched opposites as a form of analysis, but also because putting the words together with only a *versus* or an *and* between them implies that all art is Art, man's highest accomplishments, while all nature, God's or some Inhuman Force's, is rude and inferior. The contest is pointless, unwinnable, not productive of enlightenment, a relic of Renaissance and high school debates. Ariel has at least as much right to the title of artist as his master, who appears more as a cinquecento *patron* of art. Prospero's art is his power. The power of a patron is money. Ferdinand, who can lay hold of Miranda, shall, as the Nurse said to Romeo, "have the chinks," the *chinks* in this case encompassing the perquisites of monarchy. Viewing Caliban as a makeshift for Nature is altogether too indefinite to mean much more than *primitive* as a term of disapproval. Caliban is not even simple. Ignorant he may understandably be, as in his taking Stephano for a kingly figure, but practiced topers have committed more severe errors in their cups. Caliban has touched liquor for the first time—and proved himself a Dionysian. Above all, he is not a beast. He may show remainders of bestiality from earlier phases of evolution, but neo-Darwinism, as Shaw called the notion (not Darwin's) that evolution automatically meant an improved humanity, went wildly amiss.

The Trinculo-Stephano-Caliban subplot to destroy Prospero starts out awry. Caliban harms nobody *in the action*, only by report. It is falsification to present him as either a ravening dragon or a lovable, forsaken pet, the way Shaw describes Beerbohm Tree: gazing mournfully out to sea as Prospero and Miranda sail away. He has won his "highday," his freedom, as Ariel has won his (hers, its). A case could be made, as I've already implied, for Shakespeare's conception of an androgynous Ariel. In Orgel's edition, his stage direction in 4.1 has the sprite playing the goddess Ceres, with no further explanation (1987, 175). And Prospero has won his "high-day," too, so long as the audience doesn't fail to applaud.

But is the ending comic exactly? Not exactly. Antonio, Sebastian, and Alonso have not reformed or promised to, and will go unpenalized.

Trinculo and Stephano are drenched in horse piss and shivering but otherwise intact. The close is not really about forgiveness, as Bonamy Dobrée asserted nearly half a century ago (1952; reprinted in Muir [1979, 164–75]). Instead, I would say Prospero gives up. He remains unjoined to a marital partner, will go back to Milan to rule, as Vincentio does in Vienna, for a second chance.

Nuttall, who believes that Prospero intends to spend the rest of his life brooding about death, says "the ending of *The Tempest* is sick with ambiguity" and that the close is a prayer for sympathy, not just applause (in Brown and Harris 1961, 224). He has insured continuity: Miranda and Ferdinand will rule Milan-Naples, but perhaps not yet. Does Prospero need do more? He cannot be bothered to merely because of comedy's traditional demands. Leave the dangling ends open; let the play's conclusion wrap *itself* up. Hence his last speech. Like Ariel and Caliban, he wants to be set free, and because of this wish, the play taken to be Shakespeare's final complete work will represent further innovations in the history of comedy. On a more mundane plane, a director could always tell his cast that Prospero decides to retire because he has a mild stroke or seizure (like Othello's) in act 4, a reminder of his mortality. His start on remembering "that foul conspiracy Of the beast Caliban and his confederates Against my life" (4.1.139–141) is soon followed, at the end of his "Our revels now are ended" speech, by an apology for his "weakness," his troubled "old brain," and his "infirmity," leading to his intention to walk "a turn or two . . . To still my beating mind" (159–163).

To return to *The Tempest*'s unity of place: What is to be made of the island? Criticism doesn't need to place it with any accuracy; it belongs somewhere in Shakespeare's "funny geography," that invented atlas of lands and waters that, for all we know, he impishly named after existing places. Some of his geographical references, such as the confusion in *Two Gentlemen* between Naples (and its emperor) and Milan (and its duke) and Verona, are clearly not deliberate but, according to an amalgam of conjecture and research, the result of haphazard publication and production conditions. In none other of his plays do the boundaries and the separation assert themselves so strongly. Can it become both barren desert island and dab of enchantment in the ocean for different roles and for the same roles at different moments? Technically the difficulties are few. Professional set and light designers can work instant conversions, as well as gradations of them, so that at times the stage alternates, even oscillates, between degrees of contrast. Whatever else it may represent or hint at, this island is no home to any of its inhabitants but Caliban. It can breed loneliness or insure privacy, can feel like a prison or a paradise. It has features of the ideal but inaccessible dream spot yearned for in Oskar Kokoschka's color lithographs,

"The Distant Isle" and "The Sleeping Woman," and the painting of Böcklin's "Island of the Dead," which ends *The Ghost Sonata*, and H. G. Wells's *Island of Dr. Moreau*.

The Forbidden Planet (1956), screenplay by Cyril Hume, director Fred M. Wilcox, became renowned as a modern science fiction adventure in part through a main plot related to that of *The Tempest*. Correspondences are noticeable. The attraction of Prospero's foes to his island resembles a space ship's landing in 2200 on a tiny planet called Altair Four. Its human population consists of a scientist (Walter Pidgeon) and his blonde daughter. Love erupts between the daughter (Anne Francis) and the ship's commander (Leslie Nielsen), lightly reminiscent of the Miranda–Ferdinand affair. The movie also displays an Ariel figure named Robby the Robot, who has prodigious strength to do anything the scientist wishes, and an invisible monster, which proves itself invincible to the most harmful ammunition the weapons of the twenty-third century can hurl against it. The monster turns out to be invisible because in the scientist's psyche, his id came unhooked from his unconscious (which the dialogue keeps calling the subconscious). If the film's creators were suggesting that Caliban is the id of Prospero ("This darkness I acknowledge mine"), eventually tamed, they recall the obsessive Freudianism on film of the 1940s and 1950s as well as a neat clue to the play's performance as Prospero's self-conflict.

The island does combine revelry, reverie, and regret with the light and dark possibilities of science fiction. It should radiate waves of friendliness and animosity into the auditorium when either one is appropriate for the production's successions of melodrama, comedy, farce, and impassioned narration. But at other times it looks inaccessible: one might think of Mount Whitney viewed from Seattle, hovering above the horizon as if it were a volcanic peak floating on mist. Like its tidal edges, the temporary refuge undergoes transformation after transformation.

Notes

1. A number of critics have pointed out the vaunting speech as a paraphrase of the one pronounced by Ovid's Medea (*Metamorphoses*, seventh book), which Stephen Orgel reprints in Latin and in the Golding translation into English in his edition of *The Tempest* (1987, Appendix E). The play also reveals debts to *The Aeneid*, which Orgel synopsizes [39–42].

2. For an exploration of these and other lines as pointers to Prospero's role, see Orgel [1987, 14–20, 50–56].

3. Prospero's 30 percent compares with Vincentio's 30.7 percent. Dominant numbers of lines in the tragedies and histories include: Richard III, 31.2

percent of the total text; Timon of Athens, 34.8 percent; Hamlet 38 percent. More than one critic has pointed out that Vincentio is one of two of Prospero's predecessors as rulers who get a second chance, the other being Duke Senior.

4. Sprinchorn, "An Intermediate Stage Level in the Elizabethan Theatre" (1992).

5. For some of the more compelling arguments, see Harry Berger, Jr., "Miraculous Harp: A Reading of Shakespeare's *Tempest*," in Bloom [1989, 9–41]; and Stephen Orgel, "Prospero's Wife," ibid.; Nuttall, "Two Unassimilable Men," ibid; and also Nuttall's *Two Concepts of Allegory* (1967), especially the final chapter.

6. I cannot do justice here to the intricacies of Dr. Yates's thesis. She sums it up in *Shakespeare's Last Plays: A New Approach*, ibid., but draws on the conclusions of several earlier books dealing with the history of ideas in the sixteenth and seventeenth centuries. In the chapter "Ben Jonson and the Last Plays," she contrasts Shakespeare's respectful treatment of Dee's magic, linked as it was, in her view, to Hermetic magic and the Rosicrucian philosophy, with Jonson's satirical treatment in *The Alchemist*, written at about the same time. According to her, James I opposed the influence of the Rosicrucians, and "*The Tempest* was a very bold manifesto" (132).

Conclusion: Loose Ends

Halfhearted Shakespeare

Most of us acknowledge that artists are captives of their time. And yet, we like to believe that this author, whose comedies have won centuries of admiration, has oracular vision (not invariably shared by critics, including spectators); that this vision liberates the work from its time and struggles to support a glut of modern, postmodern, posed-modern, and supposed-modern Shakespeare. Plenty of justifications for updating go into talk and print, some of them defensible: the ambitions and inventiveness of directors; yawns that greet stale and lazy interpretations; the necessity to travel alongside the fashion cycle in set and costume design and technical opportunities (sand and real flames on stage, inches of water and mud to wade through, strobe lights to make theatre flicker like the movies, smoke machines to spread coughs through the auditorium); new actors and novel acting styles; flash laughs in fresh places; the controversy bug (get the public quarreling); pushing what most reviewers say they like. . .

Hard behind the belief in modernity comes disbelief in the scene or soliloquy that won't work. Directors and their unheeded advisory peons, dramaturgs, will not admit they lack inventiveness, especially when other directors have staged the material they long to cut. They rewrite, a practice cruder than cutting. Brian Gibbons mentions some of the adaptations that have scrambled different Shakespeare plays together into sunny-side-ups or homogeneous omelettes. (A French once-over-lightly some years ago was titled, "Omelette, Prince of Denmark.") In 1642 Davenant, first playwright-producer-director of Restoration theatre, whipped Beatrice and Benedick into a version of *Measure for Measure*, possibly because *Much Ado*, like *Measure*, has a young lover named Claudio and, Gibbons says, because "Shakespeare's characters are generally thought of as separable from the dramatic text in which he presents them, and are given fresh narratives and situations" (1991, 53).

Why do directors now habitually force Shakespeare into periods and countries that differ from the originals? In order, it seems, to foist on him a consistency the roles will not support without mutilation, consistency that grows more baffling to audiences than the jumps in time and motivation they were ready to allow for "because it's Shakespeare." The sponsors of productions that feature cowboys and the nineteenth-century frontier or prosperous middle America during this century's first decades (Booth Tarkington territory) or the homeless under scummy arches in an Elizabethan city like Chicago or Denver apparently want to garner the prestige of putting on undeniable classics without earning it. Even nontraditional casting, that admirable practice, can lead to tortured rewriting. For instance, if the role of Hermia goes to an African American performer, casting her father, Egeus, as African American merely to make Hermia look or sound legitimate is to stick her with a crutch she doesn't need.

Similarly, doubling resorted to as a cost-saving, cast-paring device makes sense for a poor company. But thematic doubling, which is intrinsically more fascinating and discussable, although it may also come about for financial reasons, leaves itself open to questions of judgment. Avraham Oz has written about a production of *The Merchant* in Israel in which Bassanio hastily commuted between Venice and Belmont as he also played the two other casket suitors, Morocco and Aragon (in Charney, [1980, 178–182]). Here again, the arrangement makes the director into the playwright's senior partner.

Some directors, such as Peter Brook, by cutting and sorting, impose on plays a sharper social, theological, political, or other statement than the playwright's. They may, it's true, goad us into seeing a work anew, reexamining lines and ideas that have been hitherto neglected or read superficially, but the specificity can also shorten the playwright's reach. Directors who love and long to serve the plays they stage have careers to think of: futures can hinge on novelties that cry out to be noticed. To a trendy reviewer, a director who won't peer at a comedy from new angles seems more of a slouch than one who does, even though new angles may cause cramps and distortions. Not that distortions matter much; the texts exist in numerous editions and will outlive the warpings.

More than fifty years ago Eric Bentley offered a salutary caution that remains worth heeding in these days of unapt settings; he addresses himself here primarily to "historical scholars" but his words apply keenly to unhistorical directors.

> Once we question the almost universal assumption of the timelessness of art, we may come to believe that historical interpretation is not merely an apparatus to help us fill out the details of our understanding of Shakespeare or Ibsen and that Shakespeare's individuality lies in his *Elizabethanness* and not in his timelessness. Obviously Shakespeare is not to be enjoyed merely by "an age" but by "all time," yet that is not to say that posterity cannot enjoy the Elizabethanness

of Shakespeare. There has been much confused thinking on the point, and the historical scholars have contributed to it by making remarks about the Eternal Shakespeare which reduce their own researches to insignificance. The arts are fragments of the time and place which produced them and cannot be comprehended either conceptually or imaginatively, outwardly or inwardly, without some knowledge and imaginative understanding of their context. The great generalities which unhistorical critics produce are the inevitable product of an ignorance of the relevant particularities. (1944, 33–34)

It won't do much good in an open society to condemn in principle and in advance new, up-to-date concepts that happen to bypass Shakespeare's Elizabethanness because one never knows what the current generation or the next one will turn up. But the novelties may in practice merely support more jeans, motorbikes, and slurred speaking.

Flawed Shakespeare

After Maurice Charney's conference and book on Bad Shakespeare, others got into the act. A further bout of Bard-bashing took place in 1995 at Slippery Rock University. The conference, "'Wretched Plays' and 'Miserable Fragments': Exploring the Dark Corners of the Shakespearean Canon," comprised of talks (chapters by now?) on "Unruly Women and 'Wretched' History" and "All's Not Necessarily Well." But who launched the notion that Shakespeare has *not* been attacked on almost every conceivable pretext since the 1590s? We *expect*, for heaven's sake, to find flaws in thirty-eight plays, or large parts thereof, composed in about twenty-five years. Why should we strain at what are often gnats of flaws—bugs—and after consideration, prove not to be? Suppose the author *has* left a wisp of the ending open, as happens with the fate of Antonio at the close of *Twelfth Night?* Such a "defect" hardly cripples the work.

Perhaps flaws make it harder for critics to rank the plays reliably. But what value resides in ranking the plays, anyway, other than as a device for promoting sales of books and productions and films ("Shakespeare's most gripping, most moving, most tender, most hilarious . . .") or to demonstrate the superiority of the critic to the playwright by sitting in judgment on him? Rankings—rank opinions—deserve attention only when they raise compelling questions of interpretation.

British scholars, who did sterling work before and after WWII in Oxford, Cambridge, Manchester, Glasgow, Birmingham, London, and elsewhere and formed an unofficial fraternity, with a few outstanding women, Americans, and Europeans admitted, jostled for the most part with exquisite civility over roles that did not fit the hero or villain mold. Many of the questions raised remain unresolved here, not alone because of my uncertainties but also because those very questions about flaws generally permit us to choose two or more attractive but distinctive stage answers.

A mania for consistency occasionally enlists a mania for neatness, that foe of generous criticism—and of the drama itself. When the playwright has omitted information or provided information that baffles audiences, a director's trimming the material may be in order. Even more in order is the art of doing nothing if a fault provokes spectators. At least, they remained awake. Besides, a text with omissions, oversights, or bewildering facts—conflicting dates, ages, titles, motives, relationships—will sometimes prove inhospitable to corrections. Wise directors accept the flaws they know. By tidying up they may commit new, unforeseen flaws, which do not get noticed until the first preview or, worse, the first night.

Repairs and corrections of the sort I refer to here do not include outright adaptations. These Shakespeare deserves. His defenders cannot cry foul when writers and composers return him a favor for having looted British and other literatures. But they do owe him an acknowledgment.

Narrow-Minded Shakespeare

Our author is so hallowed a dramatist and poet, so popular, so *famous* that some people who fear the spread of negative propaganda from his writings maintain that he should have created roles who can serve as exemplary figures: a perfect Portia, a model for women; Shylock as a model for Jews; Caliban and Othello as models for third-world peoples or for sizable minorities within the first world or the second. Unhappily for them, Shakespeare gives us roles who have faults and therefore uncomfortably resemble people we know and know of.

The latest and most extensive outbreak of role-rebuking occurred during the 1980s. Feminist critics in the United States wanted some of Shakespeare's less positive female parts to display more strength. They censured these helpless roles as if they were people needing advice on how to introduce a bit more steel into the spine. The roles should have taken a firmer grasp of their destinies, not allowed their lives merely to happen. One critic (Marcia Riefer) I have no reason to single out, except that she chose a telling example; she objected to the emotional high point of *Measure*, Isabella's willful self-humiliation when she kneels to Duke Vincentio to plead for Angelo's life. There is something here not dissimilar to the pretension among American men, especially politicos, lawyers, and literati, for being (or seeming) "tough," a verbal stance often mocked in other countries as at home. Professor Riefer comes closer to the play's bearing as she writes: "Regardless of the playwright's intention, *Measure for Measure* . . . exposes the dehumanizing effect on women of living in a world dominated by powerful men who would like to re-create womanhood according to their fantasies" ("'Instruments of Some More Mightier Member': The Constriction of Female Power in *Measure for Measure*").[1] The word *exposes* is well chosen.

Elitist Shakespeare

The humorous and especially the farcical roles in Shakespeare's comedies, who unintentionally make others laugh, come mostly from the lower classes, while the witty roles, who deliberately set out to amuse others, come mostly from the titled and royal levels of society. Does class-consciousness dictate Shakespeare's theatre? It certainly has a conspicuous influence, as Marxist critics have pointed out. He goes part of the way with Aristotle in distinguishing between tragic rulers and comic ordinary citizens. But he doesn't subscribe wholly to the Aristotelian analysis. Among his tragic figures, Othello, Macbeth (a literal tyrant, a "thane" who usurps the throne), Romeo, Juliet, Brutus, Cassius, and the Antony of *Antony and Cleopatra* represent non-royalty. Yet, he creates enough exceptions to justify the word *mostly* here. Sir Andrew Aguecheek, a titled idiot, and Shallow, Silence, and Slender, those upper-crust rustics, behave and speak farcically. On the lower end of the spectrum, he invests servants with wit, from Speed and Margaret (*Much Ado*) to the Dromios. And some roles are of a mixed caliber, such as Holofernes and Don Armado, who think of themselves as witty while audiences laugh at their misapprehensions. Some underclass roles, country- and city-bred, plead eloquently in prose and poetry: Corin, Silvius, and Phoebe. Bastards, debased, and self-debasing antiheroes have their defensive say, which, in the case of Iago, Richard III, or Edmund, arouses perverse delight. And even when humorous and farcical roles go through their paces and spoken pieces, we often laugh with them, not at them. Even a broad target like Holofernes may dispense sagacity and dignity. I see I've already embarked on those cherished topics, Shakespeare's mix of comedy, tragedy, melodrama, farce, and self-revelation.

Shakespeare's Awkward Comic Intrusions

Richard III's wooing of Anne . . . Hamlet's teasing Polonius about fishmongering and cloud shapes . . . Falstaff on the battlefield at Shrewsbury

. . . Iago's "bobbing" of wealth from Roderigo . . . The Roman mob's fickle willingness to follow Brutus or Antony, the latest public persuader . . . Jack Cade's aristocratic pretensions during the rebellion into which he steers his "rabblement" . . . Aaron's gleeful confessions to Lucius of cruelties so barbaric that they become funny . . . Mercutio's joking about having suffered a mortal wound . . . Pandarus hawking love and Thersites unloading his loathings . . . Not only the knocking at the gate sequence in *Macbeth* but also, and even more, the three absurdly ominous "weyerd sisters" worming their way in and out of the action . . . Why do these subversive flotsam and jetsam drift into the tragedies and the histories? Why does a witty remark or a nonsensical bit of farce like the impudence and punishment of Lucio interrupt (some would say "ruin") the serious summit of a comic resolution? Will a term like comic relief explain them? Not really. The dramatic pressure relents momentarily, then goes on around the interruption to build to a higher level, a fiercer outcome or conflict. Shakespeare used comedy and farce for their own sake but also as tools for wielding, sculpturing, punctuating, and heightening his other theatre. In his drama irregularity of role and narrative are the "order" of the day.

The Bard on What Boards?

After nearly three hundred years in which Shakespeare was performed on stages seen through a proscenium arch, and in which the plays were not only surgically molested but also gussied up with whimsical scenic romance, William Poel allowed the words to prevail as he brought some of the plays back to what he supposed to be plain, open acting platforms, which may have characterized the author's working conditions at the Globe. Harley Granville Barker in London and Jacques Copeau in Paris followed Poel's lead in pursuing an unadorned Shakespeare, most noticeably in dressing the comedies without the sort of prettification added by Augustin Daly, Max Reinhardt, and their imitators. J. L. Styan particularizes the variety of attempts during the first three-quarters of this century to present the plays pure, on a stripped-down stage at first, later on precarious constructivist bridges in Russia and elsewhere; on multiple levels and slopes; in the round, cater-cornered, out of doors; under the influence of complex thematic designs that proceeded from the allied brains of directors and designers. Staircases became prominent after Leopold Jessner's dexterity in exploiting stage depth and height with his *Jessnertreppen* in Germany after World War I.

In *Shakespeare: The Globe and the World* (1981) Schoenbaum includes a tableau from the Ashland, Oregon, production of *Two Gentlemen* in

1974: a curved staircase in what looks like blue-green marble descending to what looks like a revolve, all designed by Richard L. Hay and populated by nineteen actors in vivid costumes and artificial poses, magnificence in simplicity.

J. L. Styan advances a view, I obviously subscribe to:

> It is questionable whether the real advances in Shakespeare scholarship in this century have come through verbal and thematic studies. A stronger claim can be made for another line of scholarship more directly related to the practical business of staging a play, research which can be traced from the new interest in the Elizabethan playhouse and its conventions after the discovery of the [copy of the] Swan drawing in 1888 and W. W. Greg's publication of Henslowe's Diary and Papers between 1904 and 1908. (1977, 4)

For a time in the 1950s and 1960s the thrust or enlarged apron became *de rigueur*—so that when the Beaumont was built at Lincoln Center, it was to have had a proscenium stage. However, consultations with critics brought the dividing line between actors and audience well forward to cope with productions of Shakespeare and his contemporaries—of which there have been hardly any in that house in the past thirty-five years. The result was a stage so deep that, from sight lines on either side of the fan-shaped auditorium, upstage left and right formed invisible triangles, and the company that then occupied the building closed off altogether the rear sector of the stage.

On which type of stage do Shakespeare's comedies belong today? Do different types of acting area presuppose different implications in plays? They do, but one can hardly foresee those implications, only eulogize or grumble retrospectively as many critics have done, sometimes unjustly. The Globe imitation in Southwark may or may not change many opinions about the best methods of staging Shakespeare, and individual minds that apply themselves to the subject will surely change differently. "When you think about a variable," said Doyne Farmer, then a young scientist at Santa Cruz, "the evolution of it must be influenced by whatever other variables it's interacting with" (quoted by James Gleick in *Chaos: Making a New Science* [1987, 266]).

Shakespeare in Cyberspace

Prospero has already floated on futuristic versions of Blake's Island in the Moon or immeasurably further out in the empyrean on some enterprising starship. An invention by two young men in Westchester County of a play called CyberSpeare, "very loosely based" on *A Midsummer Night's Dream*, exemplifies what is known as hypermedia, which combines computerization with a variety of art forms.[2] A viewer can take part in the performance, as a reminder of "a time when aristocrats would sit on the stage and interact with the players." *And interfere with the players* was more like what happened in the seventeenth century, but never mind. The interactive day approaches at high velocity—may have already come—when with one move of your mouse you blank out a role on a videotape, rewrite it, and take over. You too can enjoy a rebirth as Falstaff.

The Shakespeare ID

Some shrewd assembling of biographical medleys has gone into supporting King Edward VI (if he lived in secret after 1553), Francis Bacon, Kit Marlowe, and especially of late, Edward de Vere, Earl of Oxford, as claimants to the authorship of Shakespeare's writings.[3] But the ingenuity of the various cases could prove the obverse of the claims. Because Marlowe and Shakespeare were born in the same month and because Oxford's and Bacon's lives and as much of the short life of Edward VI as is known overlapped our playwright's, we could say with some assurance that Shakespeare must have been responsible for the plays of Marlowe and the poetry of Oxford, when he was not turning out the prodigious output now attributed to him.

Notes

1. *The Shakespeare Quarterly* 35, No. 2 (Summer 1984). Reprinted in *Modern Critical Interpretations,* collection devoted to *Measure for Measure,* ed. Harold Bloom,144.

2. The information in this paragraph is taken from The Westchester-Rockland Newspapers, June 15, 1995, 11A.

3. See, for a recent sample, the symposium "The Ghost of Shakespeare: Who, in fact, was the Bard?" in *Harper's Magazine,* April 1999, backing the case for the "Oxfordians" or defending the "Stratfordians." The July 1999 issue of the magazine carried more than nine columns of responsive letters, most of them unwilling to give up the accepted Shakespeare for the unfamiliar Oxford.

Bibliography

Acocella, Joan. "The Politics of Hysteria." *The NewYorker*, April 6, 1998.

Anon. (Shakespeare?) *The Taming of a Shrew* Passages (or Christopher Sly scenes) are printed in the editions of Morris, Oliver, and Thompson. (See below.)

Arthos, John, ed. *Love's Labor's Lost*. New York, 1965.

Baker, Herschel, ed. *Twelfth Night*. New York, 1986.

Baldwin, T. W. *The Organization and Personnel of the Shakespeare Company*. New York, 1961.

Bamber, Linda. *Comic Women, Tragic Men*. Stanford, CA, 1982.

Barber, C. L. *Shakespeare's Festive Comedy*. Princeton, 1959.

Barker, Harley Granville. (1) Preface to *Twelfth Night*. Portsmouth, NH, 1995.

———. (2) Preface to *The Merchant of Venice*. Portsmouth, NH, 1995.

Barnet, Sylvan. "*Twelfth Night* on the Stage." New York, 1986.

———, ed. *All's Well that Ends Well*. New York, 1988.

Barton, Anne, ed. (1) "The Comedy of Errors" in G. Blakemore Evans edn.

———. (2) *A Midsummer Night's Dream*," in G. Blakemore Evans.

———. (3) *The Names of Comedy*. Toronto, 1990.

Barton, John. *Playing Shakespeare*. Portsmouth, NH, 1988.

Bawcutt, N. W., ed. *Measure for Measure*. Oxford, 1994.

BBC TV Series, ed. John Wilders. London, various dates.

Beckerman, Bernard. "The American Shakespearean Actor—an Endangered Species," in *Shakespeare Study Today*. New York, 1986.

———. *Shakespeare at the Globe, 1599–1609*. New York, 1962.

Bentley, Eric. (1) *The Playwright as Thinker*. New York, 1944.

———. (2) *In Search of Theatre*. New York, 1953.

Berger, Harry, Jr. "Miraculous Harp: A Reading of Shakespeare's *Tempest*," in Bloom (3).

Bergeron, David M. "Come Hell or High Water: Shakespearean Romantic Comedy," in Charney (1).

Bergson, Henri. *Laughter*, ed. Wylie Sypher. New York, 1956.

Berry, Edward. *Shakespeare's Comic Rites*. Cambridge, U. K., 1984.

Bertin, Michael. "Two *Twelfth Nights*" in *Shakespeare Quarterly*, Summer, 1981.

Bevington, David. (1) "'But We Are Spirits of Another Sort: The Dark Side of Love and Magic in *A Midsummer Night's Dream*," in *Medieval and Renaissance Studies*, Chapel Hill, NC, 1978.

———, ed. (2) *The Complete Works of Shakespeare*. New York, 1992.

———, ed. (3) *Henry IV, Part One*. New York, 1994.

Bloom, Harold, ed. (1) *Modern Critical Interpretations: Henry IV, Part I*. New Haven, 1987.

———, ed. (2) *Modern Critical Interpretations: As You Like It*. New Haven, 1988.

———, ed. (3) *Modern Critical Interpretations: The Tempest*. New Haven, 1989.

Boas, F. S. *Shakespeare and His Predecessors*. New York, 1896.

Bradbrook, M. C. *The Growth and Structure of Elizabethan Comedy*. New York, 1963.

Bradbury, Malcolm, and David Palmer, eds. *Shakespearian Comedy*. London, 1972.

Brissenden, Alan, ed. *As You Like It*. Oxford, 1994.

Brooks, Harold F. (1) "Themes and Structures in *The Comedy of Errors*," in Brown and Harris (1).

———, ed. (2) *A Midsummer Night's Dream*. London, 1983.

Brown, John Russell, ed. (1) *The Merchant of Venice*, London, 1954.

———, ed. (2) *The Tempest*. London, 1969.

———. (3) *Free Shakespeare*. London, 1974.

———. (4) *Discovering Shakespeare*. New York, 1981.

———, and Bernard Harris, eds. (1). *Early Shakespeare*. Stratford-upon-Avon Studies 3, London, 1961.

———, eds. (2). *Elizabethan Theatre*. London, 1966.

Büchner, Georg. *Gesammelte Werke*. Munich, 1964.

Carroll, William C. *The Metamorphoses of Shakespearean Comedy*. Princeton, 1985.

Chambers, Edward. *Shakespeare: A Survey*. London, 1925.

Chambers, R. W. "The Jacobean Shakespeare and *Measure for Measure*." *Proceedings of the British Academy*, XXIII. 1937.

Charlton, H. B. *Shakespearian Comedy*. London, 1938.

Charney, Maurice. (1) *Shakespearean Comedy*. New York, 1980.

———. (2) *"Bad" Shakespeare*. Cranbury, NJ, 1988.

———. (3) *All of Shakespeare*. New York, 1993.

Chevalier, Jean, and Alain Gheerbrant, eds. *Dictionnaire des symboles*. Paris, 1989.

Clemen, Wolfgang. *The Development of Shakespeare's Imagery*. New York, 1962.

Coghill, Nevill. "Six Points of Stage-Craft," in Muir (2).

Corrigan, R. W., ed. *Classical Comedy: Greek and Roman*. New York, 1987.

Craik, T. W., ed. *The Merry Wives of Windsor*. Oxford, 1990.

Cunningham, Dolora. "Conflicting Images of the Comic Heroine," in Charney (3).

David, Richard W., ed. *Love's Labour's Lost*. London, 1951.

Davison, P. H., ed. *Henry IV, Part One*. New York, 1968.

Dobrée, Bonamy. *Essays and Studies*. London, 1952.

Doebler, John, ed. *As You Like It*, in Bevington (2).

Donno, Elizabeth Story, ed. *Twelfth Night*. Cambridge, U.K., 1985.

Dorius, R. J., ed. Discussions of Shakespeare's Histories. Boston, 1964.

Dowden, Edward. *Shakespeare: A Critical Study of His Mind and Art*. London, 1875.

Driscoll, James P. *Identity in Shakespearean Drama*. Cranbury, NJ, 1983.

———. "The Shakespeare 'Metastance'" in Bloom (3).

Emerson, Ralph W. *Essays*, series 1, "Self-Reliance." New York, 1940.

Empson, William. *The Structure of Complex Words*. London, 1951.

Evans, Bertrand. (1) *Shakespeare's Comedies*. Oxford, 1960.

——— , ed. (2) *The Two Gentlemen of Verona*. New York, 1964.

Evans, G. Blakemore, ed. *The Riverside Shakespeare*. Boston, 1974.

Ewbank, Inga-Stina. (1) "The Triumph of Time in *The Winter's Tale*," in *A Review of English Literature*. April 1964.

———. (2) "Constancy and Consistency in *The Two Gentlemen of Verona*," in Bradbury and Palmer.

Faucit, Helen. *On Some of Shakespeare's Female Characters*. London, 1981. Extract in Muir (2).

Fergusson, Francis. *The Human Image in Dramatic Literature*. New York, 1957.

Foakes, R. A., ed. (1) *The Comedy of Errors*. Cambridge, MA, 1962.

——— , ed. (2) *A Midsummer Night's Dream*. Cambridge, U. K., 1984.

Fraser, Russell, ed. *All's Well that Ends Well*. Cambridge, U. K., 1985.

Freedman, Barbara. "Errors in Comedy: A Psycho-analytical Theory of Farce" in Charney (1).

French, Marilyn. *Shakespeare's Division of Experience*. New York, 1981.

Frye, Northrop. (1) *Anatomy of Criticism*. New York, 1965.

———. (2) "Recognition in *The Winter's Tale*," Reprint in Muir (2).

Garber, Marjorie. "'Wild Laughter in the Throat of Death': Darker Purposes in Shakespearean Comedy," in Charney (1).

Gardner, Helen. *More Talking of Shakespeare*. New York, 1959.

Gibbons, Brian, ed. *Measure for Measure*. Cambridge, U. K., 1991.

Gill, Roma, ed. *The Winter's Tale*. Oxford (School) series, 1996.

Gilman, Albert, ed. *As You Like It*. New York, 1963.

Girard, René. *A Theatre of Envy: William Shakespeare*. Oxford, 1991.

Goddard, Harold C. *The Meaning of Shakespeare*. Chicago, 1951.

Goldman, Michael. *Shakespeare and the Energies of Drama.* Princeton, 1972.

Gozzi, Count Carlo. *Five Tales for the Theatre.* Chicago, 1989.

Green, William. (1) *Shakespeare's* Merry Wives of Windsor. Princeton, 1962.

————, ed. (2) *The Merry Wives of Windsor.* New York, 1965.

Greer, Germaine. *The Female Eunuch.* New York, 1971.

Greg, W. W. *The Merry Wives of Windsor.* Oxford, 1910.

Hainaux, René, ed. *Stage Design Throughout the World Since 1935.* New York, 1956.

Halio, Jay L., ed. *The Merchant of Venice.* Oxford, 1994.

Hall, Peter. *Peter Hall's Diaries.* London, 1983.

Harbage, Alfred, General editor. *The Complete Pelican Shakespeare.* New York, 1969.

Heilman, Robert B., ed. *The Taming of the Shrew.* New York, 1986.

Herrick, Marvin T. *Comic Theory in the Sixteenth Century.* Urbana, IL, 1950.

Hibbard, G. R., ed. *Love's Labour's Lost,* Oxford, 1994.

Holland, Norman N., ed. (1) *Henry IV, Part Two.* New York, 1965.

Holland, Peter, ed. *A Midsummer Night's Dream.* Oxford, 1994.

Hollander, John. *"Twelfth Night and the Morality of Indulgence"* in *The Sewanee Review,* 67, LXVIII, 1959.

Holroyd, Michael. *Bernard Shaw,* Vol. 3. New York, 1991.

Hosley, Richard. (1) "Sources and Analogues of *The Taming of the Shrew,*" in *The Huntington Library Quarterly,* XXVII, 1963-64.

————. (2) "The Formal Influence of Plautus and Terence," in Brown and Harris (1).

————, ed. (3) *The Taming of the Shrew* in Harbage.

Hotson, Leslie. (1) *Shakespeare versus Shallow.* London, 1931.

————. (2) *"The First Night of* Twelfth Night." London, 1954.

Humphreys. A. R., ed. *Much Ado About Nothing.* London, 1981.

Hunter, G. K, ed. *All's Well that Ends Well.* London, 1962.

Huston, J. Dennis. *Shakespeare's Comedies of Play.* New York, 1981.

Huxley, Aldous. *Crome Yellow.* London, 1922.

Hyman, S. E. *Iago: Some Approaches to the Illusion of His Motivation.* New York, 1970.

Isaac, Dan."The Worth of a Jew's Eye: Reflections of the Talmud in *The Merchant of Venice,*" in *Maarav,* vol. 8, 1992.

Jayne, Sears. "The Dreaming of *The Shrew*" in *Shakespeare Quarterly,* No. 17, 1966.

Johnson, Samuel. *The Plays of William Shakespeare.* London, 1765.

Jorgens, Jack, J. *Shakespeare on Film.* Lanham, MD, 1991

Jorgensen, Paul A., ed. "The Comedy of Errors" in Harbage.

Kahn, Coppélia. *Man's Estate.* Berkeley, 1981.

Kermode, Frank, ed. (1) *The Tempest.* London, 1956.

————, ed. (2) *The Winter's Tale*. New York, 1963.

Kittredge, George Lyman, General editor. *Shakespeare: Complete Works*, 1939. New edition, ed. Irving Ribner, New York,1971.

Knight, G. Wilson. (1) *The Wheel of Fire*. London, 1930.

————. (2) *The Sovereign Flower*. London, 1958.

Knox, Bernard. "*The Tempest* and the Ancient Comic Tradition," in Langbaum.

Kott, Jan. *Shakespeare Our Contemporary*, tr. Boleslaw Taborski. New York, 1966.

Langbaum, Robert, ed. *The Tempest*. New York, 1964.

Latham, Agnes, ed. *As You Like It*. London, 1975.

Lawrence, W. W. *Shakespeare's Problem Comedies*. New York, 1931.

Leech, Clifford. (1) "The Theme of Ambition in *All's Well*," in Ornstein (2).

————. (2) "The Meaning of *Measure for Measure*," in *Shakespeare Survey 3*. Cambridge, U.K., 1950.

————, ed. *The Two Gentlemen of Verona*. London, 1969.

Leggatt, Alexander. *Shakespeare's Comedy of Love*. New York, 1974.

Lelyveld, Toby. *Shylock on the Stage*. London, 1961.

Levin, Harry, ed. *The Comedy of Errors*. New York, 1965.

Levin, Richard. "Shakespearean Defects and Shakespeareans' Defenses," in Charney (2).

Lewis, W. H. *The Splendid Century: Life in the France of Louis XIV*. New York, 1957.

MacCary, W. Thomas. *Friends and Lovers: The Phenomenology of Desire in Shakespearean Comedy*. New York, 1985.

McFarland, Thomas. *Shakespeare's Pastoral Comedy*. Chapel Hill, NC, 1972.

Mahood, M. M. (1) *Shakespeare's Word Play*. London, 1957.

————, ed. (2) *The Merchant of Venice*. Cambridge, U. K., 1987.

Mares, F. H., ed. *Much Ado About Nothing*. Cambridge, U. K., 1988.

Matthews, Brander. *The Development of the Drama*. New York, 1927.

May, Rollo. *Love and Will*. New York, 1974.

Midgley, Graham. "*The Merchant of Venice*: A Reconsideration" in Wilders (1).

Morris, Brian, ed. *The Taming of the Shrew*. London, 1981.

Mowat, Barbara A., ed. *The Winter's Tale*, in Bevington (2).

Muir, Kenneth, ed. (1). *Shakespeare: The Comedies*. Englewood Cliffs, NJ, 1965.

————, ed. (2) *Shakespeare: The Winter's Tale*. Nashville, TN, 1970.

————. (3) *Shakespeare's Comic Sequence*. New York, 1979.

Myrick, Kenneth, ed. *The Merchant of Venice*. New York, 1965.

Nagarajan, S., ed. *Measure for Measure*. New York, 1964.

Neely, Carol Thomas. *Broken Nuptials in Shakespeare's Plays*. New Haven, 1985.

Nevo, Ruth. *Comic Transformations in Shakespeare*. London, 1980.

Nuttall, A. D. "Two Unassimilable Men," in Brown and Harris.

Odell, G. C. D. *Shakespeare from Betterton to Irving*. New York, 1966.

Oliver, H. J., ed. (1) *The Taming of the Shrew*. Oxford, 1994.

———, ed. (2) *The Merry Wives of Windsor*. London, 1973.

Orgel, Stephen, ed. *The Tempest*. Oxford, 1987.

Ornstein, Robert, ed. (1) *Discussions of Shakespeare's Problem Comedies*. Boston, 1961.

———. (2) *Shakespeare's Comedies*. Newark, DE, 1986.

Ovid. *The Metamorphoses*, tr. Horace Gregory. New York, 1958.

Parten, Anne. "Falstaff's Horns," in *Studies in Philology*, 1985.

Pater, Walter. *Appreciations*. London, 1885.

Poel, William. *Shakespeare in the Theatre*. London, reprint, 1968.

Quiller-Couch, Arthur ("Q"), ed. *All's Well that Ends Well*. Cambridge, U.K., 1929, 1955.

Rae, Kenneth, ed. *Stage Design*, New York, 1956.

Reik, Theodor. *Of Love and Lust*. New York, 1974.

Rossiter, A. P. *Angel with Horns: Fifteen Lectures on Shakespeare*. London, 1961.

Rudlin, John. *Jacques Copeau*. Cambridge, U.K., 1986.

Rushdie, Salman. *The Moor's Last Sigh*. New York, 1995.

Salingar, Leo. *Shakespeare and the Traditions of Comedy*. Cambridge, U.K., 1974.

Sanderson, James L., ed. *Henry the Fourth, Part I*. New York, 1969.

Schanzer, Ernest. "The Structural Pattern," in Muir (2).

Schlueter, Kurt, ed. *The Two Gentlemen of Verona*. Cambridge, U. K., 1990.

Sewell, Arthur. *Character and Society in Shakespeare*. London, 1951.

Shapiro, James. *Shakespeare and the Jews*. New York, 1996.

Shaw, Bernard. (1) *Dramatic Opinions and Essays*, Vol. 2, ed. Huneker. London, 1899.

———. (2) Preface to The Dark Lady of the Sonnets.

———. Collected Works, "definitive ed." Vol. 4. New York, 1963.

Shepherd, Chuck. From *Louisville* [KY] *Eccentric Observer*, Vol. 6, No. 9, January 10, 1996.

Snyder, Susan. (1) "Wise Saws and Modern Instances: The Relevance of Donatus," in Charney (1).

———, ed. (2) *All's Well that Ends Well*. Oxford, 1994.

Spencer, Hazelton. "The Art and Life of William Shakespeare," in Ornstein (1).

Sprague, Arthur Colby. *Shakespeare and the Actors*. London, 1944.

Sprinchorn, Evert, "An Intermediate Stage Level in the Elizabethan Theatre," in *Theatre Notebook*, Vol. 46, 1992.

Stauffer, Donald. *Shakespeare's World of Images*. New York, 1949.

Stevenson, David L., ed. *Much Ado About Nothing*. New York, 1964.

Stevenson, Robert Louis. *The Strange Case of Dr Jekyll and Mr Hyde*. London, 1886.

Stewart, J. I. M. *Character and Motive in Shakespeare*. London, 1949.

Stoll, E. E. "Shylock," in *Journal of English and Germanic Philology*, No. 10, 1911.

Story, Graham, ed. *Angel with Horns: Fifteen Lectures on Shakespeare*. London, 1961.

Stubbes, Phillip. *The Anatomy of Abuses*. London, 1583.

Styan, J. L. *The Shakespeare Revolution*. Cambridge, 1977.

Suzman, Janet. *Acting with Shakespeare: Three Comedies*. New York, 1995.

Taylor, Gary. *Reinventing Shakespeare*. London, 1989.

Taylor, Michael. "The Darker Purpose of *A Midsummer Night's Dream*" in *Studies in English Literature* 9, 1963.

Terry, Ellen. *Four Lectures on Shakespeare*. London, 1932.

Tillyard, E. M. W. *Shakespeare's Last Plays*. London, 1938.

Traister, Barbara Howard, "Prospero: Master of Self-knowledge," in Bloom (3).

Traversi, Derek. (1) *An Approach to Shakespeare*. London, 1938.

————. (2) *Shakespeare: The Last Phase*. London, 1954.

Thompson, Ann, ed. *The Taming of the Shrew*. Cambridge, U.K., 1984.

Van Doren, Mark. "*The Merchant of Venice*: An Interpretation," in Wilders, John (1).

Warren, Roger, and Stanley Wells, eds. *Twelfth Night*. Oxford, 1995.

Weekley, Ernest, ed. *An Etymological Dictionary of Modern English*. London 1921, New York 1967.

Wells, Stanley, ed. *The Comedy of Errors*. New York, 1980.

Westlund, Joseph. *Shakespeare's Reparative Comedies*. Chicago, 1984.

Wheeler, Richard P., ed. *All's Well that Ends Well*, in Bevington (2).

Wilders, John, ed. (1). *The Merchant of Venice: A Casebook*. Nashville, TN, 1970.

————, ed. (2) *The Two Gentlemen of Verona*. London, 1984.

William, David. "*The Tempest* on the Stage," in Brown and Harris.

Wilson, Harold S. "Dramatic Emphasis in *All's Well*" in Ornstein (2).

Wilson, John Dover. (1) *Shakespeare's Happy Comedies*. London, 1962.

————, ed. (2) *The Merchant of Venice*. Cambridge, U. K., 1940.

Wimsatt, W. K., Jr., ed. *English Stage Comedy*. New York, 1954. (Reprinted 1964.)

Yates, Frances. *Shakespeare's Last Plays: A New Approach*. London, 1975.

Young, Stark. *Immortal Shadows*. New York, 1948.

Zitner, Sheldon P. (1) *All's Well that Ends Well*, new critical introduction. Boston, 1989.

————, ed. (2) *Much Ado About Nothing*. Oxford, 1993.

Index